2 B1

123/173000

BRITISH AND AMERICAN PLAYWRIGHTS

492355-1

OTHER VOLUMES IN THIS SERIES

Already published

TOM ROBERTSON edited by William Tydeman
W. S. GILBERT edited by George Rowell
HENRY ARTHUR JONES edited by Russell Jackson
DAVID GARRICK AND GEORGE COLMAN THE ELDER
    edited by E. R. Wood
WILLIAM GILLETTE edited by Rosemary Cullen and Don Wilmeth
GEORGE COLMAN THE YOUNGER AND THOMAS
    MORTON edited by Barry Sutcliffe
ARTHUR MURPHY AND SAMUEL FOOTE edited by George
    Taylor
H. J. BYRON edited by J. T. L. Davis
AUGUSTIN DALY edited by Don Wilmeth and Rosemary Cullen
DION BOUCICAULT edited by Peter Thomson
JAMES ROBINSON PLANCHÉ edited by Don Roy

Further volumes will include:

A. W. PINERO edited by George Rowell
CHARLES READE edited by M. Hammet
SUSAN GLASPELL edited by C. W. E. Bigsby
HARLEY GRANVILLE BARKER edited by Dennis Kennedy

Plays by
Tom Taylor

STILL WATERS RUN DEEP
THE CONTESTED ELECTION
THE OVERLAND ROUTE
THE TICKET-OF-LEAVE MAN

Edited with an Introduction and Notes by
Martin Banham

To the memory of my Father
Oswald Watson Banham

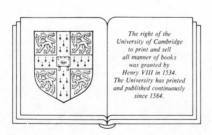

The right of the
University of Cambridge
to print and sell
all manner of books
was granted by
Henry VIII in 1534.
The University has printed
and published continuously
since 1584.

CAMBRIDGE UNIVERSITY PRESS

Cambridge

London   New York   New Rochelle

Melbourne   Sydney

Published by the Press Syndicate of the University of Cambridge
The Pitt Building, Trumpington Street, Cambridge CB2 1RP
32 East 57th Street, New York, NY 10022, USA
10 Stamford Road, Oakleigh, Melbourne 3166, Australia

First published 1985

Printed in Great Britain at
the University Press, Cambridge

Library of Congress catalogue card number: 85–5948

British Library Cataloguing in Publication Data

Taylor, Tom, 1817–1880
Plays. – (British and American playwrights
1750–1920)
I. Title   II. Banham, Martin   III. Series
822'.8   PR5549.T4
ISBN 0 521 24102 2 hard covers
ISBN 0 521 28439 2 paperback

GENERAL EDITORS' PREFACE

It is the primary aim of this series to make available to the British and American theatre plays which were effective in their own time, and which are good enough to be effective still.

Each volume assembles a number of plays, normally by a single author, scrupulously edited but sparingly annotated. Textual variations are recorded where individual editors have found them either essential or interesting. Introductions give an account of the theatrical context, and locate playwrights and plays within it. Biographical and chronological tables, brief bibliographies, and the complete listing of known plays provide information useful in itself, and which also offers guidance and incentive to further exploration.

Many of the plays published in this series have appeared in modern anthologies. Such representation is scarcely distinguishable from anonymity. We have relished the tendency of individual editors to make claims for the dramatists of whom they write. These are not plays best forgotten. They are plays best remembered. If the series is a contribution to theatre history, that is well and good. If it is a contribution to the continuing life of the theatre, that is well and better.

We have been lucky. The Cambridge University Press has supported the venture beyond our legitimate expectations. Acknowledgement is not, in this case, perfunctory. Sarah Stanton's contribution to the series has been substantial, and it has enhanced our work.

Martin Banham
Peter Thomson

Tom Taylor, Dramatist, Journalist. Third editor of *Punch*, 1874

CONTENTS

ILLUSTRATIONS

ACKNOWLEDGEMENTS

I gratefully acknowledge the generous assistance of the University of Leeds and the British Academy in the preparation of this volume. Research grants and leave of absence gave valuable time and opportunity for the original research. The staff of the Brotherton Library of the University of Leeds have been unfailingly helpful and efficient in dealing with my many requests, and I have enjoyed the facilities and helpful courtesy of the staff of the British Library and particularly the Department of Manuscripts. I am also grateful to the Humanities Research Center of the University of Texas for facilities and assistance.

The Raymond Mander and Joe Mitchenson Theatre Collection offered advice and assistance which I greatly appreciate, and I am specially indebted to Peter Cheeseman of the Victoria Theatre, Stoke-on-Trent, George Rowell, E. George Hauger and Irene Thomas for general wisdom, advice and comment. I am grateful to Tony Harrison and Matthew Scott for permission to reproduce their composition of the song 'The Maniac's Tear' specially written for the National Theatre's production of *The Ticket-of-Leave Man*. Particular thanks are due to my friend and fellow general editor Peter Thomson whose careful reading of the manuscript and helpful observations are reflected in many of the textual notes. As general editors our debt to Sarah Stanton has already been acknowledged, but as a volume editor that debt is compounded.

Finally, to my students and colleagues in the Workshop Theatre of the School of English at the University of Leeds, my warm thanks for allowing me to practise on them, and for clarifying many points. And to my family my apologies for the obsession and the mess and gratitude for their interest and support.

INTRODUCTION

Winton Tolles, in his detailed study of Tom Taylor's work,[1] summarises his contribution to the Victorian theatre:

> That his work is so representative of the English theater between 1840 and 1880 is probably its strongest claim to our attention. His writing touched every existing field of dramatic activity. The decline of the burlesque and the extravaganza from the graceful forms of Planché to the more rowdy entertainments of the Gaiety 'legs and limelight' type (entertainments soon banished from the theater to the music halls) was aided by Taylor. As long as the multiple piece bill persisted, he furnished many of the bustling farces, the clever comediettas, and the sentimental comic dramas which helped to complete the long evening's entertainment. He assisted in the development of the relatively crude 'Adelphi drama' into a more efficiently constructed type of melodrama. He aided the evolution of domestic drama by avoiding the violent and sensational scenes of physical action so prominent in native melodrama. He fostered the polished romantic drama of the school founded by Victor Hugo. His work for the Haymarket helped to popularize the eccentric type of comedy against which Robertson rebelled. As a writer for the Olympic he furthered the establishment of the various forms of mature drawing-room drama which stemmed from the *comédie-drames* of Scribe. His chronicle history plays stimulated a slight renascence of poetic drama. In all genres his work was among the best as well as the most typical. With only slight exaggeration it is true that among the playwrights of his generation Taylor, alone or in collaboration, wrote the best farce, *Our Clerks*; the best comedietta, *To Oblige Benson*; the best comic-drama, *To Parents and Guardians*; the best sentimental comedy, *Masks and Faces*; the best farce-comedy, *The Overland Route*; the best melodrama, *The Ticket-of-Leave Man*; the best drawing-room drama, *Still Waters Run Deep*; the best domestic drama, *Mary Warner*; the best romantic drama, *The Fool's Revenge*; and the best historical play, *'Twixt Axe and Crown*.[2]

Tolles' comment draws attention not only to the range of Taylor's skills as a playwright, but also to the vigorous nature of Victorian theatre, its voracious demand for entertainments of all kinds, and the importance of particular theatres and managements in determining style and taste. Most of Taylor's

1

plays were written for specific companies, and at various times he assumed the role of house playwright to such theatres as the Adelphi, the Olympic and the Haymarket. It is remarkable that one of the most popular playwrights of his day should be so forgotten a hundred years later. But Taylor himself certainly did not write with an eye to posterity: his work was practical, income-producing craftsmanship, written to serve immediate purposes. In this he was typical of his contemporaries, contributing to a period of English drama which, without being distinguished in itself, served to prepare the ground for the more substantial work of the famous playwrights of the end of the century. In Tolles' words: 'His writing . . . helped mark the roads which English drama was to take, as well as those it was to avoid.'[3]

It is fascinating to note that, although Taylor wrote over seventy plays, he was in no sense a full-time professional playwright. Having commenced an academic career, he soon qualified for the bar, and spent some time in that profession, and then became a senior civil servant. At the same time he was a prolific journalist, serving as art critic of *The Times*, a regular contributor to, and later editor of, *Punch*. He edited several large-scale works on the history of art, and on occasions acted as stage-director of his own plays. Records of him suggest that he was that most endearing of characters, the talented Victorian amateur. There is no doubt of the affection in which he was held by those who knew him, even if they sometimes found him a little solemn (as did his colleagues on the satirical journal *Punch*!) or apt to lose his temper. F. C. Burnand describes an incident when Taylor was conducting a rehearsal of one of his plays at the Olympic theatre:

> Up to a certain point Tom was excellent; his directions clear, and his manner pleasant. But as the rehearsal went on, Tom . . . losing himself in his energetic stage management, began to thunder and to scare everybody.
>
> There was one man, a 'super' who would not, or could not, comprehend the instructions given him *vivâ voce* by the author . . . Tom mastered himself with great efforts, but almost danced with rage at the man's impenetrable stupidity. At last . . . he went up to the stage and took the offender gently by the buttonhole in order to arrest his attention. The man was immensely flattered at being singled out for this special mark of courtesy, and became at once 'all ears' . . . Then Tom, still in a state of 'suppressed fury' as aforesaid, glared at him from under his bushy eyebrows, and agitating his iron-grey locks straight in front of the flattered 'super's' placid countenance, whispered – stage-whispered – severely and emphatically under his very nose –
>
> 'My dear sir' – as if he were commencing a polite letter to an utter stranger – '*My dear sir, you're a damned fool*.'[4]

The anecdote goes on to record the consternation in the company at this action, and the haste with which Taylor ('who, in effect, was the kindest-hearted creature') soothed everybody's feelings, and carried on with the rehearsal. The interest of the story lies not only in the small insight it gives us into Taylor himself, but also in the role that the Victorian playwright might be expected to play in the staging of his own plays. In a period before the director had emerged in the theatre, the organisation of the action of a play would be in the hands of a stage-manager or stage-director, serving not only the needs of the play but also the starring role of the leading players, and it is clear that the playwright himself might well undertake that responsibility. With scripts being often merely in manuscript form, with 'parts' supplied to the actors giving them only their cues, the presence of the playwright would obviously be helpful. Such association with theatres and companies, actors and actresses, inevitably brought the playwright close to the personalities of the stage. Taylor's home at Lavender Sweep, Wandsworth, clearly became a home from home for people from all the walks of literary, artistic, and theatrical life that Taylor was part of. Ellen Terry in her autobiography talks with great affection both of the Taylors and their hospitality. Taylor greatly concerned himself with her fortunes, as he had done also with her sister Kate's. Indeed from Ellen Terry's reminiscences Taylor's concern often looks more like interference – not only with her artistic life, but with her personal life. But Ellen Terry's thoughts for Taylor are all warm and kind – though not without the occasional shrewd insight: ' "Tom the Adapter" was the Terry dramatist for many years. Kate played in many of the pieces which, some openly, some deviously, he brought to the English stage from the French. When Kate married, my turn came.'[5] The charge of plagiarism implied in Ellen Terry's word 'deviously' was one that Taylor often had to face, not only because of his borrowings from the French, but also on occasions the use of materials or ideas from other British writers. Taylor defended himself robustly, and successfully, against these allegations, though in common with many of the playwrights of the period, he drew openly upon plays and novels from French and other sources. The provincial actor-manager John Coleman was another intimate of Taylor's, and a frequent visitor to Lavender Sweep. He too refers, with a sense of amusement, to Taylor's borrowings from other sources, but defends the practice: 'it must be admitted that most of his most successful works were not of native growth. In no case was he a servile translator; indeed, every play which he manipulated underwent a thorough process of transmutation.'[6] Coleman shared the high opinion of the times concerning Taylor's work, counting *The Ticket-of-Leave Man*, *Clancarty*, *Still Waters Run Deep*, *The Unequal Match* and *The Overland Route* as the best plays of their kind 'of the epoch in which he lived'.[7] Taylor's play *Arkwright's Wife*, a drama about the inventor of the spinning jenny, was first produced by Taylor at Coleman's theatre in Leeds, and the two men were associated not only professionally but as friends for many years. 'His temper was of fire', Coleman said of Taylor, 'but his heart was of gold.'[8]

Pictures of Tom Taylor offer us mainly a rather typical portrait of a sober Victorian gentleman, fully bearded, carefully dressed. But a touch of flamboyance in the dress (Ellen Terry recalls him 'dear host at the head of his dinner-table, dressed in black silk knee-breeches and velvet cutaway coat'),[9] and a Puckishness evident in a cartoon from his early days at *Punch*[10] offer an alternative view of a man essentially humorous and humane, though perhaps in later years tending to favour a sterner literary image. Though so much of his work was comedy and burlesque, if Taylor had been left to select a body of plays by which he would wish to be remembered, he might well have emphasised the historic dramas of his later years. Indeed the only collection of his plays that was published in his lifetime was a collection entitled *Historical Dramas* (1877), which included his major works in this style – *Joan of Arc*, *'Twixt Axe and Crown*, *Lady Clancarty*, *Arkwright's Wife* and *Anne Boleyn*.[11] In the preface to this collection he says that 'if this volume find readers, I may follow it up by one of Romantic Dramas, and another of Comedies and Comediettas', but he didn't, so presumably it didn't. Collected volumes of plays were, of course, unusual at that time. The historical dramas were quite successful in their time, though of variable and often uneven quality. *Arkwright's Wife*, for instance, suffers from a heavily melodramatic ending, but *'Twixt Axe and Crown*, a drama about Mary Tudor, is generally more effective. It is written in blank verse and Stephen Watt has pointed to the qualities that distinguished the play:

> it was not only to the dubious attractions of melodrama that *'Twixt Axe and Crown* owed its success, but to Taylor's emphasis of language over sensational action. Taylor's play contains no graphically realistic battles or scenes of violence, and to many reviewers this elevation of language signalled a return to the serious drama of the Kean–Macready days. In fact, few plays represented to so many commentators both the greatness of London's theatrical past and the possibility of a bright future.[12]

Taylor's historical dramas were a curious amalgam of melodrama, domestic drama, and verse drama, but at their best they offered a sensitive view of their subjects and were concerned to be faithful to historic fact. They attracted large audiences, and serious audiences, and were generally welcomed by the critics as signalling a new quality in the drama of the period. Taylor's own concern in the 1870s with the serious role of drama and the theatre is also reflected in an interesting essay *The Theatre in England, some of its shortcomings and possibilities* published in 1871.[13] This essay makes the case for a national theatre in London along the lines of the *Comédie Française*, running on a repertoire basis and forming a centre for the development of

higher standards of acting and writing. Taylor's view of the theatre to which
he himself had contributed so much was less than enthusiastic:

> 'Till the present generation the theatre was pre-eminent among
> amusements, and commanded attention and interest from all classes,
> the most instructed and cultivated as well as the most high bred.
> Their tone of thought, taste and manners was reflected on the stage,
> both in its acting and literature. The theatre of our great-grandfathers
> and grandfathers, and in a less degree that of our fathers, had, it is
> true, its bad side, both of morals and manners, in Comedy, and its
> weak places, pomposity and *pum*posity in Tragedy; but still in its
> comic vein it gave us the quintessence of wit and humour, in its
> serious a full-fed stream of poetry and passion, as compared with the
> average of what passes for stage sport and stage seriousness now.
>
> The theatre was unquestionably a place of more solid and
> satisfactory intellectual resort and relaxation in the days between
> Betterton and Macready than it has been for the last twenty years.
> The pitch of the amusement was higher. A better style of men
> engaged in management, and their search for profit was governed by
> a higher conception of the roads to it.
>
> . . . the *morale* of the English public proper, the public of the pit
> and the gallery, is still sound. Its sympathy with the good and the
> right is still strong and instinctive: it has no relish for the
> sophistication that puts a gloss on sin and confuses vice with virtue.
>
> But there are many, of all classes, who have ceased to frequent the
> theatre, because they have ceased to find what they want there –
> comedy which will amuse without disgusting by excess or offending
> by indecency; tragedy which will move and elevate without repelling
> by imperfectness and bad taste in impersonation; drama which will
> stir and enthrall without condescending to vulgar claptrap, crawling
> realism, or the mere physical excitement, now christened
> Sensation.[14]

Despite these reservations concerning the drama 'of the last twenty years',
and Taylor's implied choice of preferred work in the publication of the
historical dramas, modern taste, both in playing and reading, is more likely to
be with those earlier plays of Taylor's of the 1850s and 1860s which, whilst not
neglecting meaningful social observation and comment, illuminate that streak
of Puckish wit and humour hinted at by the Doyle drawing. This present
collection of Taylor's plays, which deliberately excludes the collaborative
plays with Charles Reade which may be represented in a further volume in
this series,[15] takes four plays from the 1850s and 1860s, all of which may be
claimed to stand up to the criterion which determines the choice of plays in
this series, namely that they were effective in their own time, and are good

enough to be effective still. All four plays have a structural dynamic that makes them good theatrical fare, are well and wittily plotted, and populated by characters who are not only fun to read but who would be fun to play.

The plays

Still Waters Run Deep

OLYMPIC – Mr Wigan has been exceedingly fortunate during his management of this theatre in his new pieces. On Monday an original drama in three acts, by Mr Tom Taylor, was produced with perfect success. Its title is 'Still Waters Run Deep'; and the moral is exemplified in the character of a north country hero, *John Mildmay* (Mr Wigan), whose usual quiet demeanour misleads his wife and household into the belief that he is 'a spoon', but who proves himself in the upshot to be a man of great practical talent. He defeats a swindler, who had plotted the ruin of his domestic peace, with the utmost coolness and courage, and saves the reputation of his wife's strong-minded aunt, who had previously ruled the family. Brought face to face with the former, whom he has to identify as a forger, he compels him to light a cigar with one that he himself is smoking, while he traces his features, and convicts him of being the guilty party. With the same *sangfroid* and dexterity, he tempts him on to demand a duel, and inflict the horsewhip, whereby the criminal is entrapped into the custody of an officer. The dialogue is equal to the situations – both are thoroughly powerful; and the piece may be accepted, on the whole, as exhibiting masterly skill equally in the construction and composition. Mr Wigan, as the hero, was admirable, and was efficiently antagonised by Mr G. Vining, as *Captain Hawksley*, so that the various collisions between them were most effectively realised.

(*The Illustrated London News*, 19 May 1855)

Taylor wrote several plays for the Olympic Theatre in the years between 1852 and 1860, when the theatre was under the management of Alfred Wigan (an actor much approved of, as George Rowell reminds us,[16] by Queen Victoria). The term 'Olympic Drama' came to describe a well-made play derivative of the form associated with Eugène Scribe, a play with clear heroes, clear villains, strong confrontations and positive resolutions. John Oxenford and Horace Wigan are identified by Tolles[17] as being, with Taylor, the leading Olympic playwrights of this period and *Still Waters Run Deep* is an excellent example of the style. *Plot and Passion* (1853) was Taylor's first drama fully to establish this form for the Olympic (though three previous plays of Taylor's had been staged there) and other significant dramas that were to follow included *Retribution* (1856), *A Sheep in Wolf's Clothing*

(1857), and *Payable on Demand* (1859). *The House or the Home?*, another play of this kind for the Wigans, was presented, in 1959, at the Adelphi. Like many plays of this style *Still Waters Run Deep* is closely adapted from another source, in this case Charles de Bernard's novel *Le Gendre*. The play was an immediate success at the Olympic and continued in the repertoire not only of the Wigans (Mrs Alfred Wigan having taken over the leading female role of Mrs Hector Sternhold from Mrs Melfort two weeks after the play opened) but of other actors for many years. It is a fascinating indication of the play's lasting powers that it emerges as a silent film in the early twentieth century, with Lady Tree as Mrs Sternhold.

The anonymous reviewer of the *Illustrated London News* gives some hint not only of the confrontations of the plot but also of the melodramatic edge that many of the situations have. The play is also generally very amusing (both the Lacy and Dicks editions describe it as a comedy) both in dialogue and incident, and theatrically it moves with pace and precision. The richness of the play is considerably helped by the characterisation. Taylor's villain, Captain Hawksley, has enough charm and wit about him to make his seduction of Mrs Sternhold, and his attempt on the honour of the hero's wife, quite plausible, and John Mildmay copes with the threats to his 'domestic peace' with the same calm skill that enables him to outwit Hawksley. Tolles claims a little more for the play, suggesting that it 'stimulates a certain amount of thought from the reader, something most Victorian plays fail to do. The action centres in the problem of a husband's behaviour when he sees his wife drifting towards infidelity. This situation contains the element necessary for a "problem play", and Taylor offers a concrete, if not very profound, solution.'[18] Tolles is right to point to this aspect of the play, but modern audiences are likely to be more attracted by the sheer fun and effectiveness of the drama, the wit of the situation, and theatrical charm of the piece, rather than by any contribution it may be claimed to make towards resolving problems of marital relationships! Indeed, as a product of its time, it assumes an attitude towards the relationship between man and wife that is positively chauvinistic. Other interesting characteristics of Taylor's work that the play illustrates include a fascination with detection and the role (albeit amateur in this play) of the detective and a delightful bias towards heroes from the north of England, characterised by that down-to-earth common sense that distinguishes them from the smooth rogues of the south! This sensible prejudice perhaps arises from Taylor's own roots in the north-east of England.

A final word on the Olympic dramas and on Taylor's contribution can again come from Tolles, who suggests that 'their deft plot construction and their experimental realism influenced the future of English Drama. Through these plays the technique of writing popular drama divorced from the absurdities of melodrama and farce passed to the generation of playwrights headed by

Pinero and Jones . . . The difference between *Still Waters Run Deep* and *The Second Mrs Tanqueray* is, after all, not so much in the basic selection and treatment of dramatic material, as it is in the technique of plotting, characterization, and style.'[19]

The Contested Election

HAYMARKET – On Wednesday a new comedy by Mr Tom Taylor was produced. It is in three acts, and entitled 'The Contested Election'. As might have been expected, it is altogether of a political character; and the author has carried it through with unmitigated spirit and a laudable intensity of purpose. His exposure of borough corruption is ruthless and unflinching. The story is the least part of the matter, and has, in fact, but little interest, being intended merely to connect the dialogues. The hero is perhaps *Mr Dodgson* (Mr C. Mathews), who, being without clients and money, willingly lends himself to the solicitation of *Mr Peckover* (Mr Buckstone) to start a new candidate in order that the borough of Flamborough may be thoroughly contested. *Peckover* is a butcher and manager of 'The Blue Lambs' – a body of corrupt voters under his leadership. *Dodgson* then contrives to inflame the ambition of the wife (Mrs C. Mathews) of *Mr Honeybun* (Mr Compton), a retired grocer, fond of his easy-chair, and through her means induces him to consent to being put forward as the new candidate. But in this he is doomed ultimately to meet with successful opposition. *Mr Wapshot* (Mr W. Farren), who is in love with *Mrs Honeybun's* stepdaughter, combines with *Honeybun* to free him from the annoyance of being elected. He commences operations by cutting the notes in half that had been sent for the bribery of the electors; and secures one set of halves for the purpose of conducting an opposition in his own person to *Honeybun's* success. By this means *Dodgson* is crippled in his operations, and 'The Blue Lambs' are thrown into a state of doubt and difficulty. All the forms, noise, and inconveniences of an election are gone through by *Honeybun*, who endures them with such grace as he can command, in the hope that he will be ultimately ousted. While expecting the arrival of the missing half notes, the time for voting passes over, and *Honeybun* rejoices in his deliverance. *Wapshot* also resigns, but manages to get possession of both halves of the notes, and thus secures his father-in-law from loss. Mr Compton played his part to admiration; and Mr C. Mathews was animated and bustling in an extreme degree. It is a character precisely suited to his abilities. The piece was perfectly successful, and the public approbation at the fall of the curtain

unmistakably unanimous and decided. There can be no doubt that
the comedy will enjoy a long run.

(*The Illustrated London News*, 2 July 1850)

As with the Olympic dramas under Wigan's management, Taylor's
association with the Haymarket theatre related to a house style – in this case
pure comedy – and a specific management, that of J. B. Buckstone.
Haymarket comedies were often written to serve the particular talents of the
company that Buckstone assembled around himself, and cherished and
familiar performances from favourite actors could be seen in one play after
another. Prominent in Buckstone's company, formed in 1853, were such
actors as Charles Mathews who, although earlier primarily concerned with his
own management ventures together with his wife Madame Vestris, joined the
Haymarket players after her death for several notable productions, and
'speciality' actors such as the 'mincing fop' Chippendale, the 'irascible old
man' Howe, Compton with his 'quiet drollery' and Buckstone himself 'calling
into action his command of facial contortion, his deep bass voice, and his
inimitable art of mimicry'.[20] In *The Contested Election* Mathews played the
attorney Dodgson, twisting and turning, wheeling and dealing, in order to
manipulate the election and rescue his own fortunes, Buckstone took the role
of Peckover, corrupt President of the Blue Lambs, preaching morality and
seeking bribes, and Compton played the poor bewildered, confused retired
grocer Mr Honeybun, forced by his wife's ambition into the heat of politics
and entirely embarrassed by the whole process. A typical Haymarket comedy
placed more emphasis on the opportunity it gave the actors to exploit their
own idiosyncratic skills than on the creation of a logical or meaningful plot. In
this respect *The Contested Election* is typical. The plot, such as it is, does not
seek to create any real suspense – as is the avowed intent in, for instance, *Still
Waters Run Deep* – but simply offers situations that can be played with by
characters in the comedy. The intent is to create a string of comic situations
sufficiently connected to allow for a rounded entertainment. It is interesting
that the reviewer of the *Illustrated London News* should invest the play with a
more noble purpose – a ruthless and unflinching exposure of borough
corruption – but one can scarcely think that the intention was paramount in
Taylor's mind. But at the same time it is an indication of Taylor's alertness to
the serious world around him that he should treat with some satire and much
ridicule contemporary practices that deserved both, rather than offer a
comedy with no teeth in it at all.

The Overland Route

HAYMARKET – Mr Tom Taylor has given another dramatic
production to the boards, under the title of 'The Overland Route'.

The piece is in three acts, but is not supported by any amount of action or incident, and principally consists of conversation and character. The scene is on board a homeward-bound steamer, sections of which pertaining to the saloon and quarter-deck are cleverly put on the stage. These occupy the first two acts; the third presents the Mazzaffa Reef, Red Sea, at midday. In the scenery we may trace the idea of the drama, which possesses both novelty and originality. The story is but a slender thread whereon to hang the dialogue. The principal character, perhaps, is *Tom Dexter* (Mr Charles Mathews), a doctor, who has been an Indian editor, and who becomes a jack-of-all-trades to the crew and passengers. The next in importance is *Mr Lovibond* (Mr Buckstone), who left his wife many years ago, threatening to commit suicide on account of her jealous disposition. That wife is now on board, believing her husband dead, and flirting with *Major McTurk* (Mr Rogers). The lady is admirably represented by Mrs Wilkins, who in the course of the play is awfully frightened by the apparition of her husband with his throat cut. *Mr Lovibond*, in fact, had gashed himself with shaving, and accidentally intruded into her cabin, but for the rest of the voyage had remained incognito under the name of *Downey* – a person whose berth he had taken, and who, it appears, had committed forgery. A detective on board arrests and handcuffs him, but at the captain's request, for the honour of the vessel, keeps him quiet. *Lovibond* and his wife become subsequently acquainted and reconciled, and some farcical fun is obtained by the impossibility of embracing his wife with his hands manacled. At length the vessel is wrecked on the reef, and all the characters in the third act are arrayed in such accidental costume as has been preserved. Many of them are modified in disposition, misfortune having done its work on all, and particularly on the *McTurk*, who from a bully changes to a coward. *Dexter* is the soul of the scene, manages the rations, and controls the destinies of others and his own. He prevents the wife of his friend Jack, *Mrs Sebright* (Mrs C. Mathews), from flirting injuriously, as a supposed widow, with *Mr Commissioner Colepepper* (Mr Chippendale) and *Sir Solomon Fraser, K.C.B.* (Mr Compton), and successfully achieves his own suit with *Miss Colepepper* (Miss M. Ternan). *Mrs Sebright's* husband, at last, appears as Captain of the *Pinnace*, which arrives to the rescue of the shipwrecked party. Mr Taylor has evinced considerable skill in the working of these materials, and causing the dialogue to culminate about the middle of each act in some point of humour that extorts the laughter of the audience, while the curtain is brought down at the end on an effective mechanical situation. The acting was equal to the writing, and the performance, notwithstanding its difficulties, unquestionably successful.

(*The Illustrated London News*, 3 March 1860)

Here again we can recognise the ingredients of the Haymarket comedy, with many of the favourite actors again allowed to exploit their particular characterisations and mannerisms. For Charles Mathews the part of Dexter must have been more satisfying than some of the cruder comic roles he had to undertake at the Haymarket, offering him a role more in tune with his taste for realistic acting. Dexter is the pivotal character in the comedy, almost a *Boys' Own Paper* hero – dashing, brave, modest, omni-competent! But the strength of the play is in the wit and verve not only of situation but also of dialogue. It also has a certain exotic appeal, with the voyage home from India of people whose experiences and recollections are of the Mutiny adding a fascinating dimension to the action. Taylor wrote one other play with a specifically Indian setting, *Up at the Hills* (1860) and this reminds us of the interest and consciousness of his audience in the affairs of Empire. *The Overland Route* was an immediate success at the Haymarket and stayed in that theatre's repertoire long after Buckstone's management ceased. The Bancrofts revived the play during their period of management of the Haymarket as late as 1882, and in their memoirs offer an interesting insight into the physical presentation of such a piece. In 1881 Squire Bancroft had taken a cruise to Constantinople on the P. & O. steamship *Deccan*. Bancroft comments:

> This trip was of wonderful service in furnishing me with all kinds of detail for a proposed revival we contemplated, in time of need, of the old Haymarket comedy, the *Overland Route*, and I did not fail to observe all that passed around me, taking copious notes, and making rough drawings of much that was enacted in the way of life on ship-board.[21]

Taylor's *Simoom* was also a supposed P. & O. steamship, and the Bancrofts' revival of the play not only benefited from Squire Bancroft's observations on the *Deccan* but also took hints for the scenery from another P. & O. steamer, as the following record of the production illustrates:

> In the *Overland Route* both the saloon and upper deck of the s.s. *Poonah*, one of the older type, of the fine P. and O. fleet, and consequently better suited to our purpose, were, as far as possible, reproduced, after months of labour, by Mr Hann . . . The Eastern . . . trip . . . now became of professional value in the reproduction of the many familiar details of life on ship-board; we were also fortunate in securing some real niggers, lascars, and ayahs, who lent great reality to the pictures. The scene of the last act, when the ship has run aground upon a coral reef in the Red Sea, was magnificently painted

by Mr Telbin, whose aquaintance with the East and the Holy Land enabled him to boldly treat the subject.[22]

Nor was the play neglected in India. The Simla Amateur Dramatic Club (claiming that its origins in 1837 make it the oldest A.D.C. in the world!) record a performance of *The Overland Route* in the Gaiety Theatre, Simla, in 1888.[23] The play was fun when produced, continued to entertain for generations and would be fun still. If an editor is allowed to express a preference for any one of his selections, this play is mine.

The Ticket-of-Leave Man

OLYMPIC – Mr Tom Taylor's new drama, which is so excellently acted that it is marked with a completeness not frequently witnessed on the stage, progresses in the good opinion of the public, and abundantly illustrates the difficulty which the criminal population have to encounter in their efforts to regain a position in society. The hero of the piece, as our readers know, is really innocent of the charge on which he was convicted and transported, and, on his return from Portland, gains a respectable position, and is about to be married to the grateful girl who had recommended him to the post. But his evil genius follows him; and his former companions in dissipation, unwilling that he should gain an advantage in which they may not partake, denounce him to his employer. The scene is very cleverly managed. There is great variety in it. Hope and fear divide the soul of the returned convict (played by Mr Neville) until all doubts end in his dismissal from his employment. It is not the detective (whose part was undertaken by Mr Horace Wigan) who denounces him, but, as we have suggested, his early acquaintances who had originally betrayed him into error. All now appears to be lost. In the further progress of the play the poor fellow is tried to the utmost, and things come to the worst. Then, by an inevitable law, they mend; and at the conclusion of the piece he has before him a future which abounds in promise of better days.

(*The Illustrated London News*, 27 June 1863)

This is certainly Taylor's best-known play, though once again with one of his major pieces we are in fact dealing with an adaptation. The source is a French play, *Léonard*, by Édouard Brisebarre and Eugène Nus. It combines melodrama, sentiment, social observation, and humour. It creates two substantial characters, that of the Ticket-of-Leave man himself, Bob Brierly (another of Taylor's northern heroes) and the detective Hawkshaw. The actor Henry Neville, who played Brierly, created his reputation with this role, and Horace Wigan as Hawkshaw set a pattern, together with the playwright, for the stage detective who was so to fascinate audiences throughout the rest of the nineteenth century and indeed to the present day. There is also a genuine social concern in the play which gives it heart and substance and which moderates the melodrama of much of the action. The prejudice in society against those with a criminal record and the near impossibility of rehabilitation is clearly depicted. Brierly's early foolishness is contrasted with his essential decency, and the peril that the former will always conspire to defeat the latter gives the play its point and edge. It is interesting to note that even this degree of concern with real social issues caused some doubt in the mind of the Lord Chamberlain's Examiner of Plays. John Russell Stephens, whilst noting that Taylor generally 'emerged virtually unscathed by censorship' records that:

> In Taylor's case the Examiner was concerned with the title *The Ticket-of-Leave Man*, fearing that Lord Sydney [the Lord Chamberlain] 'might not fancy the present one'. But he had some minor reservations as well about the kind of play that Taylor had written and its probable unsuitability for the sophisticated middle-class audience of the Olympic. As he explained to Spencer Ponsonby, 'excepting the associations, The Ticket of Leave Man, barring a few follies in Act 1, is a very estimable person, fallen into bad company. I think indeed Tom (& I shall tell him so on the very next opportunity) might as well keep from writing a kind of Victoria drama for the Olympic Theatre.'[24]

But despite the Examiner's concern for the sensitivity of Olympic audiences, the play, like Lillo's famous *George Barnwell, or The London Merchant* before it, was credited with reforming some of those who went to see it. *The Globe* newspaper, Tuesday p.m., 13 October 1863 features the following story.

THE ABSCONDING CLERK AND TOM TAYLOR'S TICKET-OF-LEAVE MAN

It is to be feared, says Sheridan, that people go to the Theatre chiefly to amuse themselves, and it may be feared that such was the chief object of a certain absconding clerk in going to the Olympic theatre with £2,500 of his employer's money in his pockets, with which 'in the ease of his heart' he had taken himself off from Liverpool. But the ease of his heart could not withstand the pressure of Mr Tom Taylor's play.

The Ticket-of-Leave Man awakened three-fifths of a conscience in this clerk's breast – he was so affected that he went out of the Theatre, got some envelopes, and sent £1,500 back to his employers. This clerk took his place in the Pit of the Olympic, if not a hardened,

Henry Neville as Bob Brierly (top right), Kate Saville as Mary Edwards (top left),
George Vincent as Moss in *The Ticket-of-Leave Man*, Olympic Theatre, 1863

yet certainly an unsoftened and unchastened offender against social
law and right. He went out of the Theatre a striking example of
instantaneous conversion from the error of his way.

  This quotation is carried in the programme of the National Theatre's
Cottesloe production of the play which opened on 12 February 1981, and
which is the latest of a series of revivals of this play. The Victoria Theatre,
Stoke-on-Trent, one of Britain's most innovative and successful regional
theatres under its director Peter Cheeseman, revived the play in 1966 (first
performance 24 May). The programme note observes: 'the plight of Bob
Brierly struggling to be accepted by a society which has already punished him
is a true fore-runner of the later social problem plays' and director Peter
Cheeseman, in a letter to the present writer, recalls:

> My deepest impression of it is the reaction of the First Night audience
> which made me understand in a blinding flash the true nature of this
> kind of melodrama and what its relation with the audience must have
> been. As is my custom, I insisted that it was played absolutely
> straight, seriously, thrillingly, and so on. I have never believed that
> this diminishes the comic potential of any text, let alone its serious
> content. At the wonderful moment of Hawkshaw's revelation of his
> true identity towards the end of the play, the First Night audience
> *genuinely* cheered and then broke into heartfelt applause.[25]

The play has also been adapted for radio, and was broadcast by the BBC in
March 1937.[26]

As I suggested earlier, this collection of Taylor's plays cannot be regarded as
truly representative, nor, in being limited to four plays, can the selection
avoid the criticism of neglecting important works that have an equal claim to
revival and attention. Perhaps foremost among these is *Our American Cousin*
which, in its day, was one of the most famous of Taylor's plays, though it
owed its fame not to its intrinsic virtues (for it is, in fact, a rather poor play)
but to the extraordinary feat of the actor E. A. Sothern in turning the part of
Lord Dundreary into a vehicle for his own talents, liberally re-writing and
readjusting the text in the course of his invention. For more than twenty years
between 1858, when the play had its premiere in Laura Keene's Theatre, New
York, and his death in 1881, Sothern starred in the play in England and
America, and after that his son, E. H. Sothern, continued to play the role.
The history of the play is extraordinary. Composed by Taylor in the early
1850s, inspired, it is suggested, by the fascination caused in London by the
Americans who flocked to the Crystal Palace Exhibition of 1851, the play,
with its simple coincidental plot of domestic intrigue and confusion, part
drama part farce, could not find a producer in England and was eventually

staged in New York only because Laura Keene's company had to fill a gap in their schedule caused by a delay in building the scenery for *A Midsummer Night's Dream*. Sothern, a member of Keene's company, was offered Lord Dundreary and was only persuaded to play what was a miniscule part by the promise that he would be allowed to 'gag' it and 'do what I please with it'.[27] The resulting performance increased daily in eccentricity and odd mannerism, particularly in speech and movement, and for the rest of its days the play rode on the back of Sothern's performance or imitations of it. A macabre footnote is that it was at a performance of *Our American Cousin* by Laura Keene's company that President Lincoln was assassinated by John Wilkes Booth on 14 April 1865 at Ford's Theatre in Washington.

Of Taylor's other plays many of the shorter burlesques and farces deserve attention, particularly perhaps *To Parents and Guardians* (1846), *Our Clerks* (1852), *To Oblige Benson* (1854) and *A Nice Firm* (1853). The collaboration with Charles Reade produced two particularly effective pieces, *Masks and Faces* (1852) and *Two Loves and A Life* (1854), and a further collaboration, this time with Augustus W. Dubourg, was *New Men and Old Acres* (1869) which is another play that would respond to a modern revival.

M. Willson Disher[28] rightly observed in his *Radio Times* article that 'The trouble is that we have been accepting his own estimate of himself. He prided himself on being the author of historical dramas, *worthy* pieces of work . . . Meanwhile we have been despising his hack-work as thoroughly as he did.' Perhaps Taylor did not feel quite so strongly as Disher suggests, though the earlier extract from *The Theatre in England* gives substance to the claim, but this collection hopes to show that in the 'hack-work' there was a quality of stagecraft that invites our enjoyment and deserves our respect.

The texts

Still Waters Run Deep is reproduced from the Lacy (vol. XXII) and Dicks' (Standard Plays no. 1,049) texts, which are identical. The Licensing copy offers a number of small corrections mainly to stage directions, which have been incorporated.

The Contested Election is based on the text published by T. Chambers, Manchester, but the Licensing copy clarifies the stage directions at the head of the play, which are confusing in Chambers, and offers an extension of the end of Act III which has been mostly brought into the present text. The Lord Chamberlain's copy, it should be noted, entitles the play *The Election*, a point echoed in the final line of the play.

The Overland Route is based on Lacy's edition (no. 1853). The Licensing copy has an alternative ending to Act II, which has been added as an appendix to the text. Certain other clarifications have been taken from the LC copy. There are substantial and important differences between Lacy's (vol. LIX) text of *The Ticket-of-Leave Man* and the Licensing copy. It has seemed to me that the original copy is more coherent and in many respects richer. I have, therefore, introduced into the text a considerable amount of material from the LC's text. I felt particularly emboldened to do so, as the two other modern publications of the text (in Michael Booth's *English Plays of the Nineteenth Century*, vol. II, and George Rowell's *Nineteenth Century Plays*) make available what is essentially the Lacy text, with which the reader can readily make comparison in selecting the most effective version.

Notes

1 *Tom Taylor and the Victorian Drama* (New York, 1940). I acknowledge my considerable debt to Winton Tolles' work. This full-length study of Taylor's plays and other writing, also serves as an admirable chronicle of the Victorian theatre.
2 *Tom Taylor and the Victorian Drama*, pp. 254–5.
3 *Ibid.*, p. 256.
4 *Records and Reminiscences*, revised edn (London, 1917), pp. 227–8.
5 *The Story of My Life* (London, 1908), p. 114.
6 *Players and Playwrights I have Known*, vol. II (London, 1888), p. 118.
7 *Ibid.*, p. 120.
8 *Ibid.*, p. 138.
9 *The Story of my Life*, p. 118.
10 See the drawing by R. Doyle, reproduced in M. H. Spielmann's *The History of Punch* (London, 1895), p. 339.
11 *Three Dramas*, which contained collaborative plays by Taylor and Charles Reade was published in 1854, and there is also a bound collection of Lacy's editions of Taylor's plays selected from those performed by 1860, and which may well have been privately collected by Taylor for distribution to his friends.
12 Stephen Watt, *The Making of the Modern History Play* (University of Illinois doctoral dissertation, 1982).
13 Reprinted in the *Dark Blue*, August 1871, published by British & Colonial Publishing Co. Ltd, London.
14 *The Theatre in England*, pp. 7–8.
15 *Plays by Charles Reade*, edited by Michael Hammet, forthcoming.
16 *The Victorian Theatre 1792–1914*, 2nd edn (Cambridge, 1978), p. 153.
17 *Tom Taylor and the Victorian Drama*, p. 117.
18 *Ibid.*, pp. 136–7.
19 *Ibid.*, p. 148.
20 *Ibid.*, pp. 150–1.
21 *Mr and Mrs Bancroft on and off the Stage* (London, new edn, 1889), p. 323.
22 *Ibid.*, p. 345.
23 See the centenary brochure of the Simla A.D.C., by Major P. H. Denyer (Simla, India, 1937). This fascinating record of amateur theatricals in India was kindly given to me by the present Secretary of the Gaiety Theatre, Simla, on a visit there in 1982. Apart from general reminiscences, the brochure lists productions from 1888 to 1936, and includes several photographs, including one of Colonel Baden Powell acting in *The Geisha* in 1897. Denyer writes: 'he went straight from the Gaiety Theatre to Mafeking and fame'.

24 *The Censorship of English Drama 1824–1901* (Cambridge, 1980), p. 125. The Victoria Theatre in the Waterloo Road (the Old Vic) being outside the West End was, by implication, a home for less sophisticated entertainment than the fashionable Olympic.
25 Letter dated 23 September 1980.
26 The *Radio Times* of 12 March 1937 carries an interesting preview of the broadcast by M. Willson Disher (p. 11).
27 Lester Wallack, *Memories of Fifty Years* (New York, 1889), p. 139.
28 See note 26.

BIOGRAPHICAL RECORD

19 October 1817	Tom Taylor born at Bishop-Wearmouth, Sunderland. His father, Thomas (1769–1843), was head partner of a brewery in Durham, having started life as a farm labourer. He became an alderman of Durham. His mother (maiden name Arnold, 1784–1858) was born in Durham though both her parents were German, born in Frankfurt-on-the-Main.
1832–36	At the University of Glasgow, where he carried off several prizes.
1837–40	Studied at Trinity College, Cambridge. Graduated B.A.
1842	Elected Fellow at Trinity College, and coached at Cambridge for two years, proceeding to his M.A. in 1843.
1844	Moved to London. His first plays, four burlesques, were produced at the Lyceum Theatre by the Keeleys. (*Valentine and Orson*, March; *Whittington and his Cat*, Easter Monday; *Cinderella*, Whit Monday; *A Trip to Kissingen*, November.)
1845	Appointed Professor of English Literature and the English Language in London University, a post he held for two years. On 28 September *To Parents and Guardians* was staged by the Keeleys at the Lyceum, and this was Taylor's first notable success.
1846	Called to the Bar, having been a student of the Inner Temple, on 20 November, and went to practise on the northern circuit.
1850	Returned to work in London upon his appointment as Assistant Secretary to the newly created Board of Health.
1852	*Masks and Faces*, written in collaboration with Charles Reade, produced at the Haymarket Theatre on 20 November.
1853	Published his three-volume biography of the historical painter Benjamin Robert Haydon. Taylor had been working as a journalist and art critic since coming to London, working for *The Times* and *The Graphic* and *Punch*, and, thereafter, apart from his playwriting wrote and edited various works which are recorded, as they occur, in this record.

1854	Promoted to Secretary of the Board of Health. He continued to hold appointments in this area until he retired (as Secretary to the Sanitary Department) in 1871.
1855	Married, 19 June, Laura Barker, daughter of the Rev. Thomas Barker of the parish of Thirkleby in Yorkshire. She was a talented musician and wrote songs and incidental music for Taylor's plays. *Still Waters Run Deep* produced at the Olympic Theatre, 14 May.
1858	*Our American Cousin* produced at Laura Keene's theatre in New York, in which Sothern created the character of Lord Dundreary. This play has the unfortunate distinction of being the drama President Lincoln was watching at Ford's Theatre, Washington, D.C. when he was assassinated in April 1865.
1859	*New Men and Old Acres* produced on 25 October at the Haymarket Theatre.
1860	*The Overland Route* produced at the Theatre Royal, Haymarket, 23 February. In December the play was staged at the Theatre Royal, Manchester, and amongst the cast – in the relatively modest role of Captain Smart – was Henry Irving. Irving, having had some early exposure to the London stage, had returned at this time to the provinces to gain experience. Taylor edited and published the late Charles Robert Leslie's 'Autobiographical Recollections'. Leslie was a successful painter, and a friend.
1863	*The Ticket-of-Leave Man*, Taylor's most famous play, produced at the Olympic Theatre, 27 May. The actor Henry Neville created the leading role of Robert Brierly and made his reputation by it. He continued playing the role until his retirement in 1910 (by which time the 'Lancashire Lad' must have mellowed somewhat). Hawkshaw, the detective, was played by Horace Wigan. The play was enormously popular, having – as Winton Tolles records – 'an initial run of more than four hundred nights'. Taylor's reward was the standard fee of £50 per act, i.e. £200 for a play that was constantly in repertoire worldwide. Although playwrights of the period had worked to establish copyright protection for their work, the adequate payment of royalties seemed to depend upon the vigour with which individual playwrights

pursued their own interests. Boucicault, for instance, earned £10,000 from *The Colleen Bawn* in 1860, but Taylor, three years later, was either unable or unwilling to secure this scale of income from his work.

1865   Completed and published Leslie's 'Life of Sir Joshua Reynolds'.

1869   Taylor persuaded the actress Mrs Rousby, famous for her beauty, to come with her husband to the Queen's Theatre in London to star in a series of historical dramas. He staged three dramas specifically for her – a revival of *The Fool's Revenge* (from Hugo's 'Le Roi s'amuse') 19 December 1869, *'Twixt Axe and Crown* (an adaptation from a German original) 22 May 1870, and *Joan of Arc* 10 April 1871. Mrs Rousby enjoyed great fame for some time and fashion items named after her enjoyed a vogue, but her acting talents did not match her beauty and she faded from the scene.

1874   Having been a contributor since the 1840s, Taylor was appointed editor of *Punch*, a position he held until his death.

1880   12 July, died at his home, Lavender Sweep, Wandsworth.

Cartoon of Tom Taylor

Title page of *Still Waters Run Deep*

STILL WATERS RUN DEEP

An original comedy in Three Acts

First performed at the Royal Olympic Theatre, 14 May 1855 with the following cast:

MR POTTER	Mr Emery
CAPTAIN HAWKSLEY	Mr George Vining
JOHN MILDMAY	Mr Alfred Wigan
DUNBILK	Mr Danvers
LANGFORD	Mr Gladstone
MARKHAM	Mr J H White
GIMLET	Mr H Cooper
JESSOP	Mr Franks
SERVANT	Mr Moore
MRS MILDMAY	Miss Maskell
MRS HECTOR STERNHOLD	Mrs Melfort

After 28 May, the role of Mrs Sternhold was played by Mrs A Wigan.

Act I

SCENE 1. *A Drawing-room in* MILDMAY'*s villa, at Brompton. Doors lead off the drawing-room to* MRS MILDMAY'*s room,* MRS STERNHOLD'*s apartment,* MILDMAY'*s dressing room, the library and the rest of the house. French windows open onto the garden, and at the back of the stage a conservatory communicates with the garden by large folding glass doors. The conservatory is stocked with flowers. It is a summer evening. The stage is furnished with a round table, an easy chair by the fireplace, a piano, a large ottoman, a small writing table, with a couch by it.* MR POTTER *is in the easy chair by the fire;* MRS MILDMAY *on the ottoman;* MRS STERNHOLD *seated by the table, and* MILDMAY *is seated, looking at a book, by the writing table.*

MILDMAY: Suppose, Emily, you gave us a little music.

MRS STERNHOLD: Music! Nonsense! That you may have the opportunity of snoring without detection, Mr Mildmay?

MILDMAY: I thought, perhaps, Emily might indulge me with 'Auld Robin Gray'.

MRS MILDMAY: 'Auld Robin Gray'! Now, aunt, only conceive his asking for a stupid old melody like that.

MILDMAY: You used to like playing it to me before we were married.

MRS MILDMAY: Before we were married! When you know I adore Beethoven.

MRS STERNHOLD: To appreciate Beethoven, Emily, requires a soul for music. Mr Mildmay has no soul for music.

POTTER: No, no, John, you know you haven't. You've no soul for anything.

MILDMAY: Very well. By the bye, Emily, what do you say to a quiet little dinner at Richmond tomorrow?

MRS STERNHOLD: It's quite out of the question, Mr Mildmay: I can't allow Emily to go. I've issued invitations for a dinner here.

MILDMAY: Oh! I thought, as it was the anniversary of our wedding-day, Emily, you might like a tête-à-tête with me at the Star and Garter.

MRS MILDMAY: But you hear it's quite impossible, and that my aunt has made a party at home.

MILDMAY: Very well; I shan't be missed, I dare say. I shall probably dine at my club.

MRS STERNHOLD: On the anniversary of your wedding-day! I'm surprised you should not see the want of proper feeling, the indecency, I may say, of such an arrangement. I shall certainly expect you to dine with us.

MILDMAY: As you please. (*rises*) Well, as we're not to have any music, I may as well go and earth up my celery.

MRS STERNHOLD: Is it such a tax to give us half an hour of your company after dinner?

MRS MILDMAY: Of course, aunt, if Mr Mildmay prefers his vegetables to our company, I should be the last person in the world to detain him.

MILDMAY: If you wish me to stay with you, Emily, you've only to say so.

MRS MILDMAY: Oh, it's perfectly indifferent to me.

MRS STERNHOLD: I'm sure your wife would be the last person to thwart your wishes.

MILDMAY: Oh, I've no particular wish on the subject. I can make myself comfortable here. (*He settles himself on the sofa.*)

MRS MILDMAY: (*to* MRS STERNHOLD) There, aunt, did you ever see anything so provokingly indifferent?

MRS STERNHOLD: My poor child! But don't distress yourself about him. Suppose you give *me* a little music.

MRS MILDMAY: With pleasure. Shall I play you the Moonlight Sonata?

MRS STERNHOLD: Anything you like. (MRS MILDMAY *sits at the piano and begins to play, glancing over her shoulder at* MILDMAY *who falls asleep. After a while she stops.*)

MRS STERNHOLD: Well, Emmy, why don't you finish the Sonata?

MRS MILDMAY: Dear me, aunt – (*angrily*) – you surely would not have me disturb Mr Mildmay! (*rises*) It's quite enough to play him to sleep, I should think, without playing him awake again.

POTTER: (*soothingly*) Come, come, Emmy, He's been working in the garden all day, you know.

MRS STERNHOLD: (*sharply*) Nonsense, Mr Potter; you know you both always fall fast asleep after dinner, though you will never allow it.

POTTER: Well, but sister –

MRS STERNHOLD: I beg we may have no discussion on the matter, brother Potter. I hate discussion. Emily has very good reason to be angry – not a year married yet. However, there's one comfort, niece, you might be a great deal worse off.

    (MR POTTER *leans back in his chair and falls into a doze.*)

MRS MILDMAY: Worse off! Now aunt, what could be worse than a husband without the least spirit, life, enthusiasm – not enough to keep himself awake even through a sonata of Beethoven?

MRS STERNHOLD: Pooh, pooh, child, what do *you* know about it? It is quite true Mr Mildmay is dull – stupid, if you like – but then, remember, he has none of those ridiculous pretensions, which most men set up, to a will of his own. That is the great point. You can do what you like with him if you'll only take the trouble.

MRS MILDMAY: Yes, aunt, but I hate taking trouble. I want a husband to interest me, to share my feelings, invest life with something of poetry – of romance!

MRS STERNHOLD: Nonsense! Poetry and romance are not half such safe investments as the three per cents.

MRS MILDMAY: Oh, look, there's a wasp right on Mildmay's nose! I'll kill it. (*She knots her handkerchief and brings it smartly down on* MILDMAY's *face.*)

MILDMAY: (*opening his eyes*) Eh?

MRS MILDMAY: It was only a wasp. I missed it.

MILDMAY: Oh, thank you! Don't try to kill the next, please. Of the two, I'd rather be stung. (MRS MILDMAY *goes to leave.*) Going into the garden?

MRS MILDMAY: No, I'm going into my own room.

MILDMAY: Oh, then, I'll go and earth up the celery! (*rises*) By the way, would you tell Jessop to pack me up a clean shirt? I'm going to Manchester tonight by the mail train.

MRS MILDMAY: Tonight! Why you never said a word about it till now!

MILDMAY: No. Why should I? I shall return by the express tomorrow. I shall see you again before I start. (*Exit* MILDMAY *leisurely, through the conservatory.*)

MRS MILDMAY: (*aside*) Provoking! But I'm glad I hurt him a little. Good night, papa – good night, Aunt Jane. (*at door*)

MRS STERNHOLD: Why, you're not going to bed child, it's hardly nine o'clock.

MRS MILDMAY: Isn't it? I'm sure the day's been long enough. (*looking for a book on table*) Did you see my Tennyson, aunt?

MRS STERNHOLD: Tennyson! Nonsense! Always at that ridiculous poetry of yours.

MRS MILDMAY: Oh, aunt, if you knew the comfort it brings to my withered heart. (*going*)

> 'She only said the day is dreary.
>
>   He cometh not, she said.
>
> She said, I am weary – a-weary –
>
>   I wish that I were dead.'

(*looking off through the conservatory*) There's Mildmay, with his coat off, just like a common market gardener. Oh, what a contrast to Hawksley! Heigho! (*Exit.*)

MRS STERNHOLD: (*rises*) Here's that brother of mine snoring now. Brother Potter! (*bawling in his ear*)

POTTER: (*waking suddenly*) Eh, my dear? Did you speak?

MRS STERNHOLD: Did I speak? Did you hear? Now Emily's gone, perhaps you will inform me, yes or no, whether you mean to do what I asked you to do before dinner? (MRS STERNHOLD *resumes her seat*; POTTER *rises and comes down to sit by the table.*)

POTTER: But, my dear sister, it's impossible!

MRS STERNHOLD: Nothing is impossible, brother Potter.

POTTER: But you won't understand that the settlement –

MRS STERNHOLD: Settlement! Stuff and nonsense!

POTTER: But, you will allow me to observe, it's anything but stuff and nonsense, sister. When Emily married, I settled eight thousand pounds on her, payable to the trustees six months from the date of the settlement. That's eight months since, and I've not paid a farthing of the money yet.

MRS STERNHOLD: And what of that, pray? She's your only child; all you have will be hers at your death.

POTTER: At my death! Well, if there *is* eighteen years' difference between your age and mine, Jane, there's no occasion to allude to my death in that cheerful way. But I'm bound to pay that eight thousand pounds over to the trustees under the settlement. Suppose Mildmay asked after this money some fine morning, a pretty figure I should cut!

MRS STERNHOLD: Mr Mildmay knows too well what is due to our position to do anything of the kind. He's not at all keen in money matters – that I must say for him.

POTTER: No: that's it. It's just because he is such an innocent, unsuspecting lamb of a man –

MRS STERNHOLD: Nonsense, brother! I don't wish for any discussion; I only want an answer – yes or no. You've already invested one thousand pounds in shares in

---

'She only said the day is dreary' misquotes a refrain from Tennyson's *Mariana*.

Captain Hawksley's Galvanic Navigation Company, and now he has very kindly offered you twenty more fifty pound shares, and I've promised you will take them up. You surely don't wish me to break my promise?

POTTER: Certainly not, sister – certainly not. It always gives me pleasure to carry out your wishes, but I really don't like to propose the thing to Mildmay.

MRS STERNHOLD: And why should you say a word to him about it? I suppose you can pay him the interest of the money? The Galvanic Navigation Company guarantees eight per cent; you pay Mildmay five, and put three per cent into your pocket by the transaction. You can't deny that.

POTTER: Well, but this Galvanic Company, you know – how can one tell it's quite safe?

MRS STERNHOLD: Do you consider Captain Hawksley a gentleman?

POTTER: Oh certainly, my dear!

MRS STERNHOLD: Do you think he would inveigle you into a dangerous speculation?

POTTER: No, I don't believe he would for a moment; but –

MRS STERNHOLD: Then what have you to say?

POTTER: Well, my dear, I say –

MRS STERNHOLD: *Black*, because I say *white*! That's always the way. I wonder what *would* happen if you could once agree with me on any one subject?

POTTER: Well, I'm sure, sister, I always do end by agreeing with you.

MRS STERNHOLD: Then why not begin with it? It would save so much disagreeable discussion. Then I consider it settled – you take up these shares. The Captain promised to call this evening. You can arrange the business with him when he comes.

POTTER: Eh! Hawksley coming here this evening?

MRS STERNHOLD: Why, have you any objection?

POTTER: No, no, no! He's a very clever fellow, Hawksley – vastly agreeable – vastly, the sort of man one's always glad to see; but still I should be just as well pleased not to see him here quite so often.

MRS STERNHOLD: Indeed! (*angrily*) May I ask why?

POTTER: Oh, if you're going to lose your temper, sister –

MRS STERNHOLD: Brother Potter, did you ever see me lose my temper?

POTTER: No, no, my dear.

MRS STERNHOLD: I wish to know what possible reason you have for objecting to Captain Hawksley's visits?

POTTER: I, sister? I object? On the contrary, I like him. I've every confidence in him, but –

MRS STERNHOLD: Well?

POTTER: I don't quite like his coming here, on Emmy's account.

MRS STERNHOLD: On Emily's account! Oh, you may be perfectly easy on that score. I grant you that before his marriage he might have shown some penchant for Emily.

POTTER: So much so that I always fancied, if it had not been for your setting your face against it, he and Emmy might have made a match of it.

MRS STERNHOLD: Captain Hawksley was not at all the man for Emily. Besides, I'm sure she never had any fancy for him.

POTTER: Perhaps not; but what I'm afraid of is she may have some fancy for him now.

MRS STERNHOLD: Brother Potter!

POTTER: Oh, I know what I'm about, sister; they're afraid of you – nothing goes on when you are there; but they don't mind me – and I've observed more than once –

MRS STERNHOLD: (*with suppressed but violent agitation*) Well – what – speak out – what have you observed?

POTTER: Well, but, sister, don't excite yourself in that manner. You know it always flies to your head. Emmy's your niece, it's true – but after all –

MRS STERNHOLD: No equivocation, brother! What have you observed?

POTTER: Well then, between ourselves, I've observed something – that is – a sort of – you know – in her manner with the Captain, and in his manner with her – Emmy's romantic, and the Captain insinuating and agreeable, and what you women call interesting – and, in short, sister, there's a sentimental sort of a – flirtation – going on between 'em already – platonic, I've no doubt, but there's no saying where that sort of thing may end – and I don't like it – and I've intended to talk to Emmy about this ever so long – only I didn't like to –

MRS STERNHOLD: (*aside*) It cannot be! (*to* POTTER) Don't say a word to Emily on the matter; you had better leave it all to me. (*rises*)

POTTER: Exactly, sister, I thought I had. (*rises*)

MRS STERNHOLD: I tell you, brother, you had better leave it all to me. Hark! There's his cab! (*Goes up to window and looks eagerly out. Aside*) Emily is watching for him at her window – he kisses his hand to her – so, so.

POTTER: I told you so. Now just see if she doesn't come down to receive him. Suppose we joined them?

MRS STERNHOLD: There's the postman with the evening paper. You know you are always anxious about the news. Go and enjoy your *Globe* in the library. Now will you oblige me by going?

POTTER: (*crossing*) Certainly, sister, certainly! (*aside*) It's a great comfort I've such a superior woman in the house as my sister. She saves one so much trouble in making up one's mind. (*Exit.*)

MRS STERNHOLD: Can this be true, or is it my silly brother's fancy? Ha! as he said, Emily joins him – she takes his arm – she leans upon it fondly. (*convulsively*) He gathers a rose – he gives it to her! Oh, I will not believe it! No, no, no! They are coming into the house. I will be satisfied. (*Retires behind the screen of plants in the conservatory.*)

        (*Enter* MRS MILDMAY, *carrying a rose in her hand, followed by* CAPTAIN HAWKSLEY.)

HAWKSLEY: And am I to have nothing for my rose?

MRS MILDMAY: Your rose shall have glass of water in my dressing-room to-night, and I promise you not to fling it away tomorrow till it is withered.

HAWKSLEY: Suppose I offered my heart on the same terms?

MRS MILDMAY: Captain Hawksley!

HAWKSLEY: Forgive me; I forgot this was London, and not Seville. I have lived so long in that land of poetry and passion that my blood has learnt its impetuosity, as my tongue its music. But you are offended. Can I wonder if, when I see you unappreciated, respect gives way to sympathy?

(*Enter* JESSOP, *with a carpet-bag.*)

JESSOP: Master's bag, ma'am. Shall I order a cab, ma'am, to take him to the station?

MRS MILDMAY: Mr Mildmay is in the garden, Jessop, you had better ask him.
(*Exit* JESSOP *through the conservatory.*)

HAWKSLEY: Is Mildmay going out of town?

MRS MILDMAY: To-night – so he told me half an hour ago, without a word of explanation, or an expression of regret at leaving me.

HAWKSLEY: And to this man you are tied for life! The law has made you his, and love has no rights in this cold, formal England. Oh, why may I not offer you that tenderness, that sympathy of which he is incapable? I ask no more, only to love you, I seek no return of love.

MRS MILDMAY: Captain Hawksley, I must not listen to this. (*sits*)

HAWKSLEY: Take care; you know not of what a man is capable whose love-code has been learnt in the hot south where passion excuses boldness. Oh, were this but Seville! sweet Seville!

MRS MILDMAY: Well, suppose this was Seville?

HAWKSLEY: Then I would insist upon your hearing an avowal of my love, when there should be none to interrupt us – at the dead of night – here!

MRS MILDMAY: You would not dare – (*rises*)

HAWKSLEY: You had better not defy me; ladies never do in Spain. At midnight I would be under your window.

MRS MILDMAY: Indeed! You would actually climb the garden wall!

HAWKSLEY: What need for that when there's a door?

MRS MILDMAY: But who would open it?

HAWKSLEY: (*taking a key from his pocket*) This!

MRS MILDMAY: The duplicate key of the garden gate that my aunt lost last week!

HAWKSLEY: It has been found, you see.

MRS MILDMAY: Then you took it?

HAWKSLEY: I did!

MRS MILDMAY: And you would dare to use it?

HAWKSLEY: This very night – if this were Seville.

MRS MILDMAY: Really, this is too absurd to be angry at.

HAWKSLEY: I fear your displeasure more than anything in the world; but even that would not change my resolution – were we in Seville.

MRS MILDMAY: Well, suppose admission secured to the garden, you forget Bruin, the savage mastiff; he is let loose after dark.

HAWKSLEY: You forget who gave him to you. Bruin knows his old master.

MRS MILDMAY: And was it for this you made us a present of him?

HAWKSLEY: Precisely. We lay our plans well in Seville.

MRS MILDMAY: Well, suppose you have played the burglar, and Bruin the traitor, what then?

HAWKSLEY: I advance on tip toe – you always sit up late, reading in this room – you start! This room opens on the conservatory – the conservatory on the garden –

MRS MILDMAY: What then? (*walking backwards and forwards across the stage*)

HAWKSLEY: Then when the moonlight trembled on the trees – when the night
winds were hushed in the petals of the flowers – when all slept but love – I
would be at your side, breathing low words of passion, and you would listen.

MRS MILDMAY: (*forcing a laugh*) Charming – were we in Seville! But here, you
forget, windows have bars, and doors have bolts.

HAWKSLEY: There are means to make them both useless.
                              (*both going up stage*)

MRS MILDMAY: Better and better! I see you are determined to destroy my night's
rest, at all events. I shall be dreaming of nothing but burglary and assassination;
imagining a bandit, duly masked, cloaked and dark-lanterned, breaking into the
house, at the least noise. (*seated on ottoman*)

HAWKSLEY: (*leaning over her*) Suppose you heard that noise at midnight?

MRS MILDMAY: And suppose others heard it besides me? A glass door bolted
inside cannot be forced without some noise.

HAWKSLEY: But if the bolt be wanting?

MRS MILDMAY: Good gracious! (*starting up and looking at door of conservatory*)
The inner bolt is removed. (*aside*)

HAWKSLEY: Well?

MRS MILDMAY: You are mad, Captain Hawksley. Ha! ha! ha! (*forcing a laugh*)
But I forget, we are playing Senor and Senora, and all this is not at Brompton,
but *might* be in Seville. (*coming down stage*) But had we not better join papa
and my aunt in the library? They must have heard your cab drive up; my aunt
will wonder what has become of us.

HAWKSLEY: Your aunt – pooh! I'll take odds she's adorning to receive me – putting
on the slightest *soupçon* of rouge. It's extraordinary how some women will be
young, in spite of nature and their looking-glasses.

MRS MILDMAY: No, no; you are too severe on poor auntie. She's a great admirer
of yours, and if I keep you so long en tête-à-tête she'll be jealous of me. Ha! ha!
ha!

HAWKSLEY: At least, let us walk round by the garden. I wish to congratulate
Mildmay on his celery – and then it's so much further. (*Exit* MRS MILDMAY
and CAPTAIN HAWKSLEY.)
                              (*Re-enter* MRS STERNHOLD *from behind the screen of plants in
                              the conservatory, suppressing signs of the most violent emotion.*)

MRS STERNHOLD: The double-faced villain! Oh, Hawksley, Hawksley! So I wear
rouge, do I? – and false hair, of course – and artificial teeth, too, I dare say!
And Emily too! They walk smiling in each other's faces. Thank Heaven I'm not
like that raw girl! I can master my emotion until the time comes, and then
beware, Captain! You do not know the woman you have trifled with! (*Exit.*)
                              (*Enter* MILDMAY, *followed by* JESSOP *with carpet-bag, through
                              conservatory.*)

MILDMAY: (*looking at his watch*) A quarter past nine! I shan't want the cab for half
an hour yet. Let's see – yes – I shall have light enough to finish painting that
trellis I think. Just bring in the ladder, Jessop. (*Exit* JESSOP.) Rather a bore
this journey to Manchester. I don't like leaving Emmy – not that she minds.
Twelve months tomorrow since we were made one. I little thought we should be
so completely two so soon. Oh these aunts and mothers-in-law! Well, patience –

patience! (*Re-enter* JESSOP *with ladder, paint, etc.*) Set it here. (JESSOP *places ladder in centre of the trellis at back of stage. Mildmay takes off his coat, and, ascending ladder, begins to paint. Exit* JESSOP *with the carpet-bag.*)

(*Enter* MR POTTER, *followed by* CAPTAIN HAWKSLEY.)

HAWKSLEY: Magnificent celery! I congratulate you, my dear Potter, on so horticultural a son-in-law. It's a pursuit at once innocent and economical.

POTTER: Yes; I calculate every bundle costs only about twice as much as in Covent Garden.

HAWKSLEY: Apropos – did Mrs Sternhold mention to you that I'd allotted you twenty more Galvanics?

POTTER: Ye-es. I think she did mention something of the kind.

HAWKSLEY: There's ten pounds paid up, you know. I suppose I may rely on the money for tomorrow?

POTTER: Why, you see, my dear Hawksley, I'm extremely obliged to you for letting me have the shares, but the fact is there's a leetle difficulty in the way. There is no making women understand money matters – not even my sister. She's a most superior woman, but she's rather of an irritable constitution; the slightest contradiction flies to her head. I'm sure she's a leetle upset at this moment by a discussion we had together this evening on the subject of these very shares.

HAWKSLEY: (*smiling*) Do you think the investment isn't a safe one?

POTTER: On the contrary – on the contrary. But, you see, all the ready money I can command just now is payable to the trustees under my daughter's settlement. In fact, it belongs, not to me, but to my son-in-law.

HAWKSLEY: Why, Mildmay must be a greater fool even than I take him for if he objects to an investment guaranteeing eight per cent.

POTTER: Well, I'll tell you what. Let me propose it to Mildmay. If he agrees, it's settled – if not, you must settle the matter with Mrs Sternhold; not that I have any objection to tell her, only contradiction does so fly to her head.

HAWKSLEY: As you please.

(*Re-enter* MRS STERNHOLD *and* MRS MILDMAY.)

Here come the ladies.

POTTER: (*in turning round, sees* MILDMAY *on the ladder*) Egad! there's Mildmay upon the ladder.

MRS STERNHOLD: Mr Mildmay? Well, sir, I suppose you don't see us?

MILDMAY: (*on ladder*) Yes, I see you. (*looking down quietly*)

MRS STERNHOLD: And do you see Captain Hawksley?

MILDMAY: Oh, yes! I don't stand on ceremony with him. I'm sure the Captain will allow me to finish my job. (*continues his painting*)

HAWKSLEY: (*sneering*) Oh, I never disturb an artist at work! Fresco, I think.

MILDMAY: No – 'flatting' – that's the technical term.

HAWKSLEY: Indeed! A punster might be provoked into saying it was proper work for a flat. (*all laugh*)

MILDMAY: Flat? Oh, I see! Very good – very good indeed. Would *you* like to try your hand?

---

flat: colloquially a dupe or a fool.

HAWKSLEY: No, thank you. I've no talent for the fine arts. Charming colour, isn't it, ladies? One would say Mildmay has a natural eye for green.

MILDMAY: You're very kind. Yes, I think it's rather a success – and when the creepers come to be trained over it –

HAWKSLEY: Why, you don't suppose any creepers will be weak-minded enough to grow there?

MILDMAY: Why not? Parasites thrive uncommonly well in this house, you know, Captain.

HAWKSLEY: Parasites!

MILDMAY: That's the technical name for what you call creepers.

HAWKSLEY: Ah! I forgot how learned you were in the *Gardeners' Chronicle*. But here's a letter for you.

MILDMAY: A letter for me?

HAWKSLEY: Yes, I looked in at the Union as I passed – and there was a letter for you, so I brought it. It's from Manchester.

MILDMAY: (*coming down*) From Manchester, eh? And *you've* taken the trouble to bring it? How very kind of you. (*Takes letter and puts it into his coat pocket.*)

POTTER: Well, if ever I saw a man so destitute of all natural curiosity!

HAWKSLEY: Well, now I've played postman, and done my devoirs to the ladies, I must be off. (*aside* to POTTER) Let me know how he decides about the shares. (*crosses*) Good night, Mrs Sternhold – Mrs Mildmay. (*bows*)

MRS MILDMAY: Adieu, Captain!

HAWKSLEY: No – not adieu – au revoir! (*Exit.*)

MRS STERNHOLD: (*up stage, looking out of the window*) What a bright moon! I feel rather tired. Good night, Emily. Take care of yourself and don't sit up late. (*crosses towards door*) Good night, Mr Mildmay. You really must go to-night? Well, take plenty of wraps. (*aside*) The unsuspecting fool! But I will watch for him! – and for myself. (*Exit.*)

      (*Enter JESSOP with carcel lamp, which he puts on the table.*)

JESSOP: The cab's at the door, sir. (*Fetches* MILDMAY's *greatcoat and hat from the dressing room, and places them on the ottoman.*)

MILDMAY: Very well, Put in my bag. (*Exit* JESSOP *with bag.*) Good night, Emmy! (*Kisses her on forehead.*)

MRS MILDMAY: Oh! Must you really go, John? Don't go – not to-night?

MILDMAY: I must, my dear. I shall be back tomorrow. Why, what's the matter? Your eyes are full of tears. Don't fret, there's a good girl. Good night.

MRS MILDMAY: (*gives a glance at the conservatory, and shudders – aside*) Oh, no! He dare not! (*Exit* MRS MILDMAY.)

POTTER: (*as* MILDMAY *is going*) Stop, Mr Mildmay, I want to speak to you.

MILDMAY: I'm rather in a hurry. (*going*)

POTTER: You *must* stop. I want to speak to you.

---

devoirs: obligations (from the French).
carcel lamp: invented by Carcel, a lamp in which oil is pumped up to the wick by clockwork (OED).

MILDMAY: (*takes out his watch*) Well, I can give you five minutes.

POTTER: (*pauses, then looks awkwardly up at the trellis*) An uncommonly neat piece of work! Do you know, Mildmay, you're a first-rate painter; and, as for celery – I do believe you'd win the medal at the Horticultural.

MILDMAY: Eh? That's not what you wanted to say!

POTTER: Eh! Well – no – you're quite right, Mildmay, that wasn't what I wanted to say, though it's quite true, all the same. But I want to talk to you on a *leetle* matter of business. You're aware I owe your trustees eight thousand pounds, under Emmy's settlement, and that the money should have been paid two months ago?

MILDMAY: I know that..

POTTER: Exactly. Well, it occurred to my sister and me – that is, to me and my sister – that you might have no objection to investing some of the money, under Emmy's settlement, in Galvanics. It's a magnificent speculation – perfectly safe – guarantees eight per cent., and so – to oblige her – I – I've been and taken forty shares.

MILDMAY: I know that.

POTTER: Good gracious! Why you know everything!

MILDMAY: Not everything.

POTTER: But who could have told you I'd taken all the shares Captain Hawksley was kind enough to allot me?

MILDMAY: Captain Hawksley himself! He thought the best way to prove to me it was a good investment was that you thought so.

POTTER: Eh? Has he been asking you to take shares, too?

MILDMAY: Should you have any objection to get rid of yours?

POTTER: Why, the fact is, it's been my sister's doing all along; and now she's undertaken for me to take twenty more shares, and, as they must be paid for out of the money due under Emmy's settlement, she thought you might have no objection to the arrangement, and, meanwhile, to take the interest of Emmy's money, instead of the principal.

MILDMAY: I've not the slightest objection. (*going up for his hat, etc.*)

POTTER: You haven't?

MILDMAY: In fact I've a few loose thousands of my own at my bankers, and as you tell me this speculation is such a good one, I should like to put a trifle into it myself, say six or eight thousand.

POTTER: Risk six or eight thousand! (*aside*) What a noodle he is! Don't be in a hurry, my dear boy! Six or eight thousand is no joke. It's not wise to risk all one's eggs in one basket, you know.

MILDMAY: But they're not all my eggs, and then it's clear, from what you say, the basket's a strong one.

POTTER: No doubt – no doubt. A magnificent speculation – as safe as the bank – but –

MILDMAY: Well?

POTTER: As a young married man, don't you think now – a good safe mortgage – though it should only bring you in five per cent. –

MILDMAY: My dear Mr Potter, if you think it a good investment, why try to dissuade me from it? If you think it a bubble, why have you put my wife's money into it?

POTTER: Eh? Well – but – confound it!

    (*Enter* JESSOP.)

JESSOP: Cabman says he can just save the mail train, sir.

MILDMAY: Very well. I'm coming. (*Exit* JESSOP.) Good night! Tell Hawksley I'll take a couple of hundred shares if he can spare 'em. I'll call at his chambers to-morrow, as soon as I get back from Manchester. Good night! (*goes up stage*)

POTTER: Good night, and a pleasant journey. (*aside*) Oh, dear! oh, dear! My sister is a most superior woman, but she has a great deal to answer for! And a contradiction does so fly to her head. (*Exit* POTTER.)

MILDMAY: Now for that letter. (*opens letter given to him by Hawksley, and reads it rapidly*) So this renders my trip to Manchester unnecessary. I must see Gimlet at once, and let him know of this discovery. (*smiling*) It was really very kind of Captain Hawksley to bring this letter. (*Exit.*) (MRS STERNHOLD *looks out of her door.*)

MRS STERNHOLD: Hark! the cab drives off! Footsteps! 'Tis Emily! (*Retires into her room, but comes out again quietly during* MRS MILDMAY'*s speech, crosses the back of the stage, and comes down to one side of* MRS MILDMAY.)

    (*Enter* MRS MILDMAY, *from her room.*)

MRS MILDMAY: Mr Mildmay! Husband! Ha! wheels! It's too late! – it's too late! Oh, I had made up my mind to tell him all – to own my folly – to ask his pardon. If Hawksley should be so rash – so wicked – so frantic, as to execute his threat, what will become of me? But he dare not! Surely he dare not! But I will be bold. I will wait here, and if he dare come – but shall I ever have the courage – oh, I shall faint – I shall go mad! (*Sinks into chair and presses her head with her hands.* MRS STERNHOLD *advances to her, surveys her fiercely, then puts her hand on her shoulder.*)

MRS STERNHOLD: Mrs Mildmay!

MRS MILDMAY: Aunt Jane! How pale you are! What is the matter? Are you ill? Shall I call my maid?

MRS STERNHOLD: What I have to say must be heard by none but you.

MRS MILDMAY: (*trying to laugh*) Nay, aunt; if you look so at me, I shall think I am a little girl again, going to be sent to the dark closet for being naughty.

MRS STERNHOLD: Emily, would to Heaven your fault was one calling but for that childish correction; for though I punished I might still esteem you.

MRS MILDMAY: What have I done that you dare speak so to me?

MRS STERNHOLD: What you have done? You dare ask what you have done? Do you think I'm blind? Do you think you can hoodwink me as you have done your doting father and your clod of a husband? I blush for you!

MRS MILDMAY: I do not understand you. (*rises*)

MRS STERNHOLD: Oh, you do not understand me! I must speak more plainly still, must I? A man has addressed you as no man dares address a married woman till he has ceased to respect her. Captain Hawksley is your lover!

---

bubble: a speculation likely to burst.

MRS MILDMAY: It is false!

MRS STERNHOLD: Is it? To-night it may be; were I not here, would it be false to-morrow? Is it false that this man has a key to the garden door? Is it false that to-night – in a few minutes, perhaps – he may be at that window – in this room – at your feet? Is that false? Answer me! (MRS MILDMAY *hides her face in her hands, and is silent.*) You cannot! Go to your room; I will wait here.

MRS MILDMAY: You wait here! – what for?

MRS STERNHOLD: To receive this man.

MRS MILDMAY: No – no!

MRS STERNHOLD: No remonstrance – go!

MRS MILDMAY: Oh, you will not –

MRS STERNHOLD: Go, I say! (*She seizes* MRS MILDMAY *by the arm and forces her off through the door. She then returns, and goes rapidly to the conservatory.*) The door unbolted! All was ready! Hark! Was that anyone stirring overhead? Let me see all is quiet upstairs – and then for *you.* (*Exit* MRS STERNHOLD *cautiously.*)

        (*Re-enter* MILDMAY, *with candle.*)

MILDMAY: Wonderful fellows, these detectives! Gimlet had got the news as soon as I did; I came full tilt upon him driving here at a gallop – we nearly smashed each other. Let me see, I must tell Mrs Sternhold at once, or she may be committing poor Potter still deeper with the fellow; she's an intelligent woman, and can keep a secret. (*goes to* MRS STERNHOLD'*s door and taps*) Mrs Sternhold – don't be frightened – it's me – Mildmay – I've come back. Eh! no answer. (*looks through keyhole*) She's not in her room. There's a light, too! Where can she be? Keeping my wife company, perhaps. Well, I'll deposit my carpet-bag in my dressing room, and then pop in on Emmy – she seemed sorry I was going – she'll be glad I've come back – poor little thing! I think sometimes she's beginning to care for me. Heigho! (*Exit with candle.*)

        (*Re-enter* MRS STERNHOLD.)

MRS STERNHOLD: All is quiet – my brother and the servants asleep. Hark! (*She turns the lamp down, and seats herself*).

        (*Enter* HAWKSLEY *through conservatory door and into the room, coming down cautiously.*)

HAWKSLEY: (springing towards MRS STERNHOLD) Emily!

MRS STERNHOLD: (*starting up – turns up lamp*) 'Tis not Emily!

        (*At this moment* MILDMAY *is seen coming from his room candle in hand. He starts, blows out the candle, and stands listening, but so as not to be seen by the others*).

HAWKSLEY: (*after a pause, recovering himself*) Good evening, Mrs Sternhold! Delighted to see you looking so brilliant – your headache is quite gone, I trust?

MRS STERNHOLD: (*rises*) Villain! adventurer! swindler! imposter! beggar!

HAWKSLEY: Your excitement makes you illogical. Allow me to observe that beggars don't ride, and that my cab is at the garden door.

MRS STERNHOLD: Thanks to the poor dupes who pay for it, of whom I have been one too long.

HAWKSLEY: You do us both injustice, my dear madam. You are too clever for a dupe – and I'm not clever enough –

MRS STERNHOLD: For a rogue? Excuse me – you have just the requisite amount of brains, but there is one quality you are deficient in.

HAWKSLEY: And what may that be, pray?

MRS STERNHOLD: Prudence – or you would have foreseen the danger of making me your enemy.

HAWKSLEY: Allow me to offer you a chair. (*placing chair by table, she sits*) I see our tête-à-tête promises to be as long as it is already interesting. (*takes chair and sits*) And now, my dear lady, I'm all attention; if you will be kind enough to explain to me the cause of all this emotion, I may perhaps succeed in calming it.

MRS STERNHOLD: You are here – and you *dare* ask the cause of my indignation.

HAWKSLEY: I understand. My presence in Mrs Mildmay's boudoir is an unpardonable crime – there might have been an excuse for me had it been yours.

MRS STERNHOLD: (*hiding her face in her hands*) If my weakness had exposed me to such an insult, a man of honour would have spared me it.

HAWKSLEY: (*contemptuously*) A man of honour! In a word, what is the meaning of this scene? Why are you here? What do you want? Where is your niece?

MRS STERNHOLD: Yonder, in her own room. You love her?

HAWKSLEY: Suppose I admit it?

MRS STERNHOLD: And you dare to tell *me* so? (*Seizes a paper knife, which lies on the table.*)

HAWKSLEY: How lucky it's not a dagger!

MRS STERNHOLD: (*In a passion of rage, breaks the paper knife, and throws away the pieces.*) The dagger's a poor revenge. It kills too soon.

HAWKSLEY: We have a variety of slow poisons.

MRS STERNHOLD: Clever as you are, you cannot give a woman a lesson in revenge. Trust the hate I feel for you from this night. My weapon shall not be dagger or poison. You see those pieces? (*pointing to fragments of paper knife*) Before a month is past I shall have broken you as I have broken that!

HAWKSLEY: You positively alarm me! Is it possible I can be so brittle?

MRS STERNHOLD: Laugh on till others laugh at *you!*

HAWKSLEY: No – really – such a capital joke deserves to be laughed at.

MRS STERNHOLD: Listen, Hawksley! Because I have been weak you have thought me blind. I have been your benefactress – yes, wince! I say your benefactress – but in your eyes I was but one dupe the more. You did not know that a woman could love a man without esteeming him. From the first day I have known you I have seen through you – your commission – your services – the credit you boast – the luxury you parade! I knew it all a lie – a shallow, transparent lie! You are nothing – you have nothing –

HAWKSLEY: By Jove, madam! (*starting up*)

MRS STERNHOLD: Sit still. I have not done yet. I say I knew you and yet was weak enough to love you. That love drew me on to serve your ends – blindly – devotedly – to give countenance to your deceptions – credit to your lies; this is what I have done for you, and thus it is I am rewarded! My blind love has made me thus guilty, and you – you, for whose sake I have done these things – upbraid me with my weakness! Heaven is just, but 'tis bitter – very bitter! (*She sobs bitterly.*)

HAWKSLEY: Don't cry! You'll spoil your complexion!

MRS STERNHOLD: (*rising*) From this moment I devote myself to your destruction with all the energy I have hitherto employed for your service. I know your heart is invulnerable. I will not strike at that.

HAWKSLEY: At my fortune, I presume?

MRS STERNHOLD: Your fortune? I have but to let in the light upon its shameful secrets and it crumbles to the ground.

HAWKSLEY: But you won't let in the light?

MRS STERNHOLD: I have done so.

HAWKSLEY: Really!

MRS STERNHOLD: The money I had wrung from my brother for your speculation, and on which you rely to meet your engagements to-morrow, will not be paid.

HAWKSLEY: Oh! at last! (*rises*) I was waiting for you to get out of the quicksands of sentiment to the solid ground of business. Be good enough to listen to me – and, above all, follow my argument closely. I am here in two characters – as a gentleman and as a man of business. As a gentleman, I confess, my conduct has been scandalous – I admit it. Call me what you like, I deserve the very worst your abundant vocabulary can supply. But, as a man of business – hands off! There I decline your jurisdiction altogether. The speculator cannot in fairness be saddled with the lover's peccadilloes. Mr Mildmay intends to invest largely, I hope, in Galvanics. You will be good enough not to prevent him from executing that laudable intention.

MRS STERNHOLD: He will not come.

HAWKSLEY: Oh, yes, he will!

MRS STERNHOLD: I will forbid him.

HAWKSLEY: And I forbid you to say a word to him in the matter! And woe to you if you breathe one syllable of my concerns to him or any other living soul! You talk of my imprudence! Have you forgotten your own? You can ruin my fortune! True. But your own reputation – that reputation so intact – so awful – kept up at such cost of hypocrisy and deceit! I am an adventurer! Granted! What are you!

MRS STERNHOLD: A most unhappy woman. (*sits*)

HAWKSLEY: You will have a better title to *that* name when I have shown you to the world in your true colours.

MRS STERNHOLD: It is not in your power! Who will believe *you*?

HAWKSLEY: Allow me to observe that I am the fortunate possessor of no less than thirteen of your letters.

MRS STERNHOLD: (*rises*) You have not burnt them, as you swore you had done, on your honour.

HAWKSLEY: *My* honour! How could *you* trust *that* security? Oh, no! One doesn't burn such letters as yours!

MRS STERNHOLD: Alas! even I did not know this man.

HAWKSLEY: (*looking at his watch*) Half-past twelve o'clock! How time flies, to be sure! I've to be up early at business, and late hours will ruin your complexion. Addio! Remember my ultimatum – peace or war, as you will. I prefer peace infinitely; I hate giving pain to a woman. But if Mildmay doesn't show tomorrow – with the money – your interesting autographs will be added to the literature of the country. En attendant – allow me to wish you a very good night. (*Goes towards the door of the conservatory, then turns.* MRS STERNHOLD *crosses, towards door.* MILDMAY *is seen to step forward and clench his fist, but checks himself and retires.*) By the way, I dine here tomorrow. I hope our little scene of to-night will not prevent your receiving me with your usual amiability. (*Exit* HAWKSLEY *by conservatory.*)

MRS STERNHOLD: Ruffian! Coward! Should he dare to expose these fatal letters, he will destroy me! But I must be calm – this girl shall not see a trace of emotion. (*goes to door and opens it*) Emily! (*Enter* MRS MILDMAY.) Emily, I – (*turns faint*)

MRS MILDMAY: Is he gone?

MRS STERNHOLD: For this night you are safe. This man dare not – dare not – Oh, what will he not dare? (*crossing towards door while speaking*)

MRS MILDMAY: Aunt – dear aunt! be composed. Come with me – come to bed! What can have passed between them? (*Exit* MRS MILDMAY, *leading* MRS STERNHOLD.)

(*Enter* MILDMAY *from room.*)

MILDMAY: So! I knew he was a rascal, but I'd no notion Mrs Sternhold had been such a fool. But when your strong-minded woman *does* break loose a Welsh river after a flood is a joke to her. Poor Emily, too! she has had a narrow escape. Perhaps, after all, I have carried the laisser aller principle too far. It's a capital rule in political economy, but it don't do in married life, I see. That wants a coup d'état now and then. So! my wife! (*goes towards conservatory*)

(*Enter* MRS MILDMAY.)

MRS MILDMAY: She's calmer now. I must go to my room for ether. (*Going towards her room she sees* MILDMAY, *and, not recognising him at first, screams.*) Stand back, sir! How dare you?

MILDMAY: (*coming forward*) Don't be alarmed, my dear; it's only John.

MRS MILDMAY: My husband? Come back? Thank Heaven! I'm safe now!

MILDMAY: I hope so. But what's the matter? Why are you up at this hour? How comes that garden door open?

MRS MILDMAY: I – I – don't know. Was it open?

MILDMAY: Yes; I found it so just now, as I came back from the station.

MRS MILDMAY: Then you're not going to Manchester. Do not leave me! Stay – do stay!

MILDMAY: My journey's unnecessary, I find. But about this open door? I must take a survey of the premises. Jessop was firing at the blackbirds today. He left his gun in the Green-house.

MRS MILDMAY: No-no! Oh, consider! If you should meet him –

MILDMAY: Him – who?

MRS MILDMAY: The – the – robber – the man!

MILDMAY: Oh! then there *is* a man?

MRS MILDMAY: No – no! Didn't you say you thought there was?

MILDMAY: Not I! But, to satisfy you, I'll make the round of the garden.

MRS MILDMAY: No – no!

MILDMAY: Don't be alarmed, Emmy. I shall take the gun, and use it – if necessary. (*going off*)

MRS MILDMAY: Oh, Heaven! If they meet! (*sinking into chair and clasping her hands. Tableau.*)

Act II

SCENE 1. *The Breakfast Room in* MR MILDMAY's *house. A door on the right. A breakfast-table and two chairs, and a small writing-table.* MRS STERNHOLD *and* MR POTTER *seated at breakfast.*

POTTER: Why, Jane you positively have eaten no breakfast! And now I look at you, I declare you are as pale as a sheet of paper, and your eyes are red, and I'm sure you're feverish. You are not well, my dear Jane! You're far from well – in fact, you're very ill. Do let me give you a globule.

MRS STERNHOLD: Nonsense, brother. I don't believe in globules. It's merely the consequence of our discussion yesterday. You know discussion always makes me ill.

POTTER: But, my dear Jane, there's not the least occasion to be ill this morning. I've agreed to do as you wished. Hawksley shall have the money for these shares this very day. It's an excellent investment, as you proved last night.

MRS STERNHOLD: And pray who ever said anything of the kind?

POTTER: Why, didn't you?

MRS STERNHOLD: Certainly not. You are always misunderstanding me.

POTTER: (*joyously*) Oh, there's time enough yet, for the matter of that. If you don't think it a good investment, say so, and I'll write to Hawksley and tell him I've changed my mind, by your advice.

MRS STERNHOLD: Of course; lay the responsibility upon me.

POTTER: Well, you see, as far as I'm concerned, I'd rather not have anything to do with the affair; there's mischief enough done as it is, particularly as Mildmay has taken it into his head to invest six or eight thousand in it himself.

MRS STERNHOLD: Mildmay invest his money in Captain Hawksley's company?

POTTER: Certainly; didn't he tell you? He was to have seen the Captain to-day about it, after his return from Manchester. As he didn't go to Manchester I suppose he'll call on him when he goes into the City this morning. He's late – poor Emmy's very unwell.

MRS STERNHOLD: Go at once, and beg Mildmay to come here before he goes.

POTTER: Yes, my dear. I'll thank you for another cup of tea.

MRS STERNHOLD: I said *at once*, brother.

POTTER: (*rising*) Certainly, my dear Jane – certainly; I'm going. (*aside*) That woman's the guardian angel of our family. (*Exit.*)

MRS STERNHOLD: (*rises*) Not satisfied with my brother's fortune, he wishes to secure Mildmay's too! And that poor silly girl fancies this man loves her – loves her for her own sake. I thought so once – fool that I was! But as long as my letters remain in his possession, I am at his mercy – I and mine. I must have those letters, be their price what it may. Oh, if I could but inspire Mildmay's sluggish nature with one spark of chivalry or sentiment! He is so dull! But he is, at least, braver and more manly than this coward. He must extort from his fears what I could never obtain from his generosity.

(*Enter* MILDMAY.)

Good morning! How is Emily?

MILDMAY: Not well; she has had a bad night; my sudden departure annoyed her, and my sudden return startled her. I recommended her to breakfast in her own room. Mr Potter told me you wanted to see me.

MRS STERNHOLD: Yes. I have a secret to confide to you – a most important secret; one I should not dare to trust to anyone in whom I had not the most implicit confidence.

MILDMAY: I'm much obliged to you; what is it? And as I've not breakfasted, if you will give me a cup of tea while you tell me. (*sits at table*)

MRS STERNHOLD: (*resuming her seat, pouring out tea*) Promise me first not to mention the subject to anyone – not even your wife.

MILDMAY: My wife! Didn't you say it was a secret? The cream, please.

MRS STERNHOLD: If your mother were alive, and a man had insulted her, what would you do?

MILDMAY: The right thing, of course. Might I trouble you for the sugar basin?

MRS STERNHOLD: You have lost your mother; so has Mrs Mildmay; but your marriage with her has given you a claim upon me, second only to that of a brother. From all I have seen of you, I feel I may expect of you a brother's devotion.

MILDMAY: Do you? Butter, please.

MRS STERNHOLD: Suppose, then, a man had insulted *me* in the most flagrant way. I am a woman – a widow; I have no son; my brother is an old man. Suppose I said to you, 'You alone can defend my cause; to you alone I can look for aid – for protection; aid me – protect me!' What would you answer?

MILDMAY: Eh! Well – really I don't know. What should you recommend me to answer?

MRS STERNHOLD: Are you a man, and ask that? You surely did not listen to the case I put.

MILDMAY: Why, you see we Lancashire folk are somewhat dull of comprehension. If you'd speak out, straightforward-like, I might understand you better.

MRS STERNHOLD: If a man gave you a blow, what would you do?

MILDMAY: Hit him again.

MRS STERNHOLD: Yes, if he were a bruiser; but if he were a gentleman you would use the weapons of a gentleman in your defence. Your honour and that of your wife's relatives are one; you have been insulted through me. Now do you understand?

MILDMAY: I see; a lady has been insulted, and she wishes me to insist on gentlemanly satisfaction on her account. Well, there's only one remark I wish to make on that point. Yesterday, after dinner, as I was lying on the sofa, asleep, as you thought, you said to my wife, 'Your husband is dull, stupid, I admit it; but then he has none of those ridiculous pretentions that most men set up to a will of his own; you could do what you like with him if you'd only take the trouble.'

MRS STERNHOLD: (*embarrassed*) I don't remember saying anything of the kind.

MILDMAY: Don't you? I do. I have no doubt that you were quite right; only I don't see how a man without any will of his own is to set up a character for pluck and energy all of a sudden, and turn fire-eater, not on his own account, but on yours; there's my difficulty!

MRS STERNHOLD: This is no answer, Mr Mildmay.

MILDMAY: Isn't it? I think I can put it into unmistakable English. I have been married for a year, and I've taken things as they came. I confess I have always had a sort of idea a man ought to be master in his own house; but I know that isn't your notion; you think a man ought to let his wife lead him by the nose; that a woman should control everything; in fact, you're the head of the family. I daren't ask a friend home to dinner without notice given, and leave obtained beforehand; the servants look to you for orders, and to me only for wages; you settle the patterns of the furniture, and the laying-out of the garden; in short, you're A 1 in the house, and I'm nobody. I've no objection; only if I'm not to have any authority, I can't think of taking any responsibility; if I am a cipher, I claim the right to act as a cipher.

MRS STERNHOLD: As I expected. (*aside*) You are right; each to his place. I knew you had abnegated the duties of head of a family; I thought it just possible you might still retain the feelings of a man. (*rises*) You have shown me my error – I am much obliged to you. Good morning, sir. (*Exit indignantly.*)

MILDMAY: I hope she understood that, at all events.

(*Re-enter* POTTER.)

POTTER: (*sits at table*) Eh! Well, Mildmay, have you settled matters with my sister?

MILDMAY: Well, I think I have pretty well; it was about those shares of Hawksley's. (*breakfasting*)

POTTER: I knew it was. Well, it appears she has changed her mind about 'em.

MILDMAY: Not that I know of. I'm off to Hawksley's directly after breakfast; and – talking of that – have you got the shares he allotted to you last week?

POTTER: Yes. (*taking out his pocket-book*) Here they are.

MILDMAY: If you like to endorse them to me, I've no objection to take them at par, on account of so much of the money owing under my wife's settlement.

POTTER: Take the shares at par! (*Rises and goes to writing-table to endorse shares.*) Delighted, my dear boy – de-lighted! But you're sure it's all right? Is my sister aware of it?

MILDMAY: Oh, Mrs Sternhold and I understand each other. There's no time to be lost – I want to catch the first 'bus to the City.

POTTER: There you are – twenty scrip certificates at par; that's one thousand pounds, and that makes seven thousand pounds I owe you now instead of eight thousand pounds. (*Gives shares.*) But, my dear boy – (*as* MILDMAY *crosses to door*) – I'd inquire about the speculation, if I were you, in the City, just by way of precaution. I would, indeed! You're not up to this sort of thing, you know.

MILDMAY: Oh, never mind me. I know I'm no conjuror; but, perhaps, after all, father-in-law, I'm not such a fool as I look. (*Exit.*)

POTTER: Poor lad! Now he thinks himself a devilish clever fellow! If he had a little of my experience! But there's no taking the self-conceit out of the young men now-a-days. (*Exit. Servants clear stage.*)

SCENE 2. CAPTAIN HAWKSLEY's *Apartments, gaily and luxuriously furnished. There is one door, and a window with chintz hangings; a profusion of prints, pictures, etc., books gaily bound, a lounging chair; fireplace; an office table, covered with papers,*

---

par: face value.
scrip: certificate of stocks or shares.

prospectuses, plans, etc.; with a drawer in it, and a chair by the table. Another table with coloured plans of the 'Inexplosible Galvanic Boats', and various other chairs.
HAWKSLEY *is discovered, writing, in a fashionable morning wrapper and smoking cap, seated at the table.*

HAWKSLEY: (*pausing from his writing to look at his watch*) Eleven o'clock and no signs of Mildmay! Surely that wildcat of a woman knows better than to carry out her threat of peaching. She ought to know I'm not a man to be trifled with. (*rises*) 'Sweet is revenge especially to woman.' But reputation is still sweeter, and thanks to her remarkably indiscreet pen, hers is in my hands – and she knows it. I'm a cool hand, I flatter myself, but, by Jove, she nearly threw me off my balance last night! That sudden turn up of the lamp was devilish well imagined. (*taking up plan*) But this infernal company. I never was so deep in a thing before without seeing my way out. After all, I should have done better to have stuck by Tattersall's and the Turf. The Ring are sharp fellows, but they're regular green 'uns compared with those blades of the Stock Exchange. Those muffs at the Home Office crow about shutting up the West-end hells; but what's chicken-hazard to time bargains? A fellow who risks his hundred on the spinning of a roulette ball is a gambler, and may be quodded by the first beak that comes handy, but let him chance his hundred thousand on the up or down of the Three per Cents every month of the twelve, and he may cultivate domestic felicity at his box at Brompton, in the respectable character of a man of business. Ha, ha, ha! John Bull is certainly a fine, practical, consistent animal. (*a knock at door*) Come in!

(*Enter* DUNBILK.)

DUNBILK: Ah, Hawksley, me boy, how are ye?
HAWKSLEY: Right as a trivet, my prince of prospectus-mongers.
DUNBILK: Ah, don't ye be putting the blarney on me, then! Look at that – (*giving newspaper*) – and see if that don't be taking the grin out of ye. Sure I've marked it wid a black edge like a mournin' letter!
HAWKSLEY: (*looking blank*) Confound it! Galvanics at two and a half discount! That's fishy!
DUNBILK: Mighty piscatorial, me boy! And betwixt you and me and the post, if you and me and the direction generally doesn't look mighty sharp the two and a half will be foive by to-morrow.
HAWKSLEY: The devil! Why, they were at two premium only yesterday!
DUNBILK: It's that blackguard, Bolter; he's blowed the gaff. I tould the direction they couldn't afford to quarrel wid the secretary!
HAWKSLEY: But how could we keep a fellow who had been robbing us to the tune of a hundred a month?

---

peaching: informing.
'*Sweet is revenge . . .*' from *Don Juan* by Byron (Stanza 124).
muff: bungler, awkward or stupid person.
chicken-hazard: game of dice (played in *West-end hells*: London gambling houses).
quodded: imprisoned.
right as a trivet: colloquially, in good health. A trivet is an iron tripod for holding cooking pots, with three steady legs.

DUNBILK: And what o' that? Sure, wasn't he the manes of getting us tin times that out o' the public? The craythur was rared for the church; why wouldn't he be taking his tithe?

HAWKSLEY: Well, there's only one thing for it – we must rig the market. Go in and buy up every share that's offered!

DUNBILK: Divilish asy to say 'buy' but where's the tin to come from? I called in at Flimsy's as I came along, and they looked so black at me in the parlour that I felt it a superfluous act of politeness to inquire after the state of our balance.

HAWKSLEY: I've a thousand in this note-case; and, besides, expect a few more thousand today.

DUNBILK: The divil you do! Hooray! Corn in Agypt! It's yourself that's the boy can do it! I'll go bail you've been dhrawing the Brompton milch cow of yours again. Sure, there's a dale of bleedin' in that ould Potter – and he's mighty polite too. Sure, he asked me to dine with him today!

HAWKSLEY: I shall meet you there. But I've a better fish on my hook than old Potter – his son-in-law.

DUNBILK: What, young Mildmay? Mind what ye're about, me boy. He's from Lancashire and thim north-country boys is as cute as Dublin car dhrivers.

HAWKSLEY: Then this fellow's a cocktail – for a greater flat was never potted!

DUNBILK: Anyhow he'd find his match in you if he was as sharp as Corney Rooney's pig, that always bolted a week after quarter day for fear he'd be made bacon of to pay the rint! The top of the mornin' to ye, my boy! I'll be off to the City and give our boord the office. By the powers! but they ought to vote you a piece of plate.

HAWKSLEY: Well, a handsome salver wouldn't look amiss on my sideboard.

DUNBILK: Divil the salver! – sure, I'd suggest a stewpan!

HAWKSLEY: A stewpan!

DUNBILK: It's nate and appropriate. Brass outside and tin at the bottom. (*Exit.*)

HAWKSLEY: Curse his bogtrotting impudence! But that's the worst of letting one's self down to this City work. At the Corner one was safe to be in a gentlemanly set, but East of Temple Bar they're such d[amne]d low fellows!
> (*Enter a* SERVANT.)

SERVANT: Mr Mildmay.

HAWKSLEY: Bravissimo! Here, bring this table down from the fire! (*The servant moves writing-table downstage, and places an easy chair beside it.*) Now show him in. (*Sits at table. Exit* SERVANT, *who re-enters immediately, showing in* MILDMAY. *Exit* SERVANT. HAWKSLEY *pretends to be absorbed in his writing and leaves* MILDMAY, *upon his entrance, standing.*)

HAWKSLEY: (*looking up*) A thousand pardons, my dear fellow! One gets so absorbed in these cursed figures. Take a chair. You'll allow me to finish what I was about.

Flimsy: slang for a banknote, so probably here means the Bank.
car: here to mean cab.
cocktail . . . potted: horse with a docked tail, not the thorough-bred it might first appear, hence the general meaning of Mildmay not being as smart as he looks and being a fool ready to be duped.
the Corner: Tattersalls' betting rooms, which were near Hyde Park Corner in London.

MILDMAY: Don't mind me. I'm in no hurry.

HAWKSLEY: (*after a minute of pretended work*) By the way, if you'll look at that table, you'll find a plan of our inexplosible galvanic boat somewhere. Just glance your eye over it, while I knock off this calculation – it will give you an idea of the machinery. (MILDMAY *approaches table, and takes up a plan, and while pretending to look at it, surveys the room, etc.*)

HAWKSLEY: (*putting away his papers and rising*) And now, my dear Mildmay, I'm at your service. But, before we come to business, how are all at Brompton? The ladies all well?

MILDMAY: Mrs Sternhold's a little out of sorts this morning.

HAWKSLEY: Ah! Had a bad night?

MILDMAY: I should think so.

HAWKSLEY: (*at table*) Well, I had a note from Potter. He tells me you had some thoughts of taking shares in our Galvanics. Ever done much in that sort of thing?

MILDMAY: No, not yet.

HAWKSLEY: I fancied not, by the style in which you seem to have talked of getting shares, as if you thought they could be had for asking. You see there's been such a run on 'em that we've had twice as many applied for as could be allotted. But there may be a few in the market still. Another week, and you'd not have had a chance. Perhaps it would be as well though, before you connect yourself with it, that I should give you, briefly, an idea of our scheme, our means of carrying it out, and its probable results. (*crosses*)

MILDMAY: If you would be so kind.

HAWKSLEY: Fetch yourself a chair, then. (*They sit.*) Steam, it has often been remarked, is yet in its infancy – galvanism, if I may be allowed the comparison, is unborn. Our company proposes to play midwife to this mysterious power, which, like Hercules, is destined to strangle steam in the cradle. But to do this effectually is the work of no mere everyday speculator. We require a plan of operations calculated on a solid and comprehensive basis. You follow me?

MILDMAY: A solid and comprehensive basis? I suppose that means a good lot of money.

HAWKSLEY: Precisely! Money is the sinews of industry, as of war. Now, to anticipate events a little, let us throw ourselves into the future, and imagine our company at work. We have created between the ports of the West of Ireland and the United States, Mexico, the West India Islands, and Brazil, a line of galvanic boats – rapid, economical, safe, and regular. For rapidity, we can give four knots an hour to the fastest steamer yet built. As for safety, our galvanic engines can't blow up.

MILDMAY: But suppose the company should? Companies do blow up sometimes, don't they?

HAWKSLEY: Bubbles do, but not such companies as this. But to resume; economy we ensure by getting rid of coal altogether.

MILDMAY: Get rid of coal! Do you really? And pray what do you use instead?

HAWKSLEY: Our new motive principle! That is *our* secret at present. But you will at once perceive, as an intelligent man of business, the incalculable consequences,

---

galvanism: electricity produced by chemical methods.

that must follow from the employment of a new motive principle, which combines the essential qualities of a motive principle – the maximum of speed and minimum of cost. (MILDMAY *bows*.) You see, there are three things to be considered – the article, the duty, and the cost of carriage. The two former being fixed, let us represent them by A and B. You understand algebra?

MILDMAY: I used to know a little of it at school.

HAWKSLEY: Then let X and $\frac{x}{2}$ denote the respective cost of the two modes of carriage – while the two rates of profit are represented by Y and Y^1.

MILDMAY: Which, in algebra, always denote an unknown quantity.

HAWKSLEY: Precisely. Well, A and B remaining constant, let $Y = A$ plus $\frac{B}{x}$ be the formula for profit in the case of steam, then $Y^1 = A$ plus $\frac{B}{x}$, divided by 2, will be the formula for profit in the case of galvanic transport – or reducing the equations $Y^1 = 2Y$, or, in plain English, the profit on galvanic transport equal to twice the profit on steam carriage. I hope that's clear!

MILDMAY: Perfectly. Only, as you began by assuming the cost of the first at only half that of the second, I don't see what need there was of any algebra to prove the double profit.

HAWKSLEY: Ah! Why, you see, some people apprehend a thing more clearly in symbols. However, to return to our plan of operations. You observe we start from a port in the west of Ireland; by this means we gain six days on Liverpool, Bristol, and the western ports of England. At one blow we destroy Liverpool.

MILDMAY: The devil you do! I've property in Liverpool.

HAWKSLEY: Next, we destroy Bristol.

MILDMAY: Destroy Bristol, too!

HAWKSLEY: That is, when I say destroy, we reduce her to a second-rate port. She will still have the coasting and fruit trade, and may do a little in turtle. We destroy Hull –

MILDMAY: But stop – stop – stop! You're going to destroy everything.

HAWKSLEY: My dear fellow, it's the law of the universe. If, by our line, we can introduce West Indian sugar into the market at two thirds the price of East Indian are we to hesitate because Ceylon may be ruined?

MILDMAY: Of course not. I suppose that would be what the political economists call sentimentalism.

HAWKSLEY: Precisely. If Ceylon is ruined on these terms so much the better for the world in general.

MILDMAY: And so much the worse for Ceylon in particular.

HAWKSLEY: Just so. I see you follow me exactly.

MILDMAY: Only I was thinking –

HAWKSLEY: Pray speak out. The suggestions of a new, fresh mind are invaluable. You were thinking –

MILDMAY: That, as the general interest is made up of particular interests, if you destroy the particular interests perhaps the general interest may not be so much benefitted, after all.

HAWKSLEY: Ah, there you get into an abstruse field of speculation.

MILDMAY: Do I? It seems clear enough to me. (*Both rise.*)

HAWKSLEY: That's because you take a shallow view of the subject.

MILDMAY: One I can see to the bottom of, in fact.

HAWKSLEY: Precisely. A man of your calibre should always distrust what he can see to the bottom of.

MILDMAY: I generally do. Well, after your very lucid demonstration, I see your company cannot fail of success. The more shares a man has the more lucky he should think himself. (*Goes up to table and puts down his hat.*)

HAWKSLEY: (*aside*) Hook'd, play'd, and landed! (*pretending to look on table for note*) I've mislaid Potter's note – but he mentioned your wanting something like two hundred shares, wasn't it?

MILDMAY: I beg your pardon – not exactly – I think –

HAWKSLEY: Why, wasn't that the figure you put it at yourself last night?

MILDMAY: Last night – yes.

HAWKSLEY: You haven't changed your mind?

MILDMAY: No.

HAWKSLEY: Then let us understand each other. Do you want more than two hundred or fewer.

MILDMAY: Neither more – nor fewer.

HAWKSLEY: What do you mean?

MILDMAY: I mean, I don't want any at all.

HAWKSLEY: (*starting with surprise*) The dev – (*recovering himself*) Oh, I suppose you've slept on it?

MILDMAY: Exactly. I've slept on it.

HAWKSLEY: Perhaps Mrs Sternhold's advice may have had something to do with your sudden change of intentions?

MILDMAY: Mrs Sternhold knows nothing about my sudden change of intentions.

HAWKSLEY: I must satisfy myself on that point. (*Comes in front of table.*)

MILDMAY: Do, by all means, if it interests you.

HAWKSLEY: (*sitting on corner of table*) Well, as you don't know your own mind for four-and-twenty hours together, there's nothing more to be said. But as you don't want these shares, may I ask what has procured me the pleasure of seeing you this morning?

MILDMAY: Certainly, I had two objects in coming. In the first place, about two months ago, my father-in-law, Mr Potter, took twenty shares in your company. Those shares have come into my hands this morning by Mr Potter's endorsement. Now, as I don't care about 'em myself, and as there seems such a rush for 'em in the market, I suppose you'll have no objection to take them off my hands at par?

HAWKSLEY: Eh? Take them off your hands at par? Ha, ha, ha! No! By Jove, that's rather too good! My dear Mr Mildmay, I know you're the most amiable of men – a consummate cultivator of that delicate vegetable, celery – a distinguished house painter and decorator – but I had no idea how great you were at a practical joke.

MILDMAY: Very well. We'll drop the shares for the present, and come to motive number two.

HAWKSLEY: Pray do – and if it's better fun than motive number one, I shall have to thank you for two of the heartiest laughs I've enjoyed for many a day.

MILDMAY: We shall see. You have in your possession thirteen letters, addressed to you by Mrs Sternhold. The second motive for my visit was to ask you to give up those letters.

HAWKSLEY: (*aside*) So! the murder's out! She prefers war! She shall have it! (*aloud*) Mr John Mildmay, your first demand was a good joke – I laughed at it accordingly; but your second you may find no joke, and I would recommend you to be careful how you persist in executing this commission of Mrs Sternhold's.

MILDMAY: I beg your pardon. I have no commission from Mrs Sternhold.

HAWKSLEY: It was not she who told you of those letters?

MILDMAY: Certainly not!

HAWKSLEY: Who did?

MILDMAY: You must excuse my answering that question.

HAWKSLEY: Then you are acting now on your own responsibility?

MILDMAY: Entirely.

HAWKSLEY: Very well – then this is my answer. Though you have married Mrs Sternhold's niece, I do not admit your right to interfere, without authority from Mrs Sternhold herself, in an affair in which she alone is interested. I refuse to give up her letters. As to your first request, my business is to sell shares, not to buy them.

MILDMAY: I was prepared for both refusals; so I have taken my measures for compelling you to grant both demands.

HAWKSLEY: The devil you have! Do let me hear what they are? I am all impatience to know how you propose to make Harry Hawksley say *yes*, when he has begun by saying *no*. You've no objection to smoke?

MILDMAY: None in the world. (HAWKSLEY *seats himself comfortably in easy-chair, putting his legs on another chair, and lights a cigar*.)

HAWKSLEY: Now, my very dear sir, fire away!

MILDMAY: (*sits, then in a very calm voice, after watching him*) When you explained the theory of your speculation just now, you thought you were speaking to a greenhorn in such matters. You were under a mistake. Some four years ago I held a partnership in a house in the City, which did a good deal in discounting shares – the house of Dalrymple Brothers, of Broad Street. You may have heard of it. (HAWKSLEY *starts*.) One day – it was the 30th of April, 1850 – a bill was presented for payment at our counting-house, purporting to be drawn on us by our correspondents, Touchet and Wright, of Buenos Ayres. (HAWKSLEY *appears uneasy*.) Though we had no advices of it, it was paid at once, for it seemed all right and regular, but it turned out to be a forgery. Our correspondents' suspicion fell at once upon a clerk who had just been dismissed from their employment for some errors in his accounts. His name *then* was Burgess – dear me, you've let your cigar out. (HAWKSLEY *puffs at his cigar with an effort*.) The body of the bill was apparently in the same handwriting as the signature of the firm; but a careful examination of it established its identity with that of the discharged clerk; and in a blotting book left accidentally behind him were found various tracings of the signature of the firm. The detectives were at once put on his track, but he had disappeared; no trace of him could ever be discovered. Well, this money was repaid, and the affair forgotten. It so

---

greenhorn: a beginner, someone lacking in experience.

happened that when the bill was presented for payment, only one person was in
the counting-house – the clerk who paid the money, and who is since dead. If
you'll allow me, I'll join you. (*taking out cigar-case*) But in the private room of
the firm, which was separated from the counting-house by a glazed door, was the
junior partner – may I trouble you for a light – (*lights his cigar by
HAWKSLEY's*) – who, through the door, saw the bill presented, and observed
the face of the person who presented it. I was that junior partner; the person
who presented the bill – Burgess, as he was then called – the forger – was *you!*

HAWKSLEY: (*falls back in his chair, then with an effort*) It is an infamous calumny!
An abominable lie! Your life shall answer for this insult!

MILDMAY: I don't think that quite. But allow me to conclude. How you have passed
your time since that 30th of April, 1850, I have not the advantage of knowing;
but I know that soon after my marriage, and retirement from business, I met you
as a visitor at my father-in-law's house. I've a wonderful memory for faces – I
remembered yours at once.

HAWKSLEY: It's a lie, I tell you! (*rises*)

MILDMAY: No, it isn't. I resolved not to speak till I could back my words by proofs. I
applied to my late partners for the forged bill. One of them was dead, the other
absent in South America; so that for eight months I found myself obliged to
receive, as a guest at my own table, as the intimate and trusted friend of my
wife's family, a person I knew to be a swindler and a forger!

HAWKSLEY: By heavens! (*aiming a blow at* MILDMAY, *which he stops and forces*
HAWKSLEY *down into easy-chair*)

MILDMAY: Take care! if we come to that game, remember it's town versus country;
a hale Lancashire lad against a battered London roué; fresh air and exercise to
smoke and speculation. You had better be quiet – a minute more and I have
done. The letter I had been so long waiting for, containing the forged bill,
arrived yesterday from Manchester. You were kind enough to bring it out to
Brompton yourself. That bill is in my pocket; if I do not deliver it into your
hands before I leave this room, it goes at once into those of the nearest police
magistrate.

HAWKSLEY: (*after a pause, gloomily*) What are your terms?

MILDMAY: The price of those shares at par, and Mrs Sternhold's thirteen letters.

HAWKSLEY: (*rises, goes round table, and takes notes out of drawer*) Here's the
money.

MILDMAY: (*at upper end of table*) You'll excuse my counting. It's a mercantile habit
I learnt in the house of Dalrymple Brothers. (*Counts notes.*) Quite correct. Here
are the scrip certificates. (*giving his shares*) And now, if you please, the letters?

HAWKSLEY: (*taking bundle of letters from drawer, and throwing them down on
table*) There!

MILDMAY: You'll excuse my counting them too. (*counts letters*) Thirteen, exactly!
And now, might I trespass on you to put them into an envelope, and seal them
with your own seal?

HAWKSLEY: Are they not safe enough as it is?

MILDMAY: Now oblige me. (HAWKSLEY *puts letters into an envelope, and is about
to light taper.*) Oh, allow me – your hand shakes. (*Takes matches from him, and
lights taper.*) I wish Mrs Sternhold to be certain that these letters have passed

through no other hand than yours. (HAWKSLEY *seals the packet, and hands it to* MILDMAY.) And there is the forged bill! (*giving bill to* HAWKSLEY)

HAWKSLEY: (*Examines the bill, then burns it by taper, and throws it to the ground, stamping on it. Aside*) Gone! And he knows nothing of the other.

MILDMAY: (*taking his hat from table*) And now, Captain Burgess – I mean Hawksley – I have the honour to wish you a very good morning.

HAWKSLEY: (*crossing to him*) Stop! A word before you go. Since we had the first pleasure of meeting I've been a soldier, and have served in countries where blood wipes out disgrace. What are your weapons?

MILDMAY: I thought it might come to that; but you needn't trouble yourself to call me out because I shan't come!

HAWKSLEY: And do you flatter yourself I can't force you? I know duelling is out of fashion in this infernal cold-blooded country: but, even here, there are insults a man can't put up with and hold his head up before the world – take care I don't put such an insult upon you! (*drawing near and lifting up his hand*)

MILDMAY: Don't try *that* on again; I may be less patient the second time. I might send you into the street without the trouble of going downstairs; there's two storey's fall, not to speak of the area spikes; you might hurt yourself.

HAWKSLEY: Very well. We are by ourselves – there would be no use in insulting you here; but take care; the first time we meet in company I will lash you across the face with my horsewhip! We shall see then if you will refuse me satisfaction!

MILDMAY: We shall. If you were only a duellist, I doubt if I should think myself bound to risk my life against yours. But I presume even the laws which you recognise absolve me from the obligation of going out with a swindler and a forger.

HAWKSLEY: (*grinding his teeth*) Do you wish to provoke me to murder you?

MILDMAY: Oh, I am not the least afraid of that! For a man who can snuff a candle at twenty paces to call out another who never fired a pistol in his life is no great piece of heroism; but to commit a murder requires some pluck. You've defied transportation, but I don't think you're the man to risk the gallows! Good morning! (*He turns to go.* HAWKSLEY *seems to meditate a rush, but checks himself, and stands biting his lip and trembling all over. Tableau.*)

Act III

SCENE 1. *Scene and furniture as in Act I. Keys in doors.* MRS STERNHOLD *seated in easy-chair by fire;* MRS MILDMAY *sitting on sofa, writing at table.* POTTER *standing, looking over her.*

POTTER: If you don't make haste, Emmy, we shan't be able to get the letter delivered putting off our dinner today in consequence of the sudden indisposition of Mrs Sternhold.

MRS MILDMAY: This is the last, papa. It's just five – Jessop will have enough time to deliver them all before six.

POTTER: (*crossing to* MRS STERNHOLD) How do you feel now, my dear Jane? (MRS STERNHOLD *turns from him impatiently*) I'm really very sorry I endorsed those shares to Mildmay, as it annoys you, but he said he had settled it with you.

MRS STERNHOLD: Dear, dear, brother – will you spare me any further allusion to the subject! My head aches dreadfully!

POTTER: Poor dear! Pull the curtains to, Emmy!

MRS STERNHOLD: No, no – leave them, pray! And leave me, do!

POTTER: I can't think what Mildmay can have meant by telling me he'd settled it all with you! Eh! here he comes to give us an explanation!

       (*Enter* MILDMAY.) Oh! here you are! Well, you're a cool hand.

MILDMAY: Eh?

POTTER: Didn't you tell me, before going into town this morning, when you asked me to endorse those shares to you, that you had settled it all with Mrs Sternhold? And now, it seems, she knew nothing about it. My dear Jane, I wish him to explain himself before you. Mildmay, I insist upon a categorical answer. Did you, or did you not, tell me it was settled between you and Mrs Sternhold?

MILDMAY: I told you so.

MRS STERNHOLD: Mr Mildmay, do you mean to say I expressed any wish of the kind? (*Rises, and comes down.*)

MILDMAY: You never said a word to me on the subject!

POTTER: (*aside*) What does he mean by contradicting himself in this extraordinary way? He must have been lunching with Hawksley. He's had too much wine!

MRS STERNHOLD: Mr Mildmay, I insist on your explaining the meaning of your conduct!

MILDMAY: With pleasure! I couldn't dispose of the shares till they came into my hands, and it occurred to me that the best way of getting them into my hands from Mr Potter's was to use your name.

POTTER: But do you mean to say you have disposed of the shares I endorsed to you?

MILDMAY: I certainly have taken that liberty.

POTTER: (*aside*) Oh! he must have been lunching! There's a coolness about him that's perfectly unnatural!

MRS STERNHOLD: I hate mystification! Will you oblige me, Mr Mildmay, by stating, simply and distinctly, what you have really done with those shares!

MILDMAY: Certainly. I was much struck last night with the justice of Mr Potter's observations on the danger of such speculations as Captain Hawksley's – so, instead of taking any new shares, I've let the Captain have the old ones back again.

MRS STERNHOLD: And do you mean to say he has taken them?

MILDMAY: Certainly – at par. Here's the money.

POTTER: (*crosses*) Do you mean to say he made no difficulty about it?

MILDMAY: Yes – he did a little – but we got over that. There is the thousand pounds you paid him. (*Gives notes to* POTTER.)

POTTER: My dear John, I've done you injustice. Would you believe it? I thought you were tipsy – that Hawksley had been making you drink, in order to humbug you into buying – and now, it seems, you've humbugged *him* into buying. Who'd have thought you had it in you? Would you have thought he had it in him, Jane?

MRS STERNHOLD: (*crossing to* MRS MILDMAY) Have you finished those letters, Emily?

MRS MILDMAY: I've only to direct them, aunt.

MRS STERNHOLD: I'll direct them if you'll tell Jessop to get ready to take them at once. (MRS MILDMAY *rises and exits.*)

POTTER: And I'll just lock up these notes in my escritoire! (*Exit* POTTER. MRS STERNHOLD *sits on sofa, and addresses a letter or two.*)

MILDMAY: Why, you're sending out a circular?

MRS STERNHOLD: It is to put off the people we had invited to dine to-day. I'm too ill to receive them. Did I understand you to say you have seen Captain Hawksley this morning?

MILDMAY: Yes. I left him not long ago.

MRS STERNHOLD: And when you offered him the shares, he took them without making any objections?

MILDMAY: I overruled his objections.

MRS STERNHOLD: Can you inform me by what means?

MILDMAY: Oh! what matter about the means, when the end's attained?

MRS STERNHOLD: Did nothing pass between you on any other subject than these shares?

MILDMAY: Oh – yes – we did touch upon other matters.

MRS STERNHOLD: (*uneasily*) But nothing of any particular interest – nothing in which any of us were concerned? (MILDMAY *takes out the packet of letters, and puts it on the table before her.* MRS STERNHOLD *snatches up the packet, and recognises* HAWKSLEY'*s seal.*) His seal! (*She tears open the packet and recognises her letters. Rises, and comes to centre.*) You have saved my good name! I owe you more than I can ever repay – more than life itself!

MILDMAY: (*quietly*) Hadn't you better lock up those letters, before anybody sees them?

MRS STERNHOLD: Stay! (*She is about to count them.*)

MILDMAY: You may save yourself the trouble – they're all there.

MRS STERNHOLD: All?

MILDMAY: Thirteen.

MRS STERNHOLD: Then you have counted them?

MILDMAY: Yes; but I've no notion what they're about. He sealed them up, as you see.

MRS STERNHOLD: John Mildmay, you have acted like a gentleman. Forgive me for my conduct to you – I cannot forgive myself. To think that I should have doubted you, at the very moment you were about to do me a service which a life of gratitude cannot pay for.

MILDMAY: I shall be satisfied with a good deal less than that. I see you're better already. Oblige me by not putting off your dinner to-day. (MRS STERNHOLD *goes to table and begins to tear up the letters written by* MRS MILDMAY, *and throws scraps into a waste paper basket. Re-enter* POTTER.)

POTTER: Jessop's ready to start. Why, if she isn't tearing up the letters! My dear Jane, what are you about? I'm sure Emmy had written them very neatly.

MRS STERNHOLD: I've changed my mind, brother. The dinner is not to be put off.

POTTER: Well, but my dear Jane – consider your headache – and allow me to observe –

MRS STERNHOLD: My dear brother, allow *me* to observe that I'm the best judge of my own state of health – and go and tell Jessop he will not be wanted to carry the letters.

POTTER: (*going*) Very well, my dear! (*aside*) Now that's sheer strength of mind! What a woman she is! 'Gad, she rises from her prostration like a – what's its name – the bird over the fire offices – a phoenix. (*Exit* POTTER.)

MRS STERNHOLD: (*crosses and sits*) And now that we are alone, tell me what has passed between you and this man. By what magic have you tamed his insolent and pitiless nature?

MILDMAY: Why dwell on details which could only give you pain? From to-day, let all that has passed relative to this affair be forgotten between us. As you said this morning, I have but paid a debt of duty to our relationship. You have got rid of a disreputable acquaintance; take my advice, and don't renew it. (*sits*)

MRS STERNHOLD: Renew it! Never! He was included in our dinner party to-day – but after what must have passed between you, I suppose there's no danger of our seeing him.

MILDMAY: I've no doubt he'll come.

MRS STERNHOLD: He dare not.

MILDMAY: Oh yes, he dare! Assurance is his strong point. But don't be afraid, I shall be here. Receive him as usual, and leave the rest to me.

MRS STERNHOLD: (*with surprise*) John Mildmay, there's something in your manner to-day I have never seen before – a coolness, a self-possession, and energy I never should have expected from – from –

MILDMAY: From such a spoon – that's what you mean, isn't it?

MRS STERNHOLD: No; that's not the word.

MILDMAY: It's about the idea though. But you're wrong. I'm the same man to-day as I was yesterday.

MRS STERNHOLD: John Mildmay, you're a perfect puzzle.

MILDMAY: Have you any curiosity about the key?

MRS STERNHOLD: Curiosity! I am a woman.

MILDMAY: I'm a man – and not an automaton, as you've always considered me – that's all! Listen to me. We *must* have an explanation – and this is the time for it. I'm neither a hero nor a conjuror, but I'm a straightforward man, and I'm not deficient in common sense. When I married your niece I looked forward to a quiet life with a woman I loved in my own undemonstrative way, and who, I thought, would have loved me – and so she would have done, but for you!

MRS STERNHOLD: But for me!

MILDMAY: Yes! She has been brought up to think you infallible. Had you treated me with respect and consideration, she would have done so, too. You thought it proper to ridicule and despise me, and she followed your lead. I saw this, even during our honeymoon. For ten months I've tried what patience, indulgence, and submission would do – that plan has been a failure. From this hour I change my tactics. You are my wife's nearest female relative, and you shall never find

---

the fire offices – a phoenix: private fire insurance companies, who had their own firemen and equipment to attend to fires at premises insured by them.
spoon: simple person.

me wanting in duty or respect, but from this day forth remember there's only one master in this house, and his name is John Mildmay. (*rises*) Now go and dress for dinner. (*She attempts to speak.*) Go and dress for dinner! (*politely handing* MRS STERNHOLD *towards door, exit* MRS STERNHOLD) And now for Emily. Poor girl! Last night's lesson was a hard one, but she brought it on herself. It will do no harm.

         (*Enter* MRS MILDMAY.)

Sit down, Emily. (MRS MILDMAY *sits*.) How well you look.

MRS MILDMAY; A compliment from you! I thought you had forgotten how to pay one.

MILDMAY: Did you, Emily? You remember what day this is?

MRS MILDMAY: Yes. (*with a sigh*) The anniversary of our marriage.

MILDMAY: Does it come round as such a day should, Emily? Do you remember the vows we both took this twelvemonth – 'To love, to honour, and obey'?

MRS MILDMAY: (*surprised*) What do you mean, John?

MILDMAY: They did well, the compilers of that solemn service, to put *love* first, for it carries with it both the others. Have you kept that vow, Emily?

MRS MILDMAY: (*agitated*) I do not understand you!

MILDMAY: Emily, I returned to this house last night, half an hour before you saw me. I overheard all that passed between your aunt and Captain Hawksley. I knew the motive of his intrusion into this house at that hour.

MRS MILDMAY: (*starting up*) Spare me! Forgive me! I was foolish! I listened to him – but I never thought he could have dared – Indeed, John, I never did! And I wished to tell you all before you went – to implore you to stay and watch over me – to guard me from the consequences of – my folly! (*sinking her head on his shoulder*)

MILDMAY: (*gravely*) Compose yourself, Emily! I have too much fairness to confound folly with guilt. Why, my poor child, I knew that fellow's game. I saw how his romantic airs, his honeyed words, and showy graces had fascinated you – how, in comparison with him, you thought me cold, awkward, uninteresting, unimpassioned. You are not the first of your sex, Emmy, who has preferred the shadow to the substance. Thank Heaven you have not been awakened from your dream by the suffering that follows upon sin! Don't speak, my love, but listen. Your father's doting fondness and your aunt's mischievous example have made you what you are. Trust to me henceforth to make you what a wife should be. I should prefer to win you by a lover's tenderness, but if I cannot do that I know how to make a husband's rights respected!

MRS MILDMAY: Oh, thank you, dearest – thank you! Tell me of my faults – I will try to correct them. I will honour and obey you, as a wife should!

MILDMAY: I've been to blame, too. I have been rough, and cold, and careless –

MRS MILDMAY: No, no; you are the kindest and most generous of men. But my father – my aunt – they have been as much mistaken in you as I was. Speak to her as you have spoken to me.

MILDMAY: (*with a smile*) I don't love her as I love you. But make yourself easy – I *have* spoken to her, and in a way I don't think she will soon forget. And now go, darling, and dry your eyes, and come down to our guests smiling as a wife should smile when she meets her husband's loving looks. (*Kisses her.*)

MRS MILDMAY: Oh, bless you – bless you for such words! How have I misjudged you!

MILDMAY: (*suppressing his emotion*) Go – go – dear! Remember, I've my eyes to dry, too (*Exit* MRS MILDMAY.) Thank Heaven, that's over! I've played a desperate game, but I've won it, and the stake was worthy of the risk! (*Exit.*)
(*Enter* POTTER: *dressed for dinner.*)

POTTER: Six o'clock, and Mildmay not dressed yet! Egad! (*rubbing his hands*) He'll be unpunctual for once! Well, I'm glad Jane's better, for we shall be a pleasant party, I flatter myself. There's Dunbilk, an uncommonly pleasant fellow, and – (*bell heard*) Oh, I daresay that's Joe Langford! Joe's always sharp – military time, as he calls it – and a military appetite!
(*Enter* JESSOP, *announcing*)

JESSOP: Mr Langford.
(*Enter* LANGFORD, *exit* JESSOP.)

POTTER: Ah! Langford, my dear fellow, delighted to see you! Mrs Sternhold will be down directly. Well – (*rubbing his hands*) – any news to-day?

LANGFORD: (*by fireplace*) Nothing particular. Uncommonly seasonable weather.

POTTER: Uncommonly seasonable weather – uncommonly seasonable – uncommonly – (*bell heard*) I shouldn't wonder if that's Markham.
(*Enter* JESSOP *announcing*)

JESSOP: Mr Markham.
(*Enter* MARKHAM, *crosses to fireplace, exit* JESSOP.)

POTTER: Ah! it is Markham! How are you all at home? – that's right! You know, Langford, I think. (LANGFORD *and* MARKHAM *bow*.) Well, anything new?

MARKHAM: No – nothing stirring but stagnation! Infernally disagreeable weather –

POTTER: Infernally disagreeable – infernally – very disagreeable weather! (*aside*) I wish Jane would come. She has such a flow of conversation.
(*Enter* MRS STERNHOLD, *and* MRS MILDMAY.)
Ah, here she is! Mr Langford – my dear – Mr Markham. (*The gentlemen bow to the ladies and enter into conversation, near fireplace. Enter* JESSOP *announcing*)

JESSOP: Mr Dunbilk. (*Enter* DUNBILK, *exit* JESSOP.)

DUNBILK: Mrs Sternhold! Mrs Mildmay! How are you, Potter? I was afraid I'd be afther me time – waiting for Hawksley. He promised to dhrive me here in his cab, and I waited till I was too late, and powdhered down in a hansom, ten miles an hour. You expect Hawksley, don't you?

POTTER: Eh? Oh, yes, we rely on the Captain! My women folk here would never forgive me if we gave a dinner without asking the Captain. I assure you, they pull caps for him – aunt and niece. Don't you, Emmy? I think I'm right in saying the Captain's a bit of a favourite – eh, Jane?

MRS STERNHOLD: (*evading the question*) We certainly did expect Captain Hawksley, but he's not always to be relied on.

DUNBILK: Ye may say that, ma'am – run afther as he is by the aristocracy. (*aside*) Not to spake of the sheriff's officers.

---

pull caps: argue over him.

(*Enter* MILDMAY.)

MILDMAY: I beg your pardon – I fear I have kept you waiting.

POTTER: Oh, Captain Hawksley hasn't come yet.

DUNBILK: Sure I wouldn't wait for him, if I was you. He'd be sorry, if he does come, to think he spoiled the fish.

MILDMAY: No; we'll give him a quarter of an hour.

MRS MILDMAY: (*aside to* MRS STERNHOLD) Surely he will not dare to show himself here, after last night!

MRS STERNHOLD: (*aside to* MRS MILDMAY) You have seen what he dares do, already!

POTTER: I hope he won't disappoint us. I never felt so anxious to see him.

MRS STERNHOLD: (*aside*) I am sick with apprehension.

MRS MILDMAY: (*aside*) Oh, what will happen if he and John meet?
(*Enter* JESSOP *with a card on a salver.*)

JESSOP: (*crosses to* MILDMAY) A gentleman wishes to see you, sir!

MILDMAY: (*coming down*) A friend of mine come to town unexpectedly. May I ask him to join us?

MRS STERNHOLD: In your own house! My dear John, you surely need not ask that question.

POTTER: Jane!

MRS MILDMAY: Show him in directly. (*Exit* JESSOP.) I'm sure we must be glad to see any friend of yours, my love.

POTTER: Emily! (*aside*) What's come to the women? (*goes up*)
(*Enter* JESSOP, *showing in* GIMLET. *Exit* JESSOP.)

MILDMAY: (*crossing*) This is my friend –

GIMLET: Maxwell.

MILDMAY: Mr Maxwell, from the North.

GIMLET: Ladies, delighted to make your acquaintance – gents all.

MILDMAY: (*aside to him*) Silence! Wait till I tell you.

GIMLET: All right! (MILDMAY *and* GIMLET *go up.*)
(*Enter* JESSOP *announcing*)

JESSOP: Captain Hawksley. (*Exit* JESSOP.)
(*Enter* CAPTAIN HAWKSLEY, *fashionably dressed.*)

HAWKSLEY: (*crossing to centre*) Ah! Mrs Sternhold, I hope you are better. No trace of yesterday's headache? Mrs Mildmay, I hope you caught no cold sitting up last night over your novel. Ah, you really should be more careful of yourself. My dear Potter, thank you particularly for letting me have those shares this morning. How do, Dunbilk? How do, Markham? Good day, Mr Langford. (*turning to* MILDMAY) Mr John Mildmay! (*a dead silence*) A word with you, sir. (MRS STERNHOLD *crosses*; MILDMAY *comes down centre.*) I told you what you must expect if ever we met in company. As you seem to have forgotten it I must remind you. (*He raises his arm to strike* MILDMAY *with horsewhip, which he draws from his pocket.* MRS STERNHOLD *stays his arm.*)

MILDMAY: Stop! My dear Mrs Sternhold, don't be alarmed – this is no scene for ladies. Oblige me by walking into the next room for a few minutes. (*The gentlemen all gather round* HAWKSLEY.)

MRS STERNHOLD: For mercy's sake –   }
MRS MILDMAY: John! Husband!   }   (*together*)

MILDMAY: I must insist on your going. (MILDMAY *puts them off, and locks door,
    then crosses and locks other door.*)

POTTER: Captain Hawksley, what is the meaning of this behaviour?

HAWKSLEY: It means that your son-in-law, after grossly insulting me this morning,
    refused me the satisfaction of a gentleman. I told him I would force it from him
    by the public outrage I have just inflicted. Dunbilk, you'll act as my friend?

DUNBILK: Delighted, my boy!   }
POTTER: If this goes on I'll send for the police!   }
MARKHAM: Gentlemen –   }   (*together*)
LANGHAM: Really, Captain Hawksley –   }

MILDMAY: (*authoritatively*) Not a word more – this is my affair! Mr Potter, you have
    pistols in the house. (*crosses*)

POTTER: Yes, but I won't allow anybody to use them – they're out of condition –
    they're dangerous – they'll burst.

MILDMAY: No matter, I have taken the liberty to bring them down. Here they are.
    (*opens box*) I'm no fire-eater, but I won't baulk Captain Hawksley of the
    satisfaction he desires; Markham, you will act for me. Mr Dunbilk, you
    represent my antagonist, I think?

POTTER: Here! police! Jessop! (*all murmer*)

MILDMAY: Be quiet, I insist – all of you. My mind is made up. Nothing can change
    it.

HAWKSLEY: (*aside*) He has more pluck than I gave him credit for. I will kill him
    though.

MILDMAY: Gentlemen, I hold you all to witness what passed. He is the insulter. I
    am the insulted. I have the choice of time, place, and weapons. I make that
    choice. Here – now – these pistols.

HAWKSLEY: I'm ready – load away, gentlemen. (DUNBILK *begins to load pistol.*)

MILDMAY: (*crossing*) You have often boasted you can hit the pip of an ace at twenty
    paces. I never fired a pistol at anything more formidable than a sparrow. I am
    willing to risk my life against yours on equal terms; but if we stand up opposite
    to each other at twelve paces, each with a loaded pistol – skill against no skill –
    what becomes of the equality of risk? (*crosses back*) Your friend has loaded one
    of these pistols – let us leave the other unloaded – put both under the cloth –
    each draw one, and fire together across the table; now, close your eyes and
    choose. You hesitate!

HAWKSLEY: Such a way of fighting was never known but in a novel. I decline this
    unheard-of mode of proceeding.

MILDMAY: I expected as much. I only wished to show these gentlemen that under
    cover of the forms of a duel you contemplate assassination. (*Goes to the door
    through which the ladies have gone and unlocks it.*) The storm is passed, ladies.

(*Re-enter* MRS STERNHOLD *and* MRS MILDMAY.)

HAWKSLEY: (*to* MILDMAY) This bravado shall not serve your turn, sir; we have
    not done with each other yet.

MILDMAY: You are right, we have not. Captain Hawksley has insulted me – I have
    challenged him – he has refused; had he challenged me, I might have refused;
    for no man, even by the code of society, is bound to go out with a felon.

ALL: A felon!

POTTER: A felon in this house! Where? Police! Police!

GIMLET: (*coming down*) Here you are, guv'nor! (*Handcuffs* HAWKSLEY.) Sorry for it, Mr Boscawen; but I've been wanting you this long time.

POTTER: Boscawen! This is Captain Hawksley! (*Goes up.*)

GIMLET: Alias Burgess – alias Boscawen. It's on a charge of forgery, committed four years ago – evidence only completed last week. It's a lifer, as sure as my name's Gimlet.

HAWKSLEY: (*aside to* GIMLET) You're done, my boy! The bill's destroyed.

GIMLET: A bill, but not *the* bill. This is the other.

HAWKSLEY: Done! – done by the wolf in sheep's clothing! (*Stands for a moment overpowered, then rouses himself.*) Some ridiculous blunder – it will be set right this evening.

GIMLET: That's right, keep your pecker up. (MILDMAY *gives key of other door to* GIMLET – *he opens it.*)

HAWKSLEY: Mrs Sternhold, I am sorry I shall not have the pleasure of dining with you; Mrs Mildmay, no chance of another tête-à-tête, I fear; Potter, my boy, you were just in time with those shares; give my compliments to the board, Dunbilk; Mildmay – (*grinding his teeth*) – if ever I come back I shall make a point of repaying all I owe you; and, till then, I shall let the debt accumulate at compound interest! (*Exit* CAPTAIN HAWKSLEY *and* GIMLET.)

POTTER: I'm bewildered! What does this mean?

MILDMAY: It means, my dear Mr Potter, that straightforward honesty is generally a match for plausible roguery in the long run.

POTTER: Jane, can you explain this? You're the only person that ever can explain things in this house!

MRS STERNHOLD: You are wrong, brother – wrong, as we have all been! Henceforth, for explanation, for advice, for guidance, look there. (*pointing at* MILDMAY)

POTTER: Why that's poor John Mildmay.

MRS STERNHOLD: Your daughter's husband. (*putting* MRS MILDMAY *across to* MILDMAY) The master of this house!

POTTER: John Mildmay the master of this house? Emily, my dear, has your aunt been – I mean has your aunt lost her wits?

MRS MILDMAY: No; she has found them, papa, as I have done, thanks to dear John. Ask his pardon, papa, as we have, for the cruel injustice we have done him. (*Gets up a little.*)

POTTER: Oh, certainly, if you desire it. John Mildmay, I ask your pardon – Jane and Emily say I ought; though what I've done, or what there is to ask pardon for –

MILDMAY: Perhaps you'll learn in time. But we're forgetting dinner. Langford, will you take my wife? (*He does so.*) Markham, you'll take Mrs Sternhold.

POTTER: My dear boy, you astonish me! But, however, there's an old proverb that says, 'All is not gold that glitters'.

MILDMAY: Yes; and there is another old proverb, and one much more to the purpose, that says, 'Still waters run deep'.

(*Disposition of the Characters at the Fall of the Curtain*)
DUNBILK
POTTER   MILDMAY
MRS STERNHOLD   MRS MILDMAY
MARKHAM   LANGFORD

THE CONTESTED ELECTION

A Comedy in Three Acts

First produced at the Theatre Royal, Haymarket, on 29 June 1859, with the following cast:

MR DODGSON, an Attorney	Mr Chas Mathews
MR WAPSHOTT, a Barrister	Mr W Farren
MR HONEYBUN, a retired Wholesale grocer	Mr Compton
PECKOVER, President of the Blue Lambs	Mr Buckstone
TOPPER, Chairman of the Green Lions	Mr Rogers
CRAWLEY ⎧ Free and Independent ⎫	Mr Cullenford
COPPERTHWAITE ⎨ Electors ⎬	Mr Worrell
OLD WINKLE ⎩ of Flamborough ⎭	Mr Moyse
MR GATHERCOLE, of the Flamborough Beacon	Mr Clark
MR SPITCHCOCK, of the Flamborough Patriot	Mr Braid
SNAPPER, a Sheriff's Officer	Mr Courtney
TRUNDLE, Clerk to Dodgson	Mr Weathersby
MRS HONEYBUN, Honeybun's second wife	Mrs Chas Mathews
CLARA HONEYBUN, her Stepdaughter	Miss Fanny Wright

Electors, servants, etc.

Act 1

SCENE 1. *Private Office of* MR DODGSON. *A door leads off on the right and there is an entrance to a safe or strong room. Writing table with papers, etc., Chairs, Desk, Law Library in bookcase. Mouth of speaking tube near door. Window on the right.*
Enter TRUNDLE, *and* SNAPPER, *disputing.*

TRUNDLE: But I tell you Mr Dodgson's not in the office.

SNAPPER: And I tell you – 'gammon!'

TRUNDLE: (*with dignity*) As a member of the legal profession, however 'umble, you ought to be above disputing another member's word; but satisfy yourself. Here's Mr Dodgson's private room – he ain't here, you see.

SNAPPER: Leastways he ain't visible. Now, you take notice, I leave a copy of the judgment that's been entered up against him at the suit of Thomas Peckover, butcher, £62.5s.3d., including costs. (*Puts copy of judgment on desk.*) Execution's issued, and I've the writ in my pocket; so you'll tell your governor, if he don't want to be locked up, he'd better settle. We've six judgments agin him, besides this!

TRUNDLE: Bless you! Mr Dodgson never pays till execution's issued. He likes the excitement.

SNAPPER: A lawyer, and fond of law! I should just as soon expect to see a doctor fond of physic.

TRUNDLE: There's no accounting for tastes; but I'm surprised that Peckover should have gone to the expense of a judgment just now.

SNAPPER: Why?

TRUNDLE: Isn't our borough election just coming off? Time's money, they say, and election time is ready money. Mr Dodgson may be a new comer in Flamborough, but he's sure of a rattling retainer from one of the candidates.

SNAPPER: Yes; if they employ lawyers.

TRUNDLE: Employ lawyers! Why, aint both Gaper and Gabbleton in the field already? Their committee room's hired, and their address is out. If they employ lawyers, indeed! Come, I like that!

SNAPPER: Well, they do say the influentials have settled among themselves that there's to be no bands, and no banners, and no bludgeon-men, and no beer.

TRUNDLE: No beer! Disgusting! Why, it's striking at the very roots of our representative system!

SNAPPER: And if there's to be neither bands, banners, bludgeon-men, or beer, I thought the next thing might be – no lawyers!

TRUNDLE: No, Mr Snapper; The British Constitution is elastic, but it never will stretch as far as that (*bell within*). But here's the office bell. A contested election without lawyers! you might as well say a sugar cask without bluebottles.
(*Exit* TRUNDLE *and* SNAPPER.)

DODGSON: (*puts his head out of the door of the safe*) All right, eh? Coast clear? (*comes out*) Out of the safe, and in safety: to have to take refuge in a receptacle for musty and old deed boxes! I must have a back door made in this room. The idea of a private office without a bolt hole, when one's liable to be intruded upon by clients or sheriff's officers at any moment, – I wish I had a few more visitors of the one sort, and not quite so many of the other. If it wasn't for this ingenious arrangement of gutta percha tubing (*pointing to speaking tube, which debouches in a closet close to* TRUNDLE's *desk*), I might have half-a-dozen writs served on me every day of the week, except Sundays. Bless this election! my retainer will enable the firm of Dodgson and Dibbs to resume cash payments. Dodgson and Dibbs! It sounds like capital. Dibbs is an imaginary personage; but a Co. imparts respectability to a concern, and that's my weak point. Very extraordinary, though, I haven't heard from either of the candidates (*goes to tube and calls*). Anything from Gaper and Gabbleton?

TRUNDLE: (*from below through tube*) Nothing, sir.

DODGSON: Astonishing how men can trifle with their interests in this way! Here's Gaper might snap me up from Gabbleton, or Gabbleton secure me under the nose of Gaper; and all for want of a little promptitude.

TRUNDLE: (*by tube*) Are you in, sir?

DODGSON: (*at tube*) Who is it?

TRUNDLE: (*by tube*) A gent, sir; won't give his name.

DODGSON: (*at tube*) I've just stepped out for a mouthful of fresh air. It's uncertain when I shall be back. (*Goes to window and peeps cautiously through hole in wire blind.* TRUNDLE *whistles up the tube.*)

DODGSON: (*goes back and speaks through tube*) What is it?

TRUNDLE: (*by tube*) He says he will come up stairs.

DODGSON: (*at tube*) Punch his head. (*row heard*)

TRUNDLE: (*by tube*) He's punched mine!

DODGSON: The deuce he has. Then here goes for the safe. (*Exit into safe.*)
(*Enter* WAPSHOTT.)

WAPSHOTT: Not here; oh, stuff! he's hiding. All right, old boy, it's only me. I know you're here – come out – (*louder*) –I say, Dodgson, old fellow – it's Charley Wapshott.

DODGSON: (*puts his head out of safe*) Delighted to see you, my dear fellow. I shall be with you directly. I'm just looking for some papers.

WAPSHOTT: Do you generally look for papers with the safe door shut, and without a candle.

DODGSON: (*coming out with papers, and down to the table*) Oh bless you, I can find my way among my papers blindfold; you know arrangement was always my strong point, (*aside*) except arrangement with my creditors. Find yourself a chair. (WAPSHOTT *sits at table.*) Well, who would have thought of seeing you in this out-of-the-way hole!

WAPSHOTT: Or you in that out-of-the-way hole, eh? (*pointing to safe*) Why, I had to make my way upstairs over your clerk's body. By Jove, Harry, if your clients find it as hard to get in as your acquaintance, I should not think they would trouble you very often.

DODGSON: My dear fellow, they don't. But I'm sorry you had any bother with my noodle of a clerk. He's got into a habit of denying me to people: he knows I don't like to be disturbed over papers (*pointing to papers he has brought out*).

WAPSHOTT: I suppose that's why you retreat to the safe, eh? Why, you old humbug, have you forgotten we chummed together for two years in the Temple?

DODGSON: Ah! that airy sky parlour in Pump-court, – I often sigh for the old snuggery. What a charming view we had! – a perfect forest of chimney-pots! Why did I ever leave? Why wasn't I called to the bar like you?

WAPSHOTT: To drag a briefless bag year after year through the weary round of session and circuit; to hide a heavy heart with a rusty gown, and an aching head under a thatch of horse hair, without earning enough to pay for patching the one or powdering the other. No; regret you're not a scavenger, or a shoe-black, if you please – but don't be sorry you're not a barrister.

DODGSON: It strikes me that we limbs of the law are all a day after the fair, Charley. People have begun to imbibe the pestilent heresy that law is meant for clients instead of lawyers. But it is no use crying over spilt milk. But what are you doing in this part of the world?

WAPSHOTT: I'll tell you. I was called down last autumn to sit on a reference at Squatterville, you know.

DODGSON: Our new country seaside resort. I hope you liked it.

WAPSHOTT: I stayed at the principal hotel – the Squatterville Arms.

DODGSON: Don't I know 'em? the extortioners!

WAPSHOTT: How much I owe that house.

DODGSON: Do you? So do I! I'm glad you haven't paid 'em! Such bills ought to be systematically resisted.

WAPSHOTT: Oh, my debt to the hotel is one of gratitude.

DODGSON: The deuce it is!

WAPSHOTT: For at its table d'hote I met Clara.

DODGSON: (*whistles*) Surname? –

WAPSHOTT: Honeybun. The family live near Flamborough.

DODGSON: I know – Easington Lodge – papa's a retired grocer.

WAPSHOTT: On a large scale, – quite on the merchant prince style. I struck up an acquaintance with Clara's stepmother. We used to discuss Tennyson, and I tried in vain to shake her faith in Tupper; but all the while I was arguing with madame I was drinking deep draughts of love from the eyes of mademoiselle.

DODGSON: Pleasant tipple, eh?

WAPSHOTT: Oh, such eyes! Clara's almost as old as her stepmother, and has property in her own right.

DODGSON: That's highly satisfactory; and then a stepmother's an immense advantage. She'll be a mother-in-law one removed.

WAPSHOTT: But she's my rock a-head, notwithstanding. She believes she's made to shine in London society, and, to crown all, she's a female Gordon Cumming in her passion for hunting lions. Naturally she wants to hitch on to a son-in-law who can lift her into what she think's her proper sphere. If I were only a rising M.P., or a popular preacher, or a fashionable author, I might have a chance; but

---

a day after the fair: too late.

reference: in law, the submission of a dispute for arbitration.

Tupper: Martin Farquhar Tupper published his 'Proverbial Philosophy' between 1838 and 1842. This was in rhythmical form and was exceedingly popular. Other published works included poems and an autobiography. Tupper's moralising platitudes underwrote Victorian acquisitiveness. Mrs Honeybun is a Tupperism.

rock a-head: used in the sense of the rock upon which I founder.

Gordon Cumming: a famous lion hunter who exhibited his trophies at the Great Exhibition, 1851.

a briefless barrister – pooh! At the first intimation of my pretensions to Clara she gave me the cut directly, and insisted on old Honeybun (who never had a will of his own, and would sacrifice his best friend for a quiet life) forbidding me his sitting room.

DODGSON: Of course you did not accept the nonsuit.

WAPSHOTT: I bowed, and from that moment never crossed their threshold again. But there was nothing to hinder my meeting Clara on the cliffs – in the retired bays of the beach – in the wooded valleys that intersect the swelling bosom of the downs –

DODGSON: Oh! cut that; you're not addressing a jury in an action for breach.

WAPSHOTT: You never had any romance in you. I soon found that Clara was dreadfully bored at home between her easy-going father and his high-pressure wife.

DODGSON: Badly-stepped team, I should say, decidedly.

WAPSHOTT: In short, that she was quite ready to take the responsibility of marrying without asking anybody's consent. Her property comes to her under her mother's will. One of the trustees, a certain Grindley, was a client of old Sharp's, and I expect there's a copy of the will among his papers. I want you to look it up, and satisfy Clara that she is free to marry when she likes without risking her little independence.

DODGSON: A job at last! Though how the deuce I am to find the will among the dusty chaos in that safe!

WAPSHOTT: Why, I thought you knew your way among the papers blindfold.

DODGSON: So I do, among my own. – (*aside*) They're only a file of bills, and as none of them are paid I can't go wrong. – But I'll direct my clerk to institute a search, on the usual terms.

WAPSHOTT: Of course. I'm delighted to bring you your first client. (*both rising*) I promised to fetch Clara to your office. She knows we're old cronies. Of course there can be no harm in my being present.

DODGSON: I say, Charley, if you find me a client, I find you a snug cage for your billing and cooing. I'm not exactly clear about the professional entry for such accommodation in the bill of costs. Oh, I know; I'll set it down as attendance on counsel with Miss H., one pound one.

WAPSHOTT: You may enter ditto to that every day the next fortnight. (*rises*, DODGSON *also*) I'll go for Clara at once. (*going*)

DODGSON: Mind always provided election business don't prevent my receiving you. I'm in momentary expectation of a summons from one committee or the other.

WAPSHOTT: Which side do you go with?

DODGSON: The one that retains me. (*Slaps his pockets.*) My motto is 'open to all parties – influenced by none.'

WAPSHOTT: Then, you regulate your politics?

DODGSON: By the golden rule, – *in medio tutissimus*, – 'stick to the medium,' 'circulating' understood.

---

nonsuit: legal term, here suggesting a withdrawal from the action.
breach: of promise to marriage.
badly-stepped team: horses that don't pull well together.

WAPSHOTT: Oh! you mercenary heathen. (*Exit.*)

DODGSON: Heathen! not I. I adore that old established divinity, the golden calf. So Charley Wapshott has picked up a girl with money. There again the bar has the advantage of us. Gives a social status, as it's called. Attornies are *infra-dig.* But I must have a copy of that will looked up. (*Calls through pipe.*) Trundle! At all events, here's a client at last. Then there'll be the girl's settlement to draw, Wapshott hasn't anything to settle. All the more reason to secure his wife's fortune from his creditors.

(*Enter* TRUNDLE.)

DODGSON: Oh! Trundle. I want the copy of the will of the late Mrs Honeybun. It should be among the papers of one Grindley, an old client of Sharp's.

TRUNDLE: Yes, sir, there is a box with that name in the safe, sir.

DODGSON: Out with it. (*Exit* TRUNDLE, *after lighting a candle, into safe,* DODGSON *calling after him.*) Nothing from Gaper or Gabbleton, eh?

TRUNDLE: (*from safe*) Not a word, sir.

DODGSON: What can be the meaning of this shilly-shallying. Why, the nomination's next week.

TRUNDLE: (*re-enter with deed box – puts it on the table*) Here's the box sir, by the name of Grindley. (DODGSON *is about to open it.*) Stop sir; you'll dirty your fingers.

DODGSON: Pooh! an attorney musn't be particular about that – (*opens box*) Now, be off down stairs – (TRUNDLE *is going*) – and, I say, Trundle, do try and be a little more discriminating.

TRUNDLE: As how sir?

DODGSON: Between creditors and clients to be sure, people who come to dun, and people who come to be done. (*Turns over papers.*)

TRUNDLE: Then there's no use in my admitting anybody. He, he! (*Laughs.*)

DODGSON: What do you mean, sir?

TRUNDLE: Don't you see, sir; 'cause I ain't to let in the creditors, and you'll let in the clients yourself. (*Exit* TRUNDLE.)

DODGSON: Now, that's the worst of being in difficulties – one's very clerk ventures to poke fun at one. (*looking at papers*) What an array of dirty sheepskin! each parchment face grinning through an inch of dust, like a Lord Chancellor's portrait in a law stationer's back parlour. (*turning over papers*) Conditions of sale, mortgage, last will and testament; – here we have it; – Martha Honeybun, etc., etc; (*running over*) In trust to Matthew Gridley and Jonas Handyside, yes, 'for my dearly beloved daughter Clara,' all right enough; but, hollo! here's an awkward reservation. (*reads*) 'In the event of my said daughter marrying against the will of my said husband, the said securities, etc., etc., to go to my said husband for the term of his natural life.' That won't suit Charley, I'm afraid, nor the young lady either. (TRUNDLE *whistles through tube.*) Hang these perpetual interruptions. (*Goes to tube, and calls impatiently through it.*) Well!

TRUNDLE: (*through tube*) Mr Peckover, and it ain't about his small account.

DODGSON: Oh! if the greasy rascal don't want his money (*through tube*), show him up. What can he be after? Eh, by Jove! I shouldn't wonder if it was about the election. Peckover is president of the 'Blue Lambs', negotiates a third of the votes for the borough – perhaps he's brought my retainer. – (*Enter

PECKOVER. *He wears a great coat, and a handkerchief over the lower part of his face.*) – My dear Mr Peckover – delighted to see you – take a chair. (PECKOVER *goes to table, struggles with his wrappers.*) Allow me to relieve you – why, how you are wrapped up! Don't sit in the draft, pray. (DODGSON *helps him off with coat etc.*)

PECKOVER: No, master Dodgson, no, I'm hearty, thank you, sir, leastways I was hearty this morning, punished a pound of prime steak at breakfast, as bad as ever I did in my life. (*Both sit at table.*)

DODGSON: Then what do you mean by swaddling yourself like an Egyptian mummy in the dog days?

PECKOVER: Ah! you may ask. It's little Peckover ever thought to see himself a-sneaking through the market place of Flamborough, disguised (unless it was in liquor, like a man). Bless you, that coat ain't mine; it's John Small's, the post boy at the Blue Lamb. I (*solemnly*) borrowed that there upper Benjamin out of the stable without asking leave of the owner. Ah! you may well stare. You'll not mention I called?

DODGSON: One moment. May I ask if I am to consider this as a professional interview?

PECKOVER: There's 6s. 8d. (*puts it down*)

DODGSON: (*is about to take it up*)

PECKOVER: (*takes it up again*) Stop, though, Muster Dodgson, we'll deduct it off my small account.

DODGSON: With pleasure – allow me to make a note of it (*at table*), strictness in money transactions, however trifling, is the virtue of our profession. (*notes*) Now, my very dear sir. (*listening*)

PECKOVER: (*leans over table*) But we're tiled, you know.

DODGSON: Make your mind easy. The attorney's office is the Protestant confessional, my client is my penitent. His communications are privileged. Neither torture, nor cross-examination can wring his secrets from the bosom of his legal adviser. Proceed Mr Peckover, proceed in confidence.

PECKOVER: Muster Dodgson, I believe this here town of Flamborough has returned a member to parliament.

DODGSON: Since a time whereof the memory of man runneth not to the contrary.

PECKOVER: Quite correct, Muster Dodgson. I believe this here borough has never returned a member to parliament without a contest.

DODGSON: The free and independent electors of Flamborough have always insisted on that right of choice, which is the heritage of every Briton paying £10 rent, free of rates, taxes, and insurance, and duly registered under the act in that case made and provided.

PECKOVER: Quite correct, Muster Dodgson; a man's vote is his property; and before he gives it he likes to know the reason why. Now unless there's at least two candidates comes forward, a free and independent elector never does get any reason why.

---

upper Benjamin: overcoat.
tiled: secure against intrusion.

DODGSON: Of course you wish to exercise your electoral rights only on due consideration.

PECKOVER: That's what I always tell our club at the Blue Lamb. 'Here's Gaper a coming forward on red principles,' say I, 'and Gabbleton on true blue; what's the odds between 'em? It's six o' one and half a dozen o' the other. What gives a man a vote? Property! What's the laws made for? to protect property! Who ought to make the laws? men of property! What's the best proof of property? ready money! Talk about your colours – show me the colour of your money! It ain't what a man stands on, but what he stands, that I look to!' Them's Tom Peckover's principles; and so long as Tom Peckover is chairman of the Blue Lambs, them's the principles the Blue Lambs goes by.

DODGSON: Most lucid and convincing. In the day of our barbarous forefathers the electors used to pay the member; our enlightened times have reversed the practice, and now the member pays the electors.

PECKOVER: And so he ought. Do you suppose if a seat in parliament weren't worth a lot, a man would go through such a deal o' dirty work to get it?

DODGSON: I trust that both Mr Gaber and Mr Gabbleton are quite prepared to back their opinions to the requisite amount.

PECKOVER: That's it! (*striking table*), the cowards! the mean rips! they're no men, Muster Dodgson, and their committees are as bad, and their agents are no better. I hope they haven't been and bagged you.

DODGSON: No, Mr Peckover, it's for a Griggs and a Crumpet to chain themselves to the chariot wheels of a Gaper or Gabbleton. I am still free to exercise my professional abilities for the good of this borough, unfettered by the sordid tie of a retainer!

PECKOVER: I know it. I says to the Blue Lambs, 'Dodgson's our man,' says I.

DODGSON: My dear sir, this confidence is most flattering.

PECKOVER: 'Griggs and Crumpet have kep' him out of his share of the swag,' sez I. 'He's as poor as a rat,' sez I, 'and as sharp set as a bull terrier.'
(DODGSON *winces*.) No offence, I 'ope sir, which I'm fond of a dawg myself.

DODGSON: The illustration is a little too familiar, though not unflattering; the tongue is the first of legal instruments, but a good set of teeth is no bad accompaniment.

PECKOVER: And, if ever two varmints wanted pinning. Gaper and Gabbleton's the men: Muster Dodgson, sir, they're fighting a cross (*rising, and speaking across the table very emphatically*).

DODGSON: What do you mean?

PECKOVER: (*solemnly*) I mean that they are going to make it all square among themselves without a contest.

DODGSON: Why, their addresses are out; their committees are working.

PECKOVER: Gammon! I tell you, sir, we've had the office; and one on 'em don't mean fighting. The cowards! They talk about election committees – about the Corrupt Practices Act – about the danger of getting the borough disfranchiselled!

DODGSON: But how do they mean to settle which is to give way!

PECKOVER: Sky a copper. I dare say they're equal to it – the sneaking rascals.

DODGSON: Commit the sacred selection of a representative to the blind hazard of a halfpenny toss! My blood boils! This accounts for my not receiving a retainer. They knew I was not the man to sanction any such iniquitous arrangement.

PECKOVER: In course the cross is to be kept dark till it's too late to find a candidate who will come down handsome.

DODGSON: Ah! there's the difficulty. Unluckily, the last two members returned for the borough were unseated on petition. Then that demoralizing Corrupt Practices Act of last session is likely to frighten timid people, and public courage is so rare now-a-days. Besides, the nomination day is close at hand.

PECKOVER: That's it, sir; and not so much as an offer to the Blue Lambs or the Green Lions! I know'd there was a screw loose somewhere. I sez to Tom Topper – he's chairman of the Lions, you know, sir – 'Tom,' sez I, 'mark my words; it ain't on the square, Tom.' But Tom he's an easy man, though he's been in the P.R. himself – champion of the light weights, Tom was, and ought to be up to crosses – so Tom laughs, 'and the longer they put it off,' sez he, 'the more it will cost 'em;' but I know'd better, and so did Mrs P., which she always has a deal to do with her money about election time. 'The children wants a new rig out,' says she; 'and my bonnet's that shabby I ain't fit to show myself in church,' says she; 'and no money comin' in,' says she. Bless you! I know'd what she meant.

DODGSON: I'm not married myself; but I can conceive a man's emotion on being forced to fob off the wife of his bosom with sighs instead of sovereigns.

PECKOVER: Ah! it's 'ard, sir; it's uncommon 'ard, I can tell you; and Mrs P. ain't a pleasant woman to say 'No!' to, at the best of times, especially at election times. And then there's the Blue Lambs.

DODGSON: A good deal bluer, I suppose, and a great deal less lamb-like than usual, on the eve of a nomination day.

PECKOVER: Why, they are fit to tear me in pieces, – me that they've always trusted to do what's right by 'em! But a candidate we will have, if we send to Brummagem to have one made.

DODGSON: A very good place to send to; great in brass goods, you know. Well, I suppose you look to me to save the borough from this scandalous compromise – to find you a candidate –

PECKOVER: Of the right sort. (*rises*, DODGSON *also*) If you'll do that Muster Dodgson!

DODGSON: By the way, though, there's one thing we must settle first, – that small account of yours.

PECKOVER: Don't mention it!

DODGSON: I'm sorry, my dear Mr Peckover, very sorry you should have thought it necessary to appeal to the law.

PECKOVER: Only find us a candidate that will do the right thing by the borough, and you shall have a receipt in full and the run of my shop for the rest of the twelvemonth.

---

sky a copper: toss a coin.
P.R.: Prize Ring – boxing.
Brummagem: slang for Birmingham.

DODGSON: Though a lawyer, I can understand the pleasure of gratitude. Far be it from me to check the tide of feeling which prompts your proposal – here's a receipt stamp.

PECKOVER: What! give you the receipt now? No! After you have found a candidate. I must see Topper, and Gathercole, and Spitchcock, and a few more of the right sort, just to put 'em up to what's going on.

DODGSON: Do. I'll let you know when I'm ready to meet them here; meanwhile your visit had better be kept dark.

PECKOVER: Oh, I'm fly. Nobody will know me in Tom Small's coat and this here wrapper. (DODGSON *helps him to muffle himself up again.*) If I am a saving this here borough, I don't want to blow a trumpet afore myself.

DODGSON: Quite right, Mr Peckover: your virtue is of that elevated order which is its own reward. Go and find your friends. Let Griggs and Crumpet chuckle in fancied security; and Gaper and Gabbleton exult in their iniquitous machinations; we shall release the borough from its thraldom. I will be your leader, and in our ranks the Lamb and the Lion shall fight side by side.

PECKOVER: Gathercole shall blaze away in the *Beacon*.

DODGSON: And Spitchcock's pen impale the traitors in the *Patriot*.

PECKOVER: You're sure you know the style of man we want?

DODGSON: A gentleman of ample means and ministerial opinions, colour not material, provided only he have enlarged notions on the subject of the currency.

PECKOVER: That's the party for Flamborough! We ain't particular whether he can open his mouth or not, if so he can keep his eyes shut.

DODGSON: Of course we must have an imposing requisition. Here's a blank form. (*Gives it to him.*) We can fill in the candidate's name and opinions when we've got him. Mind, it must be most respectably signed.

PECKOVER: I can promise you fifty-two Blue Lambs, and Topper's good for forty Green Lions, and I think I can get half-a-dozen of the heavy weight swells that never was known to vote under two figures; and if that ain't respectable, I should like to know what is. (*Exit.*)

DODGSON: Bravo! This is worth a dozen retainers from Gaper or Gabbleton. On their side I must have played second fiddle, but in opposition I shall have the orchestra to myself. Then there'll be my fees for legal agency and the incidental business and, best of all, a petition as sure as a gun whoever wins. Perhaps a commission issued to inquire into corrupt practices in the borough; in that case I'm safe for a general retainer from the Lambs and the Lions to defend their rights. If I succeed in that, who knows but the grateful electors may return me for the borough gratis! I should get called to the bar; I should rise – I feel I should. There's the solicitor-generalship open to me; the attorney-generalship; the bench; why not the woolsack? The first step's everything, and I've got that at last. Have I, though? Hold hard! First catch your candidate. There's Charley Wapshott; but where's he to find the 'necessary expenses?' and just going to be married. No, no. Suppose I run up for a man to the Reform Club, or the Carlton; no, 'tis too late for that. Besides, thanks to those two last petitions, Flamborough has such an uncommonly fishy reputation, I'm afraid the seat isn't negotiable in the borough market; – only two days before me, too. What's to be done? If I only had the money myself! I've the election in my pocket – a hundred and fifty votes will do it. Peckover and Topper are good for ninety-four. It's very hard if I can't rely on a hundred patriots besides, to resent this attempt at closing the borough. What a chance thrown away! and all for the want of a man of straw with a lining in his pocket!

TRUNDLE: (*through tube*) Gent and young lady, by appointment, sir.

DODGSON: (*calls*) Show them up. Wapshott and Miss Honeybun. Eh, by Jove! a capital idea; if I could catch old Honeybun! He's the very man to contest Flamborough: as rich as Croesus, and without an opinion to his back. This affair of Wapshott's and the girl's would be a famous opportunity for an introduction to the family.

(*Enter* WAPSHOTT *and* CLARA.)

WAPSHOTT: Miss Honeybun, Mr Dodgson – an old chum of mine, Clara; you are quite safe in his hands. (CLARA *makes an inclination to* DODGSON, *who bows.*)

DODGSON: Pray sit down, Miss Honeybun (*She sits at table.*); your case is safer in my hands, I am sorry to say, than your fortune in your own (*taking up Will*).

WAPSHOTT: Eh? (*sits*)

CLARA: My fortune not safe in my own hands!

DODGSON: There's a copy of your lamented parent's will, – I've underlined the operative parts. Wapshott, I regret to say it is expressed in unusually brief and intelligible language. (*Puts it over to him.* WAPSHOTT *examines Will.*) Your fortune (*to* CLARA) goes to your papa, if he chooses to say 'no,' when you choose to say 'yes.'

WAPSHOTT: The deuce it does! (*aside*)

CLARA: I remember papa said I must have his consent, and that means my stepmother's.

WAPSHOTT: This is very provoking. I will never agree to deprive you of your fortune, Clara; and I can't stoop to cajole Mrs Honeybun.

DODGSON: My dear Wapshott, a man can never stoop to cajole a lady, the operation is one to task the highest qualities of the diplomatic intellect. You must get Mrs Honeybun's consent – suppose you entrust me with the delicate negotiation?

WAPSHOTT: (*throws down Will on table*) Nonsense, Dodgson. Haven't I told you her character? It would be a mere waste of time.

CLARA: Let my fortune go, rather than you should do anything you think humiliating dear.

DODGSON: Depend on it, Miss Honeybun, there's nothing so humiliating in the long run as marrying without enough to live upon.

CLARA: But Charley has got his profession.

DODGSON: The profession of a barrister is like the professions of a good many christians – it don't entail practice.

WAPSHOTT: No, Clara, I will never reduce you to share the heart-sickness of hope deferred; the desperate struggle of an over-crowded calling; better anything than that. (*rises*)

DODGSON: Even softening this terrible stepmother of yours! You needn't appear in person; – you shall stoop, as you call it, by deputy. All you have to do is to procure me an introduction to Easington Lodge, and make me your plenipotentiary. There could be no harm in trying. Think of the discomfort of being married without a parent to weep over you in the vestry.

(WAPSHOTT *and* DODGSON *rise.*)

WAPSHOTT: No, no I've condescended to Mrs Honeybun's ridiculous pretensions only too much already. I won't humiliate myself further, and if Clara takes my advice –

CLARA: (*rises, goes to the window*) Good gracious!

WAPSHOTT: What's the matter, dear?

CLARA: There's the pony carriage.

DODGSON: Eh? (*interested*)

WAPSHOTT: With Mr Honeybun and your stepmother, and her favourite Skye-terrier as usual.

CLARA: Oh, she never drives out without her pet. Look how tenderly she lifts him down. Why, she's coming in here!

WAPSHOTT: No, no; she's going to the stationer's next door.

CLARA: How lucky she didn't see us together, – she would never have forgiven either of us such an act of rebellion against her sovereign will.

DODGSON: (*aside*) Now or never! (*crosses*) My dear young friends, I feel it is my duty to make one last attempt of conciliating Mrs Honeybun. You won't introduce me, you say –

WAPSHOTT: No!

DODGSON: Very well; then I must introduce myself. (*crosses*)

WAPSHOTT: Stop, Dodgson, if you don't want us to quarrel!

DODGSON: (*at tube*) Trundle, let loose the big dog!

CLARA: The big dog! What do you mean?

DODGSON: The big dog must introduce me, as you won't. (*goes to window.*) There he goes, – splendid animal, isn't he? Now, Caesar – at him, Caesar!

CLARA: Oh! he's flying at poor little Muff.

DODGSON: Yes; he has an antipathy to Skye-terriers. Your stepmother rushes out – Mr Honeybun hesitates; – I thought he wouldn't tackle Caesar. My dear young friends, common humanity demands I should rescue that interesting Skye-terrier, and bring his fainting mistress up here.

CLARA: But she'll see us together –

DODGSON: I regret there's no back door, but you'll find plenty of room in the safe. (*Opens safe, and exit.*)

CLARA: Is your friend mad?

WAPSHOTT: It looks like it; but we must bear the consequences of his folly.

CLARA: Let us hide ourselves.

WAPSHOTT: But the idea of a safe, darling!

CLARA: They're coming up stairs. (*Runs into safe.*)

WAPSHOTT: Was there ever anything so ridiculous?

CLARA: (*looking out*) Charley, dear, here's such a nice box to sit upon just big enough for two!

WAPSHOTT: If I don't pay Dodgson off for this! (*Exit into safe. Enter* DODGSON *supporting* MRS HONEYBUN, *and followed by* MR HONEYBUN *with a Skye-terrier in his arms.*)

DODGSON: Compose yourself, my dear madam, there's no harm done. (*Places her a chair.*) thanks to Mr Honeybun's heroic presence of mind.

MRS HONEYBUN: (*faintly*) Water!

DODGSON: (*to* HONEYBUN) May I trouble you?

HONEYBUN: If you'll be kind enough to hold the dog a moment.

        (HONEYBUN *crosses, gives* MRS HONEYBUN *a glass of water from table after transferring the dog to* DODGSON.)

DODGSON: The little darling is uninjured.

MRS HONEYBUN: My precious Muff! Let me see him.

        (DODGSON *gives* MRS HONEYBUN *the dog – she examines it eagerly.*)

DODGSON: We must not be interrupted. (*Locks door of the safe.*)

MRS HONEYBUN: Oh, sir, are you sure he's not hurt?

HONEYBUN: I'm afraid I am. I'm certain I felt something in the calf of my leg. (*seated*)

MRS HONEYBUN: Merciful powers! should that horrid huge beast have had hydrophobia?

DODGSON: Oh dear, no; no fear of that.

HONEYBUN: Goodness gracious!

MRS HONEYBUN: Here's a scratch on his little fore paw – I'm sure there is. (*kisses it*) My sweet Muff. Oh! sir, if he should go mad.

HONEYBUN: Appalling idea! There's only one way, – yes, one must make up one's mind to it.

MRS HONEYBUN: You torture me. What do you mean?

HONEYBUN: To have a red hot iron applied to the spot, and burn it clean out.

MRS HONEYBUN: A hot iron applied to my precious pet! (*rises*)

HONEYBUN: I meant to my own leg, my dear.

MRS HONEYBUN: I'm surprised you should make such a fuss about your own trifling inconvenience, when you see how patient this sweet little sufferer is. Look at his angelic face!

DODGSON: What a reproof to human irritability in those full calm eyes!

MRS HONEYBUN: You love dogs, sir?

DODGSON: I adore 'em, ma'am – all but one, and him I loved till to-day – I allude to my dog Caesar; I can never endure the sight of him after his unprovoked attack on your pretty favourite.

MRS HONEYBUN: Oh, sir, promise me you will never again allow your dog to go loose without a muzzle.

DODGSON: Muzzled or unmuzzled, he shall never go loose again, ma'am – he's condemned to the chain from this day forward.

HONEYBUN: He'll be much happier in a comfortable kennel with plenty of straw and regular meals, – such a very quiet life.

MRS HONEYBUN: Dear, dear, Honeybun, your love for a quiet life would reconcile you to anything.

HONEYBUN: To most things, my dear. I hate fuss. I'm afraid we've disturbed you, sir, but it's your own fault; if you will keep a great, nasty, demonstrative dog, you must take the consequences. But, if you are quite recovered, my dear, hadn't we better drive slowly home? (*rises*)

DODGSON: Better rest a few minutes; I'll tell my clerk to look after your carriage.

HONEYBUN: Oh, the pony will stand quiet, I bred him myself; he never runs away.

MRS HONEYBUN: Yes; he's a pony after your own heart, – resents being put out of a sober trot, as if six miles an hour were the extreme limit of horse power.

DODGSON: I'm afraid Mr Honeybun's is not exactly the philosophy for these railroad times.

HONEYBUN: No, sir; the old heavy coach was fast enough for me; one always got to the end of one's journey entire if one did take one's time about it. Now-a-days folks insist on being hurled from one end of the island to the other, like shot out of a gun.

DODGSON: You might say 'shells,' considering the chance of their being blown to smithereens in the transit.

HONEYBUN: A very good simile, sir. Depend upon it, pace will be the ruin of England. Look at our horses; we've bred for pace till we've lost bone, bulk, and bottom. Look at our politics: progress, progress; push a-head without looking before you, or securing the ground you've gone over. Look at our trade: small profit and quick returns, till profit and returns both are swallowed up in Basinghall-street. Instead of Old England's motto, 'slow and sure,' John Bull now-a-days spins along to the tune of 'Devil take the hindmost!' (*sits again*)

DODGSON: Ah! Mr. Honeybun, why have we not men like you in parliament to recall our headstrong generation to the 'wisdom of our ancestors.'

MRS HONEYBUN: And the triumphs of civilization, Honeybun! – the giants that have sprung from the wedlock of steam and iron! – the railway that annihilates space! – the electric telegraph that mocks at time!

DODGSON: Ah! Mrs Honeybun, we want such fervent priestesses as you to arouse an unbelieving society to have faith in the present.

MRS HONEYBUN: What is the use of preaching without an audience! I'm tired of wasting words on Honeybun; and as for the Flamborough savages! –

DODGSON: A race of benighted clodhoppers! I feel it as you do madam; accustomed as I have been to the intellectual society of the metropolis – conceive how I suffer in the provincial Boeotia –

> (*During this conversation* HONEYBUN *has settled himself comfortably in an arm chair and gone to sleep.*)

MRS HONEYBUN: What a comfort to find a person who understands one – it's like a glimpse of Paradise to the excluded Peri!

DODGSON: My dear madam, thoughts like yours would revolutionize our languid London drawing-rooms – (*turning to appeal to* HONEYBUN) – Mr Honeybun – eh? Why, he's asleep!

MRS HONEYBUN: He generally does drop off when the conversation becomes interesting. (*shrugs her shoulders*) That is one of my least trials. I was not born for the life we lead here, Mr –?

DODGSON: Dodgson, madam; another exile from Eden – if I may use the expression. London was my proper sphere, as it is yours; but I am fettered by a

---

Basinghall-street: the 'Bankrupt Office' was located in Basinghall Street in the City of London.
Boeotia: a district of Greece noted for the dullness and stupidity of its inhabitants.
Peri: a female elf or fairy, in Persian mythology, supposed to be descended from the fallen angels.

laborious profession. You are young, beautiful, rich – your husband has leisure –

MRS HONEYBUN: Leisure enough, Heaven knows. Bless me, sir, the man positively stagnates for want of occupation; look at him, his very dreams are of vacancy.

DODGSON: It is your imperative duty to rouse him. Only fancy Mr Honeybun in parliament, and you receiving the elite of London society in your drawing-room, recalling the days of a Sévigné, a Roland, or a Corinne.

MRS HONEYBUN: Ah! sir, the picture is too exciting. Take care how you encourage my ambitious dreams, for I am very ambitious, remember. The future you paint so glowingly has been the fancy of my solitude – has often helped me to bear its burden.

DODGSON: What is there to prevent its realization? The first step, at least, is within your reach.

MRS HONEYBUN: What do you mean?

DODGSON: Mr Honeybun may write M.P. after his name next week, if he pleases.

MRS HONEYBUN: Sir?

DODGSON: I tell you that Mr Honeybun may represent the borough of Flamborough if he likes to put himself in my hands.

MRS HONEYBUN: But there are two candidates in the field already – they have canvassed the borough – the contest is just at hand.

DODGSON: You are worthy of an important political confidence. (*confidentially*) There will be no contest as far as Gaper and Gabbleton are concerned; the electors have asked me to recommend them a candidate; the success of my nominee is certain – suppose I named Mr Honeybun.

MRS HONEYBUN: The suddenness of the thing takes away my breath; – I really must have time to consider.

DODGSON: It is true his aversion to trouble may stand in the way.

MRS HONEYBUN: Oh! I wasn't thinking of his aversions. There's nothing gives him so much trouble as contradicting me for long together; – if I were but satisfied of the feasibility of this project.

DODGSON: Feasible! the thing's done if you say 'do it;' your husband will have no trouble whatever. I'll draw up his address – as for all the rest –

MRS HONEYBUN: The expense for instance?

DODGSON: To his means, what the national debt is to the wealth of England – a mere flea bite – say £800; but I must have that sum soon, and in sovereigns.

MRS HONEYBUN: (*aside*) It would only be putting off the new conservatory for this year! (*aloud*) But if he stands, do you think he's certain to come in?

DODGSON: I'll guarantee his election. Suppose we awake him and propose it.

MRS HONEYBUN: No; leave that to me. I know his ways. (*aside*) A house in town, and a position in London society at last! (*aloud*) Yes; he shall stand.

DODGSON: Then I have your authority for announcing Mr Honeybun as a candidate. (HONEYBUN *moves.*)

MRS HONEYBUN: My undertaking is Mr Honeybun's. Look, he's awaking. I'll

---

Sévigné. . .Roland. . .Corinne: respectively a French noblewoman of the seventeenth century whose letters tell of the life of the nobility; the Girondist heroine of the French revolution ('O liberté! que de crimes on commet en ton nom' were her defiant words on the scaffold); and the heroine of a passionate novel (1807) by the French authoress Anne de Staël.

break the matter to him on our drive home. He'll struggle at first, but he'll end by listening to reason. (*Crosses and shakes* MR HONEYBUN *gently.*) Honeybun, darling.

HONEYBUN: Eh; what? Didn't I hear something about the triumphs of civilization. Of all the triumphs of civilization there's none greater than a perfectly easy chair. Yours is an uncommonly comfortable one, Mr –?

DODGSON: Dodgson; I shall be happy to give the address of the upholsterer.

HONEYBUN: Thank you; but I hate the trouble of ordering things. Now my dear, if you've had your talk out, I think even my pony must have had enough of standing still for the present.

MRS HONEYBUN: You're sure that dog is fastened up, Mr Dodgson?

DODGSON: For life, my dear madam. Allow me to accompany you to your carriage. (*aside to her*) Mind, I consider Mr Honeybun pledged.

MRS HONEYBUN: Certainly; – pray take care not to hurt Muff, Honeybun. (*Gives him dog.*) One would think you had never carried a delicate dog before. Bless his heart.

HONEYBUN: (*aside*) Troublesome little brute! but it's less bother to carry him than to fight about it.

DODGSON: (*from the window*) Draw up the carriage to the door, Trundle. Take care of the pony, sir, can't you.

HONEYBUN: Bless me, why he actually shied.

MRS HONEYBUN: It was that crowd of people startled him.

DODGSON: Mr Gaper's canvassers.

HONEYBUN: Ah! then, I don't wonder at his shying. The sagacious animal – he has an intuitive horror of electioneering, like his master. I don't often take the trouble of hating anything, Mr Dodgson, but I do hate an election.

DODGSON: My dear sir, electioneering is like sea bathing, unpleasant so long as you look at it from the beach, but once strip and jump in, and the whole frame seems to expand in the invigorating element. I wish you'd try the experiment.

HONEYBUN: I! do you suppose I've taken leave of my senses?

MRS HONEYBUN: (*insinuatingly*) I'm sure Honeybun, darling, you would come forward if your country called upon you.

HONEYBUN: Well, if it called very loud, and wouldn't take an answer, perhaps I might.

DODGSON: My dear sir, Cincinnatus had no idea of turning Dictator, when the Senators found him dibbling in his cabbages. Allow me. (MRS HONEYBUN *takes his arm; he leads her to door.*) Remember!

MRS HONEYBUN: (*aside to* DODGSON) Rely upon me. (*Exit with* DODGSON.)

HONEYBUN: Cincinnatus didn't hate trouble as I do, or he'd have got somebody else to dibble in the cabbages for him. (*Exit.*)

DODGSON: (*outside*) One moment madam; important papers to secure. (*rushes back*) By jove, I forgot to unlock the safe – (*Unlocks the safe and exit.*)

(*Re-enter* WAPSHOTT *and* CLARA.)

WAPSHOTT: Stop, you impudent, unprincipled –

Cincinnatus: turned in fact from the plough – not his cabbages! – to lead the Roman army in 458 B.C. in its struggle against the Aequians. Having triumphed, he returned to his land.

CLARA: Now, my dear Charley, what's the use of being in a passion. We had a delightful tête-a-tête, though it was rather dark – I didn't mind it at all.

WAPSHOTT: To think of being locked up, while he cajoled your stepmother into making a fool of your father.

CLARA: But then dear, how lucky it was we overheard the plan, – we can counterplot them you know.

WAPSHOTT: Yes, we will save your father, and sell this audacious fellow at the same time. Not a word to him of our having overheard anything. Come along Clara, who knows, I may marry you with your papa's consent yet.

CLARA: Oh! that is all we want, dear, to be quite happy. (*Exit.*)

(*Re-enter DODGSON, speaking off as he enters.*)

DODGSON: Going – eh? You'll excuse my caging you. Well, this really is the best day's work I ever did in my life. That's a woman of her word. (*looking out of window*) Here come my staff officers, and now for the dignity of a commander-in-chief, duly dashed with the suavity of a secretary of state.

(*Enter PECKOVER, cautiously.*)

PECKOVER: (*mysteriously*) They're down stairs, Muster Dodgson, unrigging themselves. There's Topper, and Gathercole, and Spitchcock, they're all wide awake, Muster Dodgson.

DODGSON: (*seating himself with dignity*) I am ready to receive them.

PECKOVER: This way, gentlemen.

(*Enter TOPPER, GATHERCOLE and SPITCHCOCK.*)

DODGSON: Good morning, gentlemen. Pray be seated. (TOPPER *fumbles with his hat.*) Mr Peckover, be good enough to relieve Mr Topper of his hat. (PECKOVER *takes all their hats and piles them on table; they all sit.*) Well, gentlemen, Mr Peckover has no doubt informed you of the unconstitutional agreement arrived at by the committees of Messrs Gaper and Gabbleton.

TOPPER: Which their backers ought to be ashamed o' themselves?

GATHERCOLE: That the scion of a bloated aristocracy, like the Hon Thomas Gabbleton, should thus trifle with the dearest interests of a constituency is not surprising, but –

SPITCHCOCK: (*interrupting*) It hardly needed the degrading example of a Gaper to teach us that the professions of the demagogue are not incompatible with the most cynical contempt for the vested rights of the electoral community –

GATHERCOLE: (*interrupting*) But that a man whom the *Flamborough Beacon* has on a former occasion powerfully commended to the favour of this constituency –

SPITCHCOCK: (*interrupting*) That one whose addresses in years gone by have been crowned with the approval of the *Flamborough Patriot* –

GATHERCOLE: Should thus venture by a dastardly compromise –

SPITCHCOCK: (*interrupting*) To deprive the free and independent electors of Flamborough of the opportunity of deciding on the choice of a representative –

DODGSON: (*who has in vain tried to edge in a word, rises*) May indeed make us blush for the profligacy of the hireling politician, but can never defeat the determination of this constituency to reap fully and freely the advantages of that electoral franchise which it holds but to promote the greatest happiness of the greatest number.

PECKOVER: That's number one!

TOPPER: I say ditto to Tom Peckover.

DODGSON: (*rises*) The unadorned eloquence of these worthy tradesmen, and the more practised oratory of these my literary friends, point I apprehend to the same conclusion; that you don't mean to be done out of your right to a contest for the honour of representing Flamborough in Parliament. (*sits*)

GATHERCOLE: (*rises*) Certainly not. Why, just look at the state of things already. I'm sure you'll agree with me, Spitchcock: here we are within two days of the nomination, and not £40 worth of printer's bills run up by either candidate. (*sits*)

DODGSON: (*rises*) Scandalous! What's a free press, if it is to be trifled with in this way!

SPITCHCOCK: And the addresses only twice repeated in my paper, and not even the names of the committee given in full. The advertisement account on both sides will be the merest trifle; nothing stirring in squibs either.

DODGSON: Disgusting! Even wit and humour paralyzed.

TOPPER: And not so much as one blessed beer ticket come into my bar at the Green Lion! and I've seen the time I've draw'd four butts extra afore the canvass was over. Talk of the British Constitution after that!

DODGSON: It's dead, sir, dead; and we're all weeping over its bier.

PECKOVER: And never a j'int of meat distributed in local charity, and me that's known an election make a difference of half-a-score of bullocks in a month's killing. Oh! it's mean, mean!

DODGSON: (*rising*) And shall all this be tamely tolerated, gentlemen? Are the electors of Flamborough bond slaves, to be delivered up, tied hand and foot, to the tender mercies of a Gaper or a Gabbleton? (OMNES: hear, hear.) It is time that we should rear the lilied flag of purity against the black banner of corruption. I am authorised to hoist that flag, gentlemen – (OMNES: hear, hear.) – I am empowered to announce to you the name of a candidate whose character is already known among you – a man who, knowing how highly you value your votes, is prepared to estimate those votes at their proper figure. (*sits*)

PECKOVER: That's the jockey for me.

TOPPER: Cut it short! Tell us at what 'ouse his money's ready, and I'm satisfied.

SPITCHCOCK: A Conservative, of course?

GATHERING: An enlightened Liberal?

DODGSON: (*rises*) Both gentlemen! His opinions are of that elastic and comprehensive kind which admit reform, while repudiating revolution; and ensure stability, while they press forward the wheels of progress.

TOPPER: Blow his opinions! What's his name?

DODGSON: Mr Honeybun, of Easington Lodge. You will appreciate with me the immense advantage of securing a resident representative.

PECKOVER: In course; you can always get at him when you want anythink.

TOPPER: Charity begins at 'ome, and never goes much furder that I see.

GATHERCOLE: He will be infinitely more amenable to the curb of local opinion.

SPITCHCOCK: And will feel more respect for its accredited organs.

DODGSON: You have anticipated my sentiments on this point. I may be told that Mr

---

squibs: printed lampoons.

Honeybun has not hitherto been an active politician; what of that? Cincinnatus was called from the plough to the Dictatorship of Rome. We summon the man of our choice from the chaff cutter and the boring machine, to parliamentary duties closely analogous. Yes, gentlemen, Mr Honeybun has consented, at your call, to abandon his elegant retirement, and in our cause to do battle with compromise and corruption! Let us support him in the struggle, and let our watchword be – 'Honeybun and purity of election.' – (OMNES: Honeybun and purity of election! huzza!) (PECKOVER *knocks over all the hats which he had piled one on top of the other.*)

Act II

SCENE 1. *A prettily furnished Drawing-room at Easington Lodge, looking through French windows on to a lawn – Doors right and left – Elegant decoration – Writing materials on table in the centre.* DODGSON *discovered.*
DODGSON: Well, I really think this address of Honeybun is about as neat a thing as I ever turned out. Constructed, as an address should be, in the pattern of a Dutchman's breeches, – to take in as much as possible.
        (*Enter* PECKOVER *from the lawn, cautiously.*)
PECKOVER: Muster Dodgson!
DODGSON: Ah, Peckover, (*rises*) what brings you here?
PECKOVER: My spring cart. I was just driving round with the day's j'ints; I see you from the sweep, and I thought you'd approve o' the cart. Look at it sir; (*points off through window*) I've turned it into a regular advertising van, posted all over with Mr Honeybun's address. It's beautiful, sir; I keep a-reading of it over to myself as I drives along, and I can't have enough of it. It's cut and come again, like a round of beef.
DODGSON: The author of this address is no common man, Mr Peckover.
PECKOVER: Just tip us it, will you, Muster Dodgson?
DODGSON: (*reads*) 'To the free and independent electors of Flamborough. – Gentlemen, – I come forward in pursuance of a requisition, numerously and respectably signed, to rescue your ancient borough from the domination of a clique:' that's Griggs and Crumpit: 'and the ignominy of a disgraceful coalition:' Gaper and Gabbleton, of course: 'bent on the practical annihilation of your electoral privileges' –
PECKOVER: Annihilation of our electoral privileges, eh! That means getting our votes for nothing, don't it?
DODGSON: Precisely. (*continues reading*) 'I have long resided among you; my opinions are well known. By principle an admirer of our glorious Constitution in Church and State; I am ready to amend with a reverent hand any proved defects in that noble structure; but, at the same time, I shall be found the steady opponent of reckless innovation. Progress is the law of the world, and you will

---

j'ints: joints of meat.
sweep: curve in the road.
tip us it: let me hear it.

find me ever ready to advocate a progressive policy; taking my stand with Bacon upon the ancient paths' –

PECKOVER: Taking his stand with Bacon! One would think he was coming out as a dead meat salesman.

DODGSON: He alludes to the Bacon of two hundred and fifty years ago.

PECKOVER: Uncommon stale that must be.

DODGSON: (*continues reading*) 'If returned as your representative, I shall be ready to give ministers an independent support; free to oppose them if their measures fail to meet the best interests of the community. On particular questions I decline to pledge myself; satisfied that, by this course, I shall be best consulting your advantage and least imperilling my own freedom of action. Your local interests will find in me a strenuous, an indefatigable, and a liberal supporter. Should these sentiments be those of a majority among you, I trust I may soon occupy the proud position of your representative – Christopher Honeybun.' – Eh?

PECKOVER: Its beautiful! How people can string words together to let out so little and take in so much, I can't think. It'll do, sir; that is, if he backs his opinions like a man; and, talking o' that, Muster Dodgson, I've a good lot o' Lambs for sale, in prime condition, you know, (*pointing over his shoulder*) if you wanted such a thing.

DODGSON: I think I know a customer for them, Mr Peckover. Of course, the less we are seen in communication the better.

PECKOVER: (*putting his finger along his nose*) I'm awake, sir. Bless you, I haven't knowed Flamborough elections these thirty years to put my foot in it at my time of life. I'd like to see the party that can say Tom Peckover ever were the man to disappoint a customer of his j'int, or a candidate of his vote – (hear, hear) if so be they paid for the article honourable and reg'lar, and I ain't a-goin' to begin the artful game now, Muster Dodgson. (*Exit to garden.*)

DODGSON: Now I've no doubt that's an honest man in his business, wouldn't give short weight or make a false entry in a customer's book for the world. What bundles of contradiction we are, to be sure!

(*Enter* MRS HONEYBUN, *right.*)

Ah! Mrs Honeybun, how radiant you are looking. It's plain enough that the prospect of a contest has no terrors for you.

MRS HONEYBUN: I see the promised Paradise beyond the battlefield Mr Dodgson, – the glorious Walhalla of London gleams before me.

DODGSON: In which your pedestal is still unoccupied. I hope you are satisfied with our address. (*shows her the address*)

MRS HONEYBUN: I could have wished for some allusion to the amendment of the laws that keep our down-trodden sex in thraldom to yours; otherwise, I have no fault to find. But I have had a great deal of trouble to keep Mr Honeybun up to the mark. He is terrified at the prospect of the labour he may be taking upon himself.

Hear, hear: probably an interjection by Dodgson.
Walhalla: Valhalla – a resting place for heroes.

DODGSON: Labour, ma'am – pooh! A legislator's is the least laborious of employments.

MRS HONEYBUN: Indeed!

DODGSON: The thing is susceptible of arithmetical demonstration. Take as your dividend the amount of work done by the House of Commons, divide it by 654 – the number employed in doing it; the quotient is infinitesimal.

(*Enter* HONEYBUN, *very dismal, right.*)

MRS HONEYBUN: Here is Mr Honeybun; you must help me to encourage him.

DODGSON: (*crossing to* HONEYBUN) Ah, my dear sir; delighted to see you looking so hearty.

HONEYBUN: Don't add insult to injury, sir. I've done it – I know I have; thanks to the advantage you two took of my unsuspecting slumber; but don't say I look as if I liked it! (*Crosses to chair and sits.*)

DODGSON: My dear sir, your address has been received with universal acclamation.

HONEYBUN: My address?

DODGSON: (*behind table*) The one I have issued in your name.

MRS HONEYBUN: I told Mr Dodgson how you hated trouble, dear.

HONEYBUN: But, bless my soul! an address in my name? I haven't got any particular opinions.

DODGSON: Don't do yourself such an injustice my dear sir – a man's opinions are written in his daily existence. Mr Honeybun, you are a constitutional Conservative.

MRS HONEYBUN: Of course you are, my dear.

HONEYBUN: Well, anything for a quiet life.

DODGSON: Concentrated Conservatism.

HONEYBUN: But I'm sure we were very well, as we were, my dear.

DODGSON: Orthodox Conservatism.

HONEYBUN: And I don't see why I should put myself out of the way.

DODGSON: *Quieta non movere.* The very motto of safe Conservatism. In this age of agitation just the class of opinion which most requires a vigorous expression.

HONEYBUN: But I'm incapable of vigorous expression, and I hate excitement and fatigue.

DODGSON: Oh! I'll take everything of that kind off your shoulders down here, and, once in Parliament, there's sure to be at least one man on the other side as averse to trouble as yourself, and you can pair off with him in perpetuity.

MRS HONEYBUN: There's one member at least you'll always vote with, my dear. The gentleman who moves that the House shall make it a rule to adjourn at twelve o'clock.

HONEYBUN: But how ever I'm to make up my mind on questions I don't know anything about, and don't care anything about if I did know –

DODGSON: (*round to back of table*) Perfectly unnecessary, my dear sir. There are always a brace of gentlemen on each side, called 'whippers in,' whose business it is to make member's minds up for them. In short, getting into parliament is

---

Quieta non movere: don't move things that are at rest – let sleeping dogs lie.
pair off: an arrangement between members of opposing parties to be absent at the same time thus maintaining the balance of the vote.

nothing more than becoming a member of the most agreeable club in London, without the preliminary of a ballot, and some people want to complete the club parallel by adding that too.

HONEYBUN: Well, well, – I've promised to let you have your way, my love, so the less said about it the better. In for a penny – in for a pound.

DODGSON: By the way talking of pounds – Mrs Honeybun may have mentioned that there'll be some trifling preliminary expense.

MRS HONEYBUN: The £800, you know, dear.

HONEYBUN: Yes, yes. I wrote to my Broker to sell out, and send down the money.

DODGSON: Not to your Bankers down here, I hope?

HONEYBUN: No; to my own address – didn't I, my dear!

MRS HONEYBUN: Yes, as you suggested, Mr Dodgson.

DODGSON: And in sovereigns.

HONEYBUN: Eh! Why really – how is a man to remember these minutiae.

DODGSON: (*aside*) I hope he won't be such a noodle as to send notes. You will be good enough to remit me the packet when it arrives, by a trustworthy messenger, – not by post.

MRS HONEYBUN: Certainly: I am sure we may trust you to see to its proper disbursement.

DODGSON: Implicitly. It is to be regretted that the legal expenses of elections should be so heavy; but, after all, when one considers the honour, and still more the collateral social advantages –

MRS HONEYBUN: They would be cheap at twice the money. You know, dear, how grateful you have been to me for doing the honours at Easington Lodge, just think what you will owe me for presiding at our house in town! I suppose the Ministers' ladies leave cards on the wives of members, Mr Dodgson.

DODGSON: (*behind table*) The wife of a member of Parliament, especially an Independent member like Mr Honeybun, is an object of most flattering ministerial civilities. You'll live in a perfect deluge of aristocratic pasteboard.

MRS HONEYBUN: Delightful.

HONEYBUN: To turn one's house out of windows.

MRS HONEYBUN: Ah! what happiness to breathe at last a congenial atmosphere; (*rises*) to soar beyond the petty vulgarities of provincial existence; to know real authors, and statesmen and poets, and artists – not in their books, or their speeches, or their pictures, but in their actual coats and waistcoats.

DODGSON: To have their illustrious feet under your own mahogany. Their wit sparkling with your own champagne (*aside*).

HONEYBUN: Good bye to my after dinner nap! Oh! Lud. (*groans*)

DODGSON: But I must leave you to attend to our interests. I've to see your canvassers; to order your colours – by the way, we haven't fixed them yet, Mrs Honeybun; what shall they be?

MRS HONEYBUN: Sky-blue – a sweet cerulean tint.

HONEYBUN: Or, what do you say to green?

MRS HONEYBUN: Green – odious. How could you think of it, dear?

To turn one's house out of windows: throw everything into confusion.

HONEYBUN: Association of ideas, I suppose, my love. I was thinking of the 'Green Man, and still' –

DODGSON: Green is the emblem of Hope you know, ma'am.

MRS HONEYBUN: But sky-blue is the colour of aspiration.

DODGSON: Sky-blue be it then – as pure as our principles, (*aside*) and as milk and waterish.

MRS HONEYBUN: I must send for the draper at once. (*Strikes gong on table.*)

DODGSON: (*taking his hat*) Au revoir, my dear madam. Mr Honeybun, I'll send you up your nomination speech in the course of the morning.

HONEYBUN: My nomination speech! (*alarmed*) You don't mean to say I shall have to learn things by heart?

> (*Enter* JAMES *right*, MRS HONEYBUN *gives him orders, aside, and he exits.*)

DODGSON: Quite superfluous. Your speech will be for the reporters. I'll take care there's row enough under the hustings to drown the lungs of a stentor. You will only have to gesticulate.

HONEYBUN: But I've a horror of gesticulation! And then if there should be a lull!

DODGSON: Oh! just come out with 'British Constitution,' at the right moment, and bring your hand down with an emphasis on the ledge in front of you, thus; – I'll show you. Just oblige me by shouting.

HONEYBUN: Hadn't you better have in the servants?

DODGSON: No, no, never admit the public at rehearsals – oblige me thus (*shouts*) Off! off! off!

HONEYBUN: (*imitates very feebly*) Off! off! off!

DODGSON: Louder, my dear sir. Mrs Honeybun, will you join the chorus? (MR *and* MRS HONEYBUN *shout off! off!*) That's it! now, repeat if you please; dropping your voice suddenly when I hold up my finger. (*They shout* off! off! *again.* DODGSON *gesticulates like a hustings speaker,* – *he holds up his finger, they stop immediately.*)

DODGSON: (*filling up the pause with hustings emphasis and manner*) 'British Constitution!' You see the plan works perfectly. Good bye, my dear sir; don't be frightened. The British hustings mob is a playful creature, (*aside*) though it sometimes does take to rather unsavoury playthings.

> (*Exit* DODGSON *right.*)

MRS HONEYBUN: Oh! what a delightful excitement, even in the anticipation of the contest. Don't you feel it, dear?

HONEYBUN: Addresses, speeches, shouting, gesticulating!

MRS HONEYBUN: Oh! these are merely on the threshold.

HONEYBUN: Yes; there's still worse to follow, the horrors of the journey to London.

MRS HONEYBUN: The delights of a season in town.

HONEYBUN: Late hours, long bills, flags like a furnace, and the Thames in a state of decomposition!

MRS HONEYBUN: Exhibition, operas, concerts, plays, parties!

'Green Man, and still': a common public-house sign.

HONEYBUN: Rushing, crushing, squalling, bawling, loving, and backbiting!

MRS HONEYBUN: To be invited to all the official receptions!

HONEYBUN: And give your vote in exchange for the invitations.

MRS HONEYBUN: To be presented at court.

HONEYBUN: And have your train torn off in the scramble.

MRS. HONEYBUN: To be asked to the balls at the palace.

HONEYBUN: And have to pay the court milliner's bill.

MRS HONEYBUN: Mr Honeybun, how can you insist on turning everything the
    seamy side out in this cynical way?

HONEYBUN: Well, my dear, as you've insisted on turning my life upside down, you
    can't wonder at my seeing things inside out. It's only a feature in the general
    derangement.
                        (*Enter* JAMES *right.*)

JAMES: Mr Glossop, ma'am!

MRS HONEYBUN: Oh! the draper, with the patterns for the banners and rosettes.
    Say, I'll come to him in the dining room. (*Exit* JAMES *right.*) Now, my dear
    Honeybun, don't agitate yourself. Leave everything to me and Mr Dodgson,
    and we'll land you at the head of the poll, as smoothly as if you had driven there
    in your own pony chaise. (*Exit left.*)

HONEYBUN: At the head of the poll, eh? Like the gentleman in flesh coloured tights
    one has seen in the streets with one end of 'la perche' in the small of his back,
    and the other in his friend's waist-belt, thirty feet below him – an enviable
    position no doubt for those that like it, but I'm not of an acrobatic turn of mind.
                        (*Enter* JAMES, *right with a registered letter on salver.*)

JAMES: By the post, sir. (*Exit left.*)

HONEYBUN: Eh! a registered letter. (*opens it*) Oh! the £800 from my broker – in
    notes after all – what a deal of money to pay for being worried to death. Oh! If I
    only could see my way out of the mess. What is to be done?
                        (*Enter* CLARA *from through window.*)
    Ah! my darling.

CLARA: Dear Papa, I'm so glad to have you to myself for once; I see so little of you
    now, you know.

HONEYBUN: Ah! my pet, you'd better make the most of me, while I can be sensible
    of your affection. I shan't be so long, I'm afraid.

CLARA: What do you mean, papa?

HONEYBUN: This election, my dear, that I've allowed myself to be persuaded into.
    I'm afraid I shall never get through it with my reason unimpaired.

CLARA: Oh! I'm so glad.

HONEYBUN: Glad that I'm likely to end my days in a lunatic asylum.

CLARA: No, no; That you've discovered how unfitted you are for a member of
    Parliament.

HONEYBUN: Oh! as to being unfitted, that's quite another matter. If I could see my
    way to avoid being returned, that is without paining Mrs Honeybun, and
    without sneaking ignominiously out of the field –

---

the gentleman in flesh coloured tights: a street acrobat who balanced on the top of a pole ('la
perche') held by his 'strong man' colleague.

CLARA: I'm sure there must be some plan, if you would only consult some experienced person, – some lawyer, say, who had a real regard for your interests.

HONEYBUN: A lawyer with a real regard for one's interests! Where is one to meet with such a phenomenon?

CLARA: I know, papa; yes, I'm sure I do – the very man.

HONEYBUN: You do! Who?

CLARA: Mr Wapshott.

HONEYBUN: Wapshott! Why, I forbade him the house.

CLARA: But I'm sure he's too generous to remember that, if you ask him to come back again; – he's in Flamborough. Indeed, James mentioned that he had called to enquire after you only this morning; in fact, I shouldn't wonder if he were still within reach, if James ran very fast.

HONEYBUN: (*aside*) Mrs Honeybun is safe with the draper, – I've a good mind. (*aloud*) Beg James to run after Mr Wapshott, my love, and to say I'm at home and shall be glad to see him. He'd better bring him in by the conservatory. (*aside*) There's no occasion for his going past the dining-room windows, right under Anna Maria's nose.

CLARA: Oh, I'm so glad! (*aside*) If we can only manage the interview before my stepmother interferes. (*Exit through window.*)

> (*Enter* MRS HONEYBUN, *from dining-room, left with blue ribbons in her hand.*)

MRS HONEYBUN: Honeybun, dear, will you help me to decide between these shades of sky-blue?

HONEYBUN: Anna Maria; they don't consult a wretch in the condemned cell about the twist of his own halter. Choose for yourself, my dear.

MRS HONEYBUN: I think the lighter tint the prettier of the two. Yes, (*going to door*) Mr Glossop, this for the rosettes, I think.

HONEYBUN: Shall you be long?

MRS HONEYBUN: Half-an-hour at least. (*Exit left.*)

HONEYBUN: That's lucky – we shan't be interrupted.

> (*Enter* CLARA *and* WAPSHOTT *through window.*)

CLARA: Mr Wapshott, papa; James just overtook him. I have explained your position; how you have allowed yourself to be put forward as a candidate –

HONEYBUN: In an unguarded moment.

WAPSHOTT: (*crossing to* HONEYBUN) And now you want to beat a retreat.

HONEYBUN: Yes, a retreat with *éclat*, like the Austrian generals!

WAPSHOTT: I must first know exactly how far you have committed yourself. Have you spent any money?

HONEYBUN: I've promised her – that is, my agent, £800 for the necessary expenses. Here's the money just sent down by my broker. (*shows letter*)

WAPSHOTT: Let me see – (*takes packet*) – ah! £10 notes; that's lucky – (*goes to table*) – oblige me, Miss Honeybun, by cutting them in two – (*she does so*) – that's as good as ham-stringing the enemy – and despatch one set of halves to Mr Dodgson at once. (CLARA *does this while the dialogue continues.*) Your only opponent, I believe is the Honourable Mr Gabbleton. I've been long enough in Flamborough to find he has disgusted the electors by his compromise with

Gaper. If you stand against him – (CLARA *after making up the packet, rings. Enter* JAMES, *left, takes packet from her, and exit.*) – thanks to your own popularity, you are certain to be returned.

HONEYBUN: That's what I am afraid of; it seems I'm so tremendously popular, I don't see how the catastrophe is to be averted.

WAPSHOTT: I'm afraid the only way is by not demanding a poll.

HONEYBUN: But if I do that, Mrs Honeybun will never let me hear the last of it. It would be as bad as being returned almost.

WAPSHOTT: If we could only bring another candidate into the field, who didn't object to winning, and had the necessary means.

HONEYBUN: How unfortunate I'm so popular!

WAPSHOTT: Perhaps another hundred might balance that.

CLARA: Oh, Mr Wapshott, why shouldn't you come forward yourself?

HONEYBUN: Ah! a capital notion, – you're young, and strong, and don't mind worry.

WAPSHOTT: Unluckily I haven't the golden key that unlocks the door of St Stephens.

HONEYBUN: Is that all? What's £800 to get myself out of this deplorable predicament! I should be delighted to find you the necessary expenses. You've the whole day before you. You'll find the House of Commons a most agreeable lounge – so I'm told; and then after you've got into parliament, you know, my wife mightn't think your marrying my girl so entirely out of the question.

WAPSHOTT: But, sir, you forget it was you who refused your consent to our marriage.

HONEYBUN: Yes; but it was Mrs Honeybun who insisted on it. She gave me the most satisfactory reasons. But only you come forward and get returned, and I'll undertake to reconcile her to the marriage. Yes; I will. (*to* CLARA) You may stare, my dear; only let me get out of this dilemma, and I feel capable of anything.

WAPSHOTT: So do I, with such a prospect. I will come forward my dear sir; and I hope I may secure your object without drawing heavily upon the purse which you so generously place at my command.

CLARA: But are you really determined on this, papa?

HONEYBUN: Firm as a rock.

CLARA: You're sure you won't change your mind; you know you do sometimes.

HONEYBUN: I'll be adamant.

CLARA: Even against Mrs Honeybun?

HONEYBUN: Even against – (*pausing*) – eh? but don't you see she won't know anything about it. She'll think Mr Wapshott's a real opponent. After her treatment of him last autumn, it would be only natural he should feel bitter against the whole family; and then I'll pretend to be very angry. I can be very angry sometimes, only I don't like to take the trouble.

WAPSHOTT: Allow me to borrow the other halves of the notes temporarily; (CLARA *hands them to him*) and now I'll be off and get my address out directly.

St Stephens: Parliament is sometimes called this because before the fire of 1834 the Commons met in the Chapel of St Stephen in the Palace of Westminster.

I'll employ Griggs as my agent; (*aside*) he's sure to know the price of every vote in the place. (*aloud*) Good morning, sir! Miss Honeybun, wish me success. Now master Dodgson, I think I shall pay you off for the safe, and in your own coin, too. (*holding up packet*) (*Exit.*)

HONEYBUN: Run after him, my dear, and see he doesn't pass in front of the dining-room windows.

CLARA: I'll take him the long way round by the shrubbery. (*aside*) What a delightful walk we shall have! (*Exit.*)

HONEYBUN: There's no use in irritating Anna Maria more than necessary. I'd do anything for that woman; but I really can't sacrifice all my peace of mind. However, my defeat's secured; what a blessing! – provided he can beat me; but I'm so popular. Well, I'll hope for the best; but I shan't be happy till I see my own name at the bottom of the poll. (*yawns*) How tired I am, to be sure. I don't think I ever spent a morning of such combined mental and bodily exertion in the whole course of my life! I really (*yawns*) must go and lie down (*yawns*) a little in the library. (*Exit, yawning, right.*)

(*Re-enter* MRS HONEYBUN *left.*)

MRS HONEYBUN: (*speaking off*) Remember, Mr Glossop, no banner under twelve feet square; and two yards to a rosette! – it is too bad of Mr Honeybun to leave the whole weight of the election on my shoulders; and yet they say women have no political capacity. I should just like to see one of our sex allowed to lead the House of Commons! What a lesson in management she would teach those lords of the creation! – (*Enter* DODGSON, *right with an air of offended dignity, carrying half-notes.*) – Ah, Mr Dodgson, just in time; I want some lessons in electioneering. I mean to canvass myself. The famous Duchess of Devonshire never did more execution in a Westminster election than I intend to do in Flamborough!

DODGSON: I presume, madam, your reliance on your own fascinations induces you to think my services superfluous.

MRS HONEYBUN: (*astonished*) Your services superfluous!

DODGSON: When confidence is at an end between principal and agent, the sooner that connection is closed the better.

MRS HONEYBUN: Confidence at an end! Why?

DODGSON: (*throwing down packet of half-notes*) There is my explanation, madam.

MRS HONEYBUN: (*examining packet*) A bundle of half-notes!

DODGSON: (*loftily*) Count them, madam. You'll find they're all correct, though they have been through my hands.

MRS HONEYBUN: What is the meaning of this?

DODGSON: That packet has just been delivered to me from your husband. It means, I suppose, that the other halves are to be retained as a guarantee, till I have effected my part of the agreement?

MRS HONEYBUN: I assure you, my dear Mr Dodgson, I knew nothing of this. (*rings*) My husband will explain it at once.

(*Enter* JAMES *right.*)

Tell your master I wish to see him, directly. (*Exit* JAMES.)

DODGSON: I trust Mr Honeybun may be able to offer some explanation which may prove satisfactory to my feelings as a man and an agent.

(*Enter* MR HONEYBUN, *yawning, right.*)

MRS HONEYBUN: Mr Honeybun – what can you mean by sending half notes to Mr Dodgson?

HONEYBUN: Why; how could I send him whole notes, my dear, when I had only half ones myself.

MRS HONEYBUN: I understand. Mr dear Mr Dodgson, this explains everything. The broker sent down the notes in halves to avoid accidents at the Post Office.

DODGSON: Oh! in that case, provided it is Mr Honeybun's intention to send me the other halves when he receives them –

HONEYBUN: Certainly – the moment I receive 'em. (*aside*) Wapshott mustn't give 'em back.

MRS HONEYBUN: Come; you are surely satisfied now, Mr Dodgson.

DODGSON: I admit I am susceptible on the point of honour. But, as Mr Honeybun assures me I shall have the other halves when they reach him, I resume my custody of this packet, (*takes it*) and all is again serene.

(*Re-enter* JAMES *right.*)

JAMES: It's Mr Peckover, sir, to speak to Mr Dodgson.

DODGSON: Tell him to call at the office.

MRS HONEYBUN: Oh! stand on no ceremony with us, Mr Dodgson, pray: we'll leave you a clear field. Beg Mr Peckover to walk in, James. Come, Honeybun.

(*Exit* JAMES *right.*)

HONEYBUN: My own house taken possession of by these greasy electors.

(*Exit* MR *and* MRS HONEYBUN, *left.*)

DODGSON: What can this blood-sucking butcher want now – the fellow's as difficult to satisfy as one of his own store pigs?

(*Enter* PECKOVER *right.*)

(*cordially*) Ah! my dear Mr Peckover.

PECKOVER: Beg your pardon for making so bold to come up here, sir; but there was no time to be lost. There's another customer in the market.

DODGSON: What do you mean?

PECKOVER: Another candidate, sir! Ah! you've opened the borough with a wengeance, you have (*unfolding a large poster*). Here's his address.

DODGSON: (*seizing the poster, and reads signature*) Charles Wapshott – Charley Wapshott, (*running over the address*) oh! this is a joke – gammon!

PECKOVER: Is it though! – why, he's retained Griggs and Crumpet. Now Gaper's out o' the market they're free, you know, sir; and half Gaper's committee, the half that was agin the compromise, with Gabbleton, when the chairman gave the casting vote for it, is acting for him. They're out canvassing already.

DODGSON: Why; he's an old friend of mine. He's hard up; in fact, as poor as Job.

PECKOVER: Then, all I can say is, he's fightin' on somebody else's stumpy. Bless you, they've been nibbling at my Lambs a'ready – three o' the Lambs has been at me, to say so. They're offering £6 a head, sir. 'But no,' – sez I. 'Five's the old established figure for a 'Blue Lamb,' sez I, 'and I've agreed with Mr Dodgson

stumpy: slang for cash.

for five. You stick to your colours,' sez I, 'and Muster Dodgson ain't the man to haggle for a pound,' sez I.

DODGSON: Quite right, Peckover! We'll make it six, if this presumptuous puppy dares to go to the poll.

PECKOVER: They've been at the Lions too, sir! I see Topper a slinkin' out of Grigg's office, as if he'd tallowed the soles of his boots.

DODGSON: That's serious! But do you really mean they've money among 'em, Peckover, or only promises?

PECKOVER: Money, sir, good hard money – leastways, notes; the Lambs said new notes – bless their new crisp faces. It wasn't easy for 'em to say 'no,' I can tell you, Muster Dodgson, specially as we haven't seen the colour of your money yet, Muster Dodgson.

DODGSON: Let me see! your Lambs count 52, don't they?

PECKOVER: Yes, sir, just the weeks in the year – but that ain't reckoning me you know, sir – I'm extra.

DODGSON: (*aside, and opening packet and counting half notes*) Nothing like striking while the iron's hot. (*aloud*) Here's £20 for yourself Peckover, and £6 a-head for the Lambs.

PECKOVER: (*beginning to count notes*) You see, I know'd you, sir, 'I sez,' sez I, 'Muster Dodgson will never stand between a poor man and his pound.' Halloa! why, what's this? (*with disgust*)

DODGSON: You shall have the other halves after the poll.

PECKOVER: (*with dignity*) Take 'em back, Muster Dodgson, I didn't think you'd ha' done it, sir. Take 'em back, sir! (*offering the half notes*)

DODGSON: Nonsense, man, put 'em in your pocket – they're not Bank of Elegance.

PECKOVER: No, sir, but they're halves. Pay us after the poll! Thomas Peckover was never insulted like this before. Done and done, is enough for Thomas Peckover, but a half note – no, Muster Dodgson, not if I never touched another 6d. for a vote, I wouldn't.

DODGSON: But don't I tell you I'm to receive the other halves to-day. The others will be of no use to me, while you keep these.

PECKOVER: And what use will these be to my Lambs, while you keep the others?

DODGSON: My good fellow, we've both a character to lose. If I don't pay you the other halves –

PECKOVER: Before the poll!

DODGSON: Before the poll – you're free to sell yourselves to any other bidder; will that satisfy you?

PECKOVER: Well, sir, if you haven't got the other halves I don't see as a gentleman can say fairer. (*Puts up the notes.*) But to talk of paying after the poll! as if I was capable of breaking my word; it hurt me, sir – naterally, it hurt me, and I dare say I looked it.

DODGSON: I can quite appreciate your virtuous indignation. Be off to the Lambs at once – there's not a moment to be lost.

PECKOVER: All right, Muster Dodgson; but it hurt me, sir, naterally, it hurt me – especially when there was another customer in the market with ready money. (*Exit* PECKOVER *right.*)

DODGSON: All this comes of sending notes. But Charley Wapshott in the field! what can be the meaning of it? Eh! now I think of it, his designs on old Honeybun's girl. Ha! yes – that's it. (*laughs*) He comes into the field to be bought out of it. Hang me if I'll put a spoke in his wheel.

(*Enter* MRS HONEYBUN, *left.*)

MRS HONEYBUN: Well! I hope Mr Peckover has brought us good news.

DODGSON: Good news, my dear madam! on the contrary, bad news! There's another candidate in the field; Charley Wapshott.

MRS HONEYBUN: Do you really think him a formidable antagonist?

DODGSON: One of the most rising young men at the bar. Has a noble future before him; perhaps, the woolsack.

MRS HONEYBUN: After all, Mr Honeybun may have been a little hasty in putting such a decided negative on his proposal for Clara. However, it's not too late to repair his hasty act. Suppose he wrote to Mr Wapshott, and intimated to him that he had been in error as to his abilities, his prospects; that he had found his daughter's attachment stronger than he thought it –

DODGSON: I quite agree with you, my dear Mrs Honeybun. Mr Honeybun might give him clearly to understand that, if he will retire you'll both agree to his marrying Miss Honeybun.

MRS HONEYBUN: An excellent suggestion; I'll write at once. (*Sits and writes.*) Mr Honeybun can sign the letter.

DODGSON: Short, my dear madam. (*looking over her*) Fire off your offer at him like a rocket. I hope Mr Honeybun won't make any difficulty about signing.

MRS HONEYBUN: Mr Honeybun hates difficulties too much ever to make any.

DODGSON: Here he comes.

(*Enter* HONEYBUN *left.*)

HONEYBUN: If you've quite done with the butcher, I suppose I may resume possession of my own drawing-room?

MRS HONEYBUN: Honeybun my dear; will you oblige me by signing this note?

HONEYBUN: Certainly! (*takes pen*) What's it about? (*sits*)

MRS. HONEYBUN: A little electioneering business – one of Mr Dodgson and my secrets; now dear. (*Puts the pen in his hand.*)

DODGSON: It will save you an immense deal of trouble.

HONEYBUN: Will it? then I'll sign it at once. (*signs*)

MRS HONEYBUN: (*sealing and directing it*) I must ask you to see it sent at once to Mr Wapshott.

HONEYBUN: To Wapshott? eh! (*with curiosity*)

DODGSON: I need no pressing on an errand of reconciliation. Wapshott shall have it in five minutes.

HONEYBUN: Wapshott. Oh! it's to Wapshott, is it? You corresponding with the enemy, my dear.

MRS HONEYBUN: Oh! you knew he was in the field against you?

HONEYBUN: (*embarrassed*) Yes! I heard so.

MRS HONEYBUN: Then you will be glad to learn my dear, that he won't long stand in your way.

HONEYBUN: Eh!

MRS HONEYBUN: That note conveyed your consent to his marriage with Clara, on condition of his retiring from the contest.

HONEYBUN: (*horror stricken*) You don't say so!

MRS HONEYBUN: A capital idea of mine, wasn't it.

HONEYBUN: Capital! (*aside*) I've signed my own death warrant. (*aloud*) Perhaps, he won't accept the offer.

MRS HONEYBUN: Oh! depend on it, he knows better than to refuse.

                     (*Enter* JAMES *right.*)

JAMES: If you please, sir, it's Mr Shears, the nurseryman.

HONEYBUN: Eh! more bother! What does he want?

JAMES: He wishes to know if you'd prefer the triumphal arch at the end of Market-street, or nearer the Lodge.

HONEYBUN: The triumphal arch! Mrs Honeybun it's all coming upon us.

JAMES: And he said if you had no objection to his taking some of our shrubs, because they are rather out of greens.

HONEYBUN: I don't wonder he thinks I must have any amount of green to spare. Send him away, and say, I want no triumphal arches, nor any such trumpery.

MRS HONEYBUN: But consider, love. The electors will be so chilled if you throw cold water on their enthusiasm in this way.

HONEYBUN: Cold water's good for plants, you know?

JAMES: He said, I was to give you his estimate of the expense, (*gives paper*) but he makes an allowance to parties finding their own greens.

MRS HONEYBUN: Tell him to go to Mr Dodgson.

HONEYBUN: Tell him to go to the devil. (*Exit* JAMES.) Didn't I tell you how it would be; turning a man of my quiet habits into a Jack-in-the-Green! (*sits*)

MRS HONEYBUN: Don't agitate yourself, dearie. After all, what is a triumphal arch, more or less.

                     (*Re-enter* JAMES.)

JAMES: Mr Peckover, sir.

MRS HONEYBUN: Oh! show him in, by all means. (*Exit* JAMES.) It's our butcher, you know; a most important voter, my dear. Mr Dodgson told me of him.

HONEYBUN: That butcher's always in my drawing-room. (*groans*) I suppose this is freedom of election.

               (*Enter* PECKOVER *right with old greasy red book.*)

PECKOVER: Servant, ma'am. Your humble, Muster Honeybun.

HONEYBUN: Well, Peckover. I suppose you have not come to bore me about evergreens?

PECKOVER: No, Mr Honeybun, greens ain't in my line, unless it was boiled with an aitch bone, or may be a sprig o' holly in a Christmas carcase. I called about the local charities, sir.

HONEYBUN: The local charities!

PECKOVER: Which the candidates is always looked to to come down handsome. Muster Gaper, he's in the tracts and flannel line, and the Hon Gabbleton, he comes the literary lecture and general good advice dodge; but I sez, when I read your address, sez I, 'Muster Honeybun, he's a Henglishman – he'll do it in beef,' and I've come to take your orders, sir.

Jack-in-the-Green: a chimney sweep, decorated in green shrubs for May-day.

HONEYBUN: Confound the local charities, if I'm to bribe my way into the House –

MRS HONEYBUN: (*soothingly*) Honeybun! (*aside*) An influential elector, my love.

PECKOVER: No, sir, – not bribe, Mr Honeybun! I don't say if you was asked to give money but where can be the harm in butcher's meat?

MRS HONEYBUN: (*hastily crosses to* PECKOVER) My good friend, if you apply to Mr Dodgson, – he is Mr Honeybun's agent, and has full authority to settle everything.

PECKOVER: Which Mr Dodgson is quite a stranger to me, ma'am; leastways, I've a heavy bill agen him, and I'm afraid he won't be quite so free in his orders as Muster Honebun might like.

MRS HONEYBUN: Say we authorise him to be most liberal. I can answer for Mr Honeybun. He has a heart as open as the day to melting charity.

PECKOVER: There's a many has their heart's open ma'am, but at election times, I've observed, they mostly have their pockets open too; and that's the main point you see, marm. Well, Mr Honeybun, then, perhaps I may say you wouldn't stick at 80 or 100 stone – prime pieces, you know. For you couldn't think of giving clods and stickings to the widders and offans. (*Exit right.*)

HONEYBUN: Thank goodness he's gone. But I can't stand much more of this; it's wearing me out – killing me by inches.

MRS HONEYBUN: You really must exercise a little common discretion, my dear. To offend these people is to risk your election.

HONEYBUN: Mercy on us. If I'm expected to be civil to all the tag, rag, and bobtail on the register –

(*Enter* JAMES *right.*)

JAMES: Mr Topper, sir. (*Exit.*)

HONEYBUN: Another influential elector, I suppose.

MRS HONEYBUN: Only be quiet, dear, and let me receive them.

(*Enter* TOPPER, *right.*)

MRS HONEYBUN: (*cheerfully*) Ah! Mr Topper; delighted to see you.

TOPPER: (*smoothing his fore-lock, and bowing awkwardly*) Ax your pardon for making bold ma'am, but at election time, you know, there's a slippery lot about; and afore I draws beer to parties, or stands goes round, I likes to have it all square from principals.

HONEYBUN: (*aside*) The muscular ruffian.

MRS HONEYBUN: I'm afraid I don't quite understand you, Mr Topper.

TOPPER: Why, you see, marm, being a Honeybun myself – I mean a supporter, marm – it's only natural Mr Honeybun should like his canvassers, and runners, and them committee-men to have their refreshments at my bar – the Green Lion, marm; – and I've called to get the office.

MRS HONEYBUN: Get the office! What office? my dear sir.

TOPPER: Beg parding, marm; which I s'ppose you don't take in Bell's Life?

MRS HONEYBUN: No!

TOPPER: Ah! pleasant Sunday reading in that paper, marm, I can tell you though the ring ain't what it was in my day; but about this matter o' business, – I want to be put up to the guv'nor's figger.

Bell's Life: 'Bell's Life in London and Sporting Chronicle' was published between 1823 and 1886.

MRS HONEYBUN: I'm afraid I am sadly stupid.

HONEYBUN: I suppose you want to know how much the hogs may swill at my expense.

TOPPER: Well, that's one way o' putting it, guv'nor.

HONEYBUN: Then, sir, let me tell you I'm an advocate of temp –

MRS HONEYBUN: (*interrupting*) Temperate enjoyment, Mr Topper; and, so long as that limit is not exceeded, you are free to supply my husband's election staff with whatever refreshments they require.

TOPPER: Well now, I do call that handsome, considerin' what some of 'em can carry. I say, guv'nor, you're agreeable to them terms – eh? (*rises*)

HONEYBUN: (*furious*) Agreeable!

MRS HONEYBUN: Oh, yes; go to my husband's agent – Mr Dodgson, and he'll give you written authority.

TOPPER: Ah! that's business, that is; nothing like articles, marm! saves a wrangle. I often wish I'd been put up to black and white myself, marm; which I was only taught to make my mark, and I've done more o' that on nobs than on paper, marm. Here's wishing you good luck to win the fight, guv'nor, – the same to you, marm, and many of 'em. (*Exit right.*)

HONEYBUN: (*rises*) My dear, this is dreadful! Not satisfied with destroying my peace of mind, you're demoralizing the community: bribery under the mask of charity; beastly intoxication in the guise of refreshments!

MRS HONEYBUN: We must all make our little sacrifices to appearance.
      (*Enter* JAMES *right.*)

JAMES: If you please, sir, it's the leader of the brass band.

HONEYBUN: Merciful powers! (*Groans, covers his face with his hand, rushes to chair and sits.*)

MRS HONEYBUN: Well, what does he want, James?

JAMES: If you'd be good enough to mention any favourite air you'd like played.

HONEYBUN: 'Down among the dead men!'

MRS HONEYBUN: Say 'The Conquering Hero,' James, as the procession approaches the hustings.

JAMES: Yes, ma'am.

HONEYBUN: And, as we drive away from it, 'The Maniac,' very loud.

JAMES: Yes sir. (*Exit.*)

HONEYBUN: Mrs Honeybun, I'm a patient man! a meek man! a submissive man, if you will; triumphal arches I might have passed over or under; to local charities I might have bled; public houses I might have winked at; but a brass band – good gracious! Mrs Honeybun, have you considered my horror of noise; what I suffer even from a stray organ grinder; and now to let loose upon me big drums, cornopeans, trombones, and ophicleides, don't expect that my brain can survive it ma'am. The electors of Flamborough may return me to parliament, but it will be as a violent and dangerous lunatic.

MRS HONEYBUN: Honeybun! Honeybun! Honeybun! how can you be so ridiculous? surely you can put cotton in your ears. – (*Enter* DODGSON, *right.*) Ah, Mr Dodgson! – but what is it? you look agitated.

DODGSON: I'm very sorry; – I've done my best to stave it off. The fact is, there's a deputation of the electors.

HONEYBUN: A deputation!

DODGSON: In fact, two deputations! one Conservative, and one Liberal. Luckily I heard of both just in time; – we'll shuffle 'em.

HONEYBUN: Shuffle 'em?

DODGSON: Introduce 'em both together! The more they contradict each other, the less they'll attend to you.

HONEYBUN: I thought nothing could go beyond the brass band.

MRS HONEYBUN: How very unfortunate; we relied on you to prevent everything of the kind, Mr Dodgson.

DODGSON: My dear madam, I've exerted all my influence; but there is a class of electors who consider candidates as cock-shies set up to be pelted with interrogatories, – a most troublesome style of men, but one can't quite keep 'em down.

MRS HONEYBUN: What is to be done? Honeybun, dear, do make an effort for once. (*Crosses to* HONEYBUN.)

HONEYBUN: An effort for once! I've been making efforts all this morning. I've no views in particular, but they're welcome to such as I have.

DODGSON: My dear sir, only be cautious; don't interrupt the speakers. Most deputations are much more anxious to talk themselves, than to get an answer from those they're talking to. I'm afraid I must ask you to retire. My dear Mrs Honeybun; it would be good policy to order them a substantial luncheon; talking makes people so hungry and thirsty.

MRS HONEYBUN: I understand. (*crossing*) Ah! women must still be dumb on public questions. (*Exit* MRS HONEYBUN *left.*)

DODGSON: (*aside*) They make it up by being anything but dumb on private ones. (*Goes to door right.*) Admit the deputations! (*Enter, right the two deputations.* SPITCHCOCK *heads the one,* GATHERCOLE *the other, followed by* CRAWLEY, COPPERTHWAITE, OLDWINKLE, *and Electors, shewn in by* JAMES *and another Servant, who place chairs on each side of stage.*) Pray be seated, gentlemen. Chairs for the deputation, James. (*introducing*) Mr Honeybun, Mr Gathercole – the enlightened editor of the *Flamborough Beacon*; Mr Spitchcock, editor and proprietor of the *Flamborough Patriot*; Mr Copperthwaite, Mr Crawley, Mr Oldwinkle, and other influential members of the constituency. (*They all sit.*) Mr Honeybun is most anxious to give the fullest explanation in answer to any questions you may put to him; at the same time, he claims the right to maintain that reserve which befits one about to enter on the arduous and responsible duty of legislation. Now, gentlemen.

GATHERCOLE: (*rises, and speaks over back of his chair*) As one of those who signed the requisition to you, sir, on this occasion, and as the mouth-piece of advanced Liberalism in this borough, I have been requested to obtain from you, sir, a categorical expression of your views on the subject of the ballot, – whether you consider that measure is not necessary to secure the humbler class of voters from oppression. (*sits*)

SPITCHCOCK: (*breaking in and rising*) Or if its effect will not be rather to give a premium to deception; to encourage cowardice, and to destroy that manly and open avowal of political opinion which has hitherto been the proud characteristic of the Englishman. (*sits*) (*While these contradictions are being exchanged,* MR HONEYBUN *keeps looking from one speaker to the other.*)

GATHERCOLE: (*interrupting and rising*) I can readily understand, with Mr
   Spitchcock's well known and hebdomadally reiterated opinions, that he should
   be averse to any change which will limit the oppressive influence of territorial
   interests. (*sits*)

SPITCHCOCK: (*rises*) And it is no secret, at least within the limited circulation of the
   Beacon, that the ballot must be acceptable to any party whose aim is to
   strengthen the hands of the demagogue, and to deprive the humble voter of the
   parental guidance of his natural protectors. I should be glad to know which of
   these two views best embodies the political sentiments of Mr Honeybun. (*sits*)

HONEYBUN: (*rises*) Well, really, gentlemen, I must observe that there seems to be a
   great deal to say on both sides. (*Sits, and wipes perspiration from his face.*)

DODGSON: (*rises*) That must be evident to all who have the advantage of perusing
   our own admirable local prints; and such has been the effect of the consummate
   power with which these organs have wielded the opposing arguments on the
   subject of the ballot, that Mr Honeybun's opinion remains suspended, and he
   demands a further opportunity for mature consideration before he commits
   himself unreservedly upon this most interesting question. (*sits*)

SPITCHCOCK: (*rises*) If Mr Honeybun is satisfied that the ballot is cowardly and un-
   English – (*sits*)

DODGSON: (*rises*) He authorized me to say that he will oppose it to the uttermost.
   (*sits*)

HONEYBUN: To the uttermost!

GATHERCOLE: (*rises*) But if he be convinced that without it the real opinions of the
   voters cannot be freely expressed – (*sits*)

DODGSON: It will find in him a strenuous and consistent supporter.

HONEYBUN: That it will.

SPITCHCOCK: The destruction of territorial and intellectual influence –

DODGSON: He holds, with you, would be most mischievous to the country.

HONEYBUN: Most mischievous.

GATHERCOLE: To impose a check on every oppressive and injurious exercise of the
   power of capital –

DODGSON: He is as firmly convinced as you or any man, is the imperative duty of an
   enlightened legislature.

HONEYBUN: Imperative. (*pause*)

DODGSON: Mr Honeybun having now stated his views on the subject of the ballot,
   he will be glad to give an equally explicit answer on any other subject to which
   the deputation may wish to direct his attention.

COPPERTHWAITE: I should like to know how you would vote on a reform bill
   disfranchising this here borough.

HONEYBUN: Well, if you ask me, I should decidedly support –

DODGSON: Any measure which might tend to secure the full representation of every
   class of the community; but as the disfranchisement of Flamborough would be a
   step in quite the opposite direction –

OMNES: Hear, hear.

---

hebdomadally: every seven days, i.e. weekly.

DODGSON: Mr Honeybun would be found, at whatever risk of forfeiting your favour, most decidedly opposed to such a proceeding.

OMNES: Hear, hear.

COPPERTHWAITE: I'm glad to hear that, sir. We're all reformers in a general way; but reform ain't like charity, sir, – it don't begin at home. We don't see why we should be reformed out of our votes. (*sits*)

CRAWLEY: (*rises*) Which, 'owever 'umble, we have always done the best with 'em for ourselves and our families. (*sits*)

DODGSON: Really this is a very original way of putting it, Mr Crawley; don't you think so, Mr Honeybun?

HONEYBUN: Oh, very!

DODGSON: The general good being the sum of individual goods, every man is only to do what is best for himself in order that the country may obtain what is best for all.

OLDWINKLE: (*rises*) I should like to hear Mr Honeybun's opinion about game laws.

HONEYBUN: (*rises*) Well, I'm not a sportsman, myself, and – (*sits*)

GATHERCOLE: (*rises*) Therefore, sir, I trust cannot advocate any system of laws which encourages poaching, leads to numerous breaches of the peace, and fills the county gaols. (*sits*)

DODGSON: Certainly not.

HONEYBUN: Certainly not!

SPITCHCOCK: At the same time, Mr Honeybun can scarcely deny that to put an end to the sports of the field would be to discourage manly activity; to remove a great inducement to resident ownership; and to largely diminish a wholesome, a favourite, and a succulent article of culinary consumption.

DODGSON: Mr Honeybun would be the last man to deny conclusions which thus stated, must commend themselves to the meanest capacity.

HONEYBUN: To the meanest capacity.

COPPERTHWAITE: How about Church-rates?

CRAWLEY: Ought refreshments to be allowed to voters?

DODGSON: Really, gentlemen, Mr Honeybun cannot be expected to answer you all at once; but one of your questions he did catch distinctly; whether refreshments ought to be allowed to voters? a question he is prepared to answer with equal distinctness, by requesting that you will do him the honour of partaking of lunch, which you will find ready in the dining-room.

OMNES: Hear, hear.

GATHERCOLE: He's very kind, I'm sure. What do you say, Spitchcock?

SPITCHCOCK: With all my heart. Political differences should never narrow the field of social intercourse.

CRAWLEY: Well, I must say, Mr Honeybun, you've met us as fair and pleasant as any gentleman could, and we shall be proud and happy to drink your very good health, sir; and success to your election, sir. (*They all rise.*)

COPPERTHWAITE: And I only wish I could be a deputation every day of the week to hear such a werry satisfactory statement of opinions as you've guv' us this morning.

DODGSON: (*showing them out*) This way, gentlemen – (*Exit deputation left –*

DODGSON *rushing back to* HONEYBUN) My dear sir, you managed them beautifully.
                    (*Enter* JAMES *right.*)
JAMES: Mr Wapshott. (*Exit.*)
DODGSON: Oh, with his answer to our proposal! (*shaking hands with* MR HONEYBUN) Keep up your pluck. You see it's nothing when you're used to it. (*Exit right.*)
HONEYBUN: So the cook said by the eels; but I never shall be used to it.
                    (*Enter* MRS HONEYBUN *right.*)
MRS HONEYBUN: Mr Wapshott has come, dear! no doubt to announce his acceptance of your proposal.
HONEYBUN: Of my proposal. Oh! yes. (*groans*)
                    (*Enter* DODGSON *right.*)
MRS HONEYBUN: You've seen Mr Wapshott?
DODGSON: Yes!
MRS HONEYBUN: He accepts, of course?
DODGSON: He maintains a diplomatic reserve.
                    (*As* MRS HONEYBUN *turns to door right to receive* WAPSHOTT, CLARA *enters rapidly from the lawn.*)
CLARA: (*aside as she passes* HONEYBUN) I've seen him, papa.
HONEYBUN: (*aside to* CLARA) He accepts?
CLARA: (*aside*) Hush!
                    (*Enter* WAPSHOTT *right.*)
MRS HONEYBUN: My dear Mr Wapshott, we parted under unpleasant circumstances; I have repented of my share in them. I have succeeded in opening Mr Honeybun's eyes to the precipitation with which he acted.
HONEYBUN: (*aside*) Oh! Anna Maria.
WAPSHOTT: And now in this note Mr Honeybun offers his consent to my marrying Miss Honeybun, which you so sternly, may I say, so offensively refused last autumn, on condition of my withdrawing from the contest for this borough.
MRS HONEYBUN: Precisely.
WAPSHOTT: Then I can only express my regret that Mr Honeybun should have placed before me so painful an alternative, between my aspirations to a seat in the legislature, and my love for Miss Honeybun. Knowing her noble nature, I am satisfied she will not consider it a proof of impaired affection if I respectfully, but firmly, decline the offer.
MRS HONEYBUN: You refuse?
CLARA: You refuse? (*altogether*)
HONEYBUN: You refuse?
DODGSON: You refuse? (*aside*) The idiot.
WAPSHOTT: Like an ancient Peruvian, I offer my heart upon the altar of my country.
CLARA: And like an ancient Spartan I applaud the sacrifice.
WAPSHOTT: I expected no less. (*taking* MR HONEYBUN's *hand*) You will not refuse my hand as a loyal antagonist?
HONEYBUN: Certainly not. (*Shakes hands with him.*) My preserver.
WAPSHOTT: Mrs Honeybun, (*Bows to her.*) Mr Dodgson, we shall meet again.

DODGSON: At Phillippi.
WAPSHOTT: No, sir, at the hustings. (*Exit.*)
MRS HONEYBUN: War to the knife.
HONEYBUN: And fork, if necessary. Huzza! (*dancing*)
DODGSON: He's mad.
MRS HONEYBUN: (*astonished*) Honeybun!

Act III

SCENE 1. *Old-fashioned panelled room in the 'King's Head', adjacent to* MR
HONEYBUN's *Committee-room. A broad window with balcony outside, looking on
Market Place. Sky blue flags etc., with placards in large letters – 'Honeybun and Purity
of Election' – 'Honeybun the friend of the people' – 'Honeybun and no coalition' – 'Poll
early for Honeybun' – 'State of the poll at one o'clock: Wapshott, 21; Honeybun, 19;
Gabbleton, 17'. Door right communicating with Committee Room, door left
communicating with staircase, door in panel up stage left. Tables, chairs, writing
materials. As the curtain rises* SPITCHCOCK, GATHERCOLE,
COPPERTHWAITE *and* OLDWINKLE *discovered (some with pipes, smoking)
clustered about the room, and near the window, from the balcony of which* DODGSON
is addressing a crowd outside, whose shouts and laughter are heard. HONEYBUN *is
trying to conceal himself behind the window curtains, afraid of being seen by the mob.
Shouts, laughter, applause, etc. at commencement.*
DODGSON: And who are our opponents? On the one side a venal member of a venal
    profession, anxious to use a seat in Parliament as the stepping stone to
    professional advancement.
PROMPTER: (*outside*) How do you like that, Wapshott? (*loud roars of laughter*)
DODGSON: On the other, the lisping scion of a bloated aristocracy, one of those who
    fatten on the sweat of the people – whose hands are too soft for any harder
    labour than dipping into John Bull's pockets.
DICK: (*outside*) Whose pockets have you been a dipping into? (*laughter, cheers, and
    counter cheers*)
DODGSON: Not into yours, my friend. I should get mighty little out of them, I
    suspect. (*laughter*)
PROMPTER: (*without*) That's a nasty one – cheekey. (*laughter, and cries of* 'oh, oh!')
DODGSON: But let them do their best, and bad is the best they can do; the sky-blue
    banner will yet wave in front of the battle, (*applause from the electors inside
    room. Cheers and groans from the outside*) and borne high upon the swelling
    billow of popular enthusiasm, Honeybun, the man of the people (*shouts*)
    Honeybun, the enemy of coalition.
DICK: (*outside*) Go it figs. (*laughter, cheers, row*)
DODGSON: A fig for you, my friend. (*laughter, calls of* 'silence,' *etc.*) Honeybun, the
    resident candidate, will assert, in the triumph of this day, that principle for
    which he has left the retirement of private life – that principle which unites his
    supporters in the irresistible might of a holy cause.

---

figs: things of little importance, but also possibly a pun on Honeybun's profession as a grocer.

PROMPTER: (*outside*) Who swallowed the blacking brush? (*row, laughter*, 'ah ah!' *and* 'silence!')

DODGSON: The principle for which a Hampden bled in the field, and a Sydney perished on the scaffold. (*immense applause, inside and out*) The principle of purity of election (*row, cheers, clapping of hands, confusion, during which* DODGSON *comes in from balcony*).

GATHERCOLE: Beautiful; my dear sir, beautiful.

SPITCHCOCK: A magnificent peroration.

    (*All crowd round and congratulate him.*)

DODGSON: Yes; I think I stuck it into them, pretty well. (*shouts without* 'Honeybun! Honeybun!') Where is he? Where's Mr Honeybun? (HONEYBUN *is discovered behind the curtain.*) Won't you address them, sir? – no matter what you say, only show yourself.

HONEYBUN: No! no! for mercy's sake – make an excuse for me; say anything only quiet 'em. (*redoubled cries of* 'Honeybun!')

DODGSON: (*steps out on balcony*) Mr Honeybun is unable to address you – (*groans*)

PROMPTER: What's he been eating on?

DODGSON: He has entirely lost his voice –

PROMPTER: Vot's the use of getting into parliament?

DODGSON: From the continued efforts of nightly addressing private meetings of the electors –

PROMPTER: Gammon! Then let him come out on the balcony and vistle us a tune.

DODGSON: But he's with you in spirit, in feeling, and sympathy.

PROMPTER: So he ought to be.

DODGSON: If his voice cannot be uplifted here, it will yet ring through the House of Commons, so long as there is an abuse to denounce, a threatened right to advocate, or a good cause to defend. (*comes in, sinks into chair exhausted – shouts*)

GATHERCOLE: You have surpassed yourself, Mr Dodgson.

SPITCHCOCK: A most chaste and nervous effort of oratory, to be sure.

CRAWLEY: I could a'most have lep out of the winder.

DODGSON: (*springing up*) And now every man to his post. I will remain here. Let me have a report of the poll every quarter of an hour.

COPPERTHWAITE: (*admiringly to* OLDWINKLE) What a beggar it is to talk.

    (*Exit all but* DODGSON *and* HONEYBUN *right.*)

Hampden . . . Sydney: John Hampden (1594–1643) was a noted parliamentarian, famous for his resistance to the Ship Tax, who was mortally wounded fighting against the forces of Charles I in the Civil War at Chalgrove Field on 18 June 1643. Shot in the shoulder, he bled to death. Sydney is likely be Algernon Sidney (or Sydney – both spellings are acceptable) (1622–82), another noted parliamentarian and republican who was executed for treason by Charles II. Sidney was suspected of complicity in the decision to execute Charles I, and the indictment in his trial accused him of having 'written a treasonable libel, affirming the subjection of the King to parliament and the lawfulness of deposing kings'. But Taylor allows some confusion to enter here, as the rather more famous Sidney – Sir Philip – himself 'bled to death in the field of battle'. Is this a subtle joke for historians in the audience or was Algernon a reasonable reference for a Victorian audience to pick up? And would Queen Victoria have been amused?

HONEYBUN: My dear sir, I do wish the next time you address the Electors, you would do it from the window of the committee-room, yonder. (*Points to door.*)

DODGSON: But this balcony immediately adjoins Wapshott's headquarters at the Black Swan. He's on the other side of that partition; every shot I fire ricochets right into the enemy.

HONEYBUN: I shouldn't mind, if I had anywhere else to go to. But I engaged this as my private room, on purpose to be able to get a little quiet, and it's been a scene of disturbance inside and out all the morning.

DODGSON: Impossible to make omelettes without eggs, Mr Honeybun. Row and disturbance are the eggs of an election omelette. But to give it the true golden colour there's one thing more wanted, and that's money.

HONEYBUN: Ah! you allude to the other halves of those notes. It's very odd I haven't received them yet.

DODGSON: It's more than odd, Mr Honeybun, it may be fatal. If I haven't these notes complete before two o'clock, your election is lost.

HONEYBUN: (*aside*) I sincerely hope so.

DODGSON: Perhaps the packet may have arrived at your house this morning.

HONEYBUN: I shouldn't wonder! Suppose I walked up to inquire. But do tell those committee-men, who smell so very strong of beer and smoke, this is my private room, and that I have a particular objection to shag tobacco. (*Exit left.*)

DODGSON: What an old muff it is! If it wasn't for his wife and his money, I'd throw him over at once.

(*Enter* PECKOVER *right.*)

Well, Peckover – how's the poll?

PECKOVER: Wapshott's still with a slight lead, – Gabbleton makin' running, sir, and your 'oss droppin astern. (*Gives paper, state of poll.*)

DODGSON: Your horse! our horse you mean!

PECKOVER: Beggin' your pardon, Muster Dodgson, the Lambs won't stir till I gives the word, and I don't give the word till I sees the money. Them's our rules, sir, and I ain't sorry to say I can't break 'em.

DODGSON: Oh! the notes are all right. Honeybun has just gone up to his house for them. By-the-bye, did you make an offer to that fellow, Haggle?

PECKOVER: Yes, sir, but he's in a difficulty. You see Haggle's a chapel man, sir, and his conscience is a werry ticklish one. He had £10 from the Honourable Gabbleton's people for his vote; and then he heard the Honourable Gabbleton was a Pooseyite, whatever that may be, but Haggle being very uncertain what he should do, went and took £10 from the other people, and since then he's been feeling very uneasy in his conscience, which of the two he ought to vote for.

DODGSON: Promise him £10 from me if he votes for neither. I've no doubt that will make his conscience quite comfortable.

PECKOVER: £30! Well, it ought to. That's a clever lad o' yours, that young Trundle. I seed him bottle a brace of Gabbleton's voters this morning, as neat as ever I see anything done in my life; hocuss'd 'em both blind; and then put 'em in the express train for London.

Pooseyite: follower of Edward Bouverie Pusey who attacked moves towards liberalism in the Church. Pusey was Regius Professor of Hebrew at Oxford.
hocuss'd 'em: made them drunk.

DODGSON: Poor devils! How astonished they'll be when they recover their senses, at the Euston Square station.

PECKOVER: Oh! Crawley wanted to know, if you'd have any dead men polled. He thinks he could manage it, as the Register wasn't very sharply looked after last year.

DODGSON: I think we had better keep our dead men till we are quite certain we want 'em.

PECKOVER: Keep the dead men as a 'corpse de resarve.' And Copperthwaite has got two more beer-shops to hang out the Honeybun colours.

DODGSON: Of course they'll want an order. (*Writes order at table.*) Send out twenty tickets for a gallon of beer each. By the way, about Topper and his Lions. You said Grigg's had been nibbling at 'em.

PECKOVER: Ah! Muster Dodgson. Topper's a greedy man – he'd do better for himself and them as goes with him, if he'd wait. But he can't stand money down. He's nailed, I'm afraid, Muster Dudgson.

DODGSON: Why, we offered as much as Griggs.

PECKOVER: Yes; but Griggs offered first.

DODGSON: If Topper carries his votes over to Wapshott, we shall have a hard pull to head him.

PECKOVER: There's a deal of the heavy weights out yet.

DODGSON: Yes; but they are such unconscionable dogs, there's no coming up to their figure.

PECKOVER: Clubs is the things depend on't, Muster Dodgson; they're easy managed, and can be kep' within a gentleman's means; and then clubs has principles. The Lambs always comes a pound a head cheaper to the Liberals.

DODGSON: (*crosses*) A very liberal discount.

PECKOVER: But principles won't keep a family, you know, sir; and I do hope you'll soon be ready with the needful, sir. The Lambs will be gettin' uncommon rampagious by about two o'clock.

DODGSON: Come along with me, (*crosses*) and I'll make 'em a speech.

PECKOVER: Bless your heart, sir, a pound o'tin is worth a ton o' talk; but you're welcome to try your best, sir.

DODGSON: We must keep an open eye on Topper.

PECKOVER: There's that young Trundle; why not lay him on the scent? He's as sharp as a ferret.

DODGSON: A good notion; he might smuggle himself into Wapshott's committee-room, and pick up some useful information. If we can bring a case home to Topper, I'll have the bribery oath administered to every Lion of the lot.

PECKOVER: Two can play at that game, sir, you know.

DODGSON: True; in case they should try it on; just give me back the notes till after the Lambs have polled; (PECKOVER *gives the half-notes*) and now they may bolt the bribery oath as easy as an oyster. (*Exit left.*)

PECKOVER: Ah! you're a cute 'un! (*Exit to committee-room right.*)
> (*Enter, from staircase, left* MR *and* MRS HONEYBUN *and* CLARA.)

MRS HONEYBUN: And so you positively refuse to drive round the town, Mr Honeybun, and give countenance to your supporters.

HONEYBUN: I'm afraid my countenance is not calculated to have an encouraging effect, my dear.

MRS HONEYBUN: Oh! if I were but a man! I would make this presumptious Wapshott tremble. To think of his being ten a-head by the last account of the poll! But you may depend upon it that whatever may be his success, I will never consent to your marrying one who has dared to stand in the way of your father's laudable ambition.

HONEYBUN: Don't mind me, my love; I shall do my best to forgive the young man; and if I succeed in doing so, surely, Anna Maria, you may.

MRS HONEYBUN: Never! I leave it to your daughter to approve of such behaviour. To me it seems as impossible to forgive as to forget; (*rings*) but he shall never see me quail, that I promise him! – (*Enter* JAMES *left.*) – Order up the phaeton.

HONEYBUN: To take you home, my dear? (*Exit* JAMES.)

MRS HONEYBUN: Home – no! to drive into the heat of the contest; to show myself, as you should; wherever I can encourage a friend or strike terror into an enemy! (*Exit left.*)

HONEYBUN: Anna Maria's energy is really alarming. Strike terror into an enemy! 'gad, it would be well if she confined herself to that; she strikes terror into me. What is to be done, my darling, to soften her feelings towards Mr Wapshott?

CLARA: Fortunately, Mr Wapshott's happiness does not depend upon my stepmother's humour so much as that of those who live with her. (*noise in adjoining room*)

HONEYBUN: Eh? (*listens*) What a noise in that next room.

CLARA: It is your consent I want; not hers!

HONEYBUN: Yes; but still, you see, if Anna Maria were to set her face dead against it, it would be very – (*violent altercation next door*) Bless me! what can be going on next door? –

> (*Altercation grows louder – a violent concussion, as if some heavy body falling against panelling, – the collison forces the door open – a shout of* 'spy! spy!' *is heard, and* TRUNDLE *is precipitated into the room, followed by* TOPPER *(who has hit him, and is preparing to repeat the blow in a scientific manner) and members of* WAPSHOTT'S *committee –* TRUNDLE *falls;* CLARA *screams;* HONEYBUN *shrinks back alarmed;* WAPSHOTT *rushes in, as if to allay the tumult.*)

WAPSHOTT: Clara! Mr Honeybun! Don't be alarmed; only a spy detected by my committee. (*to* TOPPER) Be quiet, my good good fellow; don't you see you're alarming the lady.

TOPPER: Just let me mark him, the sneaking beggar!

WAPSHOTT: No, no! You've marked him enough, already; carry him down into the yard. He'll soon come to.

> (*Exit committee-men with* TRUNDLE *through panel door.*)

TOPPER: (*apologetically to* CLARA *and* MR HONEYBUN) Beg pardon, Miss – werry sorry, Mr Honeybun, but this party was a thrustin' his nose where it didn't ought to come, so I was just givin' it a tap by way of reminder. But if I'd a know'd there was a lady, I would a polished him off private, in the passage. (*Exit.*)

WAPSHOTT: To think we should be such near neighbours. I see! The King's Head, and the Black Swan must, in old days, have been one house; the mansion of some local magnate, I suppose. I can't be angry with my friend Topper's terrific left hander, since it has opened this door of communication between us.

CLARA: How fortunate that you were there. I should have been so terrified.

HONEYBUN: And how lucky this should be my private room.

WAPSHOTT: Yes; we shall not be liable to intrusion. Well, you see, I'm going to beat you out of the field.

HONEYBUN: Yes; that's the worst of it.

WAPSHOTT: The worst of it! I thought it was what you wanted of all things?

HONEYBUN: So it is, but –

CLARA: Papa fears that if you defeat him, he will never succeed in inducing Mrs Honeybun to consent to our marriage.

HONEYBUN: Not that I'm afraid of carrying my point in the long run, but I do feel nervous, to think of what I may have to go through in the process.

WAPSHOTT: Oh! don't let me stand in the way; I thought I was doing you a service. But I can retire at any moment.

HONEYBUN: Don't dream of such a thing! Why, I should be returned.

WAPSHOTT: What if I could please both you and Mrs Honeybun?

HONEYBUN: Ah! if you could manage that.

WAPSHOTT: I presume if you are only defeated, you don't mind my retiring?

HONEYBUN: Not I.

WAPSHOTT: And you, Clara! you have no particular ambition to see your husband that is to be, in parliament?

CLARA: Well, I shouldn't be peculiarly anxious to sacrifice you to my country; – at least, till a leetle after our marriage. (*Goes to window.*)

WAPSHOTT: I say ditto to that. Then leave me to make my own terms with Mrs Honeybun?

HONEYBUN: But mind, whatever happens, I'm to be beaten.

CLARA: (*at window*) Here's the phaeton, papa.

HONEYBUN: (*at window*) Anna Maria coming back.

WAPSHOTT: No time like the present. I've had a retiring address printed in readiness for an emergency. I thought it might come to this.

HONEYBUN: But not a word of my connivance.

(*Re-enter* MRS HONEYBUN *left.*)

MRS HONEYBUN: Well; I've been to the polling booth, and that odious Mr Wapshott – (*seeing him*) You here, sir?

WAPSHOTT: Yes, Mrs Honeybun; anxious to get rid at once of your epithet, and the cause of it, I have reflected maturely on your offer of yesterday. I have determined to accept your offer on condition of your withdrawing your opposition to my marrying Clara. I am ready to retire, and turn over all the support I can command to your husband.

MRS HONEYBUN: This is a very sudden change of determination, Mr Wapshott; I thought women monopolized the right to such waywardness.

WAPSHOTT: A lover is half a woman, you know. In an hour my retiring address shall be posted all over town.

HONEYBUN: (*alarmed*) But then I may be returned after all.

MRS HONEYBUN: I hope there is no doubt of it now? Come, Mr Honeybun, we must drive round to Mr Dodgson's office, and let him know of this at once. Luckily, I told the coachman to keep the phaeton. (*Exit left followed by* CLARA.)

HONEYBUN: I say, you're sure your interest won't bring me in?

WAPSHOTT: Till these half notes come together, you are safe.

HONEYBUN: I can't understand why both you and Dodgson make such a fuss about these notes. Am I standing on purity principles, or am I not?

WAPSHOTT: Yes; but of all remedies for electoral ills the purity pill is that which needs most gilding!

HONEYBUN: I knew I hadn't enough mettle for this. (*Exit left.*)

WAPSHOTT: Now, to break my intentions to my committee, and first of all to my zealous friend Topper.

(*Goes to door in panel and calls* TOPPER! TOPPER *entering.*)

TOPPER: Yes, Muster Wapshott – I'm fly, sir; if there's another sneak to be dropped a-top of.

WAPSHOTT: No, Topper! I shall have no further occasion for your services in that way.

TOPPER: Sorry for it, sir. It's pleasant to find one's hand in agin sir! without the gloves too. (*hitting out*)

WAPSHOTT: In fact, I'm afraid I shall have no further occasion for you at all, my worthy friend.

TOPPER: Not to keep order round the booth at four o'clock, sir. There's sure to be somebody 'll want polishing off, and you'll want me to vote, sir.

WAPSHOTT: Not even to vote. In fact, I have determined on retiring.

TOPPER: Retiring! Well, to be sure.

WAPSHOTT: Yes; my offers to that most patriotic society, the Green Lions, have got wind. The very numbers of those half-notes I gave you in advance, have somehow come to the knowledge of Mr Honeybun. If I persevere I may be exposing both you and myself to the heavy penalties of the Corrupt Practices Act.

TOPPER: I see, sir; you are a-going down to avoid punishment.

WAPSHOTT: Just so; it's the safest course! Dodgson, I hear, is prepared to administer the bribery oath to you, and all the Lions who vote under your advice.

TOPPER: So Tom Peckover was a-sayin'; but I thought it was his chaff. Then you won't be wantin' us, sir? Well, to tell the truth, I ain't altogether sorry for it.

WAPSHOTT: Indeed! I flattered myself I had made a favourable impression.

TOPPER: Oh, it ain't that, sir! A nicer, civiller gentleman I wouldn't wish for a backer; but you see, sir, Dodgson's giving a pound a head higher.

WAPSHOTT: Then don't let me stand in your way for a moment. But first hand me back those half-notes.

TOPPER: (*hands him packet*) It's just as well I kep 'em sir.

WAPSHOTT: Why, the Lions couldn't have spent half-notes if you had distributed 'em.

TOPPER: No, sir; but they might have popped 'em! There ain't a pawnbroker in

Flamborough but would have advanced on 'em, if they knew they was
promised for a vote. Bless you! candidates always keep 'lection promises.

WAPSHOTT: To voters, you mean; the rule don't extend to the hustings.

TOPPER: In course not, sir. That's talk, that is; but t'other's what I call business; so
now I'll toddle down to Muster Dodgson's and see what he'll stand. It's
pleasant to think we're only selling ourselves, and not, as some does, selling
you in the bargain. (*Exit through panel.*)

WAPSHOTT: And I must explain my retirement as I best can to my committee.
Luckily they have no money to return. (*Exit through panel.*)
(*Enter* DODGSON *and* MRS HONEYBUN *left.*)

DODGSON: This is, indeed glorious news: Wapshott out of the field.

MRS HONEYBUN: At last our success, I suppose, is certain.

DODGSON: If we do our part by the electors; but, for this purpose, I must once
more earnestly impress upon you the importance of Mr Honeybun completing
his payment.

MRS HONEYBUN: What! have you never got those other half-notes yet?

DODGSON: No; and till I do I cannot answer for anything.

MRS HONEYBUN: Oh! his bankers will change them at once.

DODGSON: I have my own reasons for not wishing Mr Honeybun to apply to his
own bankers for the purpose; they support Gabbleton.

MRS HONEYBUN: But surely that is no reason.

DODGSON: There are others which I need not explain, but which are all-sufficient –
(*Enter* HONEYBUN *left.*) – My dear sir, I give you joy of Wapshott's
retirement; – (*crosses*) – that clears the way to our success.

HONEYBUN: Eh? you're satisfied of that.

DODGSON: Not a doubt of it, if – but I'll leave Mrs Honeybun to explain the one
remaining condition, which satisfied, you are the member for Flamborough.
(*aside to* MRS HONEYBUN) Remember, gold, and not from his bankers.
(*Exit into room right.*)

HONEYBUN: Only one condition of my return, eh? (*aside*) Catch me satisfying it!
(*Enter* WAPSHOTT *through panel.*)

WAPSHOTT: Well, I've convinced my committee, with some trouble, of the
expediency of my retiring, and I've got the notes from Topper.

MRS HONEYBUN: I trust you requested their support for Mr Honeybun.

WAPSHOTT: Yes, I went so far as I durst; but I'm sorry to say they didn't seem to
relish being turned over *en masse*, – I rather think they'll give their interest to
Gabbleton.

HONEYBUN: (*aside*) I hope so, devoutly.

MRS HONEYBUN: By-the-bye, dear, I understand from Mr Dodgson that money is
absolutely required for legal expenses, – suppose you gave me the £800 in gold
at once. Here are the halves.

HONEYBUN: Eh? well, but one doesn't keep £800 in gold in one's pocket, you
know. I must apply at the bank.

MRS HONEYBUN: No! that is undesirable, it seems.

WAPSHOTT: (*aside*) I should think so.

HONEYBUN: Then I'm sure I don't know where to get the money.

WAPSHOTT: Suppose you allow me to get gold for them?

MRS HONEYBUN: (*gives them*) If you would be so kind; not at the bank, you know.

WAPSHOTT: Certainly not; my practice before election committees quite explains why. (*Exit through panel.*)

MRS HONEYBUN: And now that's *en train* at last. You really must drive round the town with me Honeybun; it's absolutely necessary to show yourself; people are beginning to look upon you as a sort of Mrs Harris.

HONEYBUN: If being harassed is a qualification for the character, my love, I think they're not far wrong.

MRS HONEYBUN: Nonsense! Come along, and do be affable and cheerful; smile, and bow, and kiss your hand as we drive along.

HONEYBUN: Smile, and bow, and kiss my hand! I never thoroughly appreciated the burden of royalty till this moment. (*Exit left.*)

(*Enter* DODGSON, PECKOVER, *and* TOPPER *right.*)

DODGSON: Well, Topper, as you say Mr Wapshott's retirement leaves you quite at liberty, I don't care if I give you the same terms as I gave Peckover, though you don't deserve it.

PECKOVER: You see, Tom, you would take the £5 down; and now, just look – if your man hadn't withdrawed how you would have been out of pocket.

TOPPER: An offer's an offer; and when Griggs came out with them new notes –

DODGSON: Why you don't mean to say they were green enough to pay in notes.

TOPPER: Yes, sir.

DODGSON: And you've disgorged 'em?

TOPPER: Eh?

DODGSON: I mean, that you've given 'em back?

TOPPER: Why you see, sir, they was only halves!

DODGSON: Half-notes! (*aside*) Odd coincidence.

TOPPER: Yes; we got half down, and we was to have t'other half after polling.

PECKOVER: And you took an offer like that, Thomas Topper?

TOPPER: In course I did; why not?

PECKOVER: Then I can only say I blush for you! Why, don't you see, it was a slur on your honour, Thomas. A man in your position – head of a club of voters – ought to have knowed better. If we don't respect ourselves, Thomas, however can we expect other people to respect us? (*Mouths the last words.*)

TOPPER: Blest if I understand what you're a-whisperin' about!

DODGSON: (*who has been walking up and down*) Could you let me see those half-notes?

TOPPER: I guv' em back to Muster Wapshott; but here's their numbers. (*Gives list to* DODGSON.)

DODGSON: (*compares the two lists*) By Jove! Wapshott must have nailed parcel No. 2.

PECKOVER: Eh?

Mrs Harris: is Mrs Gamp's fictitious friend in Dickens's *Martin Chuzzlewit*. Mrs Harris never appears. It is interesting that *Punch* used Mrs Gamp and Mrs Harris to represent two publications, the *Standard* and the *Morning Herald* which it wished to ridicule. Taylor was a member of *Punch*'s editorial board.

DODGSON: Nothing, nothing! (*aside*) A splendid dodge, but risky, deuced risky; in fact, felonious.

PECKOVER: I beg pardon, Muster Dodgson; but it's getting on for half-past two, sir; and Crumpet is bidding very 'ard sir. You know I would strain any p'int for you, Muster Dodgson, after you've opened the borough; but, unless the Lambs sees their money before three, I doubt if they'll obey orders any longer.

DODGSON: I expect remittances every moment, Peckover; go and prevent your flock from bleating for the next quarter-of-an-hour.

PECKOVER: I'll do my best, sir; but my Lambs are such loyal chaps there's no keepin' 'em back when they sees a British sovereign afore 'em! (*Exit right.*)

DODGSON: And you, Mr Topper, try to induce your Lions to keep their mouths shut till feeding time; say somebody will be round with the beef by three.

TOPPER: All right, Muster Dodgson, I was bred to the P.R., sir, and, in course, I'm fly to good manners. (*Exit right.*)

DODGSON: It's as clear as daylight. By hook or by crook, Wapshott has got hold of these half-notes. The girl must have helped him. Ah! here comes Mrs Honeybun. (*Enter* MRS HONEYBUN *left.*) – On second thoughts, my dear madam, I think we may manage with the notes now, if you would let me have the packet back.

MRS HONEYBUN: I'm so sorry, but I have parted with them.

DODGSON: To Mr Honeybun.

MRS HONEYBUN: No; he was at a loss where to go for gold, unless the bank, so I gave the packet to Mr Wapshott.

DODGSON: To Wapshott! confound the fellow – why, he's got both halves now.

MRS HONEYBUN: Both halves, Mr Dodgson?

DODGSON: Yes; the whole £800. Didn't he tell you so?

MRS HONEYBUN: Not a word! I thought the other halves had not arrived from London.

DODGSON: So did I, till just now. But I've discovered that they have arrived – that they have been in Wapshott's possession ever since yesterday.

MRS HONEYBUN: Why then he must have sto–

DODGSON: Stolen 'em – madam.

MRS HONEYBUN: Yes; that's the word. But perhaps he can explain.

DODGSON: I hope so – I sincerely hope so! I knew this man in earlier life. (*aside*) It's a deuced good trick though. (*Bursts out laughing, but checks his laughter with pocket handkerchief, and pretends to be affected.*) Excuse me, Mrs Honeybun, but it's very painful to have a youthful faith thus dashed from its pedestal. (*Exit right.*)

MRS HONEYBUN: Ah! here comes Mr Honeybun; now then, I must unmask this imposter.

(*Enter* HONEYBUN *and* CLARA *left.*)

HONEYBUN: Well, Anna Maria, has Wapshott brought you those sovereigns?

MRS HONEYBUN: He has not, Mr Honeybun; and I shall be very much surprised if you ever see your notes again.

CLARA: (*angrily*) Mrs Honeybun!

HONEYBUN: What do you mean; didn't Wapshott undertake to get 'em changed?

(*Enter* WAPSHOTT *from panel.* CLARA *sees him; he makes her a sign to be silent.*)

MRS HONEYBUN: He did; but when I tell you that, at that very moment he was already in possession, surreptitious possession, of the missing halves; that by his offer he succeeds in getting possession of the other halves from me –

WAPSHOTT: (*steps forward of* HONEYBUN) Mrs Honeybun!

MRS HONEYBUN: Mr Wapshott!

WAPSHOTT: As this is my future father-in-law, and this my future wife, perhaps it would be well you should hear my defence before you pronounce me guilty of larceny. I have just received a summons from Mr Dodgson – our interview may enlighten you on this matter, and some others. Let me recommend your retiring to my room, from which you may overhear what passes between us.

MRS HONEYBUN: Overhear! Listeners, they say –

WAPSHOTT: Never hear any good of themselves, but may hear what does them good, notwithstanding. Wait, whatever passes, till I summon you by a cough, so. (*Coughs – He leads* MRS HONEYBUN *to panel, she exits.*) Mr Honeybun, Clara, I include you in the invitation.

HONEYBUN: (*aside to* WAPSHOTT, *who is showing them through panel*) Keep me clear of the business, if you can. (*Exit.*)

CLARA: You may lay all the blame on my shoulders, dear.

WAPSHOTT: Bless you; it's all right. Your stepmother shall have her eyes opened for once. (*Exit.*)

(*Re-enter* DODGSON *right.*)

DODGSON: I've sent my note to the delinquent; perhaps, it's as well we should have the row out, single-handed. Ah! the guilty party.

(*Re-enter* WAPSHOTT.)

WAPSHOTT: You want to see me, Dodgson?

DODGSON: Yes, particularly. Ah! you old fox: I've found you out.

WAPSHOTT: Found me out?

DODGSON: Yes! those half-notes, you know; I suppose it was Miss Honeybun managed to screw the other halves out of the strong-minded woman, under the pretence of getting sovereigns for 'em; upon my word, I should have been proud of the plan if I had concocted it myself.

WAPSHOTT: You are welcome to put your own interpretations on my conduct. But what do you want of me? (MR *and* MRS HONEYBUN *are seen peeping through panel.*)

DODGSON: Those notes; without them I can't carry out my promise to land Honeybun (old figs, as the little boys call him) at the head of the poll.

WAPSHOTT: But you surely don't want Mr Honeybun returned?

DODGSON: I! I don't care one of the figs he has made his fortune by, whether he's returned or not.

WAPSHOTT: A man so unsuited by his tastes and habits for a parliamentary life.

DODGSON: He's as much fitted for St Stephen's as a cow for a concert.

WAPSHOTT: Then why invest so much money in securing his return?

DODGSON: It's his money, don't you see; £800 doesn't pass through my fingers every day – and such a sum can't pass through any man's fingers without something sticking to 'em. Besides, I promised his wife. She's at the bottom of the whole business.

WAPSHOTT: Oh! indeed.

DODGSON: It's her ambition, not her old muff of a husband that's to be gratified.
Ha! ha! ha! I promised her such a success in London; ministers and their wives at
her feet – her drawing-room a hall of state, where the Flamborough Corinne was
to rule, with statesmen, poets, and artists, kissing the toe of her blue stocking.

WAPSHOTT: But you knew all this was flummery?

DODGSON: Of course I did; but I wanted a candidate, and she pulled the strings of a
puppet with the required £.s.d. and without the courage to say 'no' to this
Brummagem muse of his.

WAPSHOTT: In fact, Mr Honeybun was the gudgeon – his wife was the hook –

DODGSON: And I found the bait in a silly woman's ambition. But we are wasting
time. I've explained why I want the notes; it's nearly three o'clock, so hand 'em
over.

WAPSHOTT: Certainly; but it must be with the owner's permission. (*Makes signal by
coughing.*)
> (*Re-enter through panel,* MR *and* MRS HONEYBUN, *and*
> CLARA.)

DODGSON: But I want the money now. I can't go looking for old figs and his
precious better half.

HONEYBUN: (*coming forward*) Old Figs, and his precious better half will save you
the trouble, Mr Dodgson.

DODGSON: Ah, Mrs Honeybun! excuse my using an election nickname. You took
me by surprise.

HONEYBUN: It's only returning the compliment. You've taken us by surprise,
preciously, I can tell you. Eh! my dear.

MRS HONEYBUN: We cannot be sufficiently grateful for the frankness of the
explanation you have just given to Mr Wapshott.

DODGSON: Why, you don't mean to say you overheard.

MRS HONEYBUN: Every word.

WAPSHOTT: I'm really afraid I forgot to say they were on the other side of that door
all the while. (*Points to panel.*)

DODGSON: (*aside*) Done! Brown as a berry.

WAPSHOTT: Perhaps, you'll be kind enough to give me instructions as to these
notes, Mr Honeybun?

HONEYBUN: (*crosses to* WAPSHOTT) I think they'll not be so safe anywhere as in
Old Figs' own pocket. (*Buttons them up in his pocket.*)

MRS HONEYBUN: The pretentious blue stocking. The Brummagem muse, the
Flamborough Corinne, has the honour to thank Mr Dodgson for a very severe,
but a very useful lesson. She will do her best to profit by it.
> (*Enter* PECKOVER *and* TOPPER *right.*)

PECKOVER: Beg pardon for intrudin', ladies and gentleman. I say, Muster
Dodgson, it's three o'clock, and the Lambs is a-waitin!

TOPPER: And so is the Lions.

WAPSHOTT: Let 'em wait.

PECKOVER: Eh? (*to* DODGSON) Mind, Gabbleton's ready.

HONEYBUN: And Honeybun isn't! I'm much obliged to you, my worthy friends; but
I don't want to insist on any promises you may have given to this gentleman.

DODGSON: (*aside, recovering himself*) Come – I'll go out with a bang, (*aloud, severely*) Mr Peckover, Mr Topper, – my principal, Mr Honeybun, entered on this contest by hoisting the unsullied flag of 'Purity of Election:' you admit that was our rallying cry?

PECKOVER: Yes, Muster Dodgson, that was the flag, but that warn't the understanding.

TOPPER: Quite t'other.

DODGSON: And yet you have the assurance to come and propose to me, as Mr Honeybun's agent, a corrupt traffic in your votes! Mr Peckover, Mr Topper, – I blush for you!

HONEYBUN: (*aside*) Very kind of him, when he seems unable to blush for himself.

PECKOVER: Thomas Topper, I want to make a remark, and which remark I hope you'll 'and down to your child'n and which remark is – Did you ever?

TOPPER: No, Muster Peckover – no, I never!

WAPSHOTT: Mr Honeybun, I'm afraid this last half-hour has lost both of us the chance of a seat.

HONEYBUN: The loss wouldn't break either of our hearts, particularly if it win you a wife, eh? Anna Maria, I think we both owe a deal to Mr Wapshott.

MRS HONEYBUN: I wish it were as easy to pay the debt as to acknowledge it.

CLARA: I think, papa, he will give you a receipt in full of all demands under my hand. (*Offers it to* WAPSHOTT.)

WAPSHOTT: And own myself your debtor for life, into the bargain.

HONEYBUN: I say, my good friends, hadn't you better go to Mr Gabbleton's agent?

PECKOVER: Now, now, Mr Bunnyhun – I mean Honeybun; it ain't pleasant, under the circumstances. Why, you know we ain't worth a brass fardin to Mr Gabbleton, – he's twenty a-head o' you already.

HONEYBUN: I'm delighted to hear it!

TOPPER: I say, Tom – if the Lions was to vote for Mr Honeybun gratis?

PECKOVER: (*aside to* TOPPER) Then Gabbleton would be forced to fork out to the Lambs. But, bless you, the Lions wouldn't do it.

TOPPER: (*to* PECKOVER) They would, if you'd go halves with 'em in Gabbleton's money?

(*They retire up stage, putting their noses together.*)

DODGSON: I'm afraid these men are incurably demoralized.

MRS HONEYBUN: Demoralized! And you, Mr Dodgson? 'Oh! would some power,' prayed Burns, 'the gift but gie us, To see ourselves as other people see us.'
    Of all cold water cures, take my advice –
    None's all like a douché of truth on a pet vice.
    I've borne that shock, (*to* DODGSON) 'twas wholesome, though inhuman,
    And I'm a sadder, and a wiser, woman!
    Henceforth I'll try to curb romance by reason;
    Renounce my fond hopes of the London season;
    No longer strive to rule –

HONEYBUN: Not rule, my treasure!
    Don't abdicate –

MRS HONEYBUN: At least, I'll rule with measure.
    Till, parliamentary dreams laid on the shelf,
    I've done what parliament can't – reformed myself!

CLARA: (*to* HONEYBUN) Pa, dear, why seek the Commons' House to bore you?
WAPSHOTT: (*pointing to audience*) With this house of Uncommons here before you.
HONEYBUN: Uncommons these.
WAPSHOTT: Yes; in box, pit, and gallery – Don't all seek places, yet none look for
    salary?
DODGSON: That's not the only contrast one may trace
        Between this house and the – the other place.
        In this house all may take their seats by proxies;
        We've a box office, but no office boxes.
        Here bills are certain to come out as acts.
        And fictions pass for fictions and not facts;
        All parties smoothed by laughter's spirit-levels,
        Our only coalition's 'gainst blue devils.
WAPSHOTT: Still, on one point, the contrast's incomplete –
        In either house a man pays for his seat;
DODGSON: But here he's sure of *some* fun for his money, –
        Whatever the other house be, it's not funny.
        Our treasury, too – Unnational Institution! –
        Is filled by voluntary contribution;
        And, crowning contrast! you prove by your faces,
        That here we're 'the right men in the right places.'
HONEYBUN: I say of the House, as Head said of cocked hats
        Drilled by a Minié – 'You're well out of that.'
        To swell collective wisdom those may roam
        Who find they've more wits than they want at home:
        A rule by which the House of Commons floor
        Would require fewer seats instead of more.
        Well for our broth were senatorial cooks
        Picked more by brains – and less by Bankers' Books.
PECKOVER: I won't have my Blue Lambs held up to shame, –
        The man who buys the vote deserves the blame!
        While parliament to pelf or power's the wicket,
        Gents must expect to pay their turnpike ticket.
TOPPER: And though the Ring's gone out without a flicker.
        Coves as can't floor their man can floor their liquor.
        Put down refreshments! It's the wust of scandal
        Polls don't ought to be made into pump handles!
DODGSON: Talking of polls – the poll's not yet announced.
        It's not too late. (*aside to audience*) Old Figs may still be trounced. (*rushing
           forward*) Here; vote for Honeybun.
HONEYBUN: (*remonstrating*) For mercy's sake! Peckover – Topper – any of 'em
    take.
DODGSON: (*to audience*) You choose; the poll's to-morrow. No objection! Poll
    early, mind, –
MRS HONEYBUN: And carry 'The Election.'

Minié: a rifle

THE OVERLAND ROUTE.

A COMEDY IN THREE ACTS.

BY TOM TAYLOR.

First Performed at the Theatre Royal, Haymarket, April, 1860.

[See page 17.

Dramatis Personæ.

MR. COLEPEPPER	(Commissioner of Badgerypore District) ...	Mr. Chippendale.
MAJOR McTURK	(In Charge of Invalids) ...	Mr. Rogers.
SIR SOLOMON FRASER, K.C.B.	(Ex-Resident at Several Native Courts) ...	Mr. Compton.
MR. LOVIBOND	(A Singapore Merchant) ...	Mr. Buckstone.
TOM DEXTER	(An Adventurer) ...	Mr. Charles Mathews.
CAPTAIN SMART	(Of the P. and O. Steamer, Simoom)	Mr. Braid.
HARDISTY	(First Officer of the Simoom)...	Mr. Worrell.
CAPTAIN CLAVERING	(Of the Commander-in-Chief's Staff) ...	Mr. E. Villiers.
TOTTLE	(Head Steward of the Simoom)...	Mr. Cullenford.

No. 1,062. Dicks' Standard Plays.

Title page of *The Overland Route*

THE OVERLAND ROUTE

A Comedy in Three Acts

First produced at the Theatre Royal, Haymarket on 23 February 1860, with the following cast:

MR COLEPEPPER, Commissioner of Badgerypore District	Mr Chippendale
MAJOR McTURK, in charge of Invalids	Mr Rogers
SIR SOLOMON FRASER, KCB, ex-Resident at several Native Courts	Mr Compton
MR LOVIBOND, a Singapore Merchant	Mr Buckstone
TOM DEXTER, an Adventurer	Mr Charles Mathews
CAPTAIN SMART, of the P. and O. Steamer, Simoom	Mr Braid
HARDISTY, First Officer of the Simoom	Mr Worrell
CAPTAIN CLAVERING, of the Commander-in-Chief's Staff	Mr E. Villers
TOTTLE, Head Steward of the Simoom	Mr Cullenford
MOLESKIN, a Detective	Mr Clark
LIMPET, Sir Solomon's Man	Mr Coe
MRS SEBRIGHT	Mrs Charles Mathews
MRS LOVIBOND	Miss Wilkins
MISS COLEPEPPER	Miss L. Angel
MRS GRIMWOOD, her Maid	Miss Weekes
MRS RABBITS	Mrs Griffiths

Ayahs, Stewards, Lascars, Passengers etc.

Act I

SCENE: *The saloon of the Simoom under the poop deck. A long cabin, lighted from a large skylight in the ceiling. The doors of the berths are uniform in appearance, the upper panels closed with green Venetians. The saloon is handsomely decorated. Through the two doorways at the end, a view of the deck of the steamer. A table in the centre, with seats around it. As the curtain rises,* TOTTLE *and two steward's mates are seen dusting table and seats.* *

LIMPET: (*at door of Cabin 3 left*) Mr Tottle! 'Ow often am I to horder Sir Solomon's brandy and soda?

GRIMWOOD: (*at door of Cabin 2 right*) I've been a-calling for my young lady's tea this half-hour.

TOTTLE: Aye, aye, miss – Coming, Mr Limpet. – Jackson, brandy and soda for No. 10. (JACKSON *is going.*)

GRIMWOOD: No, we're No. 10. It's tea we want. (JACKSON *returns.*)

LIMPET: We're No. 6. (*Exit* JACKSON *perplexed.*)

TOTTLE: Aye, aye, sir. Tea for No. 6, Smiles. (SMILES *going.*)

1ST AYAH: (*from Cabin 4 left*) Missy wants doctor very bad, massa steward. (SMILES *pauses.*)

TOTTLE: Aye, aye. Smiles, the doctor for No. 3, and look alive!

2ND AYAH: (*from Cabin 4 right: re-enter* JACKSON *with soda and tea*) Miss Polly Rabbits and Massa Charley very sick. Missy Rabbits' compliments, and hope de doctor send dem powders.

TOTTLE: Aye, aye. The doctor, No. 4, Jackson, directly. (*Exit* JACKSON.)

HARDISTY: (*putting his head at entrance, door right*) Steward, bear a hand on deck here.

TOTTLE: Aye, aye, sir. Bless my heart! Here's work for one head and the usual allowance of arms and legs.

LIMPET:	(*all putting their*	Brandy and soda!
GRIMWOOD:	*heads out of*	Tea!
1ST AYAH:	*their cabins*	De doctor for missy!
2ND AYAH:	*at once*)	De powders for de babies!

HARDISTY: (*putting in his head again*) Hilloa! Saloon there!

TOTTLE: (*hastily gives* LIMPET *the cup of tea and* GRIMWOOD *the brandy and soda-water bottle*) Aye, aye, sir! (*Rushes out door right.*)

LIMPET:	Tea! I ordered soda and brandy.
GRIMWOOD:	Man – this aint' tea!

Venetians: window blinds of wooden slats.
Ayah: children's nurse or nanny, or lady's maid.
*The published texts of the play tend to cause some confusion about the placing of the cabins and their occupants. There are four down each side of the stage and I refer to them throughout as *Cabin 1 right* or *Cabin 1 left* etc., with 1 being the downstage cabin and 4 the upstage. The two doors leading to the deck are referred to as *Door right* and *Door left*.
No. 10 . . . No. 6 etc: Jackson may well be perplexed. The numbers don't relate to cabin numbers. A guess is that they are numbers on a passenger list, here used simply to heighten the sense of confusion.

LIMPET: (*coming forward with tea*) Such attendance! Here's your tea, Mrs
Grimwood, if I might trouble you for our soda and brandy.

GRIMWOOD: Really, Mr Limpet, it's disgraceful. I do 'ope your master will write to
The Times when we get 'ome.

LIMPET: That you may rely on, Mrs Grimwood; if he don't make a representation to
the guv'ment. Sir Solomon ain't used to this sort of thing.

GRIMWOOD: Nor us, neither, I can assure you, Mr Limpet. What with
Khitmuggars, Chupressiesies, and Punkah-wallahs, we'd more servants up the
country in Badgerypore than we knew what to do with.

LIMPET: Just like us. But, for all that, I shan't be sorry to be back in dear old
Hengland, if I've to do for Sir Solomon all by myself for the rest of my born
days.

GRIMWOOD: Nor me neither, Mr Limpet. But, bless me, the tea's a-getting cold.

LIMPET: And the soda water's a-getting hot.

GRIMWOOD: Good morning, Mr Limpet. (*Exit into Cabin 2 right.*)

LIMPET: Good morning, Mrs Grimwood. (*Exit into Cabin 3 left.*) (*Enter from door
right* CAPTAIN SMART, *a telescope in his hand, and* HARDISTY.)

SMART: Well, Hardisty, as we're clear of the Straits, I shall turn in for the rest of the
watch; tell the second officer to look alive, and get the new passengers shaken
down.

HARDISTY: What with the sick and sorry, there's work for three doctors among 'em,
let alone Kingston at his best; and now he's regularly on his beam ends.

SMART: What d'ye mean? The doctor down? Nothing serious, I hope.

HARDISTY: I sent Tottle to inquire, sir. Here he comes. (*Enter* TOTTLE, *door
right.*)

SMART: Well, Tottle; what's the report from the doctor?

TOTTLE: The doctor's compliments, sir, and he's got the fever, sir; and if the attack
goes on all right, he ought to be delirious about eight bells.

SMART: Delirious! And invalids on board, too! Suppose it should spread.

HARDISTY: And the ship so crowded with those Aden passengers.

SMART: By-the-bye, I've hardly overhauled the list yet, Tottle.

TOTTLE: Here it is, sir. I was a-making out the dinner places. (*Produces list.* SMART
examines it. Enter MOLESKIN *behind, door right.*) There's one on 'em, sir –
berth No. 2 there – by the name of Downy.

MOLESKIN: (*aside*) Holloa! (*listens.*)

TOTTLE: I never see a man look so green. He said it was no use my putting him
down, for his head was a-turning round so he'd be *sure* to come up t'other side of
the table.

MOLESKIN: (*coming forward*) Poor Mr Downy!

Khitmuggars: the male servant who waits at table (sp. *khid'mutgar*).
Chupressiesies: a footman. OED spelling, Chuprassy.
Punkah-wallahs: the servant who operated the swinging fan.
Badgerypore: almost certainly doesn't exist. Taylor's invention is worth savouring.
shaken down: settled.
beam ends: a nautical term meaning almost capsized or lost.
eight bells: times of the watch at sea.

SMART: Downy, eh! I remember; he's a Singapore passenger; engaged his berth at Calcutta, but came aboard at Aden.

MOLESKIN: Ah! I daresay he had some good reason; which, did you say, was his cabin?

TOTTLE: (*pointing*) No. 2, sir. Had you any business with him?

MOLESKIN: Oh dear, no! I only asked from humanity. I'm sorry he's so near the stern. He'll feel the motion very badly. (*aside*) My man, as sure as a toucher! (*Retires up and makes entries in a note-book, and strolls off, door right.*)

SMART: (*to HARDISTY*) An inquisitive customer that – always poking his nose into everybody's concerns. But about this precious business of the doctor?

HARDISTY: Here's the major in charge of the invalids, sir.

(*Enter MAJOR McTURK, door left.*)

McTURK: (*pompously*) Ah, Smart! Pleasant morning; a spanking breeze well on the quarter – she's doing ten knots. I've timed her. (*patronisingly to HARDISTY*) Good morning, Mr Hardisty.

SMART: How are your invalids, Major?

McTURK: Oh! the fellows are settling down comfortably enough. That doctor of yours is a smart hand.

SMART: (*aside*) Now for it. A capital officer, Major. But even doctors can't always keep their own bills o'health clean.

McTURK: What do you mean? Why, he's hopping about the steerage like a sanitary inspector; and there he is fumigating, and airing, and Burnet's fluiding, to say nothing of physicking.

SMART: (*aside*) The doctor must have been taken delirious at seven bells instead of eight. I'm very glad you're satisfied, Major.

McTURK: Why, the man's laugh is as good as a tonic.

SMART: His laugh! (*aside*) The doctor *must* be delirious! Didn't it sound rather wild?

McTURK: Wild! not a bit of it. Clear as a bell, and collected as a word of command. I was so pleased with the fellow that I asked for his card, a thing one's not in the habit of doing with a medico, even in the service. Here it is. (*shows card*) – Dexter – 'T. Dexter, M.R.C.S.' I said rather a good thing, *apropos* of that card. 'Well, Mr Dexter,' I said, 'you're well named, for a more dextrous practitioner I never came across.' *Dextrous* – you see. Ha, ha! Not bad, was it, for an off-hand thing?

SMART: Capital! (*aside*) Who the devil can this be, I wonder?

(*Enter MRS LOVIBOND from Cabin 1 left.*)

McTURK: Ah! Mrs Lovibond! (SMART *converses aside with* TOTTLE, *who goes off.*) In full bloom, like a rose with the morning dew on it.

MRS LOVIBOND: Now, Major, how *can* you? Good morning, Captain. Do you think I may venture on deck? You're sure those Lascars have done swabbing and swish swishing about with those dreadful rope mops without handles?

SMART: Deck as dry as a drawing-room, ma'am.

MRS LOVIBOND: Then, Major, may I ask for your arm?

---

toucher: from the game of bowls – when a bowl touches the jack.
Burnet's fluid: a patented disinfectant invented by a naval surgeon, Sir William Burnett (*sic*).
Lascars: Indian sailors.

McTURK: (*aside to her*) Both of 'em, my dearest lady.

MRS LOVIBOND: The motion of the vessel really so throws one on some kind of support.

McTURK: The more it throws you on me, the better I shall like it.

MRS LOVIBOND: Ah! Major! (*Exeunt, coquettishly, leaning on the* MAJOR, *door left.*)

SMART: That's a case, Hardisty.

HARDISTY: She's given him a full broadside, sir, at all events.

SMART: Astonishing how these widows knock over the military. But who can this extempore doctor be, I wonder? I sent Tottle to make him out.
(*Enter* TOTTLE, *door right.*)

TOTTLE: It's all right, sir. He's worth six of Dr Kingston any day; why, he makes his patients laugh on the right side of their mouths, till they quite take their physic with a appetite.

SMART: I never heard of a regular doctor doing *that*, eh, Hardisty?

TOTTLE: The women is a blessing on him, right and left, and the babies – you'd think he'd served his time in a foundling hospital, to see the way he handles the little hinnocents.

SMART: Say Captain Smart wishes to see him aft, directly he's at liberty.

TOTTLE: Aye, aye sir. (*Exit* TOTTLE *door right.*)

SMART: Why, Hardisty, this is a regular God-send.
(*Enter* 1ST AYAH *from Cabin 4 left.*)

1ST AYAH: Bless me! I wonder where dat doctor; Mem Sahib want him ever so bad.
(*Enter* 2ND AYAH *from Cabin 4 right.*)

2ND AYAH: You just wait, please, Miss, till doctor come to see my Missy babas.

1ST AYAH: ⎫ (*contemptuously*) Who your Missibabas?
2ND AYAH: ⎭ What your Mem Sahib, I like to know?

SMART: Silence! you chattering blackbirds! (*Exeunt* AYAHS, *chattering, into their respective cabins.*) Just come into my cabin, Hardisty. What with Lascar crews, Madras parrots, and up-country Ayahs, a fellow might as well sail Captain of Noah's Ark as a P.and O. steamer. (*Exeunt* HARDISTY *and* SMART *door left.*)
(*Enter* 3RD AYAH *from Cabin 1 right, knocks at* SIR SOLOMON'*s Cabin, 3 left;* LIMPET *looks out.*)

3RD AYAH: Missy Sebright's salaam to Burra Sahib Fraser, and she 'ope he gib her his arm on deck dis morning.

SIR SOLOMON: (*within*) Say I shall be happy.

LIMPET: Sir Solomon will be hap –.

SIR SOLOMON: No. On second thought, Limpet, substitute for the word happy – the word de-lighted.

LIMPET: Say Sir Solomon will be de-lighted.

Mem Sahib: the title by which a European lady would have been addressed by Indian servants. (*Sahib* being the gentleman, *Mem* his wife.)
salaam: greeting.
Burra: Great.

3RD AYAH: I tell Mem Sahib. (*Exit into Cabin 1 right.*)
(*Enter SIR SOLOMON from Cabin 3 left, attended by* LIMPET, *carrying his pith-cap and umbrella.*)

SIR SOLOMON: You, Limpet, I dare say, would not perceive any great distinctions between the expressions – I shall be happy, and I shall be delighted.

LIMPET: No, Sir Solomon. If I might make bold, I should think it were about six o'one and half-a-dozen of the other.

SIR SOLOMON: (*with a feeble laugh*) He! he! he! There are a good many men in high diplomatic positions, not a bit more discriminating than you, Limpet.

LIMPET: I dare say, Sir Solomon.

SIR SOLOMON: My solar topee, Limpet. (LIMPET *gives pith-hat.*) Have you consulted the thermometer this morning?

LIMPET: Eighty in the shade, Sir Solomon.

SIR SOLOMON: In that case, my umbrella, Limpet. (LIMPET *gives it.*) One cannot take too great precautions against exposing the brain to the sun. Limpet, the head is my weak point.

LIMPET: I should think so, Sir Solomon.

SIR SOLOMON: When I say 'the head', understand me, Limpet, I do not mean the head intellectually considered, but the material integument of the brain. Limpet, you appreciate the distinction?

LIMPET: You mean the skull, Sir Solomon?

SIR SOLOMON: Precisely. My skull is thin, Limpet – all highly organised skulls are thin – yours is thick, Limpet; you are not highly organised.

LIMPET: No, I'm only a thick-headed limpet. (*Exit* LIMPET *to Cabin 3 left.*)
(*Enter* MR COLEPEPPER *from his Cabin, 3 right.*)

COLEPEPPER: (*comes forward*) Good morning, Sir Solomon.

SIR SOLOMON: Ah! Mr Colepepper! stirring so early? Aren't you afraid of the morning air?

COLEPEPPER: No, sir; nor the morning sun neither, and that's more than you can say, to judge by your precautions. (*pointing to pith-hat and umbrella*)

SIR SOLOMON: I have still a constitution to preserve, Mr Colepepper.

COLEPEPPER: And I have one, sir, that doesn't require preservation. It's above proof, sir – tried in thirty years of hard work – cold weather and hot – kutchery and jungle – hunting field and up-country station – not dozing and dangling in lazy luxurious native courts – like some people – with nothing harder to do than nod at a nautch – or to take the air on an elephant houdah.

SIR SOLOMON: Diplomatic life, too, has its fatigues, Mr Colepepper.

COLEPEPPER: I dare say, It must be hard work to keep down yawns, and to keep up appearances.

SIR SOLOMON: You forget the delicate negotiations to conduct.

COLEPEPPER: As the fly on the wheel conducts the carriage –

---

pith-cap: to protect against the sun. Later this is referred to by the term *solar topee*, and as a *pith-hat*.
kutchery: cutchery, an Anglo-Indian term for an office of the administration, or court-house.
nautch: an Indian dancing-girl.
houdah: (or *howdah*) a seat, shaded by a canopy, carried on an elephant's back.

SIR SOLOMON: And the despatches to be written –

COLEPEPPER: From the draft of a private secretary. No, no, Sir Solomon. Don't tell an old civil servant. European diplomacy's a comedy, but Indian diplomacy's a farce very ill acted, and very well paid for. But I'm wasting my morning. (*goes to Cabin 1 right, and knocks*) Ayah, tell Mrs Sebright Mr Colepepper is ready to give her his arm on deck.

SIR SOLOMON: (*aside*) The impertinent old interloper! I regret, Mr Colepepper, that Mrs Sebright has already engaged *me* as her escort.

COLEPEPPER: That was before she knew she could command my services.

SIR SOLOMON: That you will allow the lady to decide. Here she comes!

    (*Enter* MRS SEBRIGHT, *from Cabin 1 right.*)

MRS SEBRIGHT: Ah! Sir Solomon! and Mr Colepepper, too! Was ever a poor little woman so well guarded. Two doughty squires at my beck. (MR COLEPEPPER *takes off his cap and bows*; SIR SOLOMON *does the same, embarrassed with his hat, stick and umbrella.*) The one armed cap-a-pie, the other cap-a-parapluie.

SIR SOLOMON: If Mrs Sebright will accept my escort –

MR COLEPEPPER: My arm is always at your service.

MRS SEBRIGHT: Oh! bless you! I want nobody's arm – not I – I fancy I've the best sea-legs of the three. It would be a positive sin to disappoint either of such *preux chevaliers*. So, Mr Colepepper, if you would just run to my cabin and tell my Ayah to give you the novel that's on my dressing table (MR COLEPEPPER *is going*) and my shawl, Mr Colepepper – and the footstool, please. (*Exit* MR COLEPEPPER *into her cabin.*)

SIR SOLOMON: And now, Mrs Sebright, that we're relieved of the old Commissioner – (*offers his arm*)

MRS SEBRIGHT: Dear, dear, what a head I have! Not the grey shawl. Tell the Ayah, Sir Solomon, the white one. And my poor dear little love birds, Sir Solomon – they'll be dying for want of fresh air. (*Exit* SIR SOLOMON *to Cabin 1 right, reluctantly. Re-enter* MR COLEPEPPER *with novel, shawl, and footstool.*) Oh! how very good you are! (*taking the things*)

COLEPEPPER: (*aside*) She's got rid of Fraser; now, my dear madam – (*endeavours to offer his arm. Re-enter* SIR SOLOMON *with a load of shawls, cushion, and birdcage, etc.; aside*) Here's that puppy back again!

MRS SEBRIGHT: Sir Solomon, I'm positively ashamed to see you so loaded – and Mr Colepepper, too. But you both offered me your arms, you know – and as I don't want 'em for myself – the least I can do is use 'em for my little comforts – and when I'm snugly ensconced in some shady corner, Sir Solomon shall read to me. Won't you, dear Sir Solomon?

SIR SOLOMON: With pleasure, my dear madam, if it won't bore Mr Colepepper. (*aside*) That ass Colepepper hates listening.

MRS SEBRIGHT: And Mr Colepepper shall point out to me all the objects of interest on the coast. Won't you, dear Mr Colepepper?

---

cap-a-pie: from head to foot, hence *cap-a-parapluie* (French word meaning umbrella) is a pun, 'from umbrella to foot'.
preux chevaliers: brave knights.

COLEPEPPER: I shall be delighted, my dear Mrs Sebright – if it won't interrupt Sir Solomon's reading. (*aside*) That puppy Fraser hates not being listened to!

MRS SEBRIGHT: What a pleasant trio we shall be, to be sure! Our little party will be the only one aboard the Simoom, without any jealousy or heartburning, eh, Mr Colepepper? Quite a happy family – shan't we, Sir Solomon? With poor me to play the part of the white cat. (*going*)

SIR SOLOMON: (*aside, following her*) Colepepper for the wizened old monkey!

COLEPEPPER: (*following*) And Sir Solomon, for the jackdaw!

> (*They pass up to door right, leading to deck. As* SIR SOLOMON *and* MR COLEPEPPER *try to pass out at the same door, they jostle.* DEXTER *appears and attempts to enter.*)

DEXTER: Holloa! one at a time, gentlemen!

> (*The two separate and go off,* MRS SEBRIGHT, MR COLEPEPPER, SIR SOLOMON *following, through door left.*)

DEXTER: (*comes down*) A well laden pair of pack asses – with Jenny Sebright, like the little bell mare trotting on ahead. Catch *her* carrying anything! Sir Solomon Fraser and Colepepper, too, none of the trio recognised me! How would honest Jack Sebright like to see his 'little woman', as he called her, making a fool of these two old fogies, that ought to know better? Ah, Mary Colepepper! if Tom Dexter had a good coat on his back, and a saloon berth instead of a steerage one, he might be making a beast of burden of himself at your heels, as these old boys are at saucy Jenny Sebright's. (*Enter* SMART *and* HARDISTY *from door right.*) Oh! here's the Captain! (*touches his cap, sailor fashion*) Well, Captain, you passed the word for me?

SMART: Oh! you're Mr Dexter?

DEXTER: Yes. (*Jumps on the table and sits.*)

SMART: Won't you take a chair.

DEXTER: I prefer the table – I like to swing my legs.

SMART: I've to thank you, it seems, for taking my surgeon's duty among the steerage passengers.

DEXTER: Why, as they were patients without a doctor, and I was a doctor without patients. Here's my diploma – you see – licensed to drug, dose, and draw teeth *secundem artems*, and the London Pharmacopœia! Don't be afraid! If anybody dies under my hand it won't be murder, but justifiable homicide – by medical misadventure.

SMART: Excuse me. But we don't often find professional gentlemen in the steerage.

---

the white cat . . . wizened old monkey . . . the jackdaw: I have been unable to trace this reference. Planché's extravaganza *The White Cat* offers one possibility, but the whole reference remains obscure.

But we don't often find professional gentlemen in the steerage: the LC copy carries additional material at this point, which offers an interesting comment on the historical context of the play. After SMART's line the dialogue continues:

DEXTER: Why, I meant to take a first class passage – but at Calcutta I found a lot of poor women who had lost everything in the mutiny, husbands included. They were dying to get home, but hadn't the wherewithal – and so –

SMART: You forked out for *them* and took a steerage berth for yourself. Sir – you're a trump –

DEXTER: Oh – the steerage mayn't be quite so splendid as the saloon – but it's a great deal livelier. Besides – I'm used to rough it *etc.*

DEXTER: Oh! I'm used to rough it! Come, I see you're curious to know how a smart, good-looking, well-educated young fellow like me comes into this plight. (*showing his threadbare coat sleeve*) Question and answer's slow work! I'll run my story right off the reel like a log line.

SMART: Heave ahead!

DEXTER: I was educated for a doctor. But the practice isn't so easy to come at as the profession. As I had a fancy for the pen as well as the lancet, I took to scribbling, for want of patients – but I soon got tired of penny-a-lining, and shipped as surgeon aboard a Guinea trader. There I mastered the African fever both as doctor and patient – got a sickener of Kroomen, palm oil, and mangrove swamps, and took a doctor's berth in one of Green's India ships. Left her at Kurrachee for a run up the country. Fell in with the Nawaub of Ramshacklegur, just as he was suffering from an awful indigestion of prawn curry, and physicked myself into his favour. The Nawaub was a capital fellow, but he had an awkward knack of poisoning his wives when he was tired of them, and they very naturally were inclined to return the compliment. As I wouldn't agree to help the gentlemen to poison the ladies, or the ladies to poison the gentleman, of course both parties quarrelled with me, and I had to bolt into British territory to save my bacon. Then I had a shy at all sorts of things – started a hydropathic establishment at Simla, and made money – invested it in an indigo plantation in Behar, and lost it – till, somehow or other, I one day found myself installed as editor and proprietor of a paper at Badgerypore. 'The Mild Hindoo', I called it – I hoped to succeed by sticking to truth and writing like a gentleman – but I soon found that wasn't the line for an Indian editor. My subscribers wanted their articles like their dinners, all capsicums and curry-powder. Just as I was thinking of cutting the concern, out broke the mutiny and the concern cut me. My presses were smashed, my type cast into bullets; my back stock cut up for wadding – some of my articles must have had an uncommonly wide circulation in that form – and I had to run for my life! I disguised myself as a Fakir – buff and wood ashes – and doctored my way down to Calcutta, where I soon picked up enough to pay my passage home – and here I am.

SMART: (*shakes hands with him*) By George, sir! I like a fellow who can take his life in his fist, as you've done – and none the worse if he brings a kind heart out of the tussle. My doctor's on the sick list. Will you take his place for the run to Suez? I'll enter you on the ship's books, and give you berth aft.

DEXTER: I'm your man! My traps won't take much shifting. About my outfit, though? (*looking at his coat*) Seedy, ain't it? I've some old acquaintants aft here.

---

off the reel like a log line: a marked line to find the speed of a vessel, attached to the log and wound on the [log-]reel.
Guinea trader: a ship that traded along the coast of Africa.
Kroomen: West African seamen.
Green's India ships: Green, Wigram and Green, and Eastindiaman shipping line.
Kurrachee: Karachi?
Ramshacklegur: is no doubt located in the same imagination as Badgerypore!
Fakir: a holy mendicant in India.
traps: belongings.

SMART: Never fear. We'll new rig you amongst us. Eh, Hardisty?

HARDISTY: You're welcome to anything in my chest.

DEXTER: Spoken like a man and a brother! (*Enter* CAPTAIN CLAVERING, *door right; he goes to* MISS COLEPEPPER's *Cabin, 2 right, and knocks.*) Ah! I've seen that face before. To be sure; it's Clavering – one of my old Simla acquaintances. (CLAVERING *at* MISS COLEPEPPER's *Cabin*)

CLAVERING: Miss Colepepper, your father has sent me to beg you'll come on deck. They've caught a shark.

SMART: (*to* HARDISTY) Jump up, Hardisty, and see none of the people get their legs broken skylarking with the brute's tail. (*Exit* HARDISTY, *door right.*)

DEXTER: (*coming towards* CLAVERING) Captain Clavering, I think?

CLAVERING: (*coldly and insolently*) Ya-a-a-s. (*staring at him*)

DEXTER: You ought to remember me.

CLAVERING: Ought I? I don't though. (*Turns on his heel.*)

(*Enter* MISS COLEPEPPER *from Cabin 2, right.*)

MISS COLEPEPPER: I'm quite ready. (*Sees* DEXTER, *and recognises him, but half doubtfully.*)

DEXTER: Yes, Miss Colepepper, you're quite right; it is your old Badgerypore aquaintance.

MISS COLEPEPPER: Mr Dexter! I did not know you were on board; we have not seen you in the saloon.

DEXTER: No! I'm in the steerage.

CLAVERING: Captain Smart, I didn't know steerage passengers were admitted to the saloon.

SMART: This gentleman is one of my officers from today, Captain Clavering; and my officers are company for my passengers.

CLAVERING: Ah! I say, Miss Colepepper, if you've any curiosity about the shark – (*goes up*)

MISS COLEPEPPER: Oh, yes. (*to* DEXTER) – Mr Dexter – (*embarrassed*) – I'm very glad to have met you; I'm sure my father will have pleasure in renewing his acquaintance.

DEXTER: I don't think so, or he'd not have left me to kick my heels among the Syces and Chuprassies under the verandah when I called at your house in Calcutta.

CLAVERING: I say, Miss Colepepper, if you don't come the shark will be quite cut up. (*up stage*)

DEXTER: Pray, go; neither sharks nor staff officers ought to be kept waiting.

MISS COLEPEPPER: Come, Captain Clavering; I'm very sorry, Mr Dexter. (*Exeunt* MISS COLEPEPPER *and* CAPTAIN CLAVERING, *door right.*)

SMART: Hang these young puppies of soldiers!

DEXTER: Never mind, Captain; give me five minutes to freshen his memory, and I'll make this youngster civil enough, I'll answer for it. Come along; only let me mount the P. and O. uniform. No man ever did justice to himself in a coat out at the elbows. (*Exit* DEXTER *and* SMART, *door right.*)

(*Enter* MRS SEBRIGHT *and* MRS LOVIBOND, *door left.*)

Syces: grooms.

MRS SEBRIGHT: No I can't stand it. Catching the shark was all very good fun, but cutting him up – oh!

MRS LOVIBOND: Ah! Only think, my dear Mrs Sebright, what that odious Mrs Chatterley said of you just now?

MRS SEBRIGHT: What did she say?

MRS LOVIBOND: That you had a natural sympathy with hooking –

MRS SEBRIGHT: I'm very much obliged to her, poor dear! I've heard that sharks will take any bait. But I don't think Mrs Chatterley would attract even a shark!

MRS LOVIBOND: A mere scrag of a woman, isn't she?

MRS SEBRIGHT: Yes, like all Maypoles, can't bear anybody with a figure! Perhaps you heard that spiteful question she asked Captain Smart about you at dinner yesterday – 'whether Mrs Lovibond paid for *two* berths'?

MRS LOVIBOND: Ah, my dear, people will say ill-natured things.

MRS SEBRIGHT: And people will be so good-natured in repeating 'em.

MRS LOVIBOND: It's a duty one owes one's friends – especially aboard ship! I assure you if I were to repeat half what I heard said of you –

MRS SEBRIGHT: Do, pray let me hear! I do so delight in candid criticism!

MRS LOVIBOND: Then – they say you're a dreadful flirt – and that you're trying to get two strings to your bow – Sir Solomon and Mr Colepepper. But that aiming at two birds generally succeeds in bagging neither.

MRS SEBRIGHT: Now, only think how spiteful some people are. They say *you* would be glad of my leavings.

MRS LOVIBOND: Oh! no, my dear. I have no ambition to have a pompous old fool like Sir Solomon, or a positive sexagenarian like Mr Colepepper. Really, my dear – if I might take the liberty of a friend –

MRS SEBRIGHT: Do – pray, do. If one's friends can't take liberties, who is to do it?

MRS LOVIBOND: I should advise you to be a leetle more on your guard – not to walk on deck quite so late in the evening – to be a leetle less demonstrative at dinner, and not to insist upon quite so many attentions from quite so many gentlemen. It makes other women jealous, you know. Not that I feel anything of the kind!

MRS SEBRIGHT: Oh, dear, no! I'm sure, my dear Mrs Lovibond, you must be quite satisfied with your monopoly of the Major. So pleasant, after all the trouble you've had!

MRS LOVIBOND: Trouble, my love?

MRS SEBRIGHT: In bringing such a stubborn wretch to your feet – in spite of *all* his resistance. I'm glad you've succeeded! for I like you very much, you know.

MRS LOVIBOND: Not half as much as I like you.

MRS SEBRIGHT: Never thought I could have been as fond of one so much older than myself.

MRS LOVIBOND: I assure you, I'm quite astonished to find myself overlooking in your case so much that most people would call giddiness – if not levity.

MRS SEBRIGHT: You are too kind, I'm sure, with the help of *your* experience.

MRS LOVIBOND: Oh! I'm afraid I must go to school to *you* – though you may be a year or two my junior.

MRS SEBRIGHT: Dear me! is it possible you're only twenty-seven? How the Indian climate does tell on the constitution!

MRS LOVIBOND: It has one quality to recommend it to some people. It makes a great many young widows. By-the-bye, do you know I've heard some censorious people on board wonder you don't wear your weeds.

MRS SEBRIGHT: How very odd! I've been bored to death with questions about the late Mr Lovibond. (*confusion heard without, and cry* 'A man overboard')

MRS LOVIBOND: What's that? Oh! gracious!

MRS SEBRIGHT: A man overboard!

> (*Enter* CAPTAIN CLAVERING, *door right, supporting* MISS COLEPEPPER, *who is fainting.*)

CLAVERING: Ya-as-a fellow tumbled from the main yard; Miss Colepepper went off as if she'd been shot.

MRS SEBRIGHT: We'll attend to her. You run and learn the fate of the poor sailor.

CLAVERING: I suppose the fellow can swim? Of course, everybody can swim. But I'll let you know. (*Exit, door right.*)

MISS COLEPEPPER: (*reviving*) Stay! Harry – Captain Clavering. Oh, if he should risk his life to save a drowning man.

MRS SEBRIGHT: I don't think he looks the least like it, my dear. (*cry without* – 'he's in – Huzza – huzza')

MRS LOVIBOND: Hark! a splash! Somebody has jumped in! Oh! who is it?

> (*Enter* TOTTLE, *door right.*)

TOTTLE: One of the officers! Where's the brandy? (*Exit, getting brandy off centre table.*)

MISS COLEPEPPER: The officers! Should it be Clavering!

MRS LOVIBOND: Oh! if it were my Hector! (*Cries*, 'He's got him!' 'He's down?' 'No? here he is!')

MRS SEBRIGHT: I'm very sorry – but I can't get up the slightest excitement. I'm certain it isn't Sir Solomon or Mr Colepepper!

MISS COLEPEPPER: This suspense is agony! (*Sinks into a seat.*)

MRS LOVIBOND: Oh! I can't bear it! (*imitating* MISS COLEPEPPER)

MRS SEBRIGHT: Mind! It's no use you both fainting. I can only attend to one at a time! (*cries without* – 'Huzza – Huzza')

> (*Enter* MAJOR McTURK, *door left.* MRS LOVIBOND *screams.*)

McTURK: Clarinda! Don't be alarmed, ladies. I've saved 'em.

MISS COLEPEPPER: You?

MRS LOVIBOND: I knew he had! Oh! my noble Hector! (*Rushes into his arms.*)

MISS COLEPEPPER: Then it wasn't Captain Clavering?

McTURK: Clavering! Pooh! Before he had got his eyeglass screwed into focus, I had rushed to the stern – sprang to the taffrail –

MRS LOVIBOND: Precipitated yourself into the sea?

McTURK: No; not myself – the life-buoy. They *said* they didn't want it! I knew better!

MISS COLEPEPPER: They – who?

McTURK: Why, the man who fell overboard, and the fellow who went in after him –

MRS SEBRIGHT: Oh, then, there was somebody who threw *himself* into the sea, instead of the life-buoy.

---

weeds: widow's weeds, mourning clothes.

McTURK: Yes. Saw him go in from the main chains. A shabby genteel person –
    looked like a steerage passenger.

MISS COLEPEPPER: And you don't know his name?

McTURK: Haven't the slightest idea!

MISS COLEPEPPER: Shabby genteel heroism, it seems, must be content to be
    anonymous.

(*Enter* SIR SOLOMON, *door right, goes down to* MRS
SEBRIGHT.)

MRS SEBRIGHT: But we heard it was one of the officers.

SIR SOLOMON: One of the ship's officers, ladies. If they had only listened to me, I
    recommended flinging spars to leeward, or bringing up the ship in the wind and
    lowering a boat, at the same time pointing out to the Captain the company's
    reprehensible neglect in not having the vessel furnished with Clifford's patent
    boat lowering apparatus, which I shall feel it my duty to represent in the proper
    quarter.

MRS SEBRIGHT: And while you were talking, this hasty person actually jumped
    overboard?

SIR SOLOMON: In the most reckless manner! and so risked two lives instead of one.

(*Enter* DEXTER, *door left, in uniform.*)

DEXTER: (*coming down to* MRS SEBRIGHT) It's all right, ladies. The man's come
    to – thanks to hot gruel and blankets.

MISS COLEPEPPER: And his gallant preserver?

DEXTER: Oh! he's none the worse for his ducking.

MISS COLEPEPPER: But his name?

McTURK: If you insist on knowing, I can send my orderly to inquire in the steerage?

DEXTER: You may save yourself the trouble, Major. It was I jumped after the
    man.

MISS COLEPEPPER: You, Mr Dexter?

SIR SOLOMON: Dexter – Dexter – I know that name, I think.

DEXTER: I was medical adviser to the Nawaub of Ramshacklegur while you were
    resident at his court, Sir Solomon.

SIR SOLOMON: To be sure! Let me tell you, sir, your jumping overboard was a very
    rash and reprehensible act. If you had only reflected –

DEXTER: The man would have been drowned.

McTURK: Ah! if it hadn't been for the life-buoy which I flung over –

DEXTER: Which I didn't avail myself of. Much obliged to *you* all the same!

SIR SOLOMON: (*aside*) Colepepper's engaged with the shark. Mrs Sebright (*offering
    his arm*), we're just passing Mocha. If you would like to know the statistics of
    our coffee trade with that region?

MRS SEBRIGHT: (*takes his arm*) Oh! delightful! I do so thirst for useful information!

(*Exit, door right,* MRS SEBRIGHT *and* SIR SOLOMON, *arm in arm.*)

MRS LOVIBOND: (*aside*) Especially from a K.C.B.

Mocha: a town on the Red Sea coast of the Yemen. The 'Simoom', having left Aden, is *en route*
through the Red Sea to Suez.
K.C.B.: Knight Commander of the Bath.

McTURK: (*to* MRS LOVIBOND) Suppose we take a turn on deck! I have something very particular to communicate.

MRS LOVIBOND: With pleasure, Major! Your conversation is always so instructive.

McTURK: You are such a *little* flatterer. (*Exit* MRS LOVIBOND *and the* MAJOR, *door left.*)

DEXTER: Now we're alone, Miss Colepepper, let me hand over something of yours – which I have not had an earlier opportunity of returning. (*Gives bracelet.*)

MISS COLEPEPPER: The bracelet I lost that dreadful night the mutineers broke into our bungalow. The last thing I remember was a huge sowar – tearing it from my arm. How did you recover it?

DEXTER: Oh, the fellow was cut down. I picked up his booty as we carried you into the compound.

MISS COLEPEPPER: Then you were there! – you saved me!
(*Enter* CLAVERING, *door right; comes down.*)

MISS COLEPEPPER: Captain Clavering, I have at last discovered my preserver from the mutineers.

CLAVERING: Indeed!

MISS COLEPEPPER: Let me introduce you to him. Mr Dexter, Captain Clavering.
(CLAVERING *bows haughtily.*)

DEXTER: I think Captain Clavering and I have met already?

CLAVERING: I really can't remember it.

DEXTER: Can't you? It was at a whist party in the club-room at Simla. The night of the 16th of August. You may remember, there was a little row about a missing –

CLAVERING: (*embarrassed*) Ah – yes – I recall you perfectly now – Mr Dexter, how do you do? – I'm very glad to renew an aquaintance which –

DEXTER: Begun so very pleasantly.

MISS COLEPEPPER: I must find my father, Captain Clavering; I want to tell him what we owe Mr Dexter.

DEXTER: Pray oblige me by saying nothing about it. Like most Englishmen in the mutiny, I did my duty; but I really don't deserve any credit for it.

MISS COLEPEPPER: (*aside*) As modest as he is brave. I will respect your generous wish, Mr Dexter.

CLAVERING: I hope you and I shall often meet, Mr Dexter – it will give me the greatest pleasure. (*aside*) Confound his brazen face!
(*Exeunt* MISS COLEPEPPER *and* CAPTAIN CLAVERING, *door right, to the deck.*)

DEXTER: There's one swell brought to his bearings for the rest of the voyage. It's *possible* the Captain might have known nothing about that missing card – but when a fellow holds three honours for four deals running, and has a trick of turning up aces –
(*Enter* CAPTAIN SMART, *door right.*)

SMART: You're wanted, Doctor, in the forecastle. The man you saved insists on thanking you.

DEXTER: I'm glad *he* doesn't consider my jumping after him so very rash and

---

sowar: Indian horse-soldier.

reprehensible. He isn't a diplomatist. (*Exeunt* DEXTER *and* SMART, *door, right.*)

(*Enter* MRS LOVIBOND, *door left, sits in the chair.*)

MRS LOVIBOND: A declaration from the Major at last! I've been expecting it all the way from Madras – and yet, when it does come, how it flutters one! Three hundred a year, besides his pay. The man is a little pompous certainly, and not handsome. But then one has no right to be particular after thirty. I've asked time to consider his offer. First, am I a widow? I've every reason to think so. I have passed for one during the time I have been in India. It's now ten years since Mr Lovibond left me, and since then no news of him but this melancholy letter. (*Takes out a worn letter.*) How often I've re-read it – 'Clarinda, – Meek as I am – much as I have loved you – I write this to bid you farewell for ever. If you should hear of an inquest on my remains, know that it is your jealousy and imperious disposition which have brought me to an untimely end. If ever you marry again, may you treat your second husband better than you have treated your long-suffering, but to the last affectionate – Augustus.' No date – a black-edged envelope – and the Dover postmark. I never *did* hear of an inquest – but I have always had poor Lovibond's untimely end upon my conscience. Let me endeavour to expiate my harshness to him by bringing all meekness and indulgence to his successor. I certainly do not feel that ardent attachment for the Major which young women think necessary for marriage. But do I care for him enough to make him happy? and myself, too, for that matter. That's the point I must settle, after mature deliberation – face to face with my dressing glass. (*Exits into her Cabin, 1 left.*)

MRS RABBITS: (*speaking to* AYAH *at the door of Cabin, 4 right*) Remember, Sabrina – you will insist on the doctor coming to my babies directly.

2ND AYAH: Yes, Missy Rabbits. (*Exits, door right.*)

(*Re-enter* MRS RABBITS *into her cabin. Enter* SIR SOLOMON *and* MRS SEBRIGHT, *door left.*)

MRS SEBRIGHT: And so these are really the waters where pearls come from?

SIR SOLOMON: Yes. The trade is a considerable one – employs – let me see – about ten thousand tons of small craft and a capital of –

MRS SEBRIGHT: Oh, I don't mind the figures. It's the lovely pearls I'm interested about! How I should like a handsome young diver to fish me up the finest set ever seen – bracelets, brooch, and bandeau – representing not so many pounds paid – but so many risks of life and limb – and all defied for me!

SIR SOLOMON: But why sigh for pearls – when diamonds are within your reach?

MRS SEBRIGHT: Diamonds, Sir Solomon?

SIR SOLOMON: Yes. I flatter myself that Lady Fraser's diamonds will make a sensation at the Drawing-room. What do you think of this as a specimen? (*Produces case and shows diamond necklace.*)

MRS SEBRIGHT: Oh! what a love of a necklace!

SIR SOLOMON: And what a necklace for a love – for *my* love, my dear Mrs Sebright

---

bandeau: a ribbon to bind a woman's hair – here, implicitly, set with pearls.
Drawing-room: in this context, a reception at Court.

– for *you*, if you will but say one little word! (*she is going to return the case*) No; don't pain me by refusing 'em.

MRS SEBRIGHT: But, Sir Solomon –

SIR SOLOMON: I leave you till this evening to consider your ultimatum. Haste is always undesirable – whether in love or diplomacy. (*aside*) There – I flatter myself that clinches old Colepepper. (*Exit, door right.*)

MRS SEBRIGHT: To have been within an ace of a title and diamonds like these. Oh, dear – oh, dear! If only I weren't married already. John Sebright never gave me any diamonds! And I should look so well in 'em, I'm sure. (*putting them round her arm and turns it admiringly*) The very things for my complexion! (*Enter DEXTER, door left.*) I suppose Sir Solomon didn't mean me to keep them – unless I take him into the bargain. To think the pompous empty-headed creature should be allowed to tempt poor spinsters into his toils with such baits as this! Oh! you beauties! (*Examines them in various lights.*)

DEXTER: (*aside*) Hollo! Why, that is the identical necklace the Begum of Ramshacklegur offered me to poison the Nawaub! How can *she* have come by it? (*coming forward*) Magnificent!

MRS SEBRIGHT: Oh, sir, you quite startled me!

DEXTER: I don't wonder at your being absorbed. I would recommend you not to show it on board (*points to necklace*) or I wouldn't answer for your life among so many ladies.

MRS SEBRIGHT: Oh, the necklace isn't mine! That is – if I can persuade Sir Solomon to take it back.

DEXTER: Sir Solomon – oh, ho – I'll save you all trouble on that point. (*Takes it out of her hand and pockets it.*)

MRS SEBRIGHT: (*offended*) Really, sir! This liberty from a perfect stranger.

DEXTER: Perhaps, to you; but as an old friend of John Sebright's, I mustn't allow John Sebright's wife to expose herself to misconstruction.

MRS SEBRIGHT: A friend of my husband's. Oh, sir! – how strange you must have thought it to see me passing as a widow!

DEXTER: Well – I don't think my friend John would quite like it.

MRS SEBRIGHT: Oh, yes, he would! He always likes to see his little woman petted. You know, a prudent married woman, without her husband, has no chance aboard these horrid P. and O. boats! But a widow's always sure of attentions. Mind – I never said I was one – please, don't betray me, Mr Dexter. It's only till we reach Suez – there I'm to meet Jack – and I shan't want any attentions after that. Bless him!

DEXTER: Attentions are one thing – diamonds are another. I shall return these to Sir Solomon.

MRS SEBRIGHT: I'm afraid he'll be very angry.

DEXTER: I'll pacify him.

MRS SEBRIGHT: But what shall I say when he comes for his answer and his necklace?

DEXTER: For his necklace refer him to me. For his answer – say that you've a

---

toils: net or snare.

husband already – one of the best fellows in the world, and that you're heartily ashamed of yourself for not having told him so ten days ago.

MRS SEBRIGHT: Oh, dear – oh, dear – I shall look so ridiculous!

DEXTER: If you don't like telling the truth, you must invent fibs for yourself – only, remember there's a friend of John Sebright's on board, to look after John Sebright's wife.

MRS SEBRIGHT: John Sebright's wife will look after herself, Mr Dexter! (*crosses*)

DEXTER: Bravo! I like that little bit of flare up better than anything you've said yet! Excuse me – I've some patients to attend to. (*Exit into* MRS RABBITS' *Cabin, 4 left.*)

MRS SEBRIGHT: Patients, indeed! He shan't find me among his patients, I can tell him! How dare he talk in that way! as if I were behaving in a manner my dear Jack wouldn't approve! What harm can there be in accepting all the attentions one can get! Aboard ship, too, where everybody's so selfish! If he weren't a man, I might be sure it must be all jealousy – but, he doesn't care for me! He can't be jealous. It's provoking to be so misconstrued – and by a friend of dear Jack's, too – shall I do as he told me? Tell Sir Solomon and Mr Colepepper that I'm a married woman? They'll say I've made fools of them both. I shall be talked about all over the ship – and if I say nothing about my husband, when Jack meets me at Suez, who knows what people may tell *him*! Oh! I wish I had never allowed anybody to pay me any attentions! I wish I had bored everybody to death about my husband the first day I came on board. I wish – I wish – (*passionately*) – Oh, I wish I were at the bottom of the sea! (*Exit into her Cabin, 1 right.*)

LOVIBOND: (*from his Cabin, 2 left*) Steward! steward! I say, steward! (*The door of* MR LOVIBOND'*s cabin opens, and* MR LOVIBOND *looks hastily out. He wears a white cotton night-cap, a long white flannel dressing-gown, and is endeavouring, with a towel, to staunch the blood from a cut he has given himself in shaving; comes forward calling.*) Steward! I was tormented all yesterday by an individual answering to that name, who kept harping on the disgusting subject of dinner; (*shudders*) and now that I really want him – of course he's not to be found! I wish I could get some sticking-plaster. (*Shows cut on his jaw.*) This is the sanguinary consequence of trying to shave one's self – under the mingled effects of vertigo and a swing-glass. I thought myself uncommonly lucky to secure a passage to Aden, by taking Mr Downy's berth off his hands. How I exulted over the dozen parties whose names stood on the P. and O. books before Augustus Lovibond's. What would I have given to have changed places with them yesterday! The agonies I've suffered in the last twenty-four hours on that layer of hard substance which they call a bed – in that elevated coffin, which they call a berth. The shiver of the screw, and the gnawing of the timbers, and the clashing of the chains overhead; and the pitching, and the tossing; and, worse than all, the rattle of knives and forks out here, and the notion that eating was going on within arm's length of my – (*turns sick*) I feel a leetle (*smiling*) better this morning. But my head still seems to be set on a pivot. However, let me console myself with the reflection that I'm on my way home to England after nine years broiling at Singapore. I never could have endured my exile, but that England meant Clarinda and the chains of matrimony. But it's now three years since she left London for India. Let's hope she has found another victim by this time. She could do it legally, I believe, after hearing nothing of me for seven years, even if my parting letter hadn't convinced her I was no more. Well, if she *have* married again, I wish her husband joy of her. What a temper that woman had! Oh! good heavens, what a temper to be sure! Even a Singapore sun was better than the perpetual domestic broil I endured with Mrs Lovibond. (*Door of* MRS RABBITS' *cabin opens.*)

DEXTER: (*without*) The pills at bed-time, my dear madam. The draught in the morning.

LOVIBOND: Passengers coming this way! Good gracious! I'm not fit to be seen in this pickle! Which is my cabin? Confound it! all the doors are alike – and my head's in such a whirl! This is it, I think. (*Exit into* MRS LOVIBOND's *cabin, 1 left.*)

MRS RABBITS: I shall attend most carefully to your directions, doctor. (*A shriek heard from* MRS LOVIBOND's *Cabin.* MRS RABBITS *and* DEXTER *appear on the threshold of the cabin.*) Hark! what's that?

DEXTER: A squall! (*They pause.*)

(LOVIBOND *hastily re-enters.*)

LOVIBOND: The wrong cabin, by jingo! I've frightened some unfortunate female into hysterics. Eh – this must be my door. My head is in such a whirl. (*Exit into his own cabin, 2 left.*)

MRS RABBITS: Doctor, did you see that?

(*Enter* McTURK, *door left.*)

DEXTER: A man in a dressing gown bolted into cabin No.2.

MRS RABBITS: Coming out of cabin No. 1 – and cabin No. 1 is Mrs Lovibond's!

McTURK: A man coming out of Clarinda's cabin! (*coming forward*) What's that you say, madam?

MRS RABBITS: What I blush to repeat, Major. The Doctor and I have just seen a gentleman leaving Mrs Lovibond's cabin – I repeat, a gentleman – and in a dressing gown! I will not trust myself to dwell upon the subject! (*Re-enters her cabin, with dignity.*)

McTURK: Is this true, sir?

DEXTER: I can't deny the fact – but it may have a great many explanations.

McTURK: Explanations! Don't talk to me, sir! Hector McTurk is not to be humbugged, sir! The individual who left that cabin visited it either by Mrs Lovibond's invitation, or forced his way into it against her will. In either case he must settle accounts with Hector McTurk. I'll blow out any man's brains who presumes to love Clarinda Lovibond! and as for any man who dares to insult her – I'll –

DEXTER: You can't well do more for *him*, Major. Come, it may have been only a mistake. I'll keep Mrs Rabbits quiet, if you'll promise me not to say anything to Mrs Lovibond till I've made inquiries.

McTURK: Till then, Doctor, I'll bottle up my feelings. It's right you should know I've just proposed to Mrs Lovibond! and better cross the path of a man-eater in his hunger than come between Hector McTurk and the object of his preference. (*Exit, door left.*)

DEXTER: If the lion's skin only made the lion, Hector McTurk is a very formidable personage.

MRS LOVIBOND: (*without, in a faint voice*) Ayah – Mrs Grimwood – Would anybody be good enough to go for the doctor?

DEXTER: The Doctor is here, my dear madam. (*knocks*)

(*Enter* MRS LOVIBOND, *very pale and agitated.*)

MRS LOVIBOND: Oh, Doctor – answer me one question. Do you believe in ghosts?

DEXTER: Ghosts generally resolve themselves, in medical opinion, into delirium tremens, or deranged liver.

MRS LOVIBOND: Oh – but seriously, Doctor – Do you believe the spirits of the departed are ever allowed to revisit this world?

DEXTER: Allow me. (*Feels her pulse.*) As I suspected. Quick and thready – Let me recommend a calmant.

MRS LOVIBOND: This is no case for medicine. Listen, Doctor – I'm not insane – I'm in perfect health – But not five minutes ago – in that cabin – I saw the spirit of *my* late husband.

DEXTER: A spirit!

MRS LOVIBOND: Arrayed in the habiliments of the grave – a yawning wound in his throat – oh, horrible! We were unhappy together – I was the cause. He left me with a threat of self-destruction – I have reason to believe he fell by his own hand – I was on the point of accepting a second husband. The spirit of my poor Augustus must have been sent to warn or deter me.

DEXTER: Calm yourself, my dear lady. Some one may have entered your cabin by mistake – whom your imagination invested with these ghostly attributes. I may succeed in satisfying you of this. Meanwhile, I send you a composing draught. For whom shall I say?

MRS LOVIBOND: Mrs Lovibond – No. 1.

DEXTER: Very good. You had better take care of No. 1, and keep yourself quiet for the present.

MRS LOVIBOND: I will try – but I almost dread to re-enter this cabin.

DEXTER: Never fear, madam. The ghost won't show himself while I'm here. They have a horror of doctors. (*Exit* MRS LOVIBOND *into cabin 1, left.*) Ah, ah, ah! A ghost in a white cotton nightcap!

LOVIBOND: (*puts his head out*) I really must find some sticking-plaster.

DEXTER: The ghost for a pony! Ha, ha, ha!

LOVIBOND: That's a very lively person. I beg your pardon, sir, but have you such a thing as a piece of court plaster about you?

DEXTER: (*takes out case*) Here you are, sir – black, white, or flesh coloured. Which would you prefer?

LOVIBOND: Well, I think black is the most becoming. (*Licks it and tries to stick it on.*) Oh, dear, I haven't licked the gummy side –

DEXTER: Cut yourself in shaving, I see – I'm the ship's surgeon – allow me. (*Puts on the piece of plaster.*) The yawning gash in the throat! Ha, ha, ha!

---

quick and thready: medical term meaning that the pulse is weak.
The ghost for a pony: a pony is a slang term for £25 – so literally this means 'I'll bet the man in the night cap was the ghost.'
court plaster: a sticking-plaster made of silk, originally used by Court ladies as adornment.

LOVIBOND: Really, sir – my wound may not be exactly serious. But I'm not aware that it's a fit subject for ridicule.

DEXTER: Excuse me, sir; but the lady whose cabin you entered just now –

LOVIBOND: By mistake, I assure you, sir. My brain's in such a topsy-turvy state; I'm quite incapable of such an intrusion intentionally.

DEXTER: I can quite believe it – especially in your present costume. But that lady –

LOVIBOND: I'm quite ready to make her the most ample apology, in writing, if necessary. If you'd oblige me with her name?

DEXTER: Mrs Lovibond!

LOVIBOND: (*aghast*) Eh? Mrs Lovibond?

DEXTER: Yes. Only fancy – she took you for the ghost of her late husband! Ha, ha, ha!

LOVIBOND: (*with a ghastly attempt at laughter*) Ha, ha, ha!

DEXTER: And while she takes you for a ghost, Major McTurk – who, it seems, has just proposed to her – is determined to make you one.

LOVIBOND: Eh? Major McTurk has just proposed to Clarin– to that lady?

DEXTER: Yes, and means to blow out your brains. He interprets your visit to Mrs Lovibond's cabin as the triumph of a rival – or the intrusion of a daring libertine.

LOVIBOND: My dear sir, I'm not a daring libertine. Do I look like one? I'm anything but that, I assure you. (*Enter* MOLESKIN, *behind, from the door left.*) Tell him – tell everybody – that my name is Downy – a respectable merchant of Singapore – that I'm dreadfully ill – unable to leave my cabin – I promise you I won't show my nose outside it till we're safe at Suez.

DEXTER: Oh, you'll be all right in a day or two.

LOVIBOND: I don't want to be all right in a day or two – I've the best reasons for keeping myself to myself – I hate strangers – I detest society – I'm a regular misanthrope, however little you might think so to look at me – oh, sir – if you want to save a fellow creature from the most painful consequences, help me to keep up my incognito – promise me! If money can bind you to secrecy –

DEXTER: Not the least occasion for that. We doctors are the best father confessors. Heaven bless a good many of our patients if we weren't!

LOVIBOND: Ah, sir, you've taken a load off my mind. I'm quite happy – that is – I should be – if my cabin were only a little less crowded with luggage. (*aside*) I've half of Downy's, as well as my own. If you'd only get a little of it cleared away I should think it a perfect paradise of eight feet by ten.

DEXTER: I'll send the steward to clear away some of your traps. (*Crosses, and looks into* LOVIBOND's *cabin.*)

LOVIBOND: (*aside, while* DEXTER *examines luggage*) My wife only separated from me by a slight partition! This Major thirsting for my blood! Here's a situation on the edge of two volcanoes and sea sick into the bargain. How lucky I'm down in the passengers' list under the name of Downy. (*Re-enters cabin.*)

DEXTER: (*coming out of cabin*) What the deuce can the poor devil be afraid of! I suppose it's the fire-eating Major.

MOLESKIN: (*coming down*) Doctor, I hope you respect the laws of your country.

DEXTER: Yes, in a general way.

MOLESKIN: You ain't aiding, abetting, and comforting him, are you?

DEXTER: Him? Who?

MOLESKIN: This here Downy – the party occupying this here cabin. The party that hates society – society returns the compliment, I can tell him.

LOVIBOND: (*within*) Here's a bag I can very well spare, Doctor; and a hat box I don't want. Oh! and here's a portmanteau that's always getting between my legs. (*Puts a portmanteau, hat case, black bag, etc., outside door.*)

MOLESKIN: (*seizes bag*) The very identical bag named in my instructions! (*He proceeds to pick the lock.*)

DEXTER: Hollo! what are you at?

MOLESKIN: Identifying. (*takes out papers*) All right. The missing securities – the forged bills – everything but the specie.

(*Enter* SMART, *door right.*)

DEXTER: Here, Captain, bear a hand to stop this.

SMART: What's the row? (*Comes forward.*)

DEXTER: Lunacy and larceny – rifling a passenger's luggage.

MOLESKIN: It's all right, gentlemen – I'm a detective. In the Queen's name, I charge you to aid me in arresting Thomas Downy, alias etc., etc., etc., charged in this warrant with fraudulent bankruptcy, forgery, and felony (*producing warrant*) at Colombo.

SMART: (*looks at the warrant*) A felon aboard my ship!

DEXTER: My friend the ghost! This explains his anxiety about his incognito.

MOLESKIN: Now mind, gentlemen, I look to you to help me. This here Downy's a desperate character – it's probable he'll resist. But the warrant's all regular; so if he kills any of us it'll be murder.

DEXTER: That's a comfort!

MOLESKIN: Call him, Doctor – he'll come out to you.

DEXTER: Poor devil! – but after all one mustn't pity a felon. (*knocks*) Mr Downy.

LOVIBOND: (*within*) Yes, Doctor.

DEXTER: Come out, I want to speak to you.

(*Enter* LOVIBOND.)

LOVIBOND: Strangers! Oh, Doctor, is this your fidelity?

MOLESKIN: (*laying his hand on his shoulder and handcuffing him*) Thomas Downy, I arrest you as a felon in the Queen's name!

LOVIBOND: Me – stop – this is a mistake.

MOLESKIN: Is it?

LOVIBOND: My name's not Downy – no – yes – it ain't. Oh! gracious! (*Falls into chair.*)

TABLEAU

Act II

SCENE. *The poop deck of the Simoom, towards evening; a tropical sunset sky; an awning spread; cabin skylight combings seen above the deck, with seats round them; seats at the gangways; companion seen beyond the skylight. At the back, the rail*

---

specie: gold or silver coins.
combings: raised area around a hatch to keep water out.
companion: in this context, the stairway from the deck to the cabins.

bounding the poop deck, with openings for the staircases leading to the waist of the vessel. Lounging chairs disposed about; groups of passengers seen sitting and walking; four MUSICIANS *playing the end of an overture upstage.* MRS SEBRIGHT *and* MR COLEPEPPER *discovered, she seated in a lounging chair, he seated by her – a* KHITMAGAR *in attendance.* SIR SOLOMON (*smoking a cigar on one of the seats round the skylight*) *watching them, while he pretends to read.*

MRS SEBRIGHT: (*reading from 'Don Juan', after music has ceased*)
    'They look'd up to the sky, whose floating glow
        Spread like a rosy ocean, vast and bright;
    They gazed upon the glittering sea below,
        Whence the broad moon rose circling into sight;
    They heard the waves splash, and the winds so low,
        And saw each other's dark eyes darting light
    Into each other – '
    (*she stops, and is about to shut the book*) That's quite enough!
COLEPEPPER: (*taking the book*) No; let me finish the stanza, my dear Mrs Sebright. (*he reads*)
    'And, beholding this,
    Their lips drew nearer and clung into . . . '
MRS SEBRIGHT: (*shivering*) Oh, I'm so cold!
COLEPEPPER: Good heavens! and you're not half wrapped up. (*calls*) Qui-hi! (KHITMAGAR *approaches, and salaams;* MR COLEPEPPER *whispers;* KHITMAGAR *salaams and exits by companion.*) The evenings are positively chilly. I've sent my Khitmagar for another shawl.
MRS SEBRIGHT: You're very kind, I'm sure. I'm quite ashamed to give you so much trouble; but it's very pleasant to be so devotedly waited on.
COLEPEPPER: The pleasure is entirely on the side of your attendant, my dear Mrs Sebright. Ah! when will you give me the right to offer you a life-long attention? (*Re-enter* KHITMAGAR *from below with handsome Indian shawl.* MR COLEPEPPER *takes shawl from* KHITMAGAR, *who exits.*) Allow me.
MRS SEBRIGHT: Oh, what a splendid Cashmere!
                (*Drapes herself in it. One* LADY *and* GENTLEMAN *rise and exit.*)
COLEPEPPER: It was never properly displayed till now. These shoulders are too lovely for any less costly drapery.
MRS SEBRIGHT: Oh dear! oh dear! Really, Mr Colepepper, you shouldn't show a poor weak woman such things. How is one to resist them?
COLEPEPPER: Let me hope you will continue to wear it by the best title – as –
MRS SEBRIGHT: (*rising hastily*) Hadn't we better take a turn about the deck? I should never forgive myself if you caught a chill.
COLEPEPPER: Pooh, pooh! my dear lady, I've an iron constitution; I'm no mollycoddle like Sir Solomon yonder. But if you prefer walking, I'm at your service. (*They walk up arm-in-arm.*)
SIR SOLOMON: (*comes forward*) It's astonishing how that old man can make such an

---

waist: the middle.
khitmagar: see note p. 113. The spelling, on Taylor's behalf, is obviously casual!
'Don Juan': Byron's poem, Canto II, stanza 185.

ass of himself. I wonder Mrs Sebright can tolerate his antediluvian attentions. And that shawl, too! I flatter myself my necklace will take the shine out of his old-fashioned Cashmere! (*Enter* DEXTER *from the companion.*) Ah, Dexter! Delicious evening. Allow me to offer you a cheroot. (*Presents his case.*)

DEXTER: Thank you! (*Lights cheroot; throws himself on* MRS SEBRIGHT's *chair.*) A sunset sky – a sea breeze – an easy chair – and a prime cheroot – I call this Paradise.

SIR SOLOMON: With a superabundance of Eves, Dexter.

DEXTER: (*nodding towards* MRS SEBRIGHT) Yonder goes one, at all events, with her old serpent at her side.

SIR SOLOMON: Colepepper, eh? A capital simile. Why, it's not five minutes since he tempted her with that shawl she's displaying so coquettishly.

DEXTER: Poor May! Roguish old January! (*Puffs a whiff of smoke.*)

SIR SOLOMON: A charming person, Mrs Sebright – a leetle too fond of attentions, perhaps.

DEXTER: A 'leetle', without the 'perhaps'.

SIR SOLOMON: It's melancholy to see her listening to the antiquated gallantries of an old scarecrow like Colepepper, so young as she is.

DEXTER: A mere child!

SIR SOLOMON: So inexperienced!

DEXTER: Innocence itself!

SIR SOLOMON: You know her, I think.

DEXTER: Oh, yes; we're old acquaintances.

SIR SOLOMON: It would be a charity to open her eyes to the absurdity of Mr Colepepper's attentions – he's sixty-four, if he's a day.

DEXTER: Really!

SIR SOLOMON: Hasn't a square inch of sound liver left, and no more calf to his leg than my walking-stick.

DEXTER: Then he makes up uncommonly well.

SIR SOLOMON: Wadding, Dexter; all wadding! And then, his temper! – simply detestable! He says he's going home on his pension; but, between ourselves, it's to make friends with the Council. There's a screw loose in his Badgerypore accounts – important vouchers missing. He says they were stolen in the mutiny.

> (CAPTAIN CLAVERING *and* MISS COLEPEPPER *enter and join* MRS SEBRIGHT.)

DEXTER: (*aside*) That box of papers I secured. (*to* SIR SOLOMON) The Commissioner's bungalow *was* plundered, you know.

SIR SOLOMON: Oh! of course. Depend upon it, the mutiny has been an uncommonly convenient event for a great many people.

DEXTER: Really, it would be a charity to put Mrs Sebright up to all this.

SIR SOLOMON: Well, if a friend could just hint the truth to her – not that I want to put a spoke in Colepepper's rusty old wheel –

May/January: May symbolically is the innocent young maid, January (from the Roman god Janus) two-faced, not to be trusted. Taylor is also suggesting Dexter's familiarity with 'The Merchant's Tale' from Chaucer's *Canterbury Tales*.
the Council: of the East India Company?

DEXTER: Oh! everyone who knows Sir Solomon Fraser must be aware of his disinterestedness.

SIR SOLOMON: Yes, I've been a sufferer by it all my life; but it's constitutional, and, talking of constitutions, I don't think mine will be improved by this night air; I'll just get another wrapper. Meanwhile, if you should have an opportunity to put Mrs Sebright on her guard –

DEXTER: Trust me to do justice to your hints, Sir Solomon.

SIR SOLOMON: (*rising; aside*) Now I call that diplomatically managed. (*Goes up, and exits.*)

DEXTER: (*aside*) That rascally old backbiter wants me to play the cat to get *his* chestnuts out of the fire.

(MR COLEPEPPER *leaves the group and comes forward.*)

COLEPEPPER: Good evening, Mr Dexter! I'm very glad to have an opportunity of renewing our Badgerypore acquaintance. Though a civil servant, I have never shrunk from intimacy with the Press. Your way of conducting your paper got you immense credit.

DEXTER: Did it, Mr Colepepper? I always found people eager for ready money, notwithstanding.

COLEPEPPER: I mean credit with the Governor General and the authorities at Calcutta. You set your brethren of the press an excellent example of courage and straightforwardness – noble qualities, Mr Dexter; noble qualities, sir.

DEXTER: Then I wish the authorities had paid what I lost by them.

COLEPEPPER: Ah, Mr Dexter, such virtue, I'm afraid –

(SIR SOLOMON *re-enters, comes down and joins* MRS SEBRIGHT.)

DEXTER: Is its own reward, Mr Colepepper. I've been fully repaid in that rather unsubstantial currency.

COLEPEPPER: Oh, you would have triumphed over all difficulties, my dear sir, if it hadn't been for the mutiny. We have all been sufferers by that deplorable event – civil servants, soldiers, private adventurers, women. Why, look at our passengers; observe the melancholy proportion of widows!

DEXTER: Say, rather, the uncommonly jolly proportion of some of the widows – my crummy friend, Mrs Lovibond – for example.

COLEPEPPER: Or pretty little Mrs Sebright yonder. (*aside*) Confound it! there's Sir Solomon at her elbow. A charming woman, Mr Dexter.

DEXTER: Very.

COLEPEPPER: It's a pity she should get herself talked about with that peculiarly silly old fellow, Fraser.

DEXTER: Sir Solomon is not the wisest of men, certainly; but he's a K.C.B., Mr Colepepper.

COLEPEPPER: Titles are empty things, Mr Dexter.

DEXTER: And are often appropriately bestowed on empty people.

COLEPEPPER: Too true. Sir Solomon is a melancholy example. Mrs Sebright's friends ought really to open her eyes. She's much too interesting a creature to be thrown away on a battered old beau like Sir Solomon.

---

my crummy friend: slang for rich and comely.

DEXTER: Old? Why, he don't look above five-and-forty.

COLEPEPPER: Art, Mr Dexter, all art – cosmetics, hair dyes, false teeth.

DEXTER: What a very diplomatic *tout ensemble*! But are you positive about the teeth?

COLEPEPPER: My khitmagar caught his man cleaning 'em only the other day. They're taken out at night and replaced in the morning, like his shirt studs. Then, as for his diplomatic reputation, it's all a hollow mockery, sir.

DEXTER: Like his teeth – eh?

COLEPEPPER: Exactly, and not quite so easily cleaned; for, between ourselves, there's an awkward charge hanging over him at this moment – of taking 'backsheesh' when resident at Ramshacklegur.

DEXTER: (*aside*) That accounts for the necklace.

COLEPEPPER: You know, accepting presents by civil servants is against regulations. If the charge is brought home to Sir Solomon he'll be disgraced – of course, as a friend of his, I regret to hear such things; but one can't quite shut one's ears, you know.

DEXTER: (*aside*) No, nor one's mouth neither.

> (SIR SOLOMON *is seen earnestly speaking to* MRS SEBRIGHT; *they then separate*; SIR SOLOMON *crosses, converses with a lady*; MRS SEBRIGHT, *down, approaching* DEXTER.)

COLEPEPPER: Now, it may be a melancholy duty to open her eyes, but they ought to be opened; and if you should have an opportunity – there she comes! Break it to her gently, my dear sir; but whatever you do, break it. (*aside*) Ehem! I think I've outmanoeuvred the diplomatist.

> (*Goes up, by the opposite side to that by which* MRS SEBRIGHT *comes down, and rejoins his daughter and* CAPTAIN CLAVERING.)

MRS SEBRIGHT: Oh, Mr Dexter, I'm so glad to catch you at last alone. I thought that tiresome Mr Colepepper would never have left you.

DEXTER: Don't say tiresome; he was singing your praises. I conclude from that you haven't told him the truth yet.

MRS SEBRIGHT: About John? (*hesitatingly*) No, not exactly.

DEXTER: Allow me to relieve you of *that* shawl. (*Takes off the shawl* MR COLEPEPPER *has given her; folds it up; puts it on seat.*)

MRS SEBRIGHT: Mr Dexter, how dare you take such a liberty?

DEXTER: I want it to keep company with Sir Solomon's necklace. I suppose you haven't told him the truth neither?

MRS SEBRIGHT: Not yet, Mr Dexter; you see it's so very awkward.

DEXTER: It always is awkward to get back to the hard road of facts from the soft but shifting sands of falsehood.

MRS SEBRIGHT: Oh, if you only knew the perplexity I'm in! They've both proposed. I tried everything to prevent it.

DEXTER: Everything but the truth.

MRS SEBRIGHT: I'm sure I did my best. I flirted with Sir Solomon in hopes to drive

---

'backsheesh': a bribe.

away Mr Colepepper; and then I coquetted with Mr Colepepper on purpose to disgust Sir Solomon. But it's all of no use! I'm fairly at my wit's end.

DEXTER: Then, as wit's exhausted, you may as well fall back on wisdom; and wisdom says – 'Tell truth and shame the devil.' It must be done, and better out of your mouth than other people's. Supposing I helped you to a good reason for saying 'No' to both of them?

MRS SEBRIGHT: Oh, I should be so thankful – that is, any reason but the real one.

DEXTER: Each is amiably anxious to save you from the other. According to Sir Solomon, Mr Colepepper is sixty-five – worn out in constitution – damaged in reputation – and cloudy in prospects. If I may believe Mr Colepepper, Sir Solomon is an empty made-up coxcomb – with false hair – false complexion – false teeth – and factitious reputation – and with the sword of official disgrace hanging over him by a hair. Now, you have only to hold up to *each* of your admirers the picture of him pointed by the *other*, to escape from both with flying colours. Come, you *must* get out of the scrape somehow. I've put the clue in your hand – follow it – at least it will lead you straightforward. Here comes Sir Solomon. (*Crosses behind her, retires up.* SIR SOLOMON *down.*)

SIR SOLOMON: My dear Mrs Sebright, the term for delivering your ultimatum has expired. You promised an answer to my proposal this evening.

MRS SEBRIGHT: Really, Sir Solomon – I feel quite unworthy –

SIR SOLOMON: Not unworthy. Beauty, youth, and grace have their claims, even against family, title, and diamonds.

MRS SEBRIGHT: I'm very sorry – I'm afraid you'll think me very ungrateful – but – in fact – there's an unsurmountable obstacle.

SIR SOLOMON: An obstacle? You don't mean Mr Colepepper?

MRS SEBRIGHT: Mr Colepepper! – what an idea! Why, he's sixty-five, if he's a day – a ruined constitution – a bad temper – and anything but brilliant prospects.

SIR SOLOMON: (*chuckling; aside*) Bravo! *my* thunder! Well done, Doctor!
(COLEPEPPER *comes down.*)

MRS SEBRIGHT: No, I'm sure if there were nothing more formidable in your way than Mr Colepepper –

SIR SOLOMON: Here he comes. (*aside*) We must renew this conversation. She means to say yes, or she'd have returned the necklace. (*Retires up.*)

COLEPEPPER: (*coming down*) My dear Mrs Sebright, I've been grilling over a slow fire while Sir Solomon has been bestowing his tediousness upon you. I hope you have weighed my proposal.

MRS SEBRIGHT: I'm sure, Mr Colepepper, nothing would have given me greater pleasure, but –

COLEPEPPER: 'But!' Am I to understand there's a 'but' in the way?

MRS SEBRIGHT: I'm sorry to say there is – a very great 'but'.

COLEPEPPER: I know who it is – that puppy, Sir Solomon!

MRS SEBRIGHT: He is a 'great butt' certainly; but you needn't be jealous of Sir Solomon – a battered old beau – vain – frivolous – with a made-up face – dyed hair – and false teeth!

COLEPEPPER: (*aside*) Bravo! Exactly the points I put to Dexter! (SIR SOLOMON *comes down.*) Here he comes. We'll pursue our conversation by-and-bye. (*aside*) She seems to have packed up my shawl – that must mean accepting.

SIR SOLOMON: Now, pray don't let me interrupt your *tête-à-tête*.

COLEPEPPER: Not at all, Sir Solomon. (*bugle sounds*) That's the supper bugle. Mrs Sebright was just going down for a little refreshment.

> (*The groups on deck break up and descend the companions, and through the rail by the slips at back.*)

MRS SEBRIGHT: May I trouble you to bring my things? (*They gather up shawls, footstool, etc.; aside*) How I wish I could get both off my hands!

> (*Each approaches with his load on one arm, and offers her the other; go up talking; exeunt by companion. SMART, DEXTER and MOLESKIN come forward from the rail.*)

MOLESKIN: I put it to you, Doctor, as a medical man, whether it ain't impossible for the prisoner to keep up his constitution in this 'ere climate, without fresh *h*air and *h*exercise?

DEXTER: He certainly would be all the better for '*fresh hair*' to judge by what I saw under his white cotton extinguisher. He ought to be trotted on deck at least a couple of hours every day.

MOLESKIN: So I tell him. 'Look here, Mr Downy,' I says, 'I don't want to have you die on my hands. The warrant charges me to take your body – but your dead body would be no manner of use.' But he won't listen to *me*, bless you. There he sits, moping and maundering, and declaring he's somebody else.

SMART: I'm Captain here. Come along with me, Mr Moleskin, and I'll have him on deck if I've to bouse him up by the skylight. But, remember, his arrest is to be kept quiet for the credit of the ship.

MOLESKIN: All right, Captain – mum as a mouse. Nobody needn't know anything but that we're friends – such werry good friends we can't lose sight o' one another.

DEXTER: But he can't run away from your custody here.

> (*Enter MRS LOVIBOND from companion.*)

MOLESKIN: How do I know what papers he may have stowed away? If I didn't keep a heye on him, he might throw 'em overboard, or himself either – he's artful enough.

SMART: Well, come along, Mr Moleskin. (MOLESKIN *crosses.*) The deck's all quiet now; we'll have him up in a jiffey. (*Exit SMART and MOLESKIN.*)

MRS LOVIBOND: (*coming forward*) Mr Dexter, you know Major McTurk – may I ask if he has confided to you the delicate relation in which we stand?

DEXTER: I am aware that the Major has popped – I beg your pardon – proposed to you, and I applaud his taste.

MRS LOVIBOND: Then, perhaps, he has also confided to you the reason of the strange alteration in his manner since this morning – his coldness – his estrangement?

DEXTER: Oh, yes; it was the ghost. Ha, ha, ha!

MRS LOVIBOND: Sir, that mysterious apparition is no subject for levity.

---

extinguisher: LOVIBOND was wearing a white cotton night-cap, presumably of a conical shape, and DEXTER's joke is to liken it to the extinguisher, which is a conical instrument for putting out candles.

bouse: nautical term meaning to haul with tackle.

DEXTER: Mysterious! I wish all ghosts could be explained away so easily! It turns out that the supposed ghost was a sea-sick passenger, which accounts for his cadaverous complexion; his habiliments of the grave resolve themselves into a white cotton night-cap and flannel dressing gown; and the yawning wound in his throat was a cut he had given himself in shaving. He had blundered into your cabin, and was seen by the Major making his retreat.

MRS LOVIBOND: Could the Major do me the injustice to suspect! But are you sure it was a man?

DEXTER: 'I'll take the ghost's word for a thousand pounds!' – I had it from his own lips.

MRS LOVIBOND: But the extraordinary resemblance to my late husband?

DEXTER: Accident, no doubt, or your fancy.

MRS LOVIBOND: Do you know this intruder's name?

DEXTER: Downy.

MRS LOVIBOND: Oh, what a relief! I expect the Major. My dear Doctor, may I ask you to explain this to him, and spare me painful references to the past?

DEXTER: With pleasure. (MRS LOVIBOND *retires.*) By Jove! I'm gradually becoming the pivot on which everything turns in this ship. (McTURK *comes up by the rail.*) I had no notion a P. and O. doctor's duty was to patch up more lovers' quarrels than broken heads, and to administer as many doses of calumny as of calomel. Both dangerous medicines, and both a great deal too much resorted to. Well, Major, I told you I should find an explanation of the intrusion on Mrs Lovibond's cabin this morning. I've found it.

McTURK: Satisfactory?

DEXTER: Perfectly. It turns out, as I expected, that the intruder is an entire stranger to the lady. Only came on board at Aden. He left his cabin to call the steward, and was too sea-sick to find his way back again.

McTURK: Oh, if you can satisfy me he was a stranger to Mrs Lovibond, I shall merely insist upon a public apology in the presence of all the saloon passengers. But, mind, only if he's a stranger. Let me discover any intimacy between 'em, or even acquaintanceship, and (*imitates action of firing a pistol*) one of us must fall – and I don't mean it to be me. (MISS COLEPEPPER *comes up with a book and sits near the skylight.*) But supper will be over; aren't you coming down?

DEXTER: No; I prefer solitude and a cigar. (*Exit* MAJOR; *aside*) There's Mary Colepepper– she sees me. Will she speak? I won't. If *she's* proud, so am I! (*Smokes.* MISS COLEPEPPER, *after a pause and a moment's hesitation, closes her book and approaches.*)

MISS COLEPEPPER: Mr Dexter – (*embarrassed*)

DEXTER: Miss Colepepper a truant from the supper table!

MISS COLEPEPPER: This lovely sea and sky have more attractions for me, I confess, than the saloon. (*Both sit.*)

DEXTER: I'm glad to find one person on board of my way of thinking. (*a pause*) I hope my cigar does not annoy you.

MISS COLEPEPPER: Oh, no! I don't dislike it in the open air.

'*I'll take the ghost's word* . . .': from *Hamlet* Act 3, scene 2, 'Oh good Horatio, I'll take the Ghost's word for a thousand pound. Didst perceive?'

(*Another pause; she fumbles with the book; he takes his cigar from his mouth; each is about to speak, but each, perceiving the other's intentions, pauses embarrassed.*)

DEXTER: I beg your pardon – did you speak?

MISS COLEPEPPER: No; I thought you did.

DEXTER: No; but are you sure my smoke doesn't blow in your face? Perhaps I'd better shift to leeward. (*Rises as if to go across the deck.*)

MISS COLEPEPPER: Don't stir on my account, pray. I am glad of an opportunity of expressing to you my gratitude for the preservation I owe to your courage on that terrible night of the mutiny; my admiration of the unselfish humanity with which you risked your life to-day to save a poor sailor.

DEXTER: Miss Colepepper, take my advice, and never praise a man for doing his duty. It makes him uncomfortable when it does not make him conceited.

MISS COLEPEPPER: At least let me express my regret that my father did not receive you with more hospitality at Calcutta. I'm sure, if he had known all we owed you –

DEXTER: I didn't knock at your father's door as a creditor, but as an acquaintance. I ought to have remembered Calcutta wasn't Badgerypore, and the convenient newspaper editor an altogether different personage from the out-at-elbows tramp.

MISS COLEPEPPER: But if you really knew my father, I am sure you would esteem, as well as like him. Long habits of authority have made him imperious and hasty – apt to stand on his dignity.

DEXTER: His dignity! You would laugh, perhaps, to hear me speak of mine; but I *have* such a thing. The time may come when *your father* will be as frank in owning my services as *you* are now. I will accept his recognition from his own lips, but not by proxy from yours. Meantime, forgive me if I measure our intimacy (*Enter* CLAVERING.) rather by what I know to be your father's notions of social etiquette than your kindly impulses. Here's Captain Clavering coming in search of you. *He's* up to the mark. There can be no importunity in *his* acting as your escort, and if acquaintance with him should grow into a warmer feeling – (*Both rise.*)

MISS COLEPEPPER: Mr Dexter! you have no right to suggest such a thing! Captain Clavering is an acquaintance of papa's – not of my choosing.

DEXTER: I beg your pardon. I was guilty of an impertinence; but it's difficult not to be bitter now and then, in spite of the most philosophic intentions. (CLAVERING *comes down.*)

CLAVERING: I come as a deputation, to ask if you will give us a little music downstairs. They want '*La ci darem*' – I'm ready to take the bass.

DEXTER: That I'll swear you are! (*aside*)

MISS COLEPEPPER: I don't feel in voice this evening, Captain Clavering. (*Turns away.*)

CLAVERING: Now, really, that's very provoking! I'll tell 'em so. (*Goes round to skylight, and speaks down as if to guests.*) They'll all be in despair!

DEXTER: (*aside, to* MISS COLEPEPPER) Not in voice? Oh, Miss Colepepper! The tone in which you said 'Captain Clavering,' just now, was the pleasantest music I've heard for many a day. So delightfully chilling! Do sing!

MISS COLEPEPPER: Not with him! Will *you* sing with me?

DEXTER: Will I not!

MISS COLEPEPPER: Then I'll sing.

DEXTER: But you refused Clavering?

MISS COLEPEPPER: Yes; I thought *you* would ask me.

DEXTER: (*passionately*) Mary! (*checking himself*) I beg your pardon (*ceremoniously*), Miss Colepepper. May I offer you my arm to the saloon? (*They go off arm-in-arm.*)

CLAVERING: (*looking up from the skylight down which he has been talking*) Holloa! she's taken that fellow's arm! Confound his impudence! I'll teach him. (*going violently after him*) No (*stops*), curse him! he knows too much. (*Exit sulkily.*)
> (*Enter* MOLESKIN *and* LOVIBOND; *he wears a great coat, with the collar up, and handcuffs under the long sleeve of his coat, and a large hat nearly concealing his features.*)

MOLESKIN: There's a style of toggery for the tropics! Why, it's enough to make a man perspire to look at you. How can you?

LOVIBOND: It's not for warmth – quite the contrary. I'm running away under 'em! It's the natural desire of a man in my degrading position to escape observation. You *will* cruelly force me on deck, but I hope you won't compel me to show my face. They allow masks, even to the prisoners at Pentonville.

MOLESKIN: Degrading be blowed! You're not the first or the last gent that's had a misfortune. Besides, nobody knows but *you're* a gentleman, and *I'm* a gentleman.

LOVIBOND: But you never leave me!

MOLESKIN: What o' that! It's only a case o' two gentlemen that's werry fond o' one another.

LOVIBOND: And these fetters! (*Holds up his wrists to show the handcuffs.*)

MOLESKIN: The darbies! Oh! keep your cuffs well down, and nobody will be any the wiser.

LOVIBOND: But suppose my nose should itch, and I want to scratch it?

MOLESKIN: Well, in that case, you must *rub* it against something.

LOVIBOND: I suppose it's no use asserting my innocence any more?

MOLESKIN: Not a bit of it.

LOVIBOND: Still there's a melancholy satisfaction in repeating that I'm not the felon Downy – that I was left at Aden by the breaking down of the last P. and O. boat, in which I ought to have reached Suez. I found a dozen names before mine on the list for the Simoom, and was foolish enough to jump at a berth offered me by the felon Downy, for a slight advance, little dreaming of what would be the consequence.

MOLESKIN: That's a werry feasible story, but it won't wash.

LOVIBOND: What do you mean by 'it won't wash'? (*disgusted*)

MOLESKIN: Why should you ha' come aboard by the name of Downy, if you are somebody else?

LOVIBOND: Because, Mr Moleskin, at the intermediate stations, passengers are

---

darbies: a slang term for handcuffs, from the personal name Darby, who were iron manufacturers.

booked contingent on vacancies. Now, Downy stood No. 1 for Suez; I stood No. 10. By assuming the name of Downy, I stepped into his shoes as No. 1.

MOLESKIN: Werry artful, indeed! But how do you account for your possession of that there bag?

LOVIBOND: The felon Downy begged me to take it for him. I was to leave it at Shepherd's Hotel, Cairo. What a damned fool you are!

MOLESKIN: (*admiringly*) Well, that's more than I can say of you. You *are* a cute 'un, Mr Downy! But it won't do, bless you; the likelier it looks, the less I believes it. You've got no witnesses, you see, to identify you as somebody else.

LOVIBOND: (*aside*) Identify me, eh? Good heavens! Clarinda could do it at once! But then I should only get rid of the handcuffs of justice, to put on those of matrimony. Still there's no other way of redeeming my character, so here goes. Mr Moleskin, you place me in a painful dilemma. There *is* a lady on board who can prove I'm not the felon Downy. But I must request a private interview with her, or the consequences may be awful.

MOLESKIN: Who is it?

LOVIBOND: Mrs Lovibond.

MOLESKIN: I know; the fine woman with light 'air and blue eyes. Quite the lady, *she* is. I think I might trust you with her; in course, keeping a heye on you both.

LOVIBOND: (*wiping his nose on* MOLESKIN's *shoulder*) He told me to rub it on *something!* Hem! Then let Mrs Lovibond know that a gentleman wishes to speak with her privately, on most particular business.

MOLESKIN: But I must give some name. Suppose I say 'Downy'?

LOVIBOND: Call me what you will. In my position, one name's as bad as another. (*Crosses.*)

MOLESKIN: (*goes to skylight*) Steward! Tell Mrs Lovibond to step upon deck, Mr Downy wants her. You didn't think I was agoing to lose sight of you, did you, Mr Downy? Just come back.

LOVIBOND: Yes; it's the last desperate alternative. Some people might say that it's 'out of the frying pan into the fire'. But on the whole I would rather endure penal servitude as Lovibond the married man than as the felon Downy. Both sentences would be for life; but the one will be a case of convict allowance, Carpentaria, and gray and yellow dittos. Besides, it's possible Clarinda may be changed. She may be affected by my position – this wasted form – these fettered limbs – this disgustingly familiar detective. (*Enter* MRS LOVIBOND.) Oh! how I hate that fellow!

MRS LOVIBOND: Mr Downy seeking an interview; no doubt to apologise for his intrusion.

        (MAJOR McTURK *shows his head cautiously from behind the companion hatch.*)

McTURK: A request for a private interview with Clarinda. She little thought I overheard the message. From this shelter I can watch what passes.

        (MOLESKIN *watches the interview from one of the gangway seats near top of skylight.*)

---

convict allowance, Carpentaria, etc.: a reference to convict settlements in Australia.

MRS LOVIBOND: Mr Downy, you have sought an interview. I can readily guess the motive of your request. It is granted already.

LOVIBOND: (*aside*) I'll break myself to her by gentle degrees, and alter my voice a little. Madam (*disguising his voice*), it's now some ten years ago since your husband, Augustus Lovibond –

MRS LOVIBOND: Good heavens! Mr Downy!

LOVIBOND: Left his home in Bernard Street, Russell Square, at his usual hour after breakfast, on the morning of the 10th of August.

MRS LOVIBOND: Yes; from that moment I have had no tidings of him, but one letter, from which –

LOVIBOND: You inferred that he had sought in another existence that repose denied him here.

MRS LOVIBOND: Oh, sir, how *do* you know this?

LOVIBOND: From the unhappy Lovibond in person.

MRS LOVIBOND: Then he didn't make away with himself?

LOVIBOND: He tried to do it, but couldn't; the man was very miserable.

MRS LOVIBOND: Alas, sir, by my fault, I'm afraid.

LOVIBOND: (*aside*) She owns it!

MRS LOVIBOND: I thought I had driven him to an untimely end.

LOVIBOND: You drove him as far in that direction as he was capable of going. But when it came to the point, he determined to live on.

MRS LOVIBOND: Oh, sir, you've taken a load off my mind.

LOVIBOND: He engaged a passage to Alexandria, and thence to Singapore; and there, in honest industry, strove to forget the wife whose jealousy and too great desire for sway had driven him into exile.

MRS LOVIBOND: And he still lives, sir?

LOVIBOND: He does; in hopes of one day hearing that his wife, whom he always loved, even while he trembled under her frown, had become a changed being.

MRS LOVIBOND: Oh, sir, she has; believe me, she has. Are you in communication with him?

LOVIBOND: Yes, I see him every day. He has left Singapore. Suppose I told you he was awaiting the arrival of this vessel at Suez.

MRS LOVIBOND: I should be so happy.

LOVIBOND: It wouldn't be too much for you?

MRS LOVIBOND: No!

LOVIBOND: Suppose I told you he was on board!

MRS LOVIBOND: Oh! gracious!

LOVIBOND: That he stood before you. Here! (*Strikes an attitude, removes his hat, and resumes his natural voice.*) Yes, Clarinda! Behold your long-lost Gussy!

MRS LOVIBOND: Augustus! Is it possible! You stand apart. Won't you take me to your arms?

LOVIBOND: Would if I could. (*Shows handcuffs.* McTURK *testifies by gestures his rage at the sight of the kiss and disappears.*) But I can't. These manacles! Overpowered as I am by emotion, I can't even blow my – Would you blow it for me? (*She wipes his nose with her pocket handkerchief.*)

MRS LOVIBOND: A prisoner! Why, what have you done?

LOVIBOND: Nothing; but it seems Downy has done all sorts of things. He gave me up his berth and the use of his name. No doubt he knew he was tracked, and that the officers were on board. I've been arrested for him. I've sent for you to identify me. Yonder sits the detective. Speak the word, and your Augustus once more walks abroad in the proud consciousness of freedom, and a light coat better suited to the climate.

MRS LOVIBOND: I won't lose a moment!
>   (*She goes up to* MOLESKIN, *and speaks with him earnestly. Enter* SIR SOLOMON *from companion.*)

SIR SOLOMON: Mr Downy, allow me to present my card. (*Gives card,* LOVIBOND *takes it awkwardly, owing to his handcuffs.*) As a diplomatist, it is my peculiar function to prevent fighting. But, as a gentleman, of course, I can't refuse to be the bearer of a hostile message.

LOVIBOND: A hostile message to me! Why, I've offended nobody! (*aside*) Oh, I suppose it's meant for Downy.

SIR SOLOMON: Pardon me. I am instructed to say that you have insulted a lady to whom Major McTurk stands in the most delicate relation.

LOVIBOND: I know nothing of McTurk, or his delicate relations! I've insulted nobody.

SIR SOLOMON: Pardon me. I am instructed to say that you have most grossly insulted Mrs Lovibond; first, by entering her cabin this morning; and, just now, by openly kissing her on deck, before several witnesses.

LOVIBOND: But, suppose I'm ready to explain?

SIR SOLOMON: Pardon me; I am instructed to say no explanation can be accepted. You will be good enough to refer me to a friend.

LOVIBOND: Sir, I have no friends; and if I had I wouldn't refer you to one. But surely, as a rational man, when I tell you that Mrs Lovibond is *my* wife –

SIR SOLOMON: Your wife –

LOVIBOND: Yes, sir, my wife!

SIR SOLOMON: That case was certainly not provided for in my instructions.

LOVIBOND: Perhaps you'll have the kindness to inform Major McTurk of the fact; such will be confirmed by the lady, if referred to. (*Goes to the skylight, to* MRS LOVIBOND *and* MOLESKIN.)

SIR SOLOMON: Let me see. Here I am, thrown suddenly on my own responsibility. I was charged to insist on an appointment to fight at Suez; but this relation between the parties alters the aspect of the negotiation. A man has certainly the right to enter his wife's cabin, and even kiss her before witnesses, though such conjugal endearments are in bad taste. Having, as it were, left Mr Downy a copy of my despatches, I think I may, with propriety, convey his explanation to the Major. (*Exit.* LOVIBOND, MRS LOVIBOND *and* MOLESKIN *come down.*)

MOLESKIN: Werry well. You say, ma'am, and will stake your davy, if necessary, that the prisoner is Augustus Lovibond – *your* husband – who left you ten years ago?

MRS LOVIBOND: Yes.

LOVIBOND: There, sir! Remove these degrading fetters. (*Holds out his wrists.*)

MOLESKIN: Stop a bit; don't you be in a'nurry. All you say, ma'am, may be werry

---

davy: short for affidavit.

true; I don't doubt it a bit. Only, you see, it proves nothing against this 'ere charge.

LOVIBOND: Why, it proves I'm Augustus Lovibond.

MOLESKIN: Exactly.

LOVIBOND: And, therefore, I can't be Thomas Downy?

MOLESKIN: Why not? That don't follow – Thomas Downy has no end of aliases. Why, there's six on the warrant. How do I know Lovibond mayn't be another alias of Downy – or Downy an alias of Lovibond?

MRS LOVIBOND: Oh dear! that never occurred to me! (LOVIBOND *groans*.)

MOLESKIN: Besides, you've been ten years away from your good lady here. How does she know what games you may have been up to all that time?

LOVIBOND: (*looking at* MRS LOVIBOND) Never! never! I've been up to nothing!

MOLESKIN: No, no, ma'am; I'm werry sorry for your feelings – but it won't wash!

LOVIBOND: My dear sir, what *will* wash?

MRS LOVIBOND: What *is* to be done? Oh, I know; I'll consult Mr Dexter. He's everybody's friend. Good-bye, Augustus – keep up your spirits till I return. (*Embraces him, sobbing*.) Oh dear, oh dear!

LOVIBOND: (*unable to wipe his eyes*) Clarinda, dear, do my nose again. (*She wipes his eyes, and exits*.) Here's a state of things! I've discovered myself to my wife, and I haven't got rid of my handcuffs!

(*Re-enter* SIR SOLOMON.)

SIR SOLOMON: Mr Downy, I have conveyed your explanation to my principal, Major McTurk.

LOVIBOND: Ah! of course he's satisfied?

SIR SOLOMON: Pardon me. He says that, supposing you to be the husband of Mrs Lovibond, your heartless behaviour to that lady, of which she has long ago informed him, renders it more than ever his duty to call you out. It may be as well you should know he is a dead shot, and that he labours under the impression that, in shooting you, he will be ridding the world of a monster.

LOVIBOND: Don't talk in that ridiculous manner! Do I look like a monster?

SIR SOLOMON: You will excuse my entering upon that question. May I request that you will refer me to a friend to arrange the preliminaries?

LOVIBOND: There's the Doctor. He's everybody's friend. Perhaps he won't object as mine.

SIR SOLOMON: I shall take an early opportunity of conferring with him. Sir, I have the honour to wish you a very good evening. (*Exit*.)

LOVIBOND: Good evening! I thought Mrs Lovibond would smooth everything. But she makes everything worse and worse! Here I am with a wife – a duel – and the handcuffs – all on my hands at once. Oh, Lord! – Oh, Lord!

(*Enter* DEXTER *from companion*.)

DEXTER: (*comes down*) Now, my dear sir, don't give way to despair. You're safe to be identified, sooner or later.

LOVIBOND: Later, I'm afraid.

DEXTER: The awkward part of the business is, that you've been at Singapore all the time covered by this swindler's transactions. I'm afraid the only way will be to move a postponement of your trial at the Old Bailey till we can get witnesses over from the Straits to swear that you're *not* Downy.

LOVIBOND: But my arrest isn't all, Doctor. I've got into a fresh scrape since
    Clarinda left me. Sir Solomon Fraser has brought me a challenge from Major
    McTurk.
DEXTER: A challenge! What for?
LOVIBOND: My conduct to my wife, he says –
DEXTER: Let me see. Yes, I think I can get you out of *that* mess.
LOVIBOND: Can you? Oh, my dear Doctor –
DEXTER: Certainly, We'll tell the Major you're in custody on a charge of felony. Of
    course, a man in that ignominious position forfeits all the privileges of a
    gentleman – including that of being popped off with a hair trigger.
            (LASCARS *enter with lamps from companions; hang lamps;*
            passengers and a band enter; when band is on LASCARS *exit by*
            companions.)
LOVIBOND: But the loss of my character?
DEXTER: Will be the saving of your life. Choose between 'em. (*a pause;*
    MOLESKIN *comes down.*)
LOVIBOND; Go, and blast my reputation. (*Exit* DEXTER.) My (*Passengers begin to*
    appear on deck.) wife found! My life in danger! My reputation blighted!
MOLESKIN: Here's the company coming up from supper. Now, Mr Downy (*taps him*
    on the shoulder), I think it's about time to turn in.
LOVIBOND: And a detective continually at my side! But let me hide my misery in my
    cabin. Lead on, myrmidon of the law.
MOLESKIN: Myr-midden. Come, Mr Downy, I've behaved quite the gentleman to
    you, sir, and I didn't ought to be called out of my name – and by such a hepithet
    too – 'Midden', indeed, Mr Downy, I blush for you!
LOVIBOND: That's the climax! *He* blushes for me! (*They go up. As* LOVIBOND
    approaches the companion, DEXTER *enters.*) Well, Doctor, you've seen the
    Major's friend?
DEXTER: I've seen the Major.
LOVIBOND: And, of course, the challenge is off?
DEXTER: On the contrary; he says he'll wait the result of your trial. If you're found
    guilty, he will leave you to the law. But if you're acquitted, he'll call you out the
    day after.
LOVIBOND: Good Heavens! I said the climax was attained. This caps the climax!
            (*Exeunt* LOVIBOND *and* MOLESKIN. SMART *and* HARDISTY
            come down. Enter MRS SEBRIGHT, COLEPEPPER, MRS
            LOVIBOND, SIR SOLOMON, MISS COLEPEPPER,
            CLAVERING, MRS RABBITS, *and other passengers, and*
            McTURK; *group at top.*)
DEXTER: (*to* SMART) Captain, with your permission, the passengers propose a
    dance on deck.
SMART: All right, Doctor. (DEXTER *goes up.*) I'm going to turn in, Hardisty.

---

myrmidon: policeman. The Myrmidons were the fearless followers of Achilles who went with him
to Troy, and followed his orders without questioning. A *myrmidon of the law* follows his in the
same unquestioning way.
midden: dunghill.

You'll see the look out's relieved. It's a fine night, but the moon will bring up a
   haze with it, and we're not far from the Mazaffa Reefs.
HARDISTY: Aye, aye, sir. (*Exit* SMART.)
MRS SEBRIGHT: (*coming down to* DEXTER) Oh, Doctor! both Sir Solomon and
   Mr Colepepper want to dance with me. If I accept either, I know the other will
   be so angry; so I told both I was engaged to *you*.
DEXTER: Really, as John Sebright's friend, I don't like this lavish resort to fibbing.
MRS SEBRIGHT: Please don't say fibbing.
DEXTER: Taradiddles, at all events. I've a good mind to throw you over.
MRS SEBRIGHT: Oh, please, Doctor, if you'll look over it, only this once.
DEXTER: Well, as there's no great harm done, and as you are certainly the prettiest
   partner on board – come along.
> (*A dance is formed;* SIR SOLOMON *and* MRS RABBITS;
> COLEPEPPER *and* MRS LOVIBOND; CLAVERING *and* MISS
> COLEPEPPER; DEXTER *and* MRS SEBRIGHT; *and*
> *passengers. In the middle of dance, i.e., after galop, cry from the fore*
> *part of the ship –* 'Breakers ahead on the port bow.' *Tremendous*
> *crash, which sends all the passengers reeling.*)
HARDISTY: (*seizing his trumpet at rail*) Hard aport – hard all. (*to* DEXTER) By
   heavens, Doctor, she's ashore on the Mazaffa Reef!
DEXTER: Call the Captain. I'll keep order here. (*Another heavy sound is heard, and*
   steam being let off.)
HARDISTY: (*through the trumpet*) Below there! Reverse!
DEXTER: (*snatching trumpet from him*) Go ahead – full steam! (*to engine room. To*
   HARDISTY) If we back her, she may go down in deep water.
> (*The ladies scream violently; all this passes very rapidly.*)
McTURK: ⎱ Lower the boats!
COLEPEPPER: ⎰ Mary, keep close to me!
> (*Children scream from below the skylight; confusion on board;*
> *women run about in terror.*)
DEXTER: (*very loud*) Silence all, for your lives! (*a sudden pause*) Be cool and obey
   orders, and all shall be safe on shore in an hour's time.
> (*Enter* SMART.)
SMART: Thank you for that, Doctor! (*through the trumpet*) Pipe hands to boat
   stations! (*boatswain's whistle heard*) Boat's crews stand by the tackle falls. (*They*
   do so.) Lower away and keep off! Carpenters' mates, stand by to cut away
   masts! (*Chinamen do so.*)
HARDISTY: (*coming up to* SMART) She's heeling over fast. The starboard cabins
   are filling! The doors are jammed! The women and children will be drowned!
DEXTER: We must jump down, and pass 'em up by the skylight! Here goes, to save
   the women and children! (*Throws his coat off; jumps down into the skylight and*
   passes up children.)
HARDISTY: Heads below! (*Follows* DEXTER.)
MISS COLEPEPPER: Papa! papa!

---

galop: a lively dance.

MRS SEBRIGHT: (*in terror*) Mr Colepepper! Sir Solomon! Oh dear, will nobody
save me?
MRS LOVIBOND: (*to* McTURK) Hector! (*Tries to cling to him.*)
McTURK: (*shaking both off*) Hands off! £50 for a place in the first boat!
(*Enter* LOVIBOND *and* MOLESKIN; *they cross.* LOVIBOND
sinks on the stage, flat on his back.)
MRS LOVIBOND: Augustus! you'll save me? (*Crosses to him.*)
LOVIBOND: I can't swim in handcuffs!
TABLEAU

The LC copy has an extended ending to this act, from DEXTER's line '..to save the
women and children!' This alternative ending is appended at the end of the text
of the play.

Act III

SCENE. *A coral reef coming down to the edge of the sea. Rough tents rigged out of
spars and sails, right and left. That to the right is the tent occupied by the women and
children. That to the left, which projects so as to intercept part of the sea view, is the store
tent. Barrels, cases, wine and beer bottles, and preserved meat cases are partially visible,
piled about and under it; a gong hung on a spar near it, and a flag hoisted on a flagstaff.*
TOTTLE *discovered on guard over the stores, armed with a musket and cutlass;*
HARDISTY *sitting on a case making entries in pencil in a book.*
DEXTER: (*calling from within the tent*) Four dozen soup and bouilli!
HARDISTY: (*writing in his book*) Forty-eight S. and B.
DEXTER: Three dozen roast beef.
HARDISTY: Thirty-six R.B.
DEXTER: Two dozen and a-half pheasant.
HARDISTY: Thirty pheas.
DEXTER: Forty dozen galantine.
HARDISTY: Forty-eight gal.
DEXTER: That finishes the preserved meats; and now belay, Hardisty, till I calculate
the distribution to the messes.
HARDISTY: (*putting away his book*) Well, we shan't starve yet awhile, that's a
comfort. (*Comes down.*)
(*Enter* CAPTAIN SMART, *his arm in a sling.*)
SMART: Well, Hardisty?
HARDISTY: On your pins again, Captain?
SMART: Yes, Dexter has patched me up. I thought it was all over with me when that
spar knocked me out of the chains. Well, Tottle?
TOTTLE: I'm on duty, Captain – standing sentry over the stores – or I'd have
made bold to ask for a grip of your fist, though it's clean agin discipline, I
know.
SMART: Thanks, my good fellow. I'm glad to see everything looking so ship-shape.

---

bouilli: stewed meat.

HARDISTY: Ah! we may thank Dexter for that. You may imagine the state of things on board after you were disabled.

SMART: That I can – what with lubberly Lascars, useless invalids, frightened women, and squalling babies.

HARDISTY: Officers and quartermasters did their duty like Englishmen – the passengers behaved well on the whole – but Dexter was our life and soul. She struck at nine, and thanks to him, we had every man, woman, and child ashore, tents rigged, passengers under cover, and all with a comfortable basin of soup in either holds by six in the morning.

TOTTLE: And that ain't half, Captain. Why, he's collected the stores, settled the messes, regulated the allowances, parcelled out the duty. Blest if he ain't been steward, cook, and bottle washer, to say nothing of purser, doctor, and loblolly boy. I never see such a beggar to turn his hand to things! (*Goes up with* HARDISTY.)

(*Enter* DEXTER *from the tent, left.*)

DEXTER: Belay there, Tottle! or, if you *will* sing my praises, sing 'em smaller. Well, Captain, I said I should have you afloat again in three days, and here you are.

SMART: Timbers a little battered; but good for Lloyd's A1 list for many a year to come. (*shakes hands with him*) Dexter, I owe you my life.

DEXTER: Be as long as possible in paying me then. I hope you approve of our arrangements?

SMART: Couldn't be better. I say, how about provisions?

DEXTER: We've enough for a fortnight, at least, with care.

SMART: And drinkables?

DEXTER: Ah! we might be better off there. About forty dozen of beer, half as much claret –

SMART: But water?

DEXTER: Only two hogsheads. The first nearly expended in the three days we've been here – I mean to keep the last for the children and the sick.

SMART: God help us all, if the drink runs short!

DEXTER: Oh, never fear. I think I could manage to rig up a distilling apparatus out of the ship's coppers and a few musket barrels. Besides, after consultation with Hardisty, I've sent off the second officer with the pinnace to cruise about the Straits, in hopes they may pick up a steamer and send her to our relief.

SMART: The best thing you have done yet – and everything you've done is good. By George! Dexter, I feel ashamed to take the command out of your hand.

DEXTER: I don't mean you to – for a week yet, at least. I shall have you on your beam ends again, if you go fagging about too soon. So be a good child, and go back to bye-bye.

SMART: Not I; I'm quite fit for duty, I tell you.

DEXTER: I know better. What! you won't go quietly? Here, Hardisty (HARDISTY *comes down*), carry this naughty baby to bed.

HARDISTY: Come, Captain.

SMART: I suppose I must obey orders. God bless you, my fine fellow! If prayers go

---

loblolly boy: surgeon's assistant.
hogshead: a cask, containing just over 50 imperial gallons.

the right road, *you* ought to be all safe up there. (*pointing to Heaven. Exit, leaning on* HARDISTY.)

DEXTER: There's no prayer like work, depend upon it, Captain.
                    (*Enter* COLEPEPPER *from the left.*)

COLEPEPPER: My own theory, Doctor. But you illustrate it by practice. Here's my report of the stores washed up from the wreck this last tide. (*Gives paper.*)

DEXTER: (*taking paper and glancing at it*) One of the tanks of ice, I see. Just the thing for my *coup-de-soleil* patients.

COLEPEPPER: What a mercy it is we've so few sick. For my own part, I haven't felt so well for the last twenty years.

DEXTER: Because you've never thought half so little of yourself, or half so much of other people. Hard work to a good purpose is the best *elixir vitæ* I know.

COLEPEPPER: You're right, Mr Dexter. Egad! I feel equal to anything. I could roll up a harness-cask – light a fire – cook a copper of soup – knock down Sir Solomon – Come! what have you got for me to do this morning?

DEXTER: There's the wood to chop for the fire; and the preserved meat tins to open for the mess rations.

COLEPEPPER: Oh! that's mere labourer's work. Do you know, I think I could make a sea-pie. Do let me try my hand at a sea-pie.

DEXTER: No! that's high art. Your first is safe to be uneatable; and we can't afford experiments. But I applaud your ambition.

COLEPEPPER: Ah! Mr Dexter, thanks to you for it – as for so much besides. My poor Mary, but for your care that night –

DEXTER: (*interrupting*) Look! Here comes Sir Solomon. He doesn't thrive on difficulty, like you. You must have observed the melancholy change in him?

COLEPEPPER: Melancholy change? You mean his silence? I call it the greatest change for the better I ever knew.

                    (*Enter* SIR SOLOMON, *his jaws tied up with a hankerchief, a boot on one foot and a shoe on the other, and looks generally dilapidated and seedy.*)

DEXTER: Why, Sir Solomon (SIR SOLOMON *bows*), I hope you're not suffering from toothache? (SIR SOLOMON *shakes his head ruefully, intimating that he is.*) Allow me to look at the peccant grinders.

                    (SIR SOLOMON, *with great eagerness, resists any attempt to look into his mouth.*)

COLEPEPPER: Come, Sir Solomon, don't be down in the mouth. (SIR SOLOMON *makes a grimace at the word mouth.*) Follow my example. Make yourself generally useful.

DEXTER: Come, sir, we'd better look out the meat cans for today's rations. (*They go up to store tent.*)

SIR SOLOMON: (*speaking with difficulty; as he opens his mouth an entire loss of teeth is apparent*) Toothache! I wish I had! Down in the mouth! Well I may be!

---

coup-de-soleil: sun stroke.
elixir vitæ: elixir of life.
sea-pie: a sailor's dish made of salt-meat, vegetables and dumplings baked (Chambers).
peccant grinders: offending teeth!

They may have been washed ashore! (*Enter* LIMPET, *as if searching. He wears an old pair of red plush breeches.*) Found 'em, Limpet?

LIMPET: (*in a mournful voice*) No, Sir Solomon. I've walked all round the reef; but there's no signs on 'em.

SIR SOLOMON: Continue your search. (*Exit* LIMPET, *behind tent.*)

    (*Enter* MRS SEBRIGHT *from the women's tent. She looks gay and cheerful, and wears a coquettish made-up costume, and handkerchief tied over her head.*)

MRS SEBRIGHT: Ah! good morning, Doctor; good morning, Mr Colepepper. Hard at work, I see, as usual; Sir Solomon, too. (SIR SOLOMON *turns ruefully and bows.*) No; he's *not* hard at work, as usual. (*laughs*) Oh, dear! Oh, dear! You poor, dilapidated man. Do let me take you into hospital and nurse you. What! no reply? Then you're an ungrateful monster!

    (SIR SOLOMON *intimates his thanks by signs, and strolls off sadly.* DEXTER *and* COLEPEPPER *come down.*)

MRS SEBRIGHT: I've developed such a talent for nursing since we were wrecked – haven't I, Doctor?

DEXTER: That you have. Mr Colepepper, I call this lady and your daughter my two sisters of charity. I expected a right hand in Miss Colepepper, but I confess –

MRS SEBRIGHT: You thought Jenny Sebright more ornamental than useful. I hope I've redeemed my character.

COLEPEPPER: You've not discarded the ornamental, I'm happy to see. That dress is monstrously becoming.

MRS SEBRIGHT: I'm glad you like it. I contrived it last night, when I was sitting up with Mrs Rabbits' babies. Little Polly's so much better this morning, Doctor.

DEXTER: Ah! that means that you've attended carefully to my directions through the night?

MRS SEBRIGHT: Oh, yes! I gave her her draught every half hour. Poor little darling! she was so thankful – and her poor sick mother, too. Oh! Doctor, how shall I ever thank you enough for teaching me how much pleasanter it is to wait than to be waited upon.

COLEPEPPER: What! *you've* learnt that lesson, too, my dear madam?

MRS SEBRIGHT: Oh! Doctor, it was so pitiful to hear the little darlings cry all through the night, 'Water, water!' Couldn't you allow 'em a pint a piece extra?

DEXTER: Impossible, I'm afraid.

MRS SEBRIGHT: I'll give up half mine; so will Miss Colepepper, I'm sure; and Mrs Lovibond; and all of us.

DEXTER: I've no objections to that. The more you give up the better you'll thrive on what's left. But I've work for you down at the men's hospital.

MRS SEBRIGHT: Oh, I'm so glad. What is it?

DEXTER: To attend on one of the steerage passengers. He had a *coup-de-soleil* yesterday, and is delirious this morning. I'm afraid of congestion. I want someone to keep applying ice to his head. He's an odd mysterious fellow – and nobody seems to care much about nursing him.

MRS SEBRIGHT's *costume*: the LC text describes it as a 'hybrid costume – half gypsy, half midshipman'.

MRS SEBRIGHT: I shall be ready directly. I'll just go and see my little charges tucked up comfortably, and show Mrs Rabbits' Ayah how to make arrowroot properly. I say, couldn't you allow me a leetle extra claret to mix with it, Doctor?

DEXTER: (*peremptorily*) No; I tell you!

MRS SEBRIGHT: (*coaxingly*) Only half a bottle; and every drop of it for the babies, you know!

DEXTER: Hang the woman! she'd wheedle a boatswain's mate. Here, Tottle, serve out half a bottle of claret to Mrs Sebright.

TOTTLE: Aye, aye, sir! here you are, ma'am.

MRS SEBRIGHT: (*aside, to* TOTTLE) You can stop it off my next two days' allowance, you know, Mr Tottle. (*She goes up to store tent.*)

COLEPEPPER: What a transformation!

DEXTER: No; what a revelation! It was all there; but it wanted the occasion to show itself.

COLEPEPPER: Why, there wasn't a lady on board took so much waiting on!

DEXTER: Because there wasn't a lady on board who had so much offered her. And among the civilest of her civil servants were Sir Solomon and yourself.

COLEPEPPER: I'm afraid I was very near making a fool of myself. (*Exit* MRS SEBRIGHT *into tent, right.*) But I've reflected since the wreck. Ah! Mary.
     (*Enter* MISS COLEPEPPER. *She has a pretty extempore head-dress.*)

MISS COLEPEPPER: Dear papa! (*kisses him*) Mr Dexter – (*shakes hands with him*) – how well papa's looking, isn't he?

DEXTER: And you, Miss Colepepper. Why, hardship seems to agree with your family.

MISS COLEPEPPER: Oh! I knew papa would come out under difficulties. He always does. Bless him! And with your example, Mr Dexter, we should indeed be cowards to refuse what little help we can give.

DEXTER: Then, sir, just show your daughter that ice they've got ashore. And you get a basket of it (*to* MISS COLEPEPPER), and bring it to me here. I'll walk down with you and Mrs Sebright to the hospital, and show you how to use it.

COLEPEPPER: (*going up to store tent*) I'll get you a basket, my love.

MISS COLEPEPPER: (*to* DEXTER) Oh! I'm so thankful that this accident has shown you papa in his true colours.

DEXTER: Now, for the first time, I understand how you come to be father and daughter. Ah! Miss Colepepper, this is the life – stripped to the buff. In our artificial world men are so buckrammed, and padded, and corksoled by aids and appliances, that they neither show or use their muscles. After all, we may have a few curs among us; but, on the whole, Englishmen peel well; don't they?

MISS COLEPEPPER: And Englishwomen?

DEXTER: What – *you* fishing for a compliment!

COLEPEPPER: (*coming down with basket*) Here's the basket, Mary. The ice is only a few hundred yards along the reef.

Clearly *stripped to the buff* and *peel well* are metaphorical states of nakedness in Taylor's meaning!

MISS COLEPEPPER: Come along, papa. (*Crosses to him.*) I'll be with you again
    directly, Mr Dexter. (*Exeunt* MR *and* MISS COLEPEPPER.)

DEXTER: Oh! what a wife that girl would make! It's enough to drive a fellow wild to
    think of her being wasted on a loose, idle, pleasure-loving gambler like
    Clavering; and all because he's well-born, good-looking, and has heavy interest
    to back him! But to think of old Colepepper turning up such a trump! He can't
    know this Clavering's real character, or he'd never – But Mary don't care a fig
    for him – that's a comfort! I've an enormous faith in women's wits and wills.
           (*Enter* MRS SEBRIGHT *from tent.*)

MRS SEBRIGHT: Thank you for the compliment. You so seldom pay one.

DEXTER: And that wasn't meant for *you*. But, come; don't look so vexed. I shall
    have a better account of you to give to Jack than I dared have hoped a week ago.
    Miss Colepepper is to walk down with us. She's gone for the ice with her old
    trump of a father. I say, how he *has* improved.

MRS SEBRIGHT: In all ways. Amongst others, he hasn't said a tender word to *me*
    since we were wrecked. I suppose he's too busy – but it's a great comfort.

DEXTER: And has Sir Solomon been equally sensible?

MRS SEBRIGHT: Ah! *he* hasn't said a word to anybody – I can't think what's come
    over him!

DEXTER: Let's take the good sent us, and ask no questions. Sir Solomon is what
    Sydney Smith called – a brilliant flash of silence.

MRS SEBRIGHT: At all events, I begin to hope they've both given up thinking of
    poor me – I can meet Jack so happily now.

DEXTER: Remember, you'll have to give back Sir Solomon's diamonds, and Mr
    Colepepper's shawl.

MRS SEBRIGHT: You spiteful creature! As if I'd had any pleasure out of 'em! Why,
    you've got both. But I'm so thankful you have. I feel very good now; but there's
    no saying what such temptations might do – and, you know, we may have to live
    here all the rest of our lives – and then there'd be no Jack in the way.

DEXTER: Here comes Miss Colepepper with the ice.
           (*Enter* MISS COLEPEPPER.)

MISS COLEPEPPER: Now then. Ah! Mrs Sebright, your smiling face isn't a bit
    worse for your night's nursing. Oh! Mr Dexter, if you'd seen her hushing those
    poor fretful babies!

MRS SEBRIGHT: Not half so fretful as their poor mother – and you know you were
    up half the night with her.

DEXTER: Come, I can't have any quarrelling over your respective good works.
    Hospital mates! right face; quick march! (*Takes them both on his arm, and
    exits.*)
           (*Enter* LIMPET.)

LIMPET: Not a trace of 'em. Sir Solomon's teeth have been swallowed up in the jaws
    of the hocean! Well, I hope they look better in the hocean's jaws than they did in
    Sir Solomon's. I little thought, when my guv'nor came down by the run into the

---

Sydney Smith, etc.: Smith was Canon of St Paul's, founder/contributor to *The Edinburgh Review*,
and a noted wit. Speaking of Macaulay he said 'he has occasional flashes of silence, that make his
conversation perfectly delightful'.

boat that night, that he'd knocked the whole set out of his head, as clean as a whistle. Well, it's a good job! for he can't give so many horders as he used, nor talk such a damn'd deal o' nonsense. (*Enter* MRS GRIMWOOD, *disconsolately, from the tent, right, with a cap in her hand.*) Ah! Mrs Grimwood! Good day, Mrs Grimwood!

MRS GRIMWOOD: Oh, Mr Limpet! here's a melancholy situation. I couldn't ha' believed I ever should ha' got thro' three days of it.

LIMPET: Nor me neither, Mrs Grimwood. And if master had been in his usual way, why, I couldn't – I *couldn't*.

MRS GRIMWOOD: To think of people that's been used to their comforts having to pig in tents like gipsies, or so many Robinson Crusoes.

LIMPET: No conveniences for meals, nor nothing.

MRS GRIMWOOD: Not so much as a flat-iron, if I wanted to get up any little fine thing for myself, or my young lady. Here's a cap – rough-drying is the hutmost I can manage!

LIMPET: Ah! when one *reads* of people being cast away on desolate hilands one don't realise the 'ardships of it. I give you my word, I 'aven't seen a comb or brush these three days. Just look at my head. (*Takes off hat.*)

MRS GRIMWOOD: And as I was below when the vessel struck – would you believe it? – I had to come ashore without so much as a crinoline!

LIMPET: Well, I shouldn't have noticed it if you hadn't spoke about it, Mrs Grimwood.

MRS GRIMWOOD: (*looking at his red plush breeches*) But – gracious 'evins! wot's that? (*pointing to them*) You've never gone back to livery, Mr Limpet?

LIMPET: What was a man to do? with his pantaloons a wreck, like the wessel? These disgusting things was washed on shore; and I was thankful for 'em!

MRS GRIMWOOD: Ah!

LIMPET: But my guv'nor has lost suffen what's worse nor crinolines and pantaloons, Mrs Grimwood, I can tell you!

MRS GRIMWOOD: What hever can *that* be, Mr Limpet?

LIMPET: Well, he's lost – his teeth!

MRS GRIMWOOD: Real?

LIMPET: No! they were not real; but mineral succeed-in-of-'em!

MRS GRIMWOOD: Gracious 'evins! Poor gentleman! Well, it ought to teach *us* submission. But – what's worse than all – to see one's missus so cheerful and heasy, and a-making the best of heverything to that degree – it's enough to provoke a saint!

LIMPET: Ah! Sir Solomon don't take that line, I can tell you.

MRS GRIMWOOD: Would you believe it? she actually demeans herself to wait upon the men in the hospital. Not gentlefolks, you know; but common sailors and soldiers – and such like.

LIMPET: Ah! misery – they say – makes a man acquainted with strange bedfellows!

MRS GRIMWOOD: (*offended*) Really, Mr Limpet!

LIMPET: Meaning no offence, Mrs Grimwood!

MRS GRIMWOOD: Which if one is cast on a desolate hiland, and without the common necessaries of life, one at least expects the respect due to a female! Bedfellows, indeed! Bedfellows! well, I'm sure! (*Exit into tent, right, offended.*)

LIMPET: She hevidently turned up her nose. Well, there's such a thing as being *nasty* particular. Oh! here comes Sir Solomon. I wonder if he's found his teeth? He mustn't catch me a philandering with the females, and so I'll hook it. (*Exit.*)

(*Enter* SIR SOLOMON.)

SIR SOLOMON: Can't see 'em anywhere. I've completed the round of the reef, and all in vain! I must manage till we reach Cairo. I suppose there's a dentist there. These preserved meats are a mercy! If we had been reduced to hard locusts and junk, I should have starved! I've lost everything, even my umbrella – and walking under the sun is highly dangerous to the brain. If I could provide some substitute. Ha! (*finds a hamper lid*) This, I think, with a little ingenuity, and a piece of rope-yarn – (*adjusts the hamper lid on his head, like a mushroom hat*) Let me resume my search. (*Exit.*)

Enter MAJOR McTURK. *He looks abject and dishevelled, and limps.*)

McTURK: This infernal coral cuts like a razor, and I escaped in my dress boots. What with the sun overhead, and the reef under foot – and only half enough to eat, and not near half enough to drink – I feel so low and poorly. (*Sits on a box, disconsolately.*) I'd hang myself, only there isn't a tree on the reef to fasten a rope to. That's half a bottle of beer for a fellow. I can't bear it much longer. And such a lot stored away yonder. I dare say Dexter helps himself, eh? There's only the sentry. Here! sentry, I say; I want to speak to you!

TOTTLE: (*coming forward*) Aye, aye, sir!

McTURK: I'm very bad, sentry.

TOTTLE: Which my name's Tottle, sir. I ain't a soger, sir, I'm a steward.

McTURK: Yes, Mr Tottle, I remember. I'm dying for a drop of beer, or wine, or brandy – anything strong. There's lots in store; nobody would know if we helped ourselves to a bottle apiece. (TOTTLE *is silent.*) Perhaps you don't want one. In that case, suppose you let me have both. I'd give you a five pound note – ten – twenty! Say how much?

TOTTLE: You white-livered son of a sea cook! Why, the very women ought to be let loose upon you, to scratch your eyes out! You a man!

McTURK: (*abjectly*) Oh! don't be angry, Mr Tottle; and don't speak so loud! I wasn't in earnest; I wasn't, indeed! I only wanted to try you.

TOTTLE: To *try* me! If you don't deserve six dozen at the gangway, without trial, may I never crack another biscuit! You mean, paltry –

McTURK: Oh! Mr Tottle, somebody will hear you!

TOTTLE: I wish every soul on the reef could hear me. Be off! you poor, selfish, snivelling hound! Be off! or I'll drive my bayonet through your dirty carcase!

McTURK: Oh, dear! oh, dear! What shall I do?

TOTTLE: Be off, I say!

McTURK: I'm going, Mr Tottle! (*Exit* McTURK.)

TOTTLE: And that's the chap that used to talk blood and thunder at the saloon table till you'd shake in your shoes to hear him. I suppose delirium trimmings will be the end o' him.

LOVIBOND: (*singing without*)

A light and a good pair of top boots
Will go through the world, my brave boys.

TOTTLE: Why, if it ain't that 'ere Downy. Well, he thrives on half allowance, surely.

(*Enter* LOVIBOND.)

LOVIBOND: Ah, Tottle, my boy! how d'ye do?

TOTTLE: Hearty, thank you, sir! how are you?

LOVIBOND: That's your sort. I'm charming; and the air of this watering-place makes me feel that it must be near breakfast time.

TOTTLE: Glad to see you've got your eatin' tackle aboard again, sir.

LOVIBOND: Yes, Tottle, such delightful weather; and such a nice open situation as this for enjoying the weather.

TOTTLE: And how's that werry partic'lar friend o'yourn, sir?

LOVIBOND: Moleskin, eh? Oh, *he's* all right. Came ashore in his slippers – cut his feet all to pieces on the reef – can't walk a step, I'm happy to say. That's why he isn't with me, as usual. I've got a capital pair of boots, you see. He wanted me to share 'em with him, but I declined – a pair of boots are like a man and wife – they ought never to be given. (TOTTLE *goes up, laughing*) And talking of man and wife, where's mine, I wonder? I told her I should pay her a visit this morning. Hoy, Clarinda!

(*Enter* MRS LOVIBOND *from tent, right.*)

MRS LOVIBOND: Here, Augustus, dear –

LOVIBOND: 'Here, Augustus, dear!' but you weren't *here*. I particularly told you to be waiting for me, and when I tell you a thing, I mean you to do it, my dear.

MRS LOVIBOND: I'm very sorry dear. I was all ready, but I'd some poor creatures to attend to in the tent.

LOVIBOND: You had one poor creature to attend to *out* of the tent, and that is your Augustus!

MRS LOVIBOND: I'll be careful not to keep you waiting another time, dear.

LOVIBOND: Oh, I'm not angry, Clarinda; I'm too happy to be angry! Only think that poor devil, Moleskin, limped dreadfully yesterday. But he can't stir a peg today, without my boots; and, of course, I know better than to lend him them.

MRS LOVIBOND: Oh, I'm so glad to see he's taken off the handcuffs.

LOVIBOND: He couldn't help himself. I declared if he didn't take 'em off, I wouldn't fetch him his rations. In short, my dear, for to-day, at least, I'm the master of the situation.

MRS LOVIBOND: How delightful! We can have such a nice ramble about the reef together. I've so much to tell you – ten years arrears, you know, to make up.

LOVIBOND: You won't be jealous.

MRS LOVIBOND: No, dear; I hope I've got over that folly.

LOVIBOND: When I first made myself known to you, I craned at it tremendously.

MRS LOVIBOND: Craned, dear?

LOVIBOND: Yes, I was frightened, my love. But now I'm satisfied it was the best day's work I ever did in my life. You don't bully, and you ain't jealous. You always were a duck of a woman, and if it hadn't been for your little peculiarities in that way – and now – by Jove, Clarinda, you're perfection.

---

craned: used in the sense of having to make a great effort to do something. A horse 'cranes' when it pulls up before a jump.

MRS LOVIBOND: Oh, Augustus, how happy you make me by saying that! So long as
you continue of that way of thinking, I never can be jealous!

LOVIBOND: And so long as you're not jealous, I shall continue of that way of
thinking. Yes, Clarinda, I've made a very pretty little fortune in Singapore. And
how we *will* enjoy it together! I've sowed my wild oats!

MRS LOVIBOND: Augustus, love!

LOVIBOND: Mine have been a very mild crop, I can assure you.

MRS LOVIBOND: And mine have never been sowed at all!

LOVIBOND: Then I value you all the more for it. If you've been faithful to the
memory of your Augustus, what will you be to the amiable reality? I see before
us a long vista of matrimonial felicity, dotted, at intervals, with little
Lovibonds. But, oh, gracious! (*suddenly crestfallen*) I'm forgetting the felon,
Downy, all this time – my infernal alias – who knows if the rest of my existence
mayn't be dragged out in a penal settlement!

MRS LOVIBOND: Oh, you surely must be able to prove an *alibi*?

LOVIBOND: I don't see my way to it. I've heard the strong points of the case against
me put forward so continually for the last three days by the indefatigable
Moleskin, that I begin to believe I'm safe to be convicted by any intelligent jury
of my countrymen.

MRS LOVIBOND: Let's hope you won't have an intelligent jury, dear.

LOVIBOND: I think that highly probable. Now, leave me to steel my mind for the
worst! So, kiss me quick and go, my honey.

MRS LOVIBOND: I'll do anything you bid me, dear. Goodbye, till you see me again.
(*Exit, to tent, right.*)

LOVIBOND: Now I call that a woman; and since she's so changed – she's an angel
– better than an angel! She hasn't any wings to fly away with; and she *has*
something to sit down upon! But, no; let me not indulge in idle levity. Let
me call up mental pictures of myself as a convict, or as a bleeding victim
under the bullet of Major McTurk. (*Goes towards the sea.*) Let me wander
by the sad sea wave and contemplate. There lies our noble vessel, all on one
side, like an ill roasted egg. What's that, I wonder, glittering on the sand?
Snuff-box, I hope; soap-dish, I fear (*picks up* SIR SOLOMON's *set of teeth*);
teeth, by jingo! Now, somebody must be uncommonly inconvenienced by the
loss of them. I'll be magnanimous – I'll advertise 'em. No; I won't do that,
because we're very short of provisions. Yes, I will. Here, Tottle, a pen, ink
and paper.

TOTTLE: Aye, aye, sir! (*Gets them, and puts them on box.*)

LOVIBOND: (*writes*) Lost – no! Found, a set of artificial teeth. They may be had by
owner applying to Augustus Lovibond. Confound it, though! I'm known among
the passengers in general as Downy. I suppose I must sign that hated name.
There! (*Fixes the paper on the spar by the side of the gong.*) And now to chew the
bitter cud of fancy till breakfast time. (*Exit.*)
(*Enter* COLEPEPPER.)

COLEPEPPER: So, that's off my mind. I've told Clavering the difficulty about my
accounts – and he cries off! All the better. How shall I break it to poor Mary,
though? She used to fancy this Clavering a hero. I'm glad, too, that I've had the
wisdom to break off with the pretty widow. What would she have thought if she

had found herself married to some eight lacs of debt to Government? And the poor little thing liked me – that was clear. But these *infernal* vouchers! No! as a man it is my duty to give up all idea of the widow.

(*Enter* MISS COLEPEPPER.)

MISS COLEPEPPER: Ah, papa, dear, I met Captain Clavering as I came along, looking so blank and gloomy. He merely bowed to me as he passed.

COLEPEPPER: My darling, are you brave enough to bear a great shock?

MISS COLEPEPPER: Any shock *you* can give me, I'm sure.

COLEPEPPER: Captain Clavering has proposed for you.

MISS COLEPEPPER: Oh, papa!

COLEPEPPER: As a man of honour, I felt it my duty to tell him the position of my unsettled accounts.

MISS COLEPEPPER: I know – those vouchers.

COLEPEPPER: I offered him an opportunity of renewing his offer.

MISS COLEPEPPER: (*eagerly*) And he –

COLEPEPPER: Nerve yourself, darling –

MISS COLEPEPPER: I am nerved, sir. Oh, speak! He renewed it?

COLEPEPPER: No; he declined.

MISS COLEPEPPER: Thank heaven! (*drawing a deep breath as if relieved*)

COLEPEPPER: What! you are not distressed to hear it?

MISS COLEPEPPER: Oh, you have taken such a load off my mind! I dreaded that offer – I feared you would favour Captain Clavering's suit. I once thought him all a man should be. You watched our intimacy while I lived in that delusion – I have learned better now.

COLEPEPPER: My dear girl! you've taken a load off *my* heart! With what a light heart I shall go to chop the wood to boil the soup! (*Exit.*)

MISS COLEPEPPER: Free at last! Free to let my heart follow the path it has been struggling so hard to take, yet dare not! He is here!

(*Enter* DEXTER.)

DEXTER: I've come to tell you it's nearly time for you to release Mrs Sebright. She has been managing her rebellious subject capitally. Don't be frightened at his ravings. For a delirious patient, or a kicking horse, there's nothing like a lady's hand.

MISS COLEPEPPER: Oh, I feel happy enough this morning to face a whole legion of lunatics!

DEXTER: Indeed! you do look so radiant!

MISS COLEPEPPER: If you knew what good reason I have. But are you not my best friend? Ought you not to know my happiness?

DEXTER: That's for you to answer – not me.

MISS COLEPEPPER: Yes; you shall know it. Captain Clavering has withdrawn his pretensions to my hand.

DEXTER: I'm glad to hear it – for your sake! He's a gambler – and all gamblers are mean, selfish, and unprincipled.

MISS COLEPEPPER: His conduct proves you have measured him aright. He

---

lac: 100,000 rupees.

withdrew because papa told him of the Government claims against him, on account of the vouchers he lost in the mutiny.

DEXTER: The vouchers! Then Sir Solomon's story was *not* a calumny. I really beg his pardon. But about these vouchers? If recovered, they would set your father straight with the Government?

MISS COLEPEPPER: Yes.

DEXTER: See, Miss Colepepper, what comes of people standing too much on their dignity! When I called on your father in Calcutta, it was mainly that I might restore to him a box of papers which I had recovered from the mutineers, and which I believe to have contained the very vouchers – the want of which may ruin him.

MISS COLEPEPPER: Is it possible? But where is that box now?

DEXTER: Under twenty fathoms of Red Sea water, and the stevedores only know how many tons of luggage. It went down aboard the Simoom.

MISS COLEPEPPER: Oh, hard chance! But we must face our fate without them. It will not be a harder one than I can bear. I am sure you have seen both papa and I can encounter hardship. (*Crosses.*) But I'm forgetting poor Mrs Sebright. Good-bye! Think of me as a free and happy woman. (*Exit.*)

DEXTER: Tottle! You remember a black box of mine?

TOTTLE: Yes, sir. I thought to myself – when I see you with that and a carpet-bag – well, that's the lightest lot of luggage ever came aboard a P. and O. boat, homeward bound.

DEXTER: Do you remember where it was stowed?

TOTTLE: In the after-hold, sir.

DEXTER: What water's over that part of her, do you think?

TOTTLE: About ten fathoms, sir.

DEXTER: All right. Look me out a dry suit of clothes, and bring them down to the beach when I hail. If anybody asks for me, say I shall be back soon. If perseverance and headers can do it, I may bring up these vouchers yet. (*Exit.*)
(*Enter* MRS SEBRIGHT.)

MRS SEBRIGHT: Tottle, where's the Doctor?

TOTTLE: Gone, ma'am. He'll be back soon.

MRS SEBRIGHT: I want to report my patient. (*Enter* LOVIBOND *in reflection.*) Mr Lovibond (*faces him and addresses him sharply*), stand and deliver!

LOVIBOND: Good gracious, Mrs Sebright, I was ruminating.

MRS SEBRIGHT: What a very vaccine occupation! But I'm very angry with you. You never came to the hospital, as you promised. I've had so much on these poor unassisted little hands.

LOVIBOND: (*kissing them*) Let me add the weight of that to their burdens.

MRS SEBRIGHT: You mustn't

LOVIBOND: Oh, yes I may – my wife says I may – and when a man's wife says he may – he may.

MRS SEBRIGHT: You wouldn't think, to look at them, that they have been holding down a raving maniac! Such a strong man, too!

---

vaccine: in this context, cowlike.

LOVIBOND: I should think you likelier to make madmen than to manage them!

MRS SEBRIGHT: Don't talk nonsense! Only think, my patient mixed your name up in his ravings. It was all a jumble of Lovibond and Downy – and how he was Downy and you weren't, and you were – and how he'd done the detective and a black leather bag – and bills, and money hidden away on the reef – and wanting me to let him go and dig it up and hide it again.

LOVIBOND: (*through this speech has betrayed the liveliest sign of emotion*) Describe your patient.

MRS SEBRIGHT: A plain man – about your size – in fact, a good deal like you altogether.

LOVIBOND: With a large scar on his right temple?

MRS SEBRIGHT: Yes; do you know him?

LOVIBOND: (*Sits down and begins taking off his boots*) Mrs Sebright, I want you – I want you to put on these boots.

MRS SEBRIGHT: No; I can't do that.

LOVIBOND: No; I don't mean that. May I trouble you to take these boots to Mr Moleskin, with my compliments, and beg him to put them on, and to walk down to the hospital and listen to the ravings of your patient, and act accordingly.

MRS SEBRIGHT: What do you mean?

LOVIBOND: Never *you* mind my meaning. Only carry my message. (*Crosses.*)

MRS SEBRIGHT: Is *he* mad, too?

LOVIBOND: No, he isn't; but he shortly will be, if you don't do what he asks you.

MRS SEBRIGHT: Well, I'll go; but –

LOVIBOND: But you want to be paid for your good news, I suppose? and there! (*Seizes her in his arms, and commences hugging and kissing her.*)

(*Enter* MRS LOVIBOND *from tent, right.*)

MRS LOVIBOND: Augustus!

LOVIBOND: I'm a child of impulse, Clarinda! You're *not* jealous?

MRS SEBRIGHT: No! but she has the common feelings of a woman! My dear Mrs Lovibond, I sympathise with you.

LOVIBOND: Now, don't stop to do that. Only carry my message. Insist on his putting on his boots, whether they fit him or not. Say it's to further the ends of justice, and he'll get into 'em if he grows a crop of corns for the rest of his life. I'll have another kiss if you don't go!

MRS SEBRIGHT: Mad – raving mad! another *coup-de-soleil*!

LOVIBOND: Nay, then! (*Rushes at her again.*)

MRS SEBRIGHT: Oh, Lord! (*Screams, and runs off.*)

MRS LOVIBOND: (*falling on a packing-case, and sobbing hysterically*) Augustus! if you're not insane, I am the most miserable of women.

LOVIBOND: On the contrary; I am sane, and you're the happiest of your sex! She's found the real Downy!

MRS LOVIBOND: Is it possible?

LOVIBOND: He must have shipped in the steerage under one of his many aliases.

MRS LOVIBOND: But how has he betrayed himself?

LOVIBOND: He's gone beside himself; and the insane half of him has split upon the other. Well, now I am free an' easy!

MRS LOVIBOND: That you certainly were, just now, with Mrs Sebright – you were kissing her.

LOVIBOND: Was I? Well, I'll kiss you and balance the books.

MRS LOVIBOND: Let us run and tell this good news to Mr Dexter.

LOVIBOND: By all means. (*Suddenly feels the sharp coral under his feet.*) Oh, I forgot I'd sent Moleskin my boots – I can't stir. This is the most nubbly spot on the island.

MRS LOVIBOND: Mr Dexter must be the first to congratulate us. Now, don't you move. (*Exit.*)

LOVIBOND: It's all very well to say don't move, I can't. This is the most nubbly spot on the island! This blessed news has confused my naturally lucid intellect. Let me reflect! If it wasn't for that fire-eating McTurk, my horizon would be all serene! Ha! somebody coming! McTurk! Oh! heavens! Let me conceal myself. He's capable of calling me out on the spot. (*Hides himself in tent, right.*)
(*Enter* McTURK.)

McTURK: It's no use – in spite of that brutal Tottle, I can't resist the temptation of the liquor – I must have some – beg, borrow, or steal.

DEXTER: (*without*) Tottle, ahoy!

TOTTLE: Muster Dexter a hailing. Here's his dry togs! Aye, aye, sir. (*Exit.*)

McTURK: Sentinel off his post! Now's my time! (*Steals up to store tent, rushes in, seizes a couple of bottles from store, and is retreating, when* LOVIBOND, *who has been watching him, jumps up and seizes him by the collar.*)

LOVIBOND: No, you don't! though you were ten times McTurk!

McTURK: Oh, mercy! mercy!

LOVIBOND: Drop those bottles, sir! I saw you take them.

McTURK: (*passionately*) I couldn't resist it – I feel so weak – I've such a craving for it! Oh, sir, let me go, and don't tell 'em, sir, don't; I shall be disgraced – cashiered. I'm a gentleman, sir – an officer.

LOVIBOND: Is this the fire-eater I was afraid of? Listen! I'm Mr Lovibond, the gentleman you had the impudence to challenge.

McTURK: Oh, I beg your pardon, sir! Only let me go, and I'll make any apology!

LOVIBOND: There! I forgive you! Put back that beer. For shame of you! to try and rob a poor man of his beer! (McTURK *makes an agonised gesture of entreaty, but quails under* LOVIBOND's *eye, and sneaks up to the tent, replacing the bottles, and exit.*) Poor, abject wretch! He deserves pity more than punishment.
(*Enter* MISS COLEPEPPER.)

MISS COLEPEPPER: Mr Lovibond, what is the meaning of the strange scene that has just passed in the hospital? Mrs Sebright came in with your friend.

LOVIBOND: I know – Moleskin! Then the boots *did* fit him?

MISS COLEPEPPER: They seized that poor lunatic – searched him – took him out of his bed to a neighbouring spot – to which, in the strength of his frenzy, he led the way faster than they could follow. I followed. They dug up something from the sand, and brought him back exhausted – but calmer.

LOVIBOND: (*dancing*) Huzza! huzza! huzza! Downy's done at last!
(*Enter* DEXTER, *with a small black box.*)

DEXTER: Miss Colepepper (*puts box in her hand*), your father's vouchers.

MISS COLEPEPPER: Mr Dexter, you have risked your life for them!

DEXTER: (*coolly*) Oh, dear! no. Only wetted a suit of clothes. I dive like an otter. Take them to your father.

MISS COLEPEPPER: Yes! but in your name. (*Crosses.*) How often are you to be our preserver? (*Exit.*)

DEXTER: It's time to serve out the rations. (*Goes up to tent, and strikes gong.*) Tottle!

        (*Enter* MRS LOVIBOND.)

MRS LOVIBOND: I can't find that dear Doctor.

        (*Enter* COLEPEPPER *and* MISS COLEPEPPER; *crosses to* DEXTER.)

LOVIBOND: (*down on* MRS LOVIBOND'*s side*) Because you would go to look for him. It's all right, Doctor! The real Downy's discovered! it's your mad patient!

COLEPEPPER: God bless you, sir! Mary has told me all. You have saved our good name!

DEXTER: Who was the fool who said, 'Chance ruled the world'?

        (*Enter* SMART, HARDISTY, MRS RABBITS, LIMPET, GRIMWOOD, AYAHS – *Passengers, male and female, Children, Lascars, Sailors, etc.*)

DEXTER: Now, then, ladies first. Come forward in the order of your messes. (SIR SOLOMON *gives a strange cry without.*) Hollo!

        (SIR SOLOMON *rushes in, wild and excited, his basket lid tumbling over his eyes, the handkerchief which bound his jaws waving in his hand; he gesticulates with vain efforts to speak articulately.*)

DEXTER: Another *coup-de-soleil!* Get him down – Put a quantity of ice on his head!

SIR SOLOMON: (*speaking with difficulty*) Not – sunstroke – steamer –

DEXTER: What does he say? Can anybody make it out?

LOVIBOND: (*rushing forward*) Oh, I know the physic he wants! Open your mouth. (*Produces the artificial teeth.* SIR SOLOMON *snatches the teeth and goes up and turns his back on to audience, and places them in his mouth and begins to speak volubly.*)

LIMPET: Master's minerals at last, I do declare! Well, I'm glad he got his teeth again, for they're not only *white* but they never ache!

SIR SOLOMON: As I have recently been unable to enjoy the pleasure of social intercourse, owing to the inconvenient circumstance –

DEXTER: Hang it, Sir Solomon, cut it short! You can't be allowed to pay out all your arrears at once.

SIR SOLOMON: Well, then, to cut it short, there is a steamer making for the reef.

ALL: Hurrah! hurrah! hurrah! (*Display the wildest signs of joy. All turn to face sea;* LOVIBOND *up a little;* DEXTER *seizes glass and looks out.* SMART *and* HARDISTY *do the same; the crowd gives way to them. Enter* MRS SEBRIGHT *and* MOLESKIN; *crosses to* LOVIBOND.)

MRS SEBRIGHT: What's that I hear? a steamer? (*Goes up to crowd.*)

MOLESKIN: (*to* LOVIBOND) I've got him! It's Downy, sure enough.

LOVIBOND: Of course it is! Now I'll trouble you for those boots.

'*Chance ruled the world*': Tacitus? ('chance rules all').

MOLESKIN: They're so damp I can't get 'em off. (*Exit* MOLESKIN.)

LOVIBOND: He's gone off with my boots!

MRS LOVIBOND: I'll follow him and make him give them up. (*Exit; returns immediately with one boot.*) I've only got one, dear.

DEXTER: Do you make her out, Captain?

SMART: The man-of-war steamer, 'Blazer'.

MRS SEBRIGHT: Jack's vessel! (*Jumps with joy, then half faints.* SIR SOLOMON *and* COLEPEPPER *rush up and support her; the passengers and others are watching the steamer;* DEXTER *and* MISS COLEPEPPER *converse apart.*)

COLEPEPPER: Give her air, sir, can't you?

SIR SOLOMON: Give her air yourself! I insist on my right of supporting this lady.

COLEPEPPER: On the contrary, sir; I claim that as my exclusive privilege.

SIR SOLOMON: By what title, sir?

COLEPEPPER: As her intended husband.

SIR SOLOMON: That, sir, is the foundation of my claim.

COLEPEPPER: Pooh, sir!

SIR SOLOMON: Pooh to you, sir!

COLEPEPPER: She revives – ask her?

SIR SOLOMON: My pretty Jane –

COLEPEPPER: My dearest Jane –

MRS SEBRIGHT: (*extricating herself*) Gentlemen, you mustn't.

SIR SOLOMON: You accepted my diamonds – accept me!

COLEPEPPER: Diamonds! (*contemptuously*) My shawl, and my hand with it!

MRS SEBRIGHT: Oh, Mr Dexter! (DEXTER *down centre*) I thought it was all right, and here it is as bad as ever again! Will you explain?

DEXTER: Not I – do your own explanations –

MRS SEBRIGHT: Then, gentlemen, I'm sorry I can't have either of you!

SIR SOLOMON: ⎱ You can't?
COLEPEPPER: ⎰ Why?

MRS SEBRIGHT: I've neither hand nor heart to give. I gave both, long ago, to Jack.

SIR SOLOMON: Jack?

COLEPEPPER: Who's Jack?

MISS COLEPEPPER: Mr Dexter has explained all to me – this lady is married already.

SIR SOLOMON: ⎱ Married!
COLEPEPPER: ⎰

SIR SOLOMON: But my diamond necklace, ma'am?

COLEPEPPER: Keep my shawl as a wedding-gift.

MRS SEBRIGHT: Thanks, Mr Colepepper! Sir Solomon, I'm sorry I haven't got your diamonds!

SIR SOLOMON: You haven't! Who has?

DEXTER: I have!

SIR SOLOMON: A light begins to dawn on me. (*to* COLEPEPPER) Of course, this is Jack? (*pointing to* DEXTER)

COLEPEPPER: Of course, it is! How blind I've been!

DEXTER: No, Mr Colepepper, my affections are better bestowed than on Jenny Sebright – good little soul as she is – for all her feather head!

COLEPEPPER: What! you are not Jack? And you don't love Mrs Sebright? and you do love somebody else? Why, then, it can only be – (*Looks at* MARY.)

DEXTER: It is, sir!

COLEPEPPER: Take her, my boy; you've won her fairly!

DEXTER: And, with heaven's help, as fairly will I wear her! (*embrace*)

SIR SOLOMON: But my diamonds, sir?

DEXTER: (*aside*) Which you accepted from the Nawaub of Ramshacklegur.

SIR SOLOMON: How do *you* know? I mean, how dare you insinuate?

DEXTER: I don't insinuate; I assert!

SIR SOLOMON: Only hold your tongue! I make a present of them to your wife!

DEXTER: My wife wears no diamonds less pure than her own bright eyes. I keep the necklace to return to its lawful owner. I owe the poor Nawaub some compensation for the physic I gave him.

COLEPEPPER: But, after all, we've never heard who Jack is! (*shout*)

SMART: A boat from the steamer!

        (*Enter* CAPTAIN SEBRIGHT, *Sailors, etc.*)

MRS SEBRIGHT: Jack! (*She rushes into* JACK SEBRIGHT'*s arms.*)

ALL: Hurrah! hurrah!

        TABLEAU

The alternative ending to Act II of *The Overland* Route, as in the LC's copy.

DEXTER: We must jump down, and pass 'em up by the skylight! Here goes, to save the women and children! (*Throws his coat off – jumps onto the combings of the skylight.*) Who volunteers? (*He jumps down into the skylight.*)

HARDISTY: Heads below! (*Follows* DEXTER.)

MR COLEPEPPER: (*struggling with his daughter*) Let me go too –

MISS COLEPEPPER: (*clinging to him*) Papa! Papa! – Captain Clavering! This is young men's work.

CLAVERING: I don't know the people – but of course, if you wish it. (*aside*) Horrid bore! (*Goes to hatchway and leaps down.*)

MRS SEBRIGHT: (*in terror*) Mr Colepepper!

MR COLEPEPPER: I've my own child to think of.

MRS SEBRIGHT: Sir Solomon!

SIR SOLOMON: I've my despatches – ask Limpet –

MRS SEBRIGHT: The selfish wretches! Oh dear – will nobody save me!

MRS LOVIBOND: (*to* MAJOR McTURK) Hector! (*Tries to cling to him.*)

MRS RABBITS: (*clinging to him*) For self and infants!

McTURK: (*shaking both off*) Hands off! – Fifty pounds for a place in the first boat –

MRS LOVIBOND: Augustus! You'll save me. (*Crosses to him. Enter* LOVIBOND *and* MOLESKIN *by companion.* MOLESKIN *handcuffing his own arm to* LOVIBOND'*s.*)

MRS RABBITS: And *me*! and mine! (*proffering her babies*)

LOVIBOND: What are you about? I can't swim in handcuffs –

MOLESKIN: You and me sinks or swims together!

        TABLEAU

Illustrated London News engraving of a scene from *The Ticket-of-Leave Man*

THE TICKET-OF-LEAVE MAN

A Drama in Four Acts

First produced at the Olympic Theatre, London on Wednesday, 27 May 1863, with the following cast:

The scenery by and under the direction of Mr Telbin

ROBERT BRIERLY, a Lancashire Lad	Mr H. Neville
JAMES DALTON, alias Downey, alias The Tiger	Mr Atkins
HAWKSHAW, a detective	Mr Horace Wigan
MELTER MOSS	Mr G. Vincent
GREEN JONES	Mr R. Soutar
MR GIBSON, a Bill broker	Mr Maclean
SAM WILLOUGHBY	Miss Raynham
MALTBY	Mr H. Cooper
BURTON	Mr Franks
SHARPE	
MAY EDWARDS	Miss Kate Saville
EMILY ST EVREMOND	Miss Hughes
MRS WILLOUGHBY	Mrs Stephens

Guests, navvies, etc.

Act I

SCENE: *The Bellevue Tea Gardens, in the south-west suburbs of London. Summer evening. Front of the tavern with ornamental verandah, up Left; arbours along the stage, Right and Left, with tables and seats; trees, shrubs, statues, etc. at the back, with ornamental orchestra and concert room.*

> PARTIES, *male and female, seated at the different tables, Right and Left;* WAITERS *serving refreshments. Music heard off. As the curtain rises the* PARTIES *are heard giving orders;* MALTBY *moving about with an eye to the* GUESTS, WAITERS, *etc.; two* DETECTIVES *at the table, L.C.*

1ST PARTY: Three hots with –

WAITER: (*serving another table*) Yes, sir. Brandy and Soda for you, sir.

2ND PARTY: Tea for four – shrimps and a muffin.

WAITER: Coming! (*serving another* PARTY) Pot of half-and-half for you, sir. (*at* DETECTIVES' *table*) Two sherry negus two shillings. (*Takes money.*)

MALTBY: (*moving about*) Now, James, three teas and a muffin in 5. Jackson, money in 6. (*to a* GUEST) Uncommon thirsty weather, sir, uncommon. (*to another* PARTY) If I might recommend a cobbler for the lady, sir, delicious refreshment for July. Now, James, look after them brandies in 3. (*Moves off.*)

> (*Enter* HAWKSHAW. *He strolls carelessly to the* DETECTIVES' *table, then in an undertone and without looking at them* –)

HAWKSHAW: Report.

1ST DETECTIVE: (*in same tone and without looking at* HAWKSHAW) All right.

HAWKSHAW: (*same tone*) Here's old Moss. Keep an eye on him. (*Strolls off.*)

> (*Enter* MOSS, *sits at table.*)

MOSS: (*to the* WAITER) Good evening, James. Four penn'orth of brandy, if you please, James, and a little peppermint. (*Coughs, and looks around.*) Tiger not here yet. (*Bell rings.*)

MALTBY: The concert bell, ladies and gentlemen – in the Rotunda. (*Pointing to the concert room.*) The first talent – selections from the best classical music, and original nigger melodists. This way.

> (*Exit* MALTBY, *towards concert room. Most of the* PARTIES *move off, leaving* DETECTIVES *and a* GUEST *here and there. Enter* DALTON.)

MOSS: (*stirring and sipping his brandy and peppermint*) Warm and comfortable. Tiger ought to be here before this. (*As he stirs his eye falls on the spoon; he takes it up: weighs it in his fingers.*) Uncommon neat article – might take in a good many people – plated, though, plated.

> (*While* MOSS *is looking at the spoon,* DALTON *takes his seat at* MOSS's *table, unobserved by him.*)

DALTON: Not worth flimping, eh?

MOSS: (*starting, but not recognizing him*) Eh, did you speak to me, sir?

---

cobbler: a drink made from wine and sugar, etc.
flimping: stealing.

DALTON: What, don't twig me? Then it is a good get up. (*He lifts his hat, and gives him a peculiar look.*) Eh, Melter?

MOSS: What, Tiger!

DALTON: Stow that. There's no Tigers here. My name's Downy; you mind that John Downy, from Rotherham, jobber, and general dealer.

MALTBY: (*coming down to* DALTON) Now sir, what can I have the pleasure of ordering for you, sir?

DALTON: My good friend, Mr Moss here, insists on standing a bottle of sherry.

MOSS: (*in alarm*) No, no!

DALTON: What, you will make it champagne? Very well, I'm not proud. (*to* MALTBY) I like it dry, mind, and none of your home-brewed; I buy my rhubarb-juice at the green-grocer's.

(*Exit* MALTBY.)

MOSS: Come, Ti – (DALTON *gives him a look, which stops him.*) A joke's a joke. But a bottle of real champagne at seven and six –

DALTON: That's serious, eh? Well, I've taken a serious turn, always do when it's low tide here. (*pointing to his pocket*)

MOSS: Down on your luck, eh?

DALTON: (*shrugs his shoulders*) The crushers are getting to know too much; then there's the Nailer's been after me.

MOSS: What, Hawkshaw, the 'cutest detective in the force?

DALTON: He's taken his oath on the Bow Street Office testament to be square with me for that Peckham job – (*hesitates*)

MOSS: Ah!

DALTON: When I spoiled his mate. (*Shrugs his shoulders.*)

MOSS: (*shaking his head*) Ah, I always said that life-preserver of yours would be doing somebody a mischief.

(*Re-enter* MALTBY, *with champagne and glasses.*)

DALTON: Hush, here's the tipple.

MALTBY: (*uncorking and pouring out*) And though I say it, there ain't a better bottle opened at Buckingham Palace. There's a colour – there's a bouquet. Seven and six, Mr Moss.

MOSS: (*grumbling as he pays*) There ought to be at the price.

MALTBY: Now Jackson, take orders in the Rotunda. (*Exit* MALTBY.)

DALTON: (*drinking*) Ah, tidy swizzle!

MOSS: And so you're keeping dark, eh?

DALTON: Yes, pottering about on the sneak, flimping or smashing a little when I get the chance; but the Nailer's too hard for me. There's no picking up a gentlemanly livelihood. Hang me, if I haven't often thought of turning respectable.

MOSS: No, no; it ain't so bad as that yet. (*looking around, and speaking cautiously*) Now, I have the beautifullest lot of Bank of England flimsies that ever came out of Birmingham. It's the safest paper to work, and you should have it cheap, dirt cheap, and credit till you'd planted it.

---

crushers: policemen.
smashing: passing counterfeit money.

DALTON: And how about lagging? If I'm nailed it's a lifer.

MOSS: Bless you, I wouldn't have you chance it; but in the high society you keep, you could surely pick up a flat to put off the paper.

DALTON: I've the very man. I gave him an appointment here, for this evening.

MOSS: Did you though! How pat things come about! Who is he?

DALTON: A Lancashire lad; an only son, he tells me. The old folks spoiled him as long as they lived, left him a few hundreds, and now he's got the collar over his head, and is kicking 'em down, seeing life. (*Laughs.*) And life in London ain't to be seen without paying at the doors, eh, Melter?

MOSS: Ha, ha, ha! and you're selling him the bill of the play.

DALTON: I'm putting him up to a thing or two – cards, skittles, billiards, sporting houses, sparring houses, night houses, casinos – every short cut to the devil and the bottom of a flat's purse. He's as green as a leek, and as soft as new cheese, no vice, steady to ride or drive, and runs in a snaffle. (*Rises.*)

MOSS: (*rising*) Oh, beautiful, beautiful! (*Rubs his hands.*) It would be a sin to drop such a beautiful milch cow!

DALTON: Do you think I will, if he had any milk left?

MOSS: I say, suppose we pumped him in partnership?

DALTON: Thankyou, I know *your* partnership articles, *me* all the kicks, and *you* all the half-pence. But if I can work him to plant a lot of these flimsies of yours, I don't mind; remember, though, I won't go higher than fifteen bob for a fiver.

MOSS: What, only fifteen bob, and such beauties, too, they'd take in the Bank chairman – fifteen! I'd better chance it myself! Only fifteen – it's robbery.

DALTON: Take it or leave it. (*Takes up the newspaper, and sits at table.*)

MOSS: I must take a turn and think it over. (*Going, returns.*) I'll bring you the flimsies. Come, you'll allow me a pound?

DALTON: Bid me down again, and I stand on ten shillings – now you know. It's like it or lump it. (*He returns to his paper.*)

MOSS: (*holding up his hands*) Oh dear, oh dear! What it is to deal with people that have no consciences! (*Exit.*)

BRIERLY: (*heard off*) A bottle of champagne, lad, and half a dozen Cabanas – and look sharp!

DALTON: (*looking up from paper*) Here's my pigeon!

        (*Enter* BRIERLY. *He looks feverish and dishevelled, and is dressed in an exaggerated sporting style.*)

DALTON: (*laying the paper down*) Ah, Bob, up to time as usual!

BRIERLY: Aye, nobody shall say Bob Brierly craned while he could keep't going. (WAITER *brings champagne and cigars.*) Here – yo' – a clean glass for my friend.

DALTON: (*pointing to* MOSS's *bottle*) I've had my whack already.

BRIERLY: Nay lad, you can find room for another glass. (WAITER *brings another glass –* BRIERLY *pours out wine.*)

---

lagging: being convicted.
pick up a flat: find a fool (to pass the counterfeit bank notes).
fifteen bob: fifteen shillings (75 pence).
craned: to pull up before a jump.

BRIERLY: It puts heart into a chap! (*Drinks eagerly.*) I've nearly lived on't this fortnight past.

DALTON: (*stops his hand*) Take care, Bob, or we shall have you in the doctor's hands.

BRIERLY: Doctor? Nay; I'm as game as a pebble and as stell as a tree! (*Fills DALTON's glass with a shaking hand.*) Curse the glass! Here – drink, man, drink. I can't abear drinking single-handed. I like company – always did. (*looking round uneasily*) And now, I don't know how it is – (*nervously looking down near the table*) No, no, it's nothing! Here, have a weed.

DALTON: I'll take a light from you. (*As DALTON lights his cigar at BRIERLY's the shaking of BRIERLY's hand becomes more apparent.*) Come, come, Master Bob, you're getting shaky – this won't do.

BRIERLY: It's that waking – waking. If I could only sleep. (*earnestly*) Oh, man – can't you help a chap to a good night's rest? I used to sleep like a top down at Glossop. But in this great big place, since I've been enjoying myself, seeing life – I don't know – (*passing his hand across his eyes*) I don't know how it is – I get no rest – and when I do, it's worse than none – there's great black crawling things about me. (*Gulps down a glass of wine.*) I say, Downy; do you know how a chap feels when he's going mad?

DALTON: I know the symptoms of *del.trem.* pretty well – sit down, sit down. First and foremost (*Puts him a chair.*) I prescribe a devilled biscuit – I'll doctor one for you. (*calling*) Waiter! a plate of biscuits, toasted hot – butter and cayenne. (BRIERLY *hides his head in his hands – aside, looking at him contemptuously.*) The horrors! ah, he's seen too much of life lately – Bob, are you in cash?

BRIERLY: Welly cleaned out – I've written to the lawyer-chap, down at Glossop – him that's got all my property to manage, yo' know – for more brass.

DALTON: (*aside*) Now if I'd a few of Moss's fivers – here's a chance. You must bank with me till the brass comes. Delighted to lend you a sovereign – five – ten – as much as you want.

(*Enter* MOSS.)

BRIERLY: Nay, will yo' though? That's friendly of you. Here's luck and sink the expense! (*He pours out the wine.*)

MOSS: (*aside to* DALTON) I've got the flimsies – I'll do it at seven ten.

DALTON: (*aside*) Fork over.

MOSS: (*aside, giving him a roll of notes*) There's fifty to begin with – twenty, a tenner, and four fives. Plant the big 'un first.

(*Enter* HAWKSHAW, *meets* MOSS *at back of chair – approaches the table where the* DETECTIVES *are. One of them nods towards* MOSS *and* DALTON.)

MOSS: Good evening, gentlemen; you'll find my friend, Mr Downy, excellent company, sir. Very improving for a young man from the country. (*Aside.*) That's an honestly earned seven-pun-ten! (*Exit* MOSS.)

(WAITER *brings biscuits and cayenne.*

DALTON: Now for your devil, Master Bob. (*As he prepares the biscuit,*

---

as game as a bebble . . . as stell as a tree: full of spirit and set and sturdy as a tree.
welly: well-nigh.

HAWKSHAW *approaches the table and takes up the paper which* DALTON *has put down.* DALTON *pushes the biscuit across to* BRIERLY.) Try that?

HAWKSHAW: Beg pardon, sir, but if the paper's not in hand.

DALTON: (*rudely, and pocketing the notes hastily*) Eh – sir?

HAWKSHAW: (*sitting down coolly at the table and unfolding the paper*) Papers very dull lately, don't you think so, sir?

DALTON: (*assuming a country dialect*) I never trouble 'em much, sir, except for the Smithfield Market List, in the way of business.

HAWKSHAW: Ah, much my own case. They put a fellow up to the dodges of the town, though; for instance, these cases of bad notes offered at the Bank lately. (*watching him close*)

DALTON: I never took a bad note in my life.

HAWKSHAW: You've been lucky – in the Smithfield line, too, I think you said. In the jobbing way, may I ask, sir, or in the breeding?

DALTON: Sometimes one, and sometimes t'other – always ready to turn the nimble shilling.

HAWKSHAW: My own rule.

DALTON: May I ask your business?

HAWKSHAW: The fancy iron trade. My principle is to get as much of my stock on other people's hands as I can. From the country, I think?

DALTON: Yes, Yorkshire.

HAWKSHAW: Ah! I'm Durham myself; and this young gent?

BRIERLY: What's that to you? (*pushing away the biscuit*) It's no use – I can't swallow a morsel.

HAWKSHAW: From Lancashire, I see; why; we are quite neighbours when we are at home – and neighbours ought to be neighbourly in this overgrown city, so I hope you'll allow me to stand treat – give it a name, gentlemen.

DALTON: (*roughly*) Thank you, I never drink with strangers.

BRIERLY: They've a saying down in Glossop, where I come from, 'If you want a welcome, wait to be axed'.

HAWKSHAW: Ah, quite right to be cautious about the company you keep, young man.

BRIERLY: It's a way we have where I come from, and another way we have, we don't like folks to look at us over close serious-like, as you're doing now.

HAWKSHAW: I beg your pardon. It's an old trick of mine. It's what book-learned folks call a physiognomist, one that reads characters in people's faces.

BRIERLY: I don't chose my face should be read in –

HAWKSHAW: That's a pity. I like the titlepage.

BRIERLY: Do ye though? Well now, it's more than I can say o' yours.

HAWKSHAW: Sorry for it. Perhaps I could give you a bit of good advice –

BRIERLY: Thank ye! I'm not in the way o' takin' good advice.

HAWKSHAW: Well, don't take bad; and you won't easy find a worse adviser than your thieving companion here.

---

axed: dialect form of 'asked'.

DALTON: (*firing up*) Eh? what do you mean by that?

HAWKSHAW: Not you, sir. (*tapping the champagne bottle*) This gentleman here. He robs people of their brains – their digestion – and their conscience – to say nothing of their money. But since you won't allow me to stand anything –

DALTON: And wish to keep ourselves to ourselves.

BRIERLY: And think your room a deal better than your company – meanin' no offence, you know.

HAWKSHAW: (*rises*) Not in the least. If gentlemen can't please themselves in a public establishment! I'll wish you a very good evening. (*aside*) A plant; I'll keep an eye on 'em!

DALTON: (*aside*) I don't half like the look of that fellow. There's something about his eye – I must make out if Moss knows him. Bob, will you excuse me for five minutes?

BRIERLY: Don't be long – I can't abear my own comapany.

DALTON: I've only a word to say to a customer. (*Exit.*)

> (HAWKSHAW *reappears, watches* DALTON *off and follows him after a moment's interval.*)

BRIERLY: And I'll try to sleep till he comes back. If I could only sleep without dreaming! I never close my eyes but I'm back at Glossop wi' the old folks at home – 't mother fettlin' about me, as she used when I was a brat, and father stroking my head, and callin' me his bonny boy – noa, noa – I mustn't think o' them – not here – or I shall go mad. (*sinking his head in his hands, and sobbing*)

> (*Music. Other* GUESTS *come in, and sit at other tables.*) (*Enter* MALTBY.)

MALTBY: Now then James! Jackson, take orders. Interval of ten minutes allowed for refreshment. Give your orders, gents, give your orders. The nigger melodists will shortly commence their unrivalled entertainment, preliminary to the orchestral selection from Beethoven's Pastoral Symphony.

> (*Enter* MAY EDWARDS *with her guitar. The* WAITERS *move about bringing refreshments to tables.*)

MAY: If they'll only let me sing tonight. (*tuning guitar*)

MALTBY: Halloa, halloa! what's this? Oh, it's you, is it, Edwards! Come, I'm glad to see you're about again, but I can't have you cadging here.

MAY: Oh, Mr Maltby, if you'll only allow me to try one song, and go round after it, I'll stop as soon as ever they ring up.

MALTBY: Well, well, you was always a well-behaved girl, so for once in a way –

MAY: Oh, thank you, thank you, and if you should have an opening for me, in the room, sir, when I'm quite strong again –

MALTBY: No chance of it, we're chuck full – a glut of talent; but if I *should* be able to find room for you in the chorus, and to double Miss Plantagenet when she's in the tantrums, ten shillings a week, and find your own wardrobe, you know – I'm not the man to shrink from a generous action. Now then, Jackson, money in 4. (*Exit* MALTBY.)

---

fettlin': fussing.

(MAY *sings; after her song she goes round the tables; all repulse her.*)

1ST PARTY: The concert's quite enough without catterwauling between the acts.

2ND PARTY: We've no small change, miss. Waiter! bottle pale sherry!

3RD PARTY: Be off!

4TH PARTY: Now then, what's the girl gaping at? Can't you take an answer!

MAY: (*to* BRIERLY) Please sir –

BRIERLY: Be off with thee, lass, I'm in no mood for music.

MAY: (*suppressing her tears*) Not a penny!

BRIERLY: Stop, lass; (*Feels in his pocket.*) not a farden. Where's Downy? Come here. What'st crying at?

MAY: I've not taken anything today, and I've not been well lately. (*She turns faint and grasps a seat to support herself.*)

BRIERLY: (*rising*) Poor thing; here, sit thee down; why thee looks welly clemmed. Try and eat a bit. (*He gives her a biscuit.*)

MAY: Thank you, sir, you're very kind. (*She tries to swallow but cannot.*) If I had a drink of water?

BRIERLY: Wather? Nay, a sup o' this will hearten thee up. (*Tries to give her wine from his bottle.*) Not a drop! (*He looks around and sees* WAITER *bringing a decanter of sherry.*) Here, that'll do. (*Takes decanter.*)

WAITER: Beg pardon sir, it's for No. 1.

BRIERLY: I'se No. 1.

1ST PARTY: Hollo, sir! that's my sherry.

BRIERLY: No, it's mine.

1ST PARTY: I'll let you know. (*He rises and turns up his cuffs;* BRIERLY *looks at him.*) No, I'll see the landlord. (*Exit* 1ST PARTY.)

BRIERLY: There, lass. Sup that.

MAY: (*drinks*) It's wine.

MAY sings: the words of the song reproduced below are printed in the edition of the play published in Lacy, vol. 59. The words are translated from the German of Uhland, and the music was composed by Mrs Tom Taylor.

> Where daisies blow and waters glide,
> My lonely cottage stands beside
> The willowy brook that flows along
> Its rushy bank with murmuring song.
> And near the door there grows a tree,
> So thick that scarce the cot you see,
> And screens and shades my still retreat
> From Winter's cold and Summer's heat;
> And there, at eve, a nightingale
> Will sit concealed and tell its tale –
> So sweet, that all who wander by
> Are fain to stop, and listen nigh.
> Thou gentle child, with golden hair,
> Whom long I've watched with love and care,
> The wind is cold, and rough for thee,
> Say wilt thou come and dwell with me?

farden: farthing.

welly clemmed: well-nigh starved.

BRIERLY: Sup it up.

MAY: It makes me so warm.

BRIERLY: It'll put some heart 'i thee. Sup again, thou'lt tune thy pipes like a mavis on that. Now try and eat a bit.

MAY: Oh, sir, you're too good.

BRIERLY: Good? me! nay –

(*Enter* MALTBY, *followed by* 1ST PARTY.)

MALTBY: (*soothingly*) Merely a lark, depend upon it. The gentleman will apologize. (*to* BRIERLY) The gent who ordered that bottle of sherry –

BRIERLY: Let him order another, I'll pay for it.

MALTBY: The gent can't say fairer. (*Calls.*) Bottle of sherry, Jackson; seven and six, sir.

BRIERLY: Here. (*Feels in his pockets.*) Eh? score it down.

MALTBY: Your name may be Bob Brierly, sir, or Bob Anybody, sir, but when people take wine in this establishment, sir – especially other party's wine – they pay for it.

(*Enter* DALTON, *behind.*)

BRIERLY: A tell yo' – I'll pay as soon as my friend comes back.

MALTBY: Oh, your friend! A regular case of bilk –

BRIERLY: Now yo' take care.

(*Firing up; the* PARTIES *gather round from tables.*)

MAY: (*frightened*) Oh please, sir, please Mr Maltby.

1ST PARTY: It's too bad.

2ND PARTY: Why can't you pay the man?

3RD PARTY: Police!

DALTON: (*coming forward*) Halloa, what's all this?

BRIERLY: (*seizing him*) Here, Downy, you lend me a sovereign to pay this chap.

DALTON: Sorry, I haven't change, but we'll manage it directly. (*to* MALTBY) It's all right. I'll be bail for my friend here.

MALTBY: Your word's quite enough, sir. Any friend of Mr Moss –

DALTON: Come, Bob, don't be a fool, take a turn and cool yourself. (*Drawing him off; aside.*) Now to plant the big 'un.

MALTBY: (*to* GUESTS) Sorry for this disturbance, gents, quite out of keeping with the character of my establishment. (*Bell – music, piano.*) But the concert is about to recommence; that way, gents, to the Rotunda. (GUESTS *go off – fiercely to* MAY.) This is all along of your cadging, Edwards, sitting down to drink with a promiscuous party.

MAY: Oh, I'm so sorry – he never thought – it was all his kindness.

MALTBY: (*sneeringly*) Kindness! much kindness he'd have showed you, if you'd been old and ugly. You ought to be ashamed of yourself.

MAY: (*indignantly*) You ought to be ashamed of yourself! It is cruel in you to insult a helpless and friendless girl like me.

MALTBY: Insult! ho, ho, ha, here's a lark! A half-starved street-singer cheeking me in my own establishment! You'd better apply for an engagement, *you* had, on

---

like a mavis: a song-thrush.

the first vacancy. (*looking off*) Hollo, what's that? carriage company! Heavy swells on the lark, white ties and pink bonnets! Show the ladies and gentlemen to the Rotunda, Jackson. (*Exit.*)

MAY: (*sinks down at one of the tables*) I'm foolish to be angry, my bread depends on such as he. Oh, if only I could get away from this weary work. Poor Mother! She knew the misery of the street-singer's life – Father brought her to it. And when she died, her last grief was that she was leaving me nothing but this guitar, and the songs she taught me. Oh, if only some kind lady would take me in, give me a place, or let me work for her. I'm quick at my needle; but who'd take me, a vagabond, without a friend to speak for me? I'm all alone in the world now. It's strange how people's life is made for 'em. I see so many girls, nicely dressed, well off, with parents to love and care for 'em, and everything about them soft and smooth and easy. Nay, there's many not older than me with husbands and children! Oh, it must be like heaven. I can't bear it sometimes to see them and then think what I am, and what's before me. (*Puts her hand to her face.*) I'm a silly girl: it's all because I'm so weak from the fever. There's nothing like keeping a good heart. How good he was to me; it was all through me he got into trouble; but I mustn't think of him. Ah, there's a pleasant looking party yonder. Come along old friend, you've to earn my supper yet. (*Takes her guitar and exit.*)

(*Enter* GREEN JONES *and* EMILY ST EVREMOND. *He wears evening costume, black; white tie, Gibus hat, etc.; she is gaily dressed, pink bonnet etc.*)

GREEN: Excuse me, Emily! Anything but the Rotunda! Let's leave the giddy throng – the halls – the halls of dazzling light. If your mama likes music let her enjoy it without interruption from our conversation.

EMILY: I'm sure the music's very nice, Mr Jones.

GREEN: *Mr Jones*, Miss St Evremond! What have I done to be kept at arm's length by that chevaux de frise of a mister? Was it for this that I thawed the thick-ribbed ice of Mrs Traddles?

EMILY: Thick-ribbed ain't a proper word to use to any lady, and I tell you my ma's name ain't Traddles, Mr Jones; it's the same as mine – St Evremond; she's changed it at my wish. People may change their names nowadays. *The Times* says so.

GREEN: I beg pardon of your stern parient, Mrs St Evremond, late Traddles; but I repeat, was it to be called *Mister* Jones that I treated Mrs St E. and her chyild to the Star and Garter; and her chyild without Mrs St E. to the Trafalgar, where from the moonlit balcony that overhung the fragrant river, we watched together the sunset over the Isle of Dogs?

EMILY: And very wrong it was of me to go to that whitebait dinner without ma; and preciously she blew me up about it, though I told her you couldn't have treated me with more respect if I'd been a countess instead of a coryphée.

Gibus hat: opera hat.
chevaux de frise: a *cheval-de-frise* was a barrier, formed of timber and spikes, designed to defend a passage.
coryphée: dancer in the ballet.

GREEN: Emily, you only did me justice. My intentions are honourable. If you are in
the ballet, that's no reason you shouldn't be a dear, good girl. You've been a
trump of a daughter; I don't see why you shouldn't turn out a trump of a wife.
Emily, accept my hand.
EMILY: Nonsense, Green, you don't mean it.
GREEN: I'm perfectly serious. My hand and my heart, my fortune and my future.
Don't stare, Emily. It's as true as that my name is Green. I'm quite in earnest – I
am indeed.
EMILY: Oh! Green, dear, I'm in such agitation.
GREEN: We will spend a rosy existence. You like life, and I flatter myself I
understand it.
EMILY: And don't I? I call this life – the music and the company, and the singing and
the trapeze. I thought the man must break his neck. It was beautiful.
GREEN: Yes, I like to associate with all classes. 'Survey mankind', you know, Emily
– 'from China' – to earthenware. So when Charley Punter proposed a night at
the tea gardens, I sank the swell; and here I am with my Emily and her mama.
Charley didn't seem to see the parient; but 'Propriety, Charley my boy', I said,
and he submitted with a sigh. And now what will you have?
        (*Enter* MAY. *She begins to sing.*)
Oh, anything but that. Now do oblige me by shutting up, that's a good girl.
EMILY: No, no, poor thing. Let her sing; she has a sweet voice.
GREEN: Flat, decidedly.
EMILY: (*contemptuously*) You're another. Give me a half a crown for her.
GREEN: (*gives one; she asks by gesture for another*) Two? Such a bore. I shall have to
change a note at the bar.
EMILY: You'll have to change a good many notes when we are married. (*to* MAY)
Come along, you shall have both half crowns.
        (*Exeunt* GREEN, JONES *and* EMILY. *As* MAY *is following, enter*
        BRIERLY.)
BRIERLY: Downy not here? He said I was to bring t'brass to our table.
MAY: 'Tis he! (*joyously*) Oh, sir, I'm so sorry –
BRIERLY: Why, it's t'singin' lass. I say, have you seen my friend?
MAY: No, sir.
BRIERLY: And where's t'landlord? Here's that'll make him civil enough. (*Shows a
number of sovereigns in his hand.*)
MAY: Oh, what a lot of money!
BRIERLY: Brass for a twenty pound note. I got it changed at t'cigar shop down
t'road. He's a good 'un is Downy – lends me whatever I want. Here – yo' –
landlord. Hoy!
        (*Enter* MALTBY.)
MALTBY: Coming! Coming! Oh, it's you.
BRIERLY: (*flinging a half sovereign to* MALTBY). There; seven and six is for t'wine

---

'*Survey mankind*' . . . '*from China*': Green is quoting from the opening couplet of Dr Johnson's
poem 'The Vanity of Human Wishes':
    Let observation, with extensive view,
    Survey mankind from China to Peru.

and t'other half crowns for t'thrashin' I owe you. (*Approaches him threateningly*.)

MALTBY: (*pocketing the money and retreating*) Take care – I'll teach you to insult a respectable licensed victualler, (*To* MAY, *who tries to calm* BRIERLY.) and you too, you tramp; I'll have you locked up for annoying my customers. How do I know my spoons are safe?

BRIERLY: Thou cur! (*He breaks away from* MAY *and makes a rush at* MALTBY, *who escapes, crying* 'Police!')

MAY: I can't bear you should trouble for me, indeed sir. (*concealing her tears*)

BRIERLY: Nay, never heed that muck-worm. Come, dry thine eyes. Thou's too soft for this life o' thine.

MAY: (*apologetically*) It's the fever, I think, sir – I usen't to mind unkind looks and words much once.

BRIERLY: Here, take this, (*Puts money into her hand*.) and stay thee quiet at home till thou'st i' fettle again.

MAY: Two sovereigns! oh, sir! (*Cries*.)

BRIERLY: Nay, thou'lt make better use o' t' brass than me. What, cryin' again! come, come, never heed that old brute: hard words break no bones you know.

MAY: It's not *his* hard words I'm crying for now, sir.

BRIERLY: What then?

MAY: *Your* kind ones – they're harder to bear – they sound so strange to me.

BRIERLY: Poor thing! heaven help thee – thou mindest me of a sister I lost; she'd eyes like thine, and hair, and much t' same voice, nobbut she favert redder i' t' face, and spoke broader. I'd be glad whiles to have a nice gradely lass like you to talk to.

MAY: But where I live, sir, it's a very poor place, and I'm by myself, and –

BRIERLY: (*hesitates*) No, no – you're right – I couldn't come there, but I'm loth to lose sight of yo' too.

(*Enter* DALTON *hastily*.)

DALTON: Brierly! The change for the note?

BRIERLY: Here't is – I've borrowed five o' the twenty.

DALTON: All right, now let's be off – I've a cab outside.

BRIERLY: (*to* MAY) Mind, if you want a friend, write to Bob Brierly at the Lancashire Arms, Air Street; yo'll not forget.

MAY: Never – I'll set it down (*aside*) in my heart!

DALTON: Come!

BRIERLY: And yo', tell me your name – will yo'?

MAY: May Edwards.

DALTON: Confound your billing and cooing – come!

(*As* BRIERLY *follows* DALTON, HAWKSHAW *and two of the* DETECTIVES *appear*.)

HAWKSHAW: You're wanted.

DALTON: (*aside*) The crushers! Run, Bob!

(*Music*. DALTON *attempts to escape*. DETECTIVES *detain*

---

nobbut she favert: except that she was.

BRIERLY, HAWKSHAW *seizes* DALTON. *In the scuffle* DALTON'S *hat and wig are knocked off.*)

HAWKSHAW: I know you, James Dalton!

DALTON: (*starting*) Ah!

HAWKSHAW: Remember the Peckham job.

DALTON: The Nailer! Hit out, Bob!

>(BRIERLY *has been wrestling with the two* DETECTIVES; *as* DALTON *speaks he knocks one down.*)

BRIERLY: I have. Some o' them garottin' chaps!

MAY: Help! help! (*wringing her hands*)

>(*A fierce struggle,* DALTON *escapes from* HAWKSHAW *and throws him.* HAWKSHAW *draws a pistol,* DALTON *strikes him down with a life-preserver and makes his escape through the trees.* BRIERLY *is overpowered and handcuffed.*

DETECTIVE: Look after the serjeant. This chap's all safe.

BRIERLY: (*struggling*) Let me go – What do ye mean?

DETECTIVE: That we've nailed one of the cutest smashers in London, that's all.

BRIERLY: Smashers! – what's that?

DETECTIVE: Of course *you* don't know. You're uncommon innocent you are.

MAY: Passing bad money! Oh, who would have thought it of him!

BRIERLY: And do *you* think it of me?

MAY: Oh no. I will not believe it. Let him go – he is innocent – I know he is innocent.

>(*One of the detectives has raised up* HAWKSHAW.)

HAWKSHAW: (*faintly*) Dalton!

DETECTIVE: Escaped!

HAWKSHAW: Curse him – but I'll have him yet –

>TABLEAU

Act II

SCENE: *The room occupied by* MAY EDWARDS *in* MRS WILLOUGHBY'*s house, humbly but neatly furnished; flowers in the window; a work-table; stool; door communicating with her bedroom, Right; door leading to the staircase, Left; guitar hanging against wall; needlework on the table.*

>MAY *discovered with a birdcage on the table, arranging a piece of sugar and groundsel between the bars; sofa, Right; chiffonier, Left; American clock, etc.*

MAY: There, Goldie, I must give *you* your breakfast, though I don't care a bit for my own. Ah! you find singing a better trade than I did, you little rogue. I'm sure I shall have a letter from Robert this morning. I've all his letters here. (*Takes out a packet from her work-box.*) How he has improved in his handwriting since the first. (*opening letter*) That's more than three years back. Oh, what an old woman I'm getting! It's no use denying it, Goldie. If you'll be quiet, like a good, well-bred canary, I'll read you Robert's last letter. 'Portland, February 25th, 1860. My own dearest May – (*kissing it*) As the last year keeps slipping away, I think more and more of our happy meeting; but for your love and comfort I think I should have broken down.' There, Goldie, do you hear that? (*She kisses the letter.*) 'But now we both see how things are guided for the best. But for my being sent to prison, I should have died before this, a broken-down drunkard, if not worse; and you might still have been earning hard bread as a street-singer, or carried from a hospital ward to a pauper's grave.' Yes, yes, (*shuddering*) that's true. 'This place has made a man of me, and you have found friends and the means of earning a livelihood. I count the days till we meet. Good-bye and heaven bless you, prays your ever affectionate Robert Brierly.' (*Kisses the letter frequently.*) And don't I count the days too? There! (*Makes a mark in her pocket almanack.*) Another gone! They seem so slow – when one looks forward – and yet they pass so quickly! (*taking up birdcage*) Come, Goldie, while I work you must sing me a nice song for letting you hear that nice letter.

(*Hanging up birdcage – a knock at the door.*)

EMILY: May I come in?

MAY: Oh, yes, Mrs Jones. (*Sits to work.*)

EMILY: St Evremond, please, Miss Edwards, Jones has changed his name. When people have come down in circumstances, the best way that can do is to keep up their names. Like St Evremond, it looks well in the bill, and sounds foreign. That's always attractive – and I dress my hair *à la Franĉaise,* to keep up the effect. I've brought back the shawl you were kind enough to lend me.

MAY: I hope you got the engagement, dear?

EMILY: (*sighs*) No; the proprietor said my appearance was quite the thing – good stage face and figure, and all that: you know how those creatures always flatter one; but they hadn't an opening just now in the comic duet and character dance business.

MAY: I'm so sorry; your husband will be so disappointed.

EMILY: Oh! bless you, he doesn't know what I've been after. I couldn't bear to worrit him, poor fellow! He's had so many troubles. I've been used to rough it – before we came into our fortune. (*Noise heard overhead.* MAY *starts.*)

MAY: What noise is that? It's in your room.

EMILY: Don't be alarmed – it's only Green; I left him to practise the clog-dance while I went out. He's so clumsy. He often comes down like that in the double shuffles. But he gets on very nicely in the comic duets.

MAY: It's very fortunate he's so willing to turn his hand to anything.

EMILY: Yes, he's willing enough to turn his hand, only he is so slow in turning his legs. Ah, my dear, you're very lucky only having yourself to keep.

MAY: I find it hard enough to work sometimes. But after the life I've passed through, it seems paradise.

EMILY: Oh, I couldn't a-bear it; such a want of excitement! And you that was brought up to a public life too. Every night about six, when they begin to light up the gas, I feel so fidgety, you can't think – I want to be off to the theatre. I couldn't live away from the float, that is, not if I had to work for my living – of course it was very different the three years we had our fortune. (*Sighs and gives herself an air of martyrdom.*)

MAY: I'm afraid Mr Jones ran through a great deal in a very short time.

---

live away from the float: live away from the footlights.

EMILY: Well, we were both fast, dear; and to do Jones justice, I don't think he was the fastest. You see he was used to spending and I wasn't. It seemed so jolly at first to have everything one liked. (*A knock.*)

MAY: Come in!

> (*Enter* GREEN JONES, *much dilapidated. He wears a decayed dressing-gown and a smoking cap, and carries a pair of clogs in his hand; he throws himself into a chair.*)

MAY: Your wife's here, Mr Jones.

EMILY: St Evremond, please dear.

GREEN: Yes, Montague St Evremond; that is to be in the paulo-poster-futurum. I thought you would be here, Milly. I saw you come in at the street door.

> (MAY *takes her work.*)

EMILY: Oh, you were watching for me out of the window, I suppose, instead of practising your *pas*.

GREEN: I was allowing my shins an interval of refreshment. I hope, Miss Edwards, you may never be reduced to earn a subsistence by the clog hornpipe, or if you are, that you will be allowed to practice in your stockings. The way I've barked my intractable shins!

EMILY: Poor dear fellow! There, there! He's a good boy, and he shall have a piece of sugar, he shall! (*kissing him*)

GREEN: Sugar is all very well, Emily, but I'm satisfied I shall never electrify the British public in this kind of pump. (*showing clog.*) The truth is, Miss Edwards, I'm not meant for a star of the ballet; as Emily says, I'm too fleshy.

EMILY: Stout was the word.

GREEN: Oh, was it? Anyway, you meant short-winded. My vocation is in the more private walks of existence. If I'd a nice easy light porter's place now –

EMILY: Oh, Montague, how can you be so mean-spirited?

GREEN: Or if there's nothing else open to us but the music halls, I always said we should do better with the performing dogs.

EMILY: Performing dogs? Hadn't you better come to monkeys at once?

GREEN: I've a turn for puppies. I'm at home with them. It's the thing I've been always used to, since I was at college. But we're interrupting Miss Edwards. Come along, Emily, if you're at liberty to give your Montague a lesson in the poetry of motion under difficulties. (*showing the clog*) But oh, remember your Montague has shins, and be as sparing as possible of the double shuffles. (*Rises.*)

EMILY: You poor dear soft-headed – soft-hearted – soft-shinned creature! What *would* you do without me? (*Exeunt* EMILY *and* GREEN JONES.)

MAY: (*folding up her shawl*) How times are changed since she made him give me half-a-crown that dreadful night, when Robert – I can't bear to think of it, though all has turned out well.

> (*Enter* MRS WILLOUGHBY.)

Ah, Mrs Willoughby, I was expecting a visit from you. I've the week's rent all ready. (*Gives her a folded parcel from small box on table.*)

MRS WILLOUGHBY: Which ready you always was, to the minit, that I will say, my

---

paulo-poster-futurum: Paulo post future is, in Latin grammar, the future perfect tense. Green's pun is on his future billing on theatre posters.

dear. You'll excuse me if I take a chair, these stairs is trying to an elderly woman – not that I am so old as many that looks younger, which when I'd my front tittivated only last week, Mr Miggles, that's the hairdresser at 22, he says to me, 'Mrs Willoughby,' he says, 'forty is what I'd give you with that front', he says. 'No, Mr Miggles,' I says, 'forty it was once, but will never be again, which trouble is a sharp thorn, and losses is more than time, and a shortness of breath along of a shock three years was last July.' 'No, Mr Miggles,' I says, 'fronts can't undo the work of years,' I says, 'nor yet wigs, Mr Miggles – which skin-partings equal to years I never did see, and that's the truth.' (*Pauses for breath.*)

MAY: At all events, Mrs Willoughby, you're looking very well this morning.

MRS WILLOUGHBY: Ah, my dear, you are very good to say so, which, if it wasn't for rheumatics and the rates, one a top of another, and them dustmen, which their carts is a mockery, unless you stand beer, and that boy, Sam, though which is the worst I'm sure is hard to say, only a grandmother's feelings is not to be told, which opodeldoc can't be rubbed into the 'eart, as I said to Mrs Molloy – her that has my first floor front – which she says to me, 'Mrs Willoughby', says she, 'nine oils is the thing,' she says, 'rubbed in warm', says she. 'Which it's all very well, Mrs Molloy,' says I, 'but how is a lone woman to rub it in the nape of the neck and the small of the back; and Sam that giddy, and distressing me to that degree. No, Mrs Molloy,' I says, 'what's sent us we must bear it, and parties that's reduced to let lodgings can't afford easy chairs', which well I know it, and the truth it is – and me with two beauties in chintz in the front parlour, which I got a bargain at the brokers when the parties was sold up at 24, and no more time to sit down in 'em than if I was a cherrybin.

MAY: I'm sure you ought to have one, so hard as you've worked all your life, and when Sam gets a situation –

MRS WILLOUGHBY: Sam, ah, that boy – I came here about him; hasn't he been here this morning?

MAY: No, not yet, I was expecting him – he promised to carry some things home for me.

MRS WILLOUGHBY: Ah, Miss Edwards, if you would only talk to him; he don't mind anything I say, no more than if it was a flat-iron, which what that boy have cost me in distress of mind, and clothes, and caps, and breakages, never can be known – and his poor mother which was the only one I brought up and had five, she says to me, 'Mother,' she says, 'he's a big child,' she says, 'and he's a beautiful child, but he have a temper of his own'; which 'Mary,' I says – she was called Mary, like you, my dear, after her aunt, from which we had expectations, but which was left to the Blind Asylum, and the Fishmongers' Alms Houses, and very like you she was, only she had light hair and blue eyes – 'Mary, my dear,' I says, 'I hope you'll never live to see it', and took she was at twenty-three, sudden, and that boy I've had to mend and wash and do for ever since, and hard lines it is.

MAY: I'm sure he loves you very dearly, and has an excellent heart.

---

opodeldoc: a liniment, a solution of soap in alcohol etc.
cherrybin: from cherubim, an angel. Mrs Willoughby probably thinks of busy little creatures always flying around, with no time to rest!

MRS WILLOUGHBY: Heart, my dear – which I wish it had been his heart I found in
his right-'and pocket as I was a-mending his best trowsers last night, which it was
a short-pipe, which it is nothing but the truth, and smoked to that degree as if it
had been black-leaded, which many's the time when he've come in, I've said,
'Sam,' I've said, 'I smell tobacco', I've said. 'Grandmother,' he'd say to me,
quite grave and innocent, 'p'raps it's the chimbley' – and him a child of fifteen,
and a short pipe in his right-'and pocket! I'm sure I could have broke my heart
over it, I could; let alone the pipe – which I flung it into the fire – but a happy
moment since is a thing I have not known. (*Pauses for breath.*)

MAY: Oh, he'll get rid of all his bad habits in time. I've broken him in to carry my
parcels already.

MRS WILLOUGHBY: Yes, indeed! and how you can trust him to carry parcels; but,
oh, Miss Edwards, if you'd talk to him, and tell him short pipes is the thief of
time, and tobacco's the root of all evil, which Dean Close he've proved it strong
enough, I'm sure – and I cut it out of the *Weekly Pulpit* – and wherever that
paper is now. (*Rummaging in her pocket – knock at door.*) That's at your door –
which, if you're expecting a caller or a customer –

MAY: No; I expect no one – unless it's Sam. (*Knock repeated, timidly.*) Come in.
(*Lays down her work.*)
                    (BRIERLY *opens the door, timidly.*)

BRIERLY: (*doubtfully*) Miss Edwards, please?

MAY: (*rushing into his arms*) Robert! you here!

BRIERLY: My own dear May! (*Rushes over to her.*)

MRS WILLOUGHBY: Eh? Well, I'm sure.

MAY: (*confused*) I'm so glad! But how is it that you're – I thought you said in your
letter – how well you look! (*fluttered*)

BRIERLY: Yes, I meant to surprise you, but it's all right, I'm my own master at last,
and the first place I came to is your room, and the first thing I do is take you in
my arms! –

MRS WILLOUGHBY: Well really, young man – taking a young person in your arms
– before strangers – (BRIERLY *pauses.*)

MAY: Oh, you mustn't mind, Mrs Willoughby; it's Robert.

MRS WILLOUGHBY: Oh – Robert! I suppose by the way he's a-goin' on, Robert's
your brother – leastways, if he ain't your brother –

BRIERLY: Her brother? Yes, ma'am, I am her brother! (*Kisses MAY.*)

MRS WILLOUGHBY: Indeed! And if I might make bold to ask where you come
from –

BRIERLY: I'm just discharged. (*He pauses – MAY giving him a look.*)

MRS WILLOUGHBY: Discharged! And where from – not your situation, I 'ope?

BRIERLY: From Her Majesty's Service, if you must know.

MAY: I've not seen him for three years and more. I didn't expect him so soon, Mrs
Willoughby, so it was quite natural the sight of him should startle me.

MRS WILLOUGHBY: Which well I know it – not 'avin' had brothers myself, but an
uncle that ran away for a soldier, and came back on the parish with a wooden
leg, and a shillin' a day pension, and always in arrears for liquor – which the way
that man would drink beer!

BRIERLY: I should have written to prepare you, but I thought I might be here as soon as my letter, so I jumped into the train at Dorchester, and here I am.

MAY: That was very thoughtless of you – no, it was very thoughtful and kind of you. But I don't understand –

BRIERLY: How I come to be here before the time I told you in my letter? You see, I had full marks and nothing against me, and the regulations – (MAY *gives him a look which interrupts him.*)

MAY: If Sam comes shall I tell him to go downstairs to you, Mrs Willoughby?

MRS WILLOUGHBY: I shall be much obliged to you, my dear – which I know when brothers and sisters meet they'll have a great deal to talk over, and two's company and three's none is well beknown – and I never was one to stand listenin' when other folks is talkin' – and one thing I may say, as I told Mrs Molloy only last week, when the first floor had a little tiff with the second pair front about the water – 'Mrs Molloy,' I says, 'nobody ever heard me put in my oar when I wasn't asked,' I says, 'and idle chatterin', and gossip', I says, 'is a thing that I never was given to, and I ain't a-goin' to begin now', I says, which good mornin' to you, young man, and a better girl, and a nicer girl, and a harder working girl than your sister, I 'ope and trust may never darken my doors. (BRIERLY *throws open door.*) Which her rent was ever ready to the day. No, my dear, it's the truth, and you needn't blush. (*During this last speech* BRIERLY *urges her towards door.*) Thank you, I can open the door for myself, young man. And a very nice looking head you have on your shoulders, though you have had your hair cut uncommon short, which I must say – good mornin', my dear, and anything I can do for you. (*Exit, but heard still talking till the door below is heard to shut loudly.*) I'm sure, which nobody can say but I was always ready to oblige, if reduced to let lodgings owing to a sudden shock.

BRIERLY: Phew! (*giving a sigh of relief*) One would think she'd been on the silent system for a twelvemonth! Now, we're alone at last, May. Let me have a good look at you. I gave you a bit of a squeeze, but I hadn't a good look. (*He takes her by the hand.*)

MAY: Well –

BRIERLY: Prettier than ever – you couldn't look better or kinder.

MAY: Now sit down, and don't talk nonsense.

BRIERLY: Sit down! not I – I've had a good look at you – and I must have a good look at the place. How snug it is! as neat as the cell I've just left. But it wasn't hard to keep *that* in order – I had only a stool, a basin, and a hammock. Didn't I polish the hammock-hooks neither! One must have a pride in something – you know. But here you've no end of things – a sofa – and a carpet – and chairs – and – (*going round as he spoke*)

MAY: Isn't it a nice clock, Robert? and look at the chiffonier! Picked that up a bargain – and all out of my own earnings!

BRIERLY: It's the cosiest little nest for my bird – you *were* a singing bird once, you know. (*Sees the guitar.*) And there's the old bread-winner – I'm glad you've not parted with *that*.

MAY: I should be the most ungrateful creature if I did! How many a dinner it's earned for me, how many a week's rent it's paid! But for it I never should have known

you – my friend – my brother. Yes Robert, I wanted to explain to Mrs
Willoughby when she called you my brother.

BRIERLY: So did I. But I felt it was true. If I'm not your brother born and bred,
May, you've been a true sister to me – ever since that night –

MAY: Oh, Robert – a kind word was never lost yet. No wonder I clung to you –

BRIERLY: Aye, when all stood aloof. In the prison – in the dock – to the van door.
You believed me innocent – when all but you – warders, turnkeys, fellow-
prisoners, lawyers, judge and jury – all sneered and shook their heads. But for
you, May, I should have been a desperate man. I might have become all they
thought me – a felon, in the company of felons.

MAY: Oh, do not look back to that misery – but tell me how you are out so long
before your time?

BRIERLY: Here's my ticket-of-leave – they've given me every week of my nine
months – they hadn't a mark against me. I didn't want to look forward to my
discharge – I was afraid to. I worked away; in school, in the quarry-gang first,
and in the office afterwards, as if I had to stay there for ever. I wasn't unhappy
either – all were good to me. And then I had your letters to comfort me. But
when I was sent for to the Governor's room yesterday and told I was a free man,
everything swam round and round – I staggered – they had to give me water, or I
think I should have fainted like a girl.

MAY: Ah, as I felt that night when you gave me the wine.

BRIERLY: Poor dear, I remember it as if it was yesterday. But when I passed out at
the gate, not for gang labour in my prison dress, with my prison mates, under
the warder's eye and the sentry's musket, as I had done so many a weary week –
but in my own clothes – unwatched – a free man – free to go where I liked – to do
what I liked – speak to whom I liked, I thought I should have gone crazy. I
danced, I sang, I kicked up the pebbles of the Chezzle beach– the boatmen laid
hands on me for an escaped lunatic, till I told 'em I was a discharged prisoner,
and then they let me pass – but they drew back from me; there was the convict's
taint about me – you can't fling that off with the convict's jacket.

MAY: But here no one knows you – you'll get a fresh start now.

BRIERLY: I hope so, but it's awfully up-hill work, May; I've heard enough down
yonder of all that stands between a poor fellow who has been in trouble and an
honest life. We're lepers, all of us, May – and honest people give us a wide
berth. But just let me get a chance.

MAY: Oh – if only Mr Gibson would give you one.

BRIERLY: Who's he?

MAY: The husband of the lady who was my first and best friend. (BRIERLY *looks
uneasy*.) After you, of course, you jealous thing. It was she gave me work –
recommended me to her friends – and now I've quite a nice little business. I pay
my way, I'm as happy as the day is long, and I'm thinking of taking an apprentice.

BRIERLY: How I wish I was a lass. (*taking her hand*)

Chezzle beach: Chesil Beach, a famous pebbly beach on the Dorset coast, adjoining Portland Bill,
where the prison is.

MAY: I think I see those great clumsy hands spoiling my work.

BRIERLY: You don't want a light porter, eh, May?

MAY: No – I've not quite business enough for that yet. Sam's as much as I can manage –

BRIERLY: Sam? Who's Sam?

MAY: Oh, he's a young man – a friend of mine –

BRIERLY: Oh, I'm glad you've got friends – young men friends, I mean –

MAY: Oh yes – Sam will do anything for me –

BRIERLY: Ah, will he?

MAY: Except give up suckers and short pipes –

BRIERLY: Suckers and short pipes?

MAY: Yes, a queer mixture isn't it. But never mind Sam.

BRIERLY: (*aside*) Ah, but I can't help minding him.

MAY: If Mr Gibson would only give you employment. He's something in the City – a money merchant you know – a great house I believe.

BRIERLY: No chance of that, May.

MAY: I mean as a light porter, or something of that kind of course. You can't be expected to know enough for a clerk.

BRIERLY: (*proudly*) I'm not so sure of that. The schoolmaster, down yonder, said he couldn't teach me anything more in writing and arithmetic. I'm up to book-keeping too, by single and double entry – why I kept the prison books for the last nine months I was there –

MAY: How clever of you! But if he knew the truth – that you were innocent –

BRIERLY: Oh – we're all innocent down yonder – if you take your own word for it. No, if he knows where I've been, he'll have nothing to say to me. I must begin lower down, in some line where the work's nasty and the pay low – where they don't ask questions – and when I've got a character, then I may reach a step higher, and so creep back little by little to the level of honest men. (*gloomily*) There's no help for it.

MAY: (*putting her hands upon his shoulder*) At all events you can wait and look about you a little – you've money coming in, you know.

BRIERLY: Me, May?

MAY: Yes. You forget those two sovereigns you lent me. I've put away a shilling every week out of my savings – and then there's the interest, you know – ever so much. It's all here. (*Goes to table, and puts a savings-box into his hand.*) You needn't count it. There'd have been more if you hadn't come so soon.

BRIERLY: My good, kind May, do you think I'd touch a farthing of your savings?

MAY: Oh, do take it, Robert, or I shall be so unhappy – I've had more pleasure out of that money than any I ever earned, because I thought it would go to help you.

BRIERLY: Bless your kind heart! To think of those little fingers working for me – a lusty, big-boned chap like me! Why, May, lass – I've a matter of twenty pounds in brass of my own earnings at Pentonville and Portland – overtime and allowances. The Governor paid it over to me, like a man, before I started yesterday – aye, and shook hands with me. God bless him for that.

MAY: Twenty pounds! Oh, how small my poor little earnings will look! I was so proud of them, too. (*ruefully*)

BRIERLY: Well, keep 'em May – keep 'em to buy your wedding-gown. (*Takes her in his arms and kisses her.*)

    (*Enter* SAM– *he gives a significant cough.*)

MAY: Oh! (*startled*) Sam!

BRIERLY: (*hastily*) Sam, is it? Confound him! I'll teach him. (*Sees it is a boy and pauses.*)

SAM: Now will you, though? Granny will be uncommon obliged to you. She says I want teaching – don't she? (*to* MAY)

MAY: How dare you come in like that, Sam, without so much as knocking?

SAM: How was I to know you had company? Of course I'd have knocked if I'd been aware you'd your young man.

BRIERLY: I tell you what, young 'un, if you don't make yourself scarce –

SAM: Well, what? (*retreating*) If I don't make myself scarce, you'll pitch into me. Just you try it, lanky! Yah! Hit one of your own size – do. (*squaring*)

BRIERLY: Go it, bantam! Ha, ha, ha! (*to* MAY) So this is Sam, is it?

SAM: My name's not Sam. It's Samivel Willoughby, Esquire, most respectable references given and required, (*Pulls collar up.*) as granny says when she advertises the first floor.

BRIERLY: Now be off, like a good little chap.

SAM: Come, cheeky! Don't you use bad language. I'm rising fifteen, stand five feet five in my bluchers, and I'm sprouting agin' the summer, if I ain't six foot of greens already like *you*.

MAY: Hold your tongue! Your'e a naughty, impudent little boy!

SAM: Come – I'm bigger than you are, I'll bet a bob. (*Stands on his toes.*)

    (*Enter* MRS WILLOUGHBY.)

MRS WILLOUGHBY: Oh, here's that boy at last! which upstairs and downstairs, and all along the street, have I been a-seekin' of him, and a' carryin' an 'eavy heart –

SAM: Come, come, Granny. Leave that job to the Butcher's boys.

MRS WILLOUGHBY: Which if you believe me, Miss Edwards, I left a fourpenny-bit in the chany dog-kennel on the mantelpiece downstairs only yesterday mornin' as ever was, which if ever there was a real bit of Dresden, and cost me fourteen-and-six at Hanway Yard in 'appier days, with a black and white spaniel in a wreath of roses and a shepherdess to match, and the trouble I've 'ad to keep that boy's 'ands off it since he was in long clothes – where's that fourpenny-piece – (*Seizes him.*) you young villain – which you know you took it.

SAM: Well, then, I did – to buy bird's eye with.

MRS WILLOUGHBY: Bird's-eye! and him not fifteen – and the only one left of three. (*Falls in chair.*)

SAM: If you will nobble a fellow's bacca, you must take the consequences; and just you mind – it ain't no use a-tryin' it on breaking my pipes, granny. I've given up Brosely's and started a briar root. (*Pulls it out.*) It's a stunner.

SAM: this is a 'breeches' part, that is one written to be played by an actress skilled in male impersonation. The role is crafted to this convention.

bluchers: leather boots, so called after Marshall Blücher, the Prussian general of Waterloo.

MRS WILLOUGHBY: Oh dear, oh dear! if it ain't enough to melt an 'eart of stone – no, fronts I may wear to 'ide my suffering, but my grey 'airs that boy have determined to bring with sorrow to the grave.

SAM: What? Cos I smoke? Why, there's Jem Miggles smokes, and he's a year younger than me, and *he's* allowed all the lux'ries of the season – his father's going to take him to see the badger drawn at Jeremy Shaw's one of these days – and *his* mother don't go into hysterics.

MAY: Sam, I'm surprised you should take pleasure in making your grandmother unhappy!

SAM: I don't take pleasure – she won't let me; she's always a naggin' and aggravatin' me. Here, dry your eyes, granny – and I'll be a good boy, and I won't go after the rats, and I won't aggravate old Miggles's bullfinches.

MRS WILLOUGHBY: And you'll give up that nasty tobacco and you'll keep your clothes tidy, and not get slidin' down ladders in your Sunday trowsers – which moleskins won't stand, let alone mixed woollens.

SAM: Best put me in charity leathers at once, with a muffin cap and a badge, wouldn't I look stunnin'? Oh, my!

MRS WILLOUGHBY: There, that's just him – always some of his imperent audacious chaff. I know he gets it from that young Miggles – ready to stop his poor granny's mouth with.

SAM: No. (*Kisses her.*) That's the only way to stop it. Come, I'm goin' to take myself up short, like a jibbin' cab 'oss, and be a real swell, granny, in white kids, only I'm a-waiting till I come into my fortune – *you* know, that twenty pounds you was robbed of, three years ago.

MRS WILLOUGHBY: Oh, it's all very well – a chaffin and a laughin – which heavy and hard it came upon me – the loss of that twenty pounds. Ah, my dears (*to* BRIERLY *and* MAY) I hope you may never be served so – which I've 'ad a shortness of breath ever since – in good sovereigns, that I'd saved up, by shillings at a time, as I may say, to pay my rent – gone – every farden of it!

BRIERLY: Did you say you were robbed Ma'am?

MRS WILLOUGHBY: Which robbery is too good a word for it. It was forgery, aye, and a'most as good as murder – which it might ha'been my death! Yes, my dears, as nice-looking, civil spoken a young man as you could wish to see – in a white 'at, which I never can forget, and a broad way of speaking – and, 'Would you change me a twenty pound note, ma'am,' he says' 'And it ain't very often', I says, 'you could have come into this shop' – which I was in the cigar and periodical line at the time.

BRIERLY: Where was your shop?

MRS WILLOUGHBY: In the Fulham Road, three doors outside the Bellvue Gardens, and turning twelve pound a week over the counter regular – not to speak of the ginger-beer connection – 'and it's little call I have with twenty pounds in the 'ouse', I sez, 'being a lone woman and till-robberies that frequent' – I sez – 'but twenty two sovereigns in my cash box I have' I sez – 'for the half year's rent that's due tomorrow – and hard enough it's earned' I sez – 'and me wanting the 'ouse painting and papered and nothing done, not if I was to go on my bended knees to the agent' I says, 'And a note is all the same to me,' I sez – 'if all correct', I sez – and when I looked in that young man's face, I had no more suspicion than I should of either of yours, my dears; so he gave me the note, and he took the sovereigns. And the next thing I saw was a gent, which his name he told me was Hawkshaw, and he were in the police, on'y in plain clothes, and asked to look at the note, and told me it was a bad 'un; and if that man left me on the sofa, in the back shop, or behind the counter, with my feet in a jar of brown rappee and my head among the ginger beer bottles, is more that I can tell – for fits it was for days and days, and when I worked out of 'em, then I was short of my rent, and the stock sold up, and me ruined.

(BRIERLY *shows signs of agitation while she is speaking.*)

BRIERLY: And you never recovered your money?

MRS WILLOUGHBY: Not a penny, my dear, and if it hadn't been for a kind friend that set me up in my own furniture, in the Fulham Workhouse I might have been at this moment, leastways St.George's, which that's my legal settlement – and that blessed boy – (*She cries.*)

SAM: (*gaily*) In a suit of grey dittoes, a-stepping out with another chap, a big 'un and a little 'un together, like a job lot at an auction, to church of a Sunday, to such a jolly long sermon! Shouldn't I like it! (*consolingly, and changing his tone*) I say, don't cry, granny, we ain't come to skilly yet.

MRS WILLOUGHBY: Which if that young man knew the mischief he'd done –

MAY: Perhaps he does, and is very sorry for it.

MRS WILLOUGHBY: Not he, the wretch! What do the likes o' them care for the poor creatures they robs – hangin's too good for 'em, the villains.

BRIERLY: (*taking his hat, and going*) Goodbye, May.

MAY: You're not going?

BRIERLY: I've a little bit of business that can't wait – some money to pay.

MAY: You'll not be long?

BRIERLY: No; I'll be back directly. (*aside*) Thank heaven, I *can* make it up to *her*! (*Exit.*)

MAY: (*aside*) Poor fellow! he can't bear it – she little thinks –

MRS WILLOUGHBY: You'll excuse me, it's not often I talk about it, Miss Edwards, which it's no use a-cryin' over spilt milk, and there's them as tempers the wind to the shorn lamb – and if it wasn't for that boy –

SAM: There, she's at me again.

MRS WILLOUGHBY: Which if I'd only the means to put him to school, and out of the streets, and clear of that Jem Miggles and them rats –

SAM: (*half crying*) Bother the rats!

MAY: You see, Sam, how unhappy you make your grandmother.

SAM: And don't you see how unhappy she makes me, talkin' of sendin' me to school.

MAY: (*forcing him to* MRS WILLOUGHBY) Come, kiss her, and promise to be a good boy. Ah, Sam, you don't understand the blessing of having one who loves you as she does.

SAM: Then what does she break my pipes for?

MRS WILLOUGHBY: Oh, them pipes! (*A knock.*)

---

brown rappee: snuff.
to skilly: skilly is a thin soup, the whole phrase meaning 'haven't come to poverty and the workhouse'.

MAY: More visitors! What a busy morning this is! Come in!
>(*Enter* MR GIBSON.)
MR GIBSON: Miss Edwards – eh?
MAY: Yes, sir.
MR GIBSON: Glad I'm right – I thought it was the third floor front – a woman told me downstairs. I'm afraid I pulled the wrong bell. (*Looks about him, takes off his hat, gloves etc.* MAY *sets him a chair, he sits.*)
MRS WILLOUGHBY: And a nice way Mrs Molloy would be in if you brought her down to another party's bell, which, asking your pardon, sir, but was it the first floor as opened the street door?
MR GIBSON: I don't know. It was a lady in a very broad cap border and still broader brogue.
MRS WILLOUGHBY: Which that is the party, sir, as I was a-speakin' of; and I do 'ope she didn't fly out, sir, which Mrs Molloy of a morning – after her tea – she says it's her tea – is that rampageous –
MR GIBSON: No, no; she was civil enough when I said I wanted Miss Edwards.
MRS WILLOUGHBY: Which I do believe, my dear, you've bewitched every soul in the 'ouse, from the kitchens to the attics.
MR GIBSON: Miss Edwards doesn't confine her witchcraft to your lodgers, my good lady. She's bewitched my wife. My name's Gibson.
MAY: Oh, sir; I've never been able to say what I felt to your good kind lady; but I hope you will tell her I am grateful.
MR GIBSON: She knows it by the return you have made. You've showed you deserved her kindness. For fifty people ready to help there's not one worth helping – that's my conclusion. I was telling my wife so this morning, and she insisted that I should come and satisfy myself that she had helped one person at any rate who was able and willing to help herself, and a very tidy, nice-looking girl you are, and a very neat, comfortable room you have, I must say.
MRS WILLOUGHBY: Which you can tell your good lady, sir, from – Miss Edwards' rent were always ready to the days and minits – as I was telling her brother just now.
MR GIBSON: Brother? My wife said you were alone in the world.
MAY: I was alone, sir, when she found me. He was (*She hesitates.*) away.
MR GIBSON: (*pointing to SAM, who has put down a chair, and is balancing himself acrobatically*) Is this the young gentleman?
>(SAM *pitches over with chair, and* MRS WILLOUGHBY *lugs him up.*)
MRS WILLOUGHBY: Oh, dear no, sir, begging your pardon, which that is my grandson, Samuel Willoughby, the only one of three and will be fifteen the twenty-first of next April at eight o'clock in the morning, and a growing boy – which take your cap out of your mouth, Samuel, and stand straight, and let the gentleman see you.
SAM: (*sulkily*) The old gent can see well enough – it don't want a telescope. (*Slinks across at back.*) I ain't a-going to be inspected. I'll mizzle. (*Takes flying leap over chair, Exit.*)
MRS WILLOUGHBY: Which Miss Edwards' brother is grown up, and only come back this mornin' as ever was, discharged from Her Majesty's Service, and five

foot nine in his shoes, by the name of Robert – which well he may, for a sweeter
complexion –

MR GIBSON: With a good character, I hope.

MAY: Oh, yes! (*Eagerly*) The very best, sir.

(*Re-enter* BRIERLY.)

BRIERLY: (*aside*) I've done it! I can face her now.

MR GIBSON: So – I suppose this is Robert – a likely young fellow.

MAY: This is Mr Gibson, Robert, the husband of the lady who was so good to me.

BRIERLY: Heaven bless her, and you too, sir, for your kindness to this poor girl,
while I was unable to help her.

MR GIBSON: But now you've got your discharge, she'll have a protector.

BRIERLY: I hope so, sir – as long as I live, and can earn a crust. I suppose I shall be
able to do that.

MR GIBSON: What do you mean to do?

BRIERLY: Ah, there it is; I wish I knew what I could get to do, sir. There are not
many things in the way of work that would frighten me, I think.

MR GIBSON: That's the spirit I like – your sister speaks well of you, but I shouldn't
mind *that*. It's enough for me that you've come out of (BRIERLY *looks
startled*.) Her Majesty's Service with a good character. (BRIERLY *gives a sigh
of relief*.) You write a good hand? (MAY *gets letters from box*.)

BRIERLY: Tolerably good, sir.

MAY: Beautiful sir: here are some of his letters, look, sir. (*Going to show him, but
pauses, seeing date of letter*.) Portland! not this, sir. (*Turns page*.) This side is
better written.

MR GIBSON: A capital hand. Can you keep accounts?

BRIERLY: Yes, sir, I helped to keep the books – yonder.

(*Re-enter* SAM, *comes over rapidly to* MRS WILLOUGHBY.)

SAM: Holloa, granny, here's a parcel I found for you in the letter-box; ain't it heavy,
neither.

MRS WILLOUGHBY: For me! (*Takes it*.) Whatever is it! Eh, money? Oh, Sam, you
hadn't been and gone and done anything wrong?

SAM: Bother! Do you think if I had I'd a-come to *you* with the swag?

(MRS WILLOUGHBY, *who has opened the packet, screams, and
lets a paper fall from the packet*.)

MAY: What's the matter, Mrs Willoughby?

MRS WILLOUGHBY: Sovereigns! real golden sovereigns!

MAY:
MR GIBSON: } Sovereigns!

SAM: Oh, crikey! (*Goes up and down in exultation*.)

MAY: (*picks up the paper* MRS WILLOUGHBY *has let fall*) Here's a note – 'For Mrs
Willoughby – £20 in payment of an old debt.'

MR GIBSON: Yes, and no signature. Come, don't faint, old lady! Here, give her a
glass of water.

MRS WILLOUGHBY: (*recovering*) Sovereigns! for me? Oh, sir, let me look at 'em –
the beauties – eight, nine, ten, twelve, fifteen, eighteen, twenty! Just the money
I lost.

SAM: There granny – I always said we was comin' into our fortune.

Gillian Brown as Sam Willoughby and Ron Daniels as Green Jones in
The Ticket-of-Leave Man, produced at the Victoria Theatre, Stoke-on-Trent,
24 May–9 July 1966. Directed by Peter Cheeseman

MRS WILLOUGHBY: (*with a sudden flash of doubt*) I shouldn't wonder if it was some nasty ring dropper. Oh! are they Bank of Elegance, or only gilt washed? Which I've seen 'em at London Bridge a-sellin' sovereigns at a penny a-piece.

MR GIBSON: Oh, no, they're the real thing.

BRIERLY: Perhaps it's somebody that's wronged you of the money and wants you to clear his conscience.

MR GIBSON: Ah, eccentric people will do that sort of thing – even with income tax. Take my advice, old lady, keep the cash.

MRS WILLOUGHBY: Which in course a gentleman like you knows best, and I'm sure whoever sent the money, all I wish is, much good may it do him, and may he never know the want of it.

BRIERLY: Amen!

MRS WILLOUGHBY: Which, first and foremost – there's my silver teapot I'll have out of pawn this blessed day, and I'll ask Mrs Molloy to a cup of tea in my best blue chany, and then this blessed boy shall have a year of finishin' school.

SAM: I wish the party had kept his money, I do! (MRS WILLOUGHBY *is counting the sovereigns over and over*.)

MAY: (*aside to* BRIERLY) Robert – this money – it's your savings?

BRIERLY: Yes, it's conscience money, May.

SAM: I say, granny, you couldn't spare a young chap a couple of them, could you?

MRS WILLOUGHBY: Drat the boy's impertinence! Him askin' for sovereigns as natural – Ah! they'll all be for you, Sam, one of these days.

> (SAM *makes a grab at the sovereigns playfully, and runs to back, followed by* MRS WILLOUGHBY, *whom he dodges behind a chair.* MR GIBSON *writes at table*.)

MRS WILLOUGHBY: (*half hysterically, throwing herself into a chair*) Oh, Sam! Which that boy will be the death of his poor grandmother, he will.

SAM: (*jumping over chair-back, on which he perches, gives back money and kisses her*) There, granny, it was only a lark.

MRS WILLOUGHBY: (*admiringly and affectionately*) Oh, what a boy you are. (*Exeunt* MRS WILLOUGHBY *and* SAM.)

MR GIBSON: (*gives note to* BRIERLY) Here, young man, bring this note to my office, 25 St Nicholas Lane, at ten o'clock tomorrow. I've discharged my messenger – we'll see if you are fit for the place.

BRIERLY: Oh, sir!

MR GIBSON: There – there – don't thank me. (*to* MAY) I like gratitude that shows itself in acts like yours to my wife. Let's hope your brother will repay me in the same coin. (*Exit*.)

MAY: Robert, the money has brought us a blessing already.

> (*He takes her in his arms exultingly – music, piano*.)

Act III

SCENE: MR GIBSON'*s Bill-broking office in St Nicholas Lane, City. A mahogany railing runs up the stage, separating compartment, left (in which stand across the stage*

---

ring dropper: trickster.

two large mahogany desks, set round with wire and a brass rail at the top to support books) from the compartment, right, at the side of which is the door leading to MR GIBSON's *private office. In front of the compartment, left, runs a mahogany counter, with a place for writing at, divided off. A large iron safe for books, right, another safe near door; door communicating with passage and street, centre; a small desk down stage right, two windows left. As the curtain rises,* SAM *is discovered carrying the ledgers out of safe, right through an entrance in the railings to compartment, left, and arranging them on the desks.* BRIERLY *is discovered at the counter numbering cheques in a cheque-book.*

SAM: There they are, all ship-shape. I say, Bob –

BRIERLY: Thirty-four, thirty-five-(*to* SAM) *Mr* Robert – thirty-six, thirty-seven –

SAM: Well, *Mr* Robert – you have grown such a swell since we came into the City, there's no talking to you. I say, if granny could see these big chaps, all full of £.s.d, and me as much at home with them as old Miggles with his toy terriers. (*Puts book on desk.*)

BRIERLY: Only the outsides, Sam – fifty – fifty-one –

SAM: Everything must have a beginning. I'm only under-messenger now, at six bob a week – but it's the small end of the wedge. I don't mean to stay running errands and dusting books long, I can tell you. I intend to speculate – I'm in two tips already.

BRIERLY: Tips?

SAM: Yes. (*Takes out betting book.*) I stand to win a fiver on Pollux for the Derby, and a good thing on the Count for the Ascot Cup – they were at Pollux last week, but he's all right again, and the Count's in splendid form, and the stable uncommon sweet on him.

BRIERLY: Bring me those pens. (*As* SAM *comes to him with the pens he catches him by the collar and shakes him.*) You young rascal! Now, you mark me, Master Sam. If ever I hear of you putting into a tip again, I'll thrash you within an inch of your life, and then I'll split on you to Mr Gibson, and he'll discharge you.

SAM: Now I call that mean. One City gent interfering with another City gent's amusements.

BRIERLY: (*bitterly*) Amusements. When you've seen as much as I have, you'll know what comes of such amusements, lad.

SAM: As if I didn't know well enough already. Lark, lush, and a latch-key – a swell rig-out, and lots of ready in the pockets – a drag at Epsom, and a champagne lunch on the hill! Oh, my – ain't it stunning!

BRIERLY: Ah! Sam, that's the fancy picture – mine is the true one. Excitement first, then idleness and drink, and then bad companions – sin – shame – and a prison.

SAM: Come, I don't want to be preached to in office hours – granny gives me quite enough of that at home – ain't it a bore, just!

BRIERLY: Oh, my lad, take my advice, do! Be steady – stick to work and home. It's an awful look out for a young chap adrift in this place, without them sheet anchors. (*Returns to counter.*)

SAM: Oh, I ain't afraid. I cut my eye-teeth early. Tips ain't worse than time bargains – and they're business. But don't look glum, Bob; you're the right sort, you are, and sooner than rile you, I'll cut tips, burn *Bell's Life*, and take to Cape Court and the *Share List*, and that's respectable, you know. (*Sits on counter.*)

BRIERLY: (*looking over cheque book*) You young rascal! you've made me misnumber my cheque.

SAM: Serves you jolly well right for coming to business on your wedding day.

BRIERLY: Oh, I've two hours good before I'm wanted for that.

SAM: I say, Bob, you don't mean to say you've been to the Bank for the petty cash this morning?

BRIERLY: Yes.

SAM: And didn't leave the notes on the counter?

BRIERLY: No.

SAM: And didn't have your pocket picked?

BRIERLY: No.

SAM: Well, you *are* a cool hand. I've often wondered how the poor chaps in Newgate managed to eat a good breakfast before they're turned off. But a fellow coming to office the morning he's going to be spliced – and when the Governor has given him a holiday too – by Jove, it beats the Old Bailey by lengths. I hope I shall be as cool when I'm married.

BRIERLY: You – you young cock-sparrow.

SAM: Yes. I've ordered the young woman I want down at Birmingham. Miss Edwards ain't my style.

BRIERLY: No – isn't she though? I'm sorry it's too late to have her altered.

SAM: She's too quiet – wants go. I like high action. Now I call Mrs Jones a splendid woman. Sam Willoughby, Esquire, must have a real tip-top lady. I don't mean to marry till I can go to church with my own brougham.

BRIERLY: I suppose that means when you've set up as a crossing sweeper. And now, Sam, till your brougham comes round for you, just trot off to the stationers' and see if Mr Gibson's new bill-case is ready.

SAM: (*vaulting over the counter, sees* MAY *through the glass door, Left*) All right. Here's Miss Edwards a-coming in full tog. I twig – I ain't wanted. Quite correct – Samivel is fly. (*Puts his finger to his nose and exit.*)

(*Enter* MAY *in wedding dress.*)

BRIERLY: Ah, May, darling! (*Takes her by the hand and kisses her.*)

SAM: (*looking in*) I saw you! (*Exit.*)

BRIERLY: Hang that boy! But never mind his impudence, my own little wife.

MAY: Not yet, sir.

BRIERLY: In two hours.

MAY: There's many slip between cup and lip, you know. But as the clerks aren't come yet, I thought I might just look in and show you – (*Displays her dress.*)

BRIERLY: Your wedding gown!

MAY: Yes. It's Mrs Gibson's present, with such a kind note – she insists on providing the wedding breakfast – and she's sent in the most beautiful cake, and flowers from their own conservatory. My little room looks so pretty.

BRIERLY: It always looks pretty when thou art in it. I shall never miss the sun, even in Nicholas Lane, after we are married, darling.

MAY: Oh, Robert, won't it be delightful? Me, house-keeper here, and you

---

Newgate . . . turned off: Newgate was a London prison, and *turned off* is slang for hanged.

messenger, and such a favourite, too! And to think we owe all to these good, kind, generous – There's only one thing I can't get off my mind.

BRIERLY: What's that?

MAY: Mr Gibson doesn't know the truth about you. We should have told him before this.

BRIERLY: It's hard for a poor chap that's fought clear of the mud to let go the rope he's holding to and slide back again. I'll tell him when I've been long enough here to try me, only wait a bit.

MAY: Perhaps you are right, dear. Sometimes the thought comes like a cloud across me. But you've never said how you like my dress. (*displaying it*)

BRIERLY: I couldn't see if for looking at thy bonny face – but it's a grand gown.

MAY: And my own making! I forgot – Mrs Jones is come, and Mrs Willoughby. They're going to church with us, you know. Emily looks so nice – she would so like to see the office, she says, if I might bring her in?

BRIERLY: Oh, yes, the place is free to the petticoats till business hours.

MAY: (*calls at door*) Come in, Emily.
            (*Enter* EMILY.)

EMILY: Oh, Mr Brierly!

MAY: While Robert does the honours of the office, I'll go and help Mrs Willoughby to set out the breakfast. The white service looks so lovely, Robert, and my canary sings as I haven't heard him since I left the old lodgings. He knows there's joy in the wind.

MRS WILLOUGHBY: (*calling without*) Miss Edwards!

MAY: There! I'm wanted. I'm coming, Mrs Willoughby. Oh dear! If I'd known the trouble it was to be married, I don't think I should have ventured. I'm coming. (*Exit.*)

EMILY: (*who has been looking about her*) I did *so* want to see an office – a real one, you know. I've seen 'em set on the stage often, but they ain't a bit like the real thing.

BRIERLY: They are but dull places. Not this one, though, since May's been housekeeper.

EMILY: Yes, they are dull, but *so* respectable – look so like money, you know. I suppose, now, there's no end of money passes here?

BRIERLY: A hundred thousand pounds a day, sometimes.

EMILY: Gracious goodness! All in sovereigns?

BRIERLY: Not a farthing – all in cheques and bills. We've a few thousands that a queer old-fashioned depositer insists on Mr Gibson keeping here, but except that and the petty cash, there's no hard money in the place.

EMILY: Dear me! I thought you City people sat on stools all day shovelling sovereigns about. Not that I could bear to think of Jones sitting on a stool all day, even to shovel about sovereigns, though he always says something in the City would suit him better than the comic duet business. But he doesn't know what's good for him – never did, poor fellow.

BRIERLY: Except when he married you.

And my own making: presumably the material was Mrs Gibson's present!

EMILY: Well, I don't know about that, but I suppose he would have got through the property without me – he's so much the gentleman, you know.

BRIERLY: He's coming to church with us?

EMILY: Oh, yes! You know he's to give away the bride. But he was obliged to keep an appointment in the City first; so queer for Jones, wasn't it? He wouldn't tell me what it was.

GREEN: (*heard without*) Two and six, my man. Very good, wait.

BRIERLY: Here's your husband.

EMILY: (*looking through door*) In a cab – and a new coat, and waistcoat, and trousers! Oh, Jones! Well, I shan't pay for them.
                    (*Enter* GREEN JONES, *in a gorgeous new suit.*)

GREEN: (*speaking off*) Now hand me out those parcels – yah stupid, give me hold. (*Hands in parcels one by one.*) Hear, bear a hand.
                    (*He pitches parcels to* BRIERLY, *who pitches them on to* EMILY, *who deposits them on the counter.*)

EMILY: (*as first bonnet box comes in*) Jones! (*As second bonnet box comes in.*) Green! (*As case of Eau-de-Cologne comes in.*) Green Jones! (*Glove box comes in.*) Oh! (*Two bouquets in paper are given in.*) Gracious goodness!

GREEN: There – all out. Let's see – bonnets, Eau-de-Cologne, gloves, bouquets – seven ten; two and six the cab – my own togs, five ten – that's thirteen two and six in all.

EMILY: Jones, are you mad?

GREEN: Is your principal here, Brierly?

BRIERLY: The governor? No, it's not his time yet.

GREEN: You couldn't advance me thirteen-two-six, could you?

BRIERLY: What! lend you the money? I'm afraid –

EMILY: (*reproachfully*) Oh, Jones!

GREEN: Emily, be calm. It's not the least consequence. They can wait – the shopman, I mean – that is – the two shopmen and cabby.

EMILY: Oh, he's gone crazy.

GREEN: The fact is, I've had a windfall. Choker Black has turned up trumps. He was put in the hole in California's year, had to bolt to Australia – struck an awfully full pocket at the diggings, and is paying off his old ticks like an emperor. He let me in for two thousand, and he has sent me bills for five hundred as a first instalment.

EMILY: Five hundred! And you've got the money?

GREEN: I've got the bills on his agent. Here they are. Emily, embrace your husband! (*He kisses her.*)

BRIERLY: I wish you joy – both of you. Mr Gibson will discount the bills for you as soon as he comes in.

GREEN: But I say, cash, you know, no curious sherry – no old masters, or patent filters. I've had rather too much of that sort of thing in my time.

EMILY: (*who has been peeping into bonnet box*) What a duck of a bonnet!

---

put in the hole in California's year: the longer version of this speech in the LC text makes it clear that Choker Black's 'hole' was a predicament he got into losing badly at gambling during the Californian gold rush, and then went to Australia and 'struck an awfully full pocket' of gold there.

BRIERLY: No, you're not among your old sixty percent. friends here – we only do good bills at the market rate.

EMILY: (*who has opened glove box*) And what loves of gloves!

GREEN: That's your sort. I feel now the full value of the commercial principle.

EMILY: Oh, Green! But you'll be careful of the money?

GREEN: Careful! I'm an altered man. Henceforth, I swear – you'll allow me to register a vow in your office? – to devote myself to the virtuous pursuit of money-making. I'm worth five hundred pounds, I've fifteen hundred more coming in. Not one farthing of that money shall go in foolish extravagance.

EMILY: But how about these things, Jones?

GREEN: Trifles: a *cadeau de noce* for the ladies, and a case of Eau-de-Cologne for myself. I've been running to seed so long, and want watering so much. (*Sprinkles himself with Eau-de-Cologne.*)

EMILY: Oh dear, Green! I'm afraid you're as great a fool as ever.

BRIERLY: Nay, nay, Mrs Jones – no man's a fool with five hundred pounds in his pocket. But here come the clerks; band-boxes and bouquets ain't business-like. You must carry these down to May.

GREEN: (*loading* EMILY *with the parcels*) Beg her acceptance of a bonnet, a bouquet, and a box of Piver's seven and a quarters – and accept the same yourself, from yours ever affectionately, G.J. (*Tries to kiss her over the parcels but cannot.*)

EMILY: (*from over the parcels.*) Oh, go along with your nonsense! I'll give you one downstairs. (*Exit.*)

(*Enter* BURTON *and* SHARPE, *clerks.*)

SHARPE: Good morning. Governor come yet?

BRIERLY: Not yet, Mr Sharpe; it's getting near his time, though.

(CLERKS *hang up their hats, coats, etc., and seat themselves at desks.*)

SHARPE: (*to* GREEN JONES) Can we do anything for you sir?

BRIERLY: This gentleman's waiting to see Mr Gibson. Here he is.

(*Enter* MR GIBSON.)

MR GIBSON: (*rubbing his feet on the mat*) Good morning, morning, Mr Sharpe – good morning Burton. Well, Robert – didn't expect to find you at the office this morning.

BRIERLY: Here's a gentleman waiting for you, sir, on business.

MR GIBSON: If you'll walk into my room, sir?

(*Exit* GREEN JONES *into* MR GIBSON'*s room.*)

BRIERLY: I thought I might as well number the cheques, sir, and go for the petty cash. Somehow, I felt I shouldn't like anything to go wrong today.

MR GIBSON: Well, that's a very proper feeling. I hope May likes my wife's present. She is a first-rate housekeeper; though she *did* call *you* her brother, the little rogue – and I've every reason to be satisfied with you.

BRIERLY: I'm right proud of that, sir.

MR GIBSON: You won't mind my giving you a word of advice on your wedding day? Go on as you've begun – keep a bright eye and an inquiring tongue in your head – learn how business is done – watch the market – and from what I've seen of you the six months you've been here, I shouldn't wonder if I found a better berth than messenger for you one of these days.

BRIERLY: Mr Gibson – sir – I can't thank you – but a lookout like that – it takes a man's breath away.

MR GIBSON: Many a man has risen in the city from errand boy to millionaire – with a good head on your shoulders, and a good character –

BRIERLY: (*aside*) Ah – there it is –

MR GIBSON: I know there's no gap between the first round of the ladder and the top of the tree. But that gentleman's waiting. (*Pauses – goes to the door.*) By the way, I expect a call a from Mr Hawkshaw.

BRIERLY: (*starting*) Hawkshaw!

MR GIBSON: Yes, the famous detective. Show him in when he comes. I've a particular appointment with him. (*Exit* MR GIBSON *into his own room.*)

BRIERLY: Hawkshaw coming here! The principal witness against me at my trial. Perhaps he won't know me – I'm much changed. But they say at Portland, he never forgets a face. If he knows me, and tells Mr Gibson, he'll discharge me – and today, just when we looked to be so happy! It would break May's heart. But why should I stay? I'm free for the day – I will not wait to meet my ruin. (*Going up.*)

> (*Enter* HAWKSHAW.)

HAWKSHAW: Mr Gibson within?

BRIERLY: Yes, sir but he has a gentleman with him.

HAWKSHAW: Take in my name. (*Writes on a card with pencil and gives it to* BRIERLY.)

BRIERLY: (*takes card and sees name on it – aside*) Hawkshaw! It is too late! Would you like to look at the paper, sir? (*Offers him one from desk.*)

HAWKSHAW: (*as he takes it, gives a keen look of recognition at* BRIERLY, *who shrinks under his eye, but represses his agitation by an effort*) I've seen you before, I think!

BRIERLY: I don't recollect you, sir.

HAWKSHAW: (*carelessly*) Perhaps I'm wrong – though I've a good memory for faces. Take in my card. (BRIERLY *goes off, with card.*) It's Dalton's pal, the youngster who got four years for passing forged Bank of England paper at the Bellvue Tea Gardens. I owe Master Dalton one for that night. Back from Portland, eh? Looks all the better for his schooling. But Portland's an odd shop to take an office messenger from. I wonder if his employer got his character from his last place.

> (*Re-enter* BRIERLY.)

BRIERLY: Mr Gibson will see you in a moment, sir.

HAWKSHAW: Very well. (*Gives him a look.*)

> (*Re-enter* GREEN JONES *from* MR GIBSON's *room, with cheque.*)

GREEN: (*to* BRIERLY) All right! Market rate – and no old masters. I'll drive to the bank – cash this – settle with those counter-skippers, and rattle back in time to see you turned off. I say – you must allow me to order a little dinner at the Star and Garter, and drive you down – all right you know. Mail phaeton and pair – your wife and my wife. I want to show you the style G.J. *used* to do it in. Now cabby, pull round – (*speaking loudly*) London Joint-Stock Bank – best pace. (*Exit.*)

BRIERLY: (*aside*) He little thinks what may be hanging over me.

MR GIBSON: (*appearing at the door of his room*) Now, Mr Hawkshaw, I'm at your service.

HAWKSHAW: (*returning* BRIERLY *the paper*) Cool case of note passing, that, at Bow street yesterday. (BRIERLY *winces – aside*.) It's my man, sure enough.
(*Exit into* MR GIBSON's *room*.)

BRIERLY: He knows me – I can read it in his face – his voice. He'll tell Mr Gibson! Perhaps he's telling him now! I wish I'd spoken to him – but they have no mercy. Oh, if I'd only made a clean breast of it to Mr Gibson before this!
(*Enter* MR GIBSON *and* HAWKSHAW.)

MR GIBSON: Mr Sharpe, will you go round to the banks and see what's doing? (SHARPE *takes his hat and exit.*) Mr Burton, you'll be just in time for morning's clearance.

BURTON: (*getting his hat – aside*) By Jove! the governor wants to make a morning's clearance of us, I think. I'm half an hour too soon for the Clearing House. Time for a tip-top game at billiards. (*Exit.*)

MR GIBSON: Robert! (*writing at desk*)

BRIERLY: Yes, sir.

MR GIBSON: Before you leave, just step round into Glynn's and get me cash for this. You'll have time enough before you're wanted downstairs, you rascal.

BRIERLY: (*aside*) He knows nothing. (*Aloud*) I'll be back in five minutes, sir.
(*As* MR GIBSON *is about to give him the cheque,* HAWKSHAW, *who is standing between* MR GIBSON *and* BRIERLY, *interposes, and takes cheque carelessly.*)

HAWKSHAW: Your messenger, eh?

MR GIBSON: Yes.

HAWKSHAW: Had him long?

MR GIBSON: Six months.

HAWKSHAW: Good character?

MR GIBSON: Never had a steadier, soberer, better-behaved lad in the office.

HAWKSHAW: Had you references with him?

MR GIBSON: Why, I think I took him mainly on the strength of his own good looks and his sweetheart's. An honest face is the best testimonial after all.

HAWKSHAW: H'm – neither is always to be relied on.

MR GIBSON: You detectives would suspect your own fathers. Why, how you look at the lad. Come, you've never had *him* through your hands. (*A pause.*)

HAWKSHAW: No, he's quite a stranger to me. (*Turns away.*) Here's the cheque, young man. Take care you make no mistake about it.

BRIERLY: (*aside, going*) Saved, saved! Heaven bless him for those words. (*Exit.*)

HAWKSHAW: (*aside*) Poor devil, he's paid his debt at Portland. (*Aloud*) Now to business. You say a bill drawn by Vanzeller & Co., of Penang, on the London Joint-Stock Bank was presented for discount here last night, which you know to be a forgery?

MR GIBSON: Yes. As it was after hours the clerk told the presenter to call this morning.

HAWKSHAW: Bill-forging is tip-top work. The man who did this job knows what
    he's about. We mustn't alarm him. What time did the clerk tell him to call?

MR GIBSON: At eleven.

HAWKSHAW: It's within five minutes. You go to your room. I'll take my place at
    one of these desks as a clerk, and send the customers in to you. When the forged
    bill is presented, you come to the door and say, loud enough for me to hear –
    'Vanzeller and Co., Penang', and leave the rest to me.

MR GIBSON: (*nervously*) Hadn't I better have assistance within call?

HAWKSHAW: Oh dear no – I like to work single-handed – but don't be excited.
    Take it coolly, or you may frighten the bird. (*Goes to desk.*)

MR GIBSON: Easy to say take it coolly! I haven't been thief-catching all my life. (*Exit
    MR GIBSON into his room.*)
                    (*Enter MOSS.*)

MOSS: (*at the counter, getting out his bills*) Let me see – Spelter and Wayne. Fifty, ten,
    three – thirty days after sight. That's commercial. (*examining another bill*) For
    two hundred at two months – drawn by Captain Crabbs – accepted the
    Honourable Augustus Greenway: that's a thirty per center. Better try that at
    another shop. (*Takes out another.*) Mossop and Mills – good paper – ninety-
    nine, eight, two – at sixty days. That'll do here.

MR GIBSON: (*at the door of his room*) Mr Hawkshaw!

HAWKSHAW: H – sh!
                (*Crosses, warns him against using his name, but obeys his call, and
                goes in.*)

MOSS: (*on hearing his name*) Hawkshaw! (*with a quick glance as HAWKSHAW
    passes into MR GIBSON's room*) A detective here! Ware – hawk! (*alarmed, but
    recovering*) Well, it ain't for me – I'm all on the square now. If bills will go
    missing it ain't me that steals 'em – Tiger does that. I'm always a *bona fide*
    holder for value – I can face any examination, I can. But I should like to know
    Hawkshaw's little game, and I shouldn't mind spoiling it.
                (*Re-enter HAWKSHAW.*)

Mr Gibson, if you please?

HAWKSHAW: He's in his office, sir. (*As MOSS passes in, he recognises him.*) Melter
    Moss here! Can he be the forger? He heard my name. Dear, dear, to think that a
    business-man like Mr Gibson should be green enough to call a man like me by
    his name.
                (*Re-enter MOSS.*)

Here he comes; now for the signal. (*Goes to desk.*)

MOSS: (*coming down with cheques and bill-book*) All right! Beautiful paper, most of
    it. Only two of 'em fishy. Well, I'll try *them* three doors down – they ain't so
    particular.

HAWKSHAW: (*aside*) No signal!

MOSS: If you'll allow me, I'll take a dip of your ink, young man; I've an entry to make
    in my bill-book. (HAWKSHAW *pitches him a pen.*) Thank you. (MOSS *writes.*)
             (*Enter DALTON dressed as a respectable elderly commercial man,
             in as complete contrast as possible with his appearance in first Act.*)

DALTON: Mr Gibson? (*Takes out his bill case.*)

HAWKSHAW: You'll find him in his office, sir.

DALTON: (*aside*) That's not the young man I saw here yesterday afternoon. (*aloud*) Let me see first that I've got the bill. (*rummaging for bill*)

MOSS: (*recognizing* DALTON) Tiger here, in his City get-up. Oh, oh! If this should be Hawkshaw's little game! I'll drop him a line.
> (*Writes, crosses, and passes paper secretly to* DALTON, *with a significant look, and taking care to keep behind the railing of the counter.*)

DALTON: (*recognizing him*) Moss! (*Taking paper, reads.*) 'Hawkshaw's at that desk.' Forewarned, forearmed!

MOSS: There, I hope I've spoiled Hawkshaw's little game. (*Exit* MOSS.)
> (MR GIBSON *appears at door of office.*)

MR GIBSON: (*about to address* HAWKSHAW *again*) Mr –

HAWKSHAW: (*hastily interrupting him*) H'sh! a party wants to see you, sir, if you could step this way for a moment.

DALTON: Would you oblige me, Mr Gibson, by looking very particularly at this bill?

MR GIBSON: 'Vanzeller and Co., Penang.' (*Glances at* HAWKSHAW *aside, who seats himself at desk.*) He don't stir! 'Vanzeller and Co., Penang'. (*aside*) Confound it, I haven't made a blunder, have I? 'Vanzeller and Co., Penang.'
> (HAWKSHAW *prepares handcuffs under the desk.*)

DALTON: Yes, a most respectable firm. But all's not gold that glitters. I thought the paper as safe as you do; but, unluckily, I burnt my fingers with it once before. You may or may not remember my presenting a bill drawn by the same firm for discount two months ago.

MR GIBSON: Yes, particularly well.

DALTON: Well, sir, I have now discovered that was a forgery.

MR GIBSON: So have I.

DALTON: And I'm sadly afraid, between you and me – by the way, I hope I may speak safely before your clerk?

MR GIBSON: Oh, quite.

DALTON: I'm almost satisfied that this bill is a forgery too. The other has been impounded, I hear. My object in coming here yesterday was first to verify, if possible, the forgery in the case of this second bill; and next to ask your assistance, as you had given value for the first as well as myself, in bringing the forger to justice. (HAWKSHAW *looks up as in doubt.*)

MR GIBSON: Really, sir –

DALTON: Oh, my dear sir! If we City men don't stand by each other in these rascally cases! But before taking any other step, there is one thing I owe to myself, as well as to you, and that is to repay you the amount of the first forged bill.

MR GIBSON: But you said you had given value for it?

DALTON: The more fool I! But if I am to pay twice, that is no reason you should be a loser. I've a memorandum of the amount here. (*Looks at his bill-book.*) Two hundred and twenty – seven – and one – two – three. (*counting out coppers*)

MR GIBSON: Oh, pray, sir, don't trouble yourself about the coppers.

DALTON: I'm particular in these matters. Excuse me – it's a little peculiarity of mine – three – four – five. There, that's off my conscience! But you've not examined the notes. (HAWKSHAW *pockets handcuffs.*)

MR GIBSON: Oh, my dear sir. (*putting them up*)

DALTON: Ah, careless, careless! (*Shakes his head.*) Luckily, I *had* endorsed 'em.

MR GIBSON: Really, sir, I had marked that two hundred and twenty off to a bad debt a month ago. By the way, I have not the pleasure of knowing your name.

DALTON: Wake, sir – Theophilus Wake, of the firm of Wake Brothers, shippers and wharfingers, Limehouse and Dock street, Liverpool. We have a branch establishment at Liverpool. Here's our card. (*Gives card.*)

MR GIBSON: So far from expecting you to repay the money, I thought you were coming to bleed me afresh with forged bill No. 2 – for a forgery it is, most certainly.

DALTON: Quite natural, my dear sir, quite natural. I've no right to feel the least hurt.

MR GIBSON: And what's more, I had a detective at that desk ready to pounce upon you.

DALTON: No, really!

MR GIBSON: You can drop the clerk, now Mr Hawkshaw. (HAWKSHAW *comes down.*)

DALTON: Hawkshaw! Have I the honour to address Mr Hawkshaw, the detective, the hero of the great gold dust robberies, and the famous Trunk-line transfer forgeries?

HAWKSHAW: I'm the man, I believe – (*modestly*)

DALTON: Sir, the whole commercial world owes you a debt of gratitude it can never repay. I shall have to ask your valuable assistance in discovering the author of these audacious forgeries.

HAWKSHAW: Have you any clue?

DALTON: I believe they are the work of a late clerk of ours, who got into gay company, poor lad, and has gone to the bad. He knew the Vanzellers' signature, as they were old correspondents of ours.

HAWKSHAW: Can you give me a description of him? Age – height – hair – eyes – complexion – last address – haunts – habits – associates – (*significantly*) any female connection?

DALTON: Unluckily I know very little of him personally. My partner, Walker Wake, can supply all the information you want.

HAWKSHAW: Where shall I find him?

DALTON: Here's our card. We'll take a cab and question him at our office. Or (*as if struck by a sudden thought*) suppose you bring him here – so that we may all lay our heads together.

HAWKSHAW: You'll not leave this office till I come back?

DALTON: If Mr Gibson will permit me to wait.

MR GIBSON: I shall feel extremely obliged to you.

HAWKSHAW: You may expect me back in half an hour at farthest – (*Going up, returns.*) egad. sir, you've had a narrow escape. I had the darbies open under the desk. (*showing handcuffs*)

DALTON: Ha, ha, ha, how very pleasant. (*Takes and examines handcuffs curiously.*)

HAWKSHAW: But I'll soon be down on this youngster.

MR GIBSON: If only he hasn't left London.

HAWKSHAW: Bless you – they can't leave London. Like the moths, they turn and turn about the candle till they burn their wings.

DALTON: Ah, thanks to men like you. How little society is aware of what it owes its detective benefactors.

HAWKSHAW: There's the satisfaction of doing one's duty – and something else now and then.

MR GIBSON: Ah, a good round reward.

HAWKSHAW: That's not bad; but there's something better than that.

DALTON: Indeed!

HAWKSHAW: Paying off old scores. Now, if I could only clinch the darbies on Jem Dalton's wrists.

DALTON: Dalton! What's your grudge against him in particular?

HAWKSHAW: He was the death of my pal – the best mate I ever had – poor Joe Skirrit. (*Draws his hands across his eyes.*) I shall never work with such another.

MR GIBSON: Did he murder him?

HAWKSHAW: Not to say murder him right out. But he spoiled him – give him a clip on the head with a neddy – a life-preserver. He was never his own man afterwards. He left the force on a pension, but he grew sort of paralysed, and then got queer in his head. I was sitting with him the week before he died – 'Jack,' he says – it was Joe and Jack with us, 'Jack,' he says, 'I lay my death at the Tiger's door' – that was the name we had for Dalton in the force. 'You'll look after him, Jack,' – he says, 'for the sake of your old mate.' By – no, I won't say what I said, but I promised him to be even with Jem Dalton, and I'll keep my word.

DALTON: You know this Dalton?

HAWKSHAW: Know him! He has as many outsides as he has aliases. You may identify him for a felon today, and pull your hat off to him for a parson tomorrow. But I'll hunt him out of all his skins, and my best night's sleep will be the day I've brought Jem Dalton to the dock!

DALTON: Mr Hawkshaw, I wish you every success!

HAWKSHAW: But I've other fish to fry now. (*Looks at card.*) Wake Brothers, Buckle's Wharf, Limehouse. (*Exit* HAWKSHAW.)

DALTON: Ask anybody for our office. (*aside*) And if anybody can tell you I *shall* be astonished.

MR GIBSON: I'm really ashamed to keep you waiting, sir.

DALTON: Oh, I can write my letters here. (*pointing to the counter*) If you don't mind trusting me all alone in your office.

MR GIBSON: My dear sir, if you were Dalton himself – the redoubtable Tiger – you couldn't steal ledgers and day-books, and there's nothing more valuable here – except, by the way, my queer old depositer Miss Faddle's five thousand, that she insists on my keeping here in the office in gold, as she believes neither in hands nor bank-notes. And, talking of notes, I may as well lock up these you so handsomely paid me. (*Goes to safe.*)

DALTON: Not believe in notes! Infatuated woman! (*aside*) I hope he'll like mine.

MR GIBSON: (*locks safe*) I'll leave you to write your letters. (*Exit* MR GIBSON *into his office.*)

DALTON: Phew! (*Whistles low.*) That's the narrowest shave I ever had. So Jack Hawkshaw, you'll be even with Jem Dalton yet, will you? You may add this day's work to the score against him. How the old boy swallowed my soft sawder and Brummagem notes! They're beauties! It would be a pity to leave them in his hands – and five thousand shiners, p'raps, alongside of 'em. Come – I've my wax handy – never travel without my tools. Here goes for a squeeze at the lock of this safe.

> (*Goes to safe, and by means of a pick-lock applies wax to the wards of the lock by the key-hole. Music.*)
> (*Enter* BRIERLY.)

BRIERLY: (*hangs up hat*) Clerks not returned. Hawkshaw gone? (*Sees* DALTON *at safe.*) Holloa, who's this? Tampering with the safe? Hold hard there. (*He seizes* DALTON, *who turns.*)

DALTON: (*aside*) Brierly! Hands off, young 'un. Don't you know a locksmith when you see him?

BRIERLY: Gammon! Who are you? How came you here? What are you doing with that safe?

DALTON: You ask a great deal too many questions.

BRIERLY: I'll trouble you to answer 'em.

DALTON: By what right?

BRIERLY: I'm messenger in this office, and I've a right to know who touches a lock here.

DALTON: You messenger here? Indeed! and suppose I took to asking questions – you mightn't be so keen of answering them yourself – Robert Brierly!

BRIERLY: You know me!

DALTON: Yes. And your character from your last place, Port –

BRIERLY: (*terrified*) Hush!

DALTON: Your hair hasn't grown so fast but I can see traces of the prison crop.

BRIERLY: For mercy's sake!

DALTON: Silence for silence. Ask me no questions and I'll press for no answers.

BRIERLY: You must explain your business here to Mr Gibson. I suspected you for a thief.

DALTON: And I know you for a jail-bird. Let's see whose information will go the farthest. There, I'll make you a fair offer, Robert Brierly. Let me pass, and I leave this place without breathing a word to your employer that you're fresh from a sentence of penal servitude for four years. Detain me, and I denounce you for the convict you are. (*A knock at the door.*)

MRS WILLOUGHBY: (*without*) Mr Brierly!

BRIERLY: Hush! Coming, Mrs Willoughby.

DALTON: Is it a bargain?

BRIERLY: Go – go – anything to escape this exposure. (*giving him his hat, etc., from counter*)

DALTON: (*at door*) There's Aby Moss waiting for me outside. He shall blow the lad to Gibson. He may be useful to us, and I owe him one for spoiling my squeeze. (*Exit* DALTON.)

> (*Enter* MRS WILLOUGHBY.)

MRS WILLOUGHBY: Which, I've to ask pardon for intruding, not bein' used to an

---

Gammon: nonsense.

office, and knowing my place I 'ope. But it's gettin' on for a quarter past eleven, Mr Robert, and twelve's the latest they will do it, and the breakfast all set out beautiful – and some parties is a-gettin' impatient, which it's no more than natural, bless her, and Sam, that rampageous – but whatever's the matter? You look struck all of a heap like!

BRIERLY: Oh, nothing, nothing. It's natural, you know, a man should look queer on his wedding morning. There, go and tell May I'll be with her directly.
          (*Enter* SAM.)

SAM: Come along, Bob, we're all tired of waiting, especially this child. (*Sings nigger song.*) Come along!

MRS WILLOUGHBY: (*admiringly*) Oh, that boy! If it ain't enough to make any grandmother's 'eart proud.

BRIERLY: Go – go – I'll follow – I've some business matters to attend to.

SAM: A nice state for business you're in – I don't think. There, granny. (*Looks at him.*) This is what comes of getting married! If it ain't an awful warning to a young fellow like me!

MRS WILLOUGHBY: Drat your imperence.

SAM: But the party's waiting downstairs, and we're wanted to keep 'em in spirits, so come along, granny. (*Polks out with* MRS WILLOUGHBY.)

BRIERLY: Known! Threatened! Spared by Hawkshaw – only to be denounced by this man.
          (*Enter* MOSS.)

MOSS: Mr Gibson, if you please?

BRIERLY: He's in his office, sir – that way.

MOSS: I remember the young man now. A convict get himself into a respectable situation! It is a duty one owes to society to put his employer on his guard. (*Exit.*)

BRIERLY: Yes – he's gone – I can draw my breath again. I was wrong to let him go. But to have the cup at one's lip, and see it struck away – I couldn't – I couldn't – even the detective had mercy. When we're married, I'll tell Mr Gibson all.
          (*Re-enter* MOSS *and* MR GIBSON *from his office.*)

MOSS: You can question him, sir, if you don't believe me: any way I've done my duty, and that's what I look to. (*Exit.*)

BRIERLY: Here's the money for the cheque, sir. (GIBSON *takes money –* BRIERLY *is going.*)

MR GIBSON: Robert.

BRIERLY: Sir.

MR GIBSON: Where are you going?

BRIERLY: To dress for church, sir.

MR GIBSON: Stay here.

BRIERLY: Sir.

MR GIBSON: You have deceived me.

BRIERLY: Mr Gibson –

Polks out: dances out. SAM's 'nigger song' is a minstrel song, a popular music hall entertainment.

MR GIBSON: I know all – your crime – your conviction – your punishment.
BRIERLY: Mercy, mercy!
MR GIBSON: Unhappy young man.
BRIERLY: Ah, unhappy you may well call me. I was sentenced, sir, but I was not guilty. It's true, sir, but I don't expect you to believe it. I've worked out my sentence, sir – they hadn't a mark against me at Portland – you may ask 'em – here's my ticket-of-leave, sir. You own I've been steady and industrious since I came here. By heaven's help I mean to be so still – indeed I do.
MR GIBSON: I dare say, but I must think of my own credit and character. If it was buzzed about that I kept a ticket-of-leave man in my employment –
(*Enter* GREEN JONES, MAY, EMILY, MRS WILLOUGHBY, *and* SAM.)
MRS WILLOUGHBY: Which, axin' your pardon, Mr Gibson, we're all ready, and the cab is waitin' –
SAM: And the parson getting cold.
MAY: Robert, why are you not dressed? What is the matter?
BRIERLY: Heaven help thee, my poor lass.
MAY: You are pale – you tremble – you are ill – oh, speak! what is it?
BRIERLY: Bear up, May. But our marriage – cannot – be – yet – awhile.
ALL: The wedding put off! (MAY *stands aghast.*)
EMILY: No bonnets!
MRS WILLOUGHBY: And no breakfast!
GREEN: By Jove! ⎫
SAM: Here's a go! ⎭ (*Together.*)
MAY: Am I dreaming? Robert, what does this mean?
BRIERLY: It's hard to bear. Keep up your heart – I'm discharged. He knows all.
MAY: Oh, sir, you couldn't have the heart – say it is not true.
MR GIBSON: Sorry for it. You have both deceived me – you must both leave the place.
BRIERLY: You hear – come, May.
MAY: I'll go, sir. It was I deceived you, not he. Only give him a chance –
(*Music, piano, till end.*)
BRIERLY: Never heed her, sir. She'd have told you long ago, but I hadn't the heart. My poor lass – let her bide here, sir. I'll leave the country – I'll 'list.
MAY: Hush, hush, Robert! We were wrong to hide the truth – we are sorely punished – if you've courage to face what's before us, I have.
BRIERLY: My brave wench! Thank you for all your kindness, sir. Goodbye, friends. Come, May, we'll go together.

Act IV

SCENE 1. *The Bridgewater Arms. A large gaily decorated Coffee Room set out with tables and benches; a bar crosses the corner of room, up Left, with gaily painted hogsheads ranged above it; beer engine, etc., at the head of bar, Left Centre; door to street, Right; door to parlour, Right; curtained windows; a piano, Left; a trap leading to cellar, practicable, up stage Centre, near the end of the bar; table and three chairs in front Right; table and benches, up Left; table and benches at back, Right.*

MOSS *with bags of silver, and* DALTON *seated at table, Right.*
MALTBY *waiting upon them.*

MALTBY: Pint of sherry. (*putting it down*) Very curious! Yes, Mr Moss, it's a pleasure to see you, sir, at the Bridgewater Arms; though it ain't the Bellevue Gardens, worse luck.

MOSS: Ah, ups and downs is the lot of life, Mr Maltby. You'll let me know when Mr Tottie comes?

MALTBY: Ah, the subcontractor for the main sewer in the next street. Such nuisance! stops all traffic –

MOSS: But sends you all the navvies. It's here they're taken on and paid, you know.

MALTBY: Connection not aristocratic, but beery; we do four butts a week at the bar, to say nothing of the concert room upstairs.

DALTON: What, the navvies like music to their malt, do they?

MALTBY: Oh yes, sir! I introduced the arts from the West End. The roughs adore music, especially selections from the Italian Opera, and as for sentiment and sensation, if you could hear Miss St Evremond touch them up with the 'Maniac's Tear', the new sensation ballad by a gifted composer attached to the establishment, and sold at the bar, price one shilling. Why, we've disposed of three dozen 'Maniac's Tears' on a pay-night – astonishing how it goes down!

DALTON: With the beer?

> (*Enter* EMILY. *She wears handsome evening dress under her shawl.*)

MALTBY: Here comes Mrs Jones – gentlemen, this is the great and gifted creature I was alluding to.

EMILY: Go along with your nonsense!

MALTBY: Miss St Evremond, the great sensation balladist, formerly of the Nobility's Concerts and Her Majesty's Theatre – (*aside*) in the ballet.

MOSS: Proud to make the acquaintance of so gifted an artiste.

EMILY: You're very obliging, I'm sure. (*taking off her bonnet and shawl and smoothing her hair, to* MALTBY) How's the room tonight?

MALTBY: Tidy, but nothing to what it will be. It's the navvies' pay-night, you know.

EMILY: Navvies! Oh Lord, (*Sighs.*) to think of Emily St Evremond wasting her sweetness upon an audience of navigators!

DALTON: They are not aristocratic, but they are appreciative.

EMILY: Yes, poor creatures, they do know a good thing when they hear it!

DALTON: If Miss St Evremond will oblige us with a ballad –

MALTBY: The 'Maniac's Tear'.

EMILY: If these gentlemen wouldn't mind.

DALTON: On the contrary – we like music; don't we, Moss?

MOSS: I doat upon it; especially Handel.

EMILY: But where's the accompanist?

MALTBY: I regret to say the signor is disgracefully screwed.

EMILY: Oh, never mind, Jones can accompany me. Come in, Green Jones; you're wanted! (MALTBY *opens piano.*)

> (*Enter* GREEN JONES *with basket of trotters.*)

GREEN: In the trotter line, or the tuneful?

EMILY: To accompany me on the piano. (*She arranges her hair.*)

GREEN: Till you're ready, these gentlemen wouldn't like to try a trotter, would they? A penny a set, and of this morning's boiling – if I might tempt you? They're delicious with a soupcon of pepper.

MALTBY: No, no, Mr Jones, these are not *your* style of customers.

GREEN: Excuse me, Mr Maltby. I'm aware trotters are not known in good society; but they go down as a relish, even with people accustomed to entrees. I liked 'em as a swell before I was reduced to them as a salesman.

MALTBY: Perhaps you'd give us the 'Maniac's Tear'?

EMILY: I can't do it without letting down my back hair.

DALTON: Oh, down with the back hair, by all means.

EMILY: You're very kind. Jones! Where's the glass?

> (GREEN JONES *procures a hand-glass from basket.* EMILY *arranges her hair by glass.*)

GREEN: (*seating himself at the piano*) One word of preface, gentlemen. It's a sensation ballad. Scene – Criminal Ward, Bedlam! Miss St Evremond is an interesting lunatic – with lucid intervals. She has murdered her husband – (*Finds basket in his way.*) Emmy, if you'd just shift those trotters – and her three children, and is supposed to be remonstrating with one of the lunacy commissioners on the cruelty of her confinement!

> (*Music.* EMILY *sings 'The Maniac's Tear', accompanied by her husband – all applaud.*)

MALTBY: Now look sharp, Miss St Evremond. The Wisconsin Warblers are at their last chorus. (*Exit* MALTBY.)

EMILY: (*to her husband*) Bye-bye, dear, till after the concert – you know I can't be seen speaking to you while you carry that basket.

GREEN: True – in the humble trotter-man who would suspect the husband of the brilliant St Evremond! There's something romantic in it. I hover round the room – I hear you universally admired – visibly applauded – audibly adored. Oh, agony!

EMILY: Now, Jones – you are going to be jealous again! I do believe jealousy's at the bottom of those trotters! (*Exeunt* EMILY *and* GREEN JONES.)

MOSS: Now's our time – while the fools upstairs are having their ears tickled. You've the tools ready for jumping that crib in St Nicholas Lane?

DALTON: Yes, but tools ain't enough – I must have a clear stage, and a pal who knows the premises.

MOSS: I've managed that – nobody sleeps in the place but the old housekeeper and her precious grandson.

'*The Maniac's Tear*' was composed for the play by James Howard Tully (1814-68). I am indebted to E. George Hauger for the following note. 'Tully was essentially a theatre musician. Beginning life as a performer, he settled down as a chorus master and/or musical director, working at the Bower Saloon, the Alhambra, Covent Garden and Drury Lane. He composed songs, dance music, incidental music and several stage works, none of which is nowadays performed. A highlight in his career was his conducting the first performance in English of Verdi's *Il Trovatore* which was presented at Drury Lane in 1856 under the title of *The Gypsy's Vengeance*.'

The version of the song written for the National Theatre's production in London in 1981 is produced on p. 223.

DALTON: He's as sharp as a terrier dog – and can bite too – a young varmint. If
I come across him – (*threateningly*)

MOSS: No occasion for that – you're so violent. I've made the young man's
acquaintance. I've asked him to meet me here tonight for a quiet little game –
his revenge, I called it. I'll dose the lad till he's past leaving the place. You drop
a hint to the old lady – she'll come to take care of him. The coast will be clear
yonder.

DALTON: And the five thousand shiners will be nailed in the turning of a jemmy.
If we had that young Brierly in the job – he knows the way about the
place blindfold. But he's on the square, he is – bent on earning an honest
livelihood.

MOSS: But I've blown him wherever he's got work. He *must* dance to our tune at
last!

DALTON: Ah, if *you've* got him in hand! Work *him* into the job, and I'll jump the
crib tonight.

MOSS: He's applied to be taken on at the contract works near here. This is the pay-
night – Tottie, the subcontractor, is a friend of mine –

DALTON: He's lucky!

MOSS: Yes, I find him the cash at twenty per cent. till his certificates are allowed by
the engineer. 'Tain't heavy interest, but there's no risk – a word from me, and
he'd discharge every navvy in his gang. But I've only to breathe jail-bird, and
there's no need of a discharge. The men themselves would work the lad off the
job. They are sad roughs, but they've a horror of jail-birds.

DALTON: Ah, nobody likes the Portland mark. I know that – I've tried the honest
dodge, too.

MOSS: It don't answer.

DALTON: It didn't with me. I had a friend, like you, always after me. Whatever I
tried, I was blown as a convict and hunted out from honest men.

MOSS: And then you met me – and I was good to you – wasn't I?

DALTON: Yes. You were very kind.

MOSS: Always allowed you handsome for the swag you brought, and put you up to no
end of good things, and I'll stick by you, my dear – I never drop a friend.

DALTON: No, till the hangman takes your place at his side.
(*Presses his elbows to his side in the attitude of a man pinioned.*)

MOSS: Don't be disagreeable, my dear – you give me a cold shiver. Hush! here come
the navvies.
(*Enter the* NAVIGATORS *noisily. They seat themselves at their
tables, calling, some for pots of beer, some for quarterns of gin. The*
POTMAN *and* WAITERS *bustle about with* MALTBY
superintending and taking money. BRIERLY *follows. Enter*
HAWKSHAW, *disguised as a navvy. He appears flustered with
drink – goes to one of the tables, and assuming a country dialect, calls
swaggeringly.*)

HAWKSHAW: Gallon o' beer, measter.

MALTBY: A gallon?

HAWKSHAW: Aye, and another when that's done – I'm in brass tonight, and I stand
treat. Here, mates, who'll drink? (NAVVIES *crowd, with loud acclamations, to*

his table – beer is brought – HAWKSHAW *to* BRIERLY, *who is seated.*) Come, won't thou drink, my little flannel-back?

BRIERLY: No, thank you; I've a poor head for liquor and I've not had my supper yet.

HAWKSHAW: Thou'st sure it's not pride?

BRIERLY: Pride? I've no call for pride – I've come to try and get taken on at the works.

HAWKSHAW: Well, thou look'st like a tough 'un. There's Cast-iron Jack was smashed in the tunnel this morning. There'll be room for thee if thou canst swing the old anchor.

BRIERLY: The old anchor?

HAWKSHAW: Ha, ha! It's easy to see thou'st no banker. Why, the pick to be sure – the groundsman's bread-winner. Halloa, mates, keep a drop of grog for Ginger. (*Goes back to table.*)

NAVVIES: Aye, aye!

HAWKSHAW: Here's the old anchor, boys, and long may we live to swing it.

ALL: The pick forever. Hip, hip hurrah!

MALTBY: Mr Tottie's in the parlour, and wishes particularly to see you, Mr Moss.

MOSS: I should think he did – say I'm coming. (*Exit* MALTBY.)

DALTON: (*aside to* MOSS) You look after the Lancashire lad – yonder he sits – and I'll drop a hint to the old woman. Stay; we'd better work from the old church-yard of St Nicholas – there's a door opens into it from the crib. I'll hide the tools behind one of the tombstones.

MOSS: Beautiful! Sacred to the memory of Jem Dalton's jack-in-the-box! Ha, ha, ha! (*Exeunt* MOSS *into parlour*, DALTON *by the street door.*)

HAWKSHAW: Here, landlord, take your change out of that. (*Flings a sovereign on the table.*) Call for more beer, mates, till I come back. (*aside*) Yes – it's Jim Dalton – or the Devil! Whichever it is he shall find Jack Hawkshaw a match for him. I've marked him down here! Now – I'll stalk him like his shadow. (*Exit, staggering like a drunken man after* DALTON.)

1ST NAVVY: Thou'lt come back, mate?

HAWKSHAW: Aye, aye, boys, directly. (*at door*) Contractor's in t'parlour wi' the week's pay.

1ST NAVVY: Here's thy health!

ALL: (*sing*) 'For he's a jolly good fellow', etc.
               (*Enter* GREEN JONES.)

GREEN: Emily is bringing down the house in the 'Maniac'. I can't stand it; my feelings as a husband are trampled on! But she's a trump, too – and what a talent! By heaven, if ever I get my head above water again, I won't fool away my money as I have done; no, I'll take a theatre at the West End, and bring out my wife in everything. It will be an immense success; meanwhile, 'till the pounds present themselves, let me look after the pence. Trotters, gents, trotters – penny the set, and this morning's boiling.

1ST NAVVY: Stop till we get brass; we'll clear out thy basket.
               (*Exeunt* NAVVIES, *followed by* GREEN JONES.)

---

flannel-back: presumably slang for navvy, referring to the poor but tough quality clothing.

BRIERLY: Yes, the old anchor is my last chance – I've tried every road to an honest livelihood, and one after another they are barred in my face. Everywhere that dreadful word, jail-bird, seems to be breathed in the air about me – sometimes in a letter, sometimes in a hint, sometimes a copy of the newspaper with my trial, and then it is the same story – sorry to part with me – no complaint to make – but can't keep a ticket-of-leave man. Who can it be that hunts me down this way? Hawkshaw spared me. I've done no man a wrong – poor fellows like me should have no enemies. I wouldn't care for myself, but my poor lass, my brave, true-hearted May; I'm dragging her down along with me. Ah! here she is.

> (*Enter* MAY EDWARDS, *poorly dressed. She has a can, and some food in a bundle.*)

MAY: (*cheerfully*) Well, Robert, dear, I said I shouldn't be long. I have brought your supper.

BRIERLY: Thank thee, darling – I'm not hungry. Thou'st been out after work all the day – eat thyself – thou need'st strength most.

MAY: Nay, dear, what will become of me if you lose heart? But if you'll be a good boy, and take your tea (*Opens tin and takes bread from bundle.*) I'll tell you a piece of good news – for you – for both of us.

BRIERLY: That will be something new.

MAY: I've got a promise of work from the Sailor's Ready Made Clothing Warehouse near here. It won't be much, but it will keep the wolf from the door till you get another situation. Have you tried if the contractor here will take you on?

BRIERLY: Not yet. He's in yonder paying the men. He'll send for me; but I scarcely dare to ask him. Oh, May, lass, I've held on hard to hope, but it feels as if it was slipping out of my hand at last.

MAY: Robert, dear Robert, grasp it hard; so long as we do what is right, all will come clear at last; we're in kind hands, dear – you know we are.

BRIERLY: I begin to doubt it, lass – I do, indeed.

MAY: No, no; never doubt that, or my heart will give way too –

BRIERLY: And thou that has had courage for both of us. Every blow that has fallen, every door that has been shut between me and an honest livelihood, every time that clean hands have been drawn away from mine, and respectable faces turned aside as I came near them, I've come to thee for comfort and love and hope, and I've found them till now.

MAY: Oh, yes! what's the good of a sunshine wife? It's hard weather tries us women best, dear; you men ain't half so stout-hearted.

BRIERLY: I'd not mind the misery so much for myself; 'tis for thee.

MAY: I don't complain – do I?

BRIERLY: Never! But, nevertheless, I've brought thee to sorrow and want and shame. Till I came back to thee thou hadst friends, work and comforts. But since Mr Gibson turned us off, the plight that has followed me has reached thee too, the bravest, honestest, brightest lass that ever doubled a man's joys, and halved his burdens. Oh! it's too bad – it kills the heart of me – it makes me mad.

MAY: I tell you, 'twill all come clear at last, if we are only true to ourselves – to each other. I've work promised, and perhaps you may be taken on here. I spy bright days before us still.

BRIERLY: Bright days! I can't see them through the prison cloud that stands like a

dark wall between me and honest labour. May, lass, I sometimes think I had
better let it all go – run – 'list – make a hole in the water, anything that would rid
thee of me; thou could'st make thy way alone.

MAY: Oh, Robert, that is cruel! Nothing others could do to us could hurt me like
those words from you; we are man and wife, and we'll take life as man and wife
should, hand-in-hand. Where you go, I will go, where you suffer, I will be there
to comfort; and when better times come, as come they will – we will thank God
for them together.

BRIERLY: I'll try to hope.

MAY: And you won't heed the black thoughts that come over you when you're alone?

BRIERLY: I'll do my best to fight 'em off.

MAY: That's a brave dear. I'm only going to the warehouse; I shall be back soon.
Goodbye, dearest. Remember, when the clouds are thickest, the sun still shines
behind them. (*Exit.*)

BRIERLY: Bless that brave bright heart; she puts strength into me, in spite of the
devilish doubts that have got their claws about my throat. Yes, I *will* try once
more.

> (*The* NAVIGATORS *come noisily out of parlour, and re-seat
> themselves at the tables.*)
> (*Enter,* MOSS, *from parlour.*)

MOSS: (*speaking off*) So, all paid at last?

> (*Re-enter* DALTON, *and* HAWKSHAW *after him.*)

DALTON: (*to* MOSS) All right, the lad's coming. I've tipped the old woman the
office, and planted the tools.

HAWKSHAW: (*tapping* BRIERLY *on the shoulder*) All the gang ha' gotten their
brass – Tottie's takin' on men now, my little flannel-back. Then go in, and put
on a bold face – Tottie likes chaps as speaks up to him. (HAWKSHAW *returns
to his mates.*)

BRIERLY: If this chance fail – God help us both.

> (*Exit into parlour.* NAVVIES *at the table clamour and fight, and
> shout over their drink.* MOSS *glances at* BRIERLY *as he passes.*)

MOSS: There he goes!

DALTON: It would be a pity to let a ticket-of-leave man in among all those nice,
sober, well-behaved young men.

MOSS: I must blow him again; he ought to be near the end of his tether now. (*Enter*
SAM WILLOUGHBY.) Here comes our young friend. (*coaxingly*) Ah, my
dear – so you've come out for a little hanky-panky with old Moss. Sit down. My
friend, Mr Walker. What'll you have?

SAM: I don't care – I'm game for anything from sherry to rum-shrub. Suppose we
begin with a brandy and soda, to cool the coppers?

DALTON: Brandy and soda, Maltby.

SAM: I had an awful go in of it last night at the balls, and dropped into a lot of 'em like
a three-year-old! (*Imitates action of billiard play, with his walking-cane for a
cue.*)

MOSS: Billiards, too! Lord, what a clever young chap you are. (MALTBY *brings soda
water and brandy.*)

SAM: (*sits at back of table*) Yes, I know a thing or two. (*Takes glass.*) I wasn't born blind, like a terrier pup – I rayther think. But you promised me my revenge, you old screw. (*Drinks.*) That's the tipple to steady a chap's hand. Now fork out the pictures, old boy.

MOSS: (*shuffling cards*) Oh, what a boy you are! What shall it be this time?

SAM: A round or two of brag to begin with, and a few deals at Blind Hookums for a wind up. (*As he deals, enter* BRIERLY *from inner room.*)

BRIERLY: Heaven be thanked, another chance yet!

HAWKSHAW: Well, my little flannel-back, has he taken you on?

BRIERLY: Yes, I'm to come to work tomorrow morning. I'm in Ginger's gang.

HAWKSHAW: I'm Ginger. Come, let's wet thy footing.

BRIERLY: My last shilling! (*Throws it down.*) It's all I have, but you're welcome.

HAWKSHAW: Nay, it shan't be said Ginger Bill ever cleared a chap out neither. I'll pay for thy footing, and thou'lt stand beer thy first pay-night. Here, measter, a gallon to wet t'new chap's name. Bob, we'll christen thee, 'cause thou hadst but a shillin' – Ha, ha, ha!

NAVVIES: (*laugh – they all drink*) Here's Bob's health!

BRIERLY: Sam Willoughby, in this place, and over the devil's books, too. Oh, I'm sorry to see this – sorry – sorry. Poor old woman! If she knew!

SAM: Best card. (*showing a card*) First stake.

DALTON: Stop a minute – ace of diamonds.

SAM: First stake to you. Hang it! never mind, (*Deals.*) one can't lose much at this game – I go a tizzy.

MOSS: A shilling.

SAM: Five.

DALTON: I stand.

MOSS: Ten.

SAM: A sovereign. Thirty-one. Third stake and the brag. (*Shows his cards.*) Pair royal – pair – ace of spades. Fork over the shiners.

MOSS: Oh, dear, oh, dear! I'm ruined – ruined. (*Pays sovereign.*)

DALTON: (*calls*) Two colds without.

SAM: Now for my deal. (*He deals three cards to each.* MALTBY *brings brandy.*)

MOSS: Best card? First stake. I stand.

SAM: I brag. Hang peddling with tizzies-half a crown.

DALTON: Five. (MOSS *looks at* SAM's *hand, and signals to* DALTON.)

SAM: Ten.

DALTON: A sovereign.

MOSS: Oh! Oh, dear, what a boy it is! How much have you got in your pocket?

SAM: Lots! I'm paid quarterly now. Had my quarter today. Another cold without. (*Calls.*) Let's see – I'll hold on. (*Draws card.*) Thirty-four – overdrawn – confound it! Now let's see your hand. (*to* DALTON)

DALTON: Three pairs – fives, trays, deuces, and the knave of clubs.

SAM: Hang it all! How is a man to stand against such cards?

BRIERLY: How is a man to stand against such play?

Blind Hookums: a card game (Blind-hookey).
a tizzy: sixpence.
colds without: brandy with cold water.

SAM: ⎱
MOSS: ⎰ Holloa!

BRIERLY: Why, Sam, don't you know me . . . Brierly?

SAM: Bob, in this dress – who could have thought of seeing you here?

BRIERLY: Who'd have thought of seeing *you* here, Sam, and at *this* work?

SAM: Oh, come, I'm not going to be preached to –

MOSS: Certainly not.

DALTON: The youngster is his own master.

SAM: I should think I was, rayther, so if you've got nothing better to do than to look black and talk good . . . your room's a great deal better than your company, master Bob. I've cut – deal away, old 'un. (BRIERLY *falls back.*)

MOSS: (*dealing*) What a spirit! What a spirit!

SAM: Best card! – Now for the brag –

MOSS: Half a crown.

SAM: Five.

MOSS: (*looking over* SAM's *cards*) Ten –

SAM: (*catching him in the act*) Holloa – you're looking over my cards.

MOSS: Ah, my dear – you're dreaming.

SAM: Dreaming! I saw you –

MOSS: Oh, a man old enough to be your grandfather.

BRIERLY: And look. (*seizing a card from* MOSS's *lap*) Here's a knave of clubs – handy to make pairs royal. Ah, you'd not believe me Sam, believe your own eyes: you're being cheated, robbed. You old villain – you ought to be ashamed of yourself!

MOSS: Oh, dear, oh, dear!

DALTON: We're not to be bullied.

SAM: (*threateningly*) You give me back my money! (MALTBY *comes down.*)

MOSS: I shan't! Here, Mr Maltby.

MALTBY: Come, we can't have any disturbance here. Mr Moss is a most respectable man, and his friends are as respectable as he is, and as for you – if you won't leave the room quietly – you must be made to.

SAM: Who'll make me? Come on, (*squaring*) both of you! Stand up to 'em, Bob, I'm not afraid! (NAVIGATORS *gather round.*)

(*Enter* MRS WILLOUGHBY.)

MRS WILLOUGHBY: It's his voice – which well I know it. Oh, Sam – Sam, I've found you at last!

SAM: Well, suppose you have – what then?

MRS WILLOUGHBY: What then! Oh, dear – oh, dear! And I've run myself into that state of trimmle and perspiration, and if it hadn't been for the gentleman I might have been east, and west, and high and low, but it's at the Bridgewater Arms you'll find him, he says – and here I *have* found you, sure enough – and you come 'ome with me this minute.

MOSS: Ah! you'd better go home with the old lady.

DALTON: And if you take my advice, you'll send him to bed without his supper.

SAM: (MRS WILLOUGHBY *pushing him away*) I ain't a-going. Now, you give me my money – I'm not going to stand any nonsense.

MRS WILLOUGHBY: And this is what he calls attending elocution class of a night, and improvin' of his mind – and me a-toilin' and a-moilin' for him – which I'm his own grandmother, gentlemen, and him the only one of three. (*still holding him*)

SAM: It's no use, granny. I'm not a child to be tied to your apron strings – you've no right to be naggin' and aggravatin', and coming after a chap, to make him look small this way. I don't mind – I shan't stir. There! (*He flings his cap on the table, and sits on it, swinging his legs.*)

MRS WILLOUGHBY: Oh, dear, oh, dear. He'll break my heart, he will.

BRIERLY: Sam, my lad, listen to me, if you won't harken to her. A bad beginning makes a bad end, and you're beginning badly; the road you're on leads downwards, and once in the slough at the bottom o't – oh! trust one who knows it – there's no working clear again. You may hold out your hand – you may cry for help – you may struggle hard – but the quick-sands are under your foot – and you sink down, down, till they close over your head.

HAWKSHAW: Hear the little flannel-back. He talks like a missionary, he do. (*All laugh.*)

BRIERLY: Go home, my lad – go home with her – be a son to her – love her as she has loved thee – make her old days happy – be sober, be steady and when you're a grown man, and her chair's empty at t'chimney corner, you'll mayhap remember this day, and be thankful you took the advice of poor, hunted-down, broken-hearted Bob Brierly.

SAM: (*who has betrayed signs of feeling while he has been speaking*) I don't know – I feel so queer – and – don't look at me. (*To* MRS WILLOUGHBY – *gets off table, crosses to her.*) I've been a regular bad 'un, granny – I'm very sorry – I'll put on the curb – I'll pull up – that is, I'll try.

MRS WILLOUGHBY: Oh, bless him for those words! Bless you, my own dear boy. And you too, Mr Brierly – which, if the widow's blessing is worth while, it's yours, and many of them. Oh, dear, oh, dear! (*Cries – gets out her handkerchief, and in doing so drops her purse and keys.* MOSS *picks up the purse.* MRS WILLOUGHBY *catches his eye as he does so.* DALTON *unobserved by all, picks up the keys.*)

BRIERLY: Nay, don't thank me. It's late now. Go home – Sam, give her your arm.

MOSS: Here's your purse, old lady. (*making a final attempt on* SAM) What, you won't stay and make a night of it?

MRS WILLOUGHBY: I'll trouble you not to speak to my grandson. If ever an old man was ashamed of his grey hairs, it's *you* ought to be. Come, Sam.

MOSS: (*aside*) Baulked.

DALTON: No – I didn't give her back her keys.

SAM: (*turning to* MOSS) If I wasn't a-going to turn over a new leaf – oh, wouldn't I like to pitch into you! (*Exeunt* SAM *and* MRS WILLOUGHBY.)

HAWKSHAW: (*pretending to be very drunk*) And so should I – an old varmint – and so would all of us – you're bad enough for a tommy shopkeeper.

NAVVIES: Aye, that he is – ought to be ashamed of himself.

MOSS: And who accuses me? A nice chap, this, to take away honest folk's characters!

---

tommy shopkeeper: a tommy shop is a truck shop, i.e. a junkshop.

HAWKSHAW: Stow that! He's one of *us* now – a regular blue-stocking – Tottie's taken him on! He's paid his footing – eh, mates?

ALL: Aye – aye.

HAWKSHAW: Here's Bob's health, mates.

ALL: Aye – aye.

MOSS: Stop. Before you drink that health, best know the man you're drinking to. You're a rough lot, I know, but you're honest men.

BRIERLY: Oh, man, if you've a heart –

MOSS: I owe you one – I always pay my debts. (*to* NAVVIES) You're not felons, nor company for felons – for jail-birds.

ALL: Jail-birds!

MOSS: Aye – jail-birds. Ask him how long it is since he served his four years at Portland. Look! he turns pale – his lip falls; he can't deny it. (BRIERLY *turns away.*)

HAWKSHAW: Who knows, lads – perhaps he's repented.

ALL: No, no. (*grumbling*) No jail-bird – no convict – no ticket-of-leaver. (*They turn away from* BRIERLY.)

BRIERLY: Aye, mates – it's true I was convicted, but I wasn't guilty. I served my time. I came out an altered man. I tried hard to earn an honest livelihood. (*They all turn away.*) Don't all turn away from me! Give me a chance – only a chance.

ALL: No – no.

BRIERLY: Nay, then, my last hope is gone – I can fight no longer! (*Throws his head on his hands in despair.* HAWKSHAW, *pretending to be very drunk, appears to sleep with head on table. The* NAVIGATORS *drop off and exit one by one.*)

MOSS: (*to* DALTON) Honesty's bowled out at last! It's our game now. (*Puts his hand on* BRIERLY'S *shoulder.*) I say my friend –

BRIERLY: Eh! (*looking up*) You! The man who told them! (*fiercely*)

MOSS: Yes – yes; but don't put yourself in a passion.

BRIERLY: Only tell me – is it you who have followed me in this way, who have turned all against me, who have kept me from earning honest bread?

MOSS: Yes.

BRIERLY: But why, man why? I had done you no wrong.

MOSS: Ask him. (*pointing to* DALTON) He's an old friend of yours.

BRIERLY: I don't know him – yet – I've seen that face before. Yes, it is – Jem Downy! Thou villain! (*He seizes him.*) I know thee now. Thou shalt answer to me for all this misery.

DALTON: Easy does it, Bob. Hands off, and let's take things pleasantly.

BRIERLY: Not content with leading me into play and drink and devilry – with making me your tool – with sending me to a prison, it's you that have dogged me – have denounced me as a convict.

DALTON: Of course – you didn't think any but an old friend would have taken such an interest in you.

BRIERLY: Did you want to close all roads against me but that which leads to the dock?

DALTON: Exactly.

MOSS: Exactly.

DALTON: You see, when a man's in the mud himself and can't get out of it, he don't like to see another fight clear. Come, honest men won't have anything to do with you – best try the black sheep – we ain't proud. We've a job in hand will be the making of all three. (*Fills his glass.*) Here, drink, and put some heart into you. (BRIERLY *drinks.*) That's your sort – a lad of spirit – I said there was real grit in him – didn't I, Mossey?

MOSS: You always gave him the best of characters.

DALTON: Is it a bargain?

BRIERLY: Yes.

DALTON: There! Tip us the cracksman's crook – so! (*Shakes hands with a peculiar grip.*)

(*Enter* MAY EDWARDS.)

MAY: Robert – not here? Ah, there he is. (*Going – pauses.*) who are those with him?

DALTON: Now a caulker to clinch the bargain. (DALTON *and* BRIERLY *drink.*)

MAY: (*in pain*) Ah! Robert.

BRIERLY: You here, lass?

MOSS: Oh, these petticoats!

DALTON: You're not wanted here, young woman.

MAY: He is my husband, sir. He is not strong – the drink will do him harm.

DALTON: Ha, ha, ha! Brandy do a man harm! It's mother's milk – take another sip. (*Fills* BRIERLY'*s glass again.*) To your girl's good health!

MAY: Robert, dear – come with me.

BRIERLY: Have you got work?

MAY: No – not yet.

BRIERLY: No more have I, lass. The man took me on – it was the old story.

MAY: Oh, Robert – come!

BRIERLY: (MAY *clings to him*) Stand off, lass. You used to do what I bid you – stand off, I say. (*He shakes himself free of her.*)

MAY: Oh, Robert, Robert!

BRIERLY: (*aside*) I must – or they'll not trust me.

MAY: (*aside*) These men? to what have they tempted him in his despair? But I won't leave him. They shan't drive me away.

(*Enter* EMILY *with a guitar.*)

EMILY: Green – Green Jones – Trotters – where is that husband of mine? I'm so tired, and Green can put the guitar in his basket. Two encores – and the wretches wanted another – How I shall enjoy my supper. (*Sees* MAY *and recognizes her.*) Who's this? Eh, no, it can't be – Miss Edwards – *you* here? – Oh – I'm so glad – I mean – I'm so sorry to see you looking so pale and ill. Oh, whatever has happened? What are you doing here? – What are you crying at? – Do tell me.

MAY: Hush, hush, dear – I'm waiting for my husband –

EMILY: Your husband?

MAY: Yes – Robert – he's yonder –

EMILY: Then you *were* married, after all –

MAY: Yes, yes – but we've had sad trouble lately. But you, you're looking well and happy?

EMILY: Oh yes – I've a first rate engagement – and Jones is so steady – you can't think –

MAY: He has an engagement too?

EMILY: Well, not exactly – he's in business – as a sort of – a – sheep farmer –

MAY: Indeed! I'm so glad – well, I daresay you're tired – I won't keep you – goodbye –

EMILY: (*aside*) Poor thing! How shabby she is – if only I durst – I say I hope you won't be offended, but you know, you lent me many a half-crown once – when I was the worst off of the two – if it would be of any use.

MAY: God bless you – you're very kind – but it's not want. Oh, Emmy, dear – I'm afraid Robert's trouble has driven him wild. Look – those men he's drinking with – I'm afraid of them – if only I could get him away from them!

EMILY: Then whatever you do, don't go nagging after him – they can't bear *that*, my dear. He hasn't taken to drink I hope?

MAY: Never 'till tonight. It's want of work.

EMILY: Jones was just as bad when he couldn't learn the clog dance – But I've earned for both –

MAY: So would I – But I've been out of work too – lately –

EMILY: You had a nice voice – I'm the great creature here – twist Maltby round my finger. Miss Beaumaris has just left him – and I daresay I could get you the engagement.

MAY: Oh! – that's a good kind thought of yours – (*aside*) my voice might remind Robert of old days – Ask leave for me to try a song – say it's Miss Edwards – Maltby will remember. I used to sing at the Bellevue long ago. Will you lend me your guitar?

EMILY: Of course I will. And I'll get leave for you to take the plate round. A sort of little extempore benefit, eh, dear? Miss Edwards' night, you know! The navvies are perfect gentlemen – they come down splendidly – when they like one – and I'm an immense favourite! (*Exit* Emily.)

    (*As* MAY *strikes a chord* BRIERLY *looks round.*)

BRIERLY: What, lass, come down to the old work – like me, eh? Sing away – light heart should make sweet music.

    (MAY *sings. At the end of the first verse –*)

DALTON: That's personal!

MAY sings: The LC manuscript has MAY's song in it. It is the same song from which she will sing a snatch towards the end of the play.

You leave my side in quest of dangers
With men of desperate fate and fame,
To all my cares and fears a stranger
You dare the sin and scorn the shame.

Then from the tempter turn away
And be his lures – his efforts vain,
The voice you love is tuned to pray
Oh let it not be tuned in vain.

How glad our lot though dark and dreary
So we but meet it side by side,
No way so long – no way so weary
But still there's hope and heaven to guide.
Then from the tempter turn away *etc.*

(MAY *sings again. At the end of the second verse she goes round
     the tables.*)

BRIERLY: I can't bear her voice!

DALTON: Drink men – (*Fills his glass.*) and drive away the blue devils – Her
     catterwauling is enough to give one the horrors!

MOSS: Don't say that – it's beautiful. I'm so fond of music.
     (*The navvies disperse after the song.*)

MAY: (*coming up with the money she has collected*) Here – Robert, darling – you may
     take it without shame – it's your wife's earnings.

MOSS: Now, did he ask for anything?

MAY: I was speaking to my husband. Come with me –

BRIERLY: (*getting to his feet*) I shall stay – with my friends here – you, go home – and
     don't sit up for me –

MAY: Robert!

BRIERLY: I've my reasons. (*Takes her hand.*) Perhaps you'll know 'em some day.

DALTON: (*getting between them*) Come – are you going?

MOSS: Really, Mr Maltby – it's too bad that your customers are to be annoyed in this
     sort of way –

MALTBY: (*coming up*) Come, come, Miss Edwards – You've been round – it's time
     to shut up this house – I must trouble you to clear out. I can't have any crying
     here – 'Taint the liquor I deals in. (*Hustles her out.*)

MAY: (*calling*) Robert! Robert! – (*aside*) At least I'll watch. (*Exit* MAY.)
     (*The tables have before this been cleared of all the* NAVVIES *except*
     HAWKSHAW, *who lies with his head on the table as if dead drunk.*)
     (*Enter* MALTBY *from bar.*)

MALTBY: (*shaking* HAWKSHAW *by the shoulder*) Now, my man, we're shutting up
     the bar.

HAWKSHAW: Shut up. I'm shut up. Good night. (*Lets his head fall.*)

MALTBY: It's no use – he won't go, and I'm wanted in the concert room. (*Exit*
     MALTBY, *calling.*) Bar closed.

MOSS: (*to* DALTON, *suspiciously pointing to* HAWKSHAW) There's a party –

DALTON: Eh? (*shaking* HAWKSHAW) Holloa, wake up. (HAWKSHAW *grunts.*)

MOSS: He's in a deplorable state of intoxication.

DALTON: Yes, he's got his cargo – no danger in him – now for business. First and
     foremost, no more of this. (*Pockets bottle – to* BRIERLY.) You've heard the
     job we have in hand?

BRIERLY: Yes, but you have not told me where it is, or why you want my help.

DALTON: It's old Gibson's office. The five thousand, you know – you know where
     it's kept?

BRIERLY: Well.

DALTON: And you'll take us to it?

BRIERLY: Yes.

DALTON: That's the ticket. Then we may as well start.

BRIERLY: Now?

DALTON: My rule is, never put off till tomorrow the crib I can crack today. Besides,
     you might change your mind.

MOSS: One has heard of such things.

BRIERLY: But –

DALTON: You crane –

BRIERLY: No.

DALTON: I'll get a cab. (*going*)

MOSS: And I'll get another – we'd best go single. (*following him*)

DALTON: No, it wouldn't be polite to leave Mr Brierly. (*aside*) I don't half trust him – don't let him out of your sight. (*Exit.*)

BRIERLY: (*aside*) If he'd only leave me for a moment.

MOSS: He's carried off the bottle, and the bar's shut up; or we might have a little refreshment.

BRIERLY: Perhaps if you went to the landlord –

MOSS: No, I'd rather stay with you – I like your company uncommon.
  (*Enter* MALTBY, *with a wine basket and a candle.*)

MALTBY: Here's Mr Tottie standing champagne round to the Wisconsin Warblers, and the bar stock all out, and the waiters in bed! I must go down to the cellar myself – very humiliating! (*Goes to trap near bar.*) What with the light, and what with the liquor – I say, Mr Moss, if you would lend me a hand.

BRIERLY: (*aside*) I might give him the information. (*to* MALTBY) Let me help you, sir. (*Goes to trap.*)

MOSS: Then I'll go too. (MALTBY *opens trap.*)

BRIERLY: The stairs are steep – two's quite enough.

MOSS: But I'm so fond of your company.

MALTBY: If you'll hold the light. (BRIERLY *takes it and* MALTBY *goes down.*)

BRIERLY: (*aside*) A word'll do it. (MOSS *takes candle from him and gets between him and* MALTBY.)

MOSS: Allow me. The light will do best in the middle. (MOSS *descends.*)

MALTBY: (*from below*) Now then!

BRIERLY: (*rapidly closes the trap, and stands upon it*) Now's the time. (*Seizes the pen that stands on the bar, and writes, reading as he writes quickly.*) 'To Mr Gibson, Peckham. The office will be entered tonight; I'm in it to save the property and secure the robbers – R. Brierly.) But who'll take it?

HAWKSHAW: (*who has got up and read the letter over his shoulder*) I will.

BRIERLY: You?

HAWKSHAW: (*pulls off his rough cap, wig, and whiskers, and speaks in his own voice.*) Hawkshaw, the detective. (*Gives a pistol.*) You may find this useful – I shall be in the way. (BRIERLY *has left the trap for moment – it is raised from below.*)

MOSS: (*from below*) Holloa! Brierly! (*The street door opens at the same moment. Enter* DALTON. HAWKSHAW *lets his head fall again on the table and snores stentoriously.*)

DALTON: (*sees* BRIERLY *conceal the pistol*) A six shooter! So – hm –

MOSS: (*coming up from trap followed by* MALTBY) Why didn't you come down?

BRIERLY: The trap fell. I couldn't find the ring.

DALTON: I've two cabs at the door – Come. (*aside to* MOSS) He's got a pistol – flimp it – and nail the caps!

MOSS: All right, – Goodnight, Mr Maltby. (*Exit* MOSS, DALTON, *and* BRIERLY.)

MALTBY: Goodnight, Mr Moss. (*shaking* HAWKSHAW) Come, you can't sleep here all night. We're shut up.

HAWKSHAW: (*staggering to his feet*) Sh-h-ut up –

SCENE 2. *A street in the city – moonlight. Enter* MRS WILLOUGHBY *and* SAM, *she searching her pocket.*

SAM: You're sure you had 'em at the public?

MRS WILLOUGHBY: Certain sure, my dear, leastwise, I let myself out with the big street door, so I couldn't have left that in the kitchen window, and I'd the little ones all in my pocket, which I noticed a hole in it only yesterday – and it's best holland at one and six, and only worn three years, and they ain't dropped into my skirt, nor they ain't a-hanging to my crinoline.

SAM: Oh, bother, granny; we can't have a regular Custom House search in the street. Let's go back to the public – perhaps they've found them.

> (*Enter* EMILY *and* GREEN JONES, *she with shawl and bonnet, he with his basket and guitar.*)

GREEN: There's only one set left; perhaps Providence has sent a customer. Trotters, mum? One penny a light and wholesome refreshment.

MRS WILLOUGHBY: Trotters, man. Go along with your trotters – I ain't in a state for trotters –

EMILY: Why – if it isn't Mrs Willoughby – and Sam! Why, don't you know us? The St Evremonds –

MRS WILLOUGHBY: Lor, bless me, and so it is! And that dear blessed man that was born to keep his carriage – and him reduced to a trotter-basket! Which ups and downs in life, as the trout says –

GREEN: My dear Madam – I flatter myself – even the trotter trade may be elevated by politeness and attention to seasoning.

EMILY: But whatever are you doing here?

MRS WILLOUGHBY: Oh, my dear, it's a long story – and if you wears pockets, mend 'em, is my advice – which, whether they dropped, or whether they was picked –

SAM: (*impatiently*) We can't get in – granny's lost her keys.

EMILY: And *you* haven't a latch? Well, I wouldn't have thought it of you. Where did she lose them?

SAM: At the Bridgewater Arms – and the house is shut up now.

EMILY: I don't mind knocking Maltby up – I rather like it. Come along, Jones, it's only a step. (*Exeunt* EMILY, SAM *and* MRS WILLOUGHBY.)

GREEN: (*shifting his basket*) I'd rather carry four trotters than one guitar, any time. (*Exit.*)

> (*Enter* HAWKSHAW.)

HAWKSHAW: This should be Crampton's beat. (*Gives a peculiar whistle, and enter a* DETECTIVE.) Take the fastest Hansom you can find; tear down with this to Peckham. (*Gives note.*) Bring the old gent back to St Nicholas Lane. Say he'll be wanted to make a charge. There's a crib to be jumped. I'm down on 'em. By the by, lend me your barker. (DETECTIVE *gives him a pistol, and exit.*) Jem Dalton's a tough customer. I always feel rather ashamed to burn powder. Any fool can blow a man's brain out. (*Tries caps and charges.*) So that lad's true blue after all. I had no idea that he tumbled to their game. He managed that letter uncommonly neat. Now for St Nicholas Churchyard. When Jem Dalton planted his tools he never thought Jack Hawkshaw admired his gardening. (*Exit.*)

            (*Enter* MAY, *breathless.*)

MAY: I've followed the cab as far as I could. I saw them get out, and lost them at the last turning. If I could only keep them in sight – if he could but hear my voice – Robert! Robert! (*Exit.*)

SCENE 3. *The Churchyard of St Nicholas with tombstones and neglected trees; wall at back, Left Centre: up Left side of stage an iron railing supposed to separate the churchyard from the street; Right Centre, the wall of* MR GIBSON'*s office, with practicable back door.*

DALTON: (*showing his head over the wall*) All serene – Now for it. (*He drops over followed by* BRIERLY *and* MOSS.)

MOSS: (*aside, as he puts something into* DALTON'*s hands*) There are the caps – I've muzzled the barker.

DALTON: (*getting black leather bag from behind tombstone*) Now to transplant the tools. Moss, you be crow – two whistles if the coast ain't clear – *we'll* work the crib. Lucky I nailed the old woman's keys. They'll save tools and time. Give me the glim. (MOSS *takes out small lanthorn and gives it to him.*) Now, my lad (*to* BRIERLY) take care; I'm a man of few words. The pal who sticks to me, I stick by him, till death. But the man who tries to double on me had better have the hangman looking after him than Jem Dalton. (*Exit into office by back door, followed by* BRIERLY.)

            (HAWKSHAW, *whose head has been seen over wall during this speech drops noiselessly down and hides behind the tombstone.*)

MOSS: (*on the look out*) Nice quiet place – I like working in the City; I wish everybody lived out of town, and left their premises in charge of their housekeepers. (MAY *is heard singing the refrain of her song.*) What's that? That girl! She must have followed us. Here she is.

            (*Enter* MAY *in the street.*)

MAY: Oh, sir, you were with him! Where is he?

MOSS: I'm just taking a little walk in my garden before retiring for the night; they've gone on to the Cave of Harmony – first turn on the left; there's a red lamp over the door, you can't miss it.

MAY: Oh, thank you – thank you!

MOSS: That's neat! Trust old Moss when anybody's to be made safe.

            (HAWKSHAW *seizes* MOSS *from behind, stops his mouth with one hand, and handcuffs him.*)

HAWKSHAW: Stir or speak, and you're a dead man!

DALTON: (*appearing at back door*) Hang the cloud! I can't see. Moss!

HAWKSHAW: (*imitating*) All serene!

DALTON: We've done the job. (*calling to* BRIERLY) Now, the box.

BRIERLY: (*within*) I'll bring it. (*Comes from door with cash box.*)

DALTON: We'll share at the Pigeons in Duck Lane. The box, quick!

BRIERLY: A word or two first.

DALTON: We can talk in the cab.

BRIERLY: No, here. You were my ruin four years ago.

DALTON: I've paid you back twice over tonight. Come, the box.

BRIERLY: I suffered then for *your* crime. Ever since, you've come between me and honest life – you've broke me down – you've brought me to this.

DALTON: I suppose you mean you've a right to an extra share of the swag?

BRIERLY: No, I mean that you're my prisoner, or you're a dead man. (*Seizes him and presents pistol.*)

DALTON: Hands off, you fool!

BRIERLY: Nay then – (*Snaps pistol.*)

DALTON: You should have asked me for the caps. Here they are. (*Holds them up.*)

BRIERLY: No matter; armed or unarmed, you don't escape me. (*A struggle.* DALTON *strikes down* BRIERLY *as* HAWKSHAW *rushes from his concealment.*)

HAWKSHAW: Now, Jem Dalton! It's my turn!

DALTON: Hawkshaw! (*They struggle;* HAWKSHAW *is forced down on a tombstone and nearly strangled.* SAM *appears outside the rails, springs over them, seizes* DALTON *by the legs and throws him over.* HAWKSHAW *rises and puts the handcuffs on* DALTON. MAY *appears in the street.*)

MAY: Robert! Husband!

SAM: (*over* DALTON) Lie still, will you? You're a nice young man! (*crossing and looking over* MOSS) You're a pair of nice young men!

HAWKSHAW: Now Jem Dalton, remember poor Joe Skirrit – I promised him I'd do it. I've done it at last.

(*Enter* MR GIBSON *from back door of house, followed by* MAY, *who has gone round.*)

MR GIBSON: This way! Here they are! The safe open! The cash-box gone!

HAWKSHAW: No, saved. (*Gives it to him.*)

MR GIBSON: By whom?

HAWKSHAW: The man who is bleeding yonder, Robert Brierly.

MAY: My husband – wounded! Oh, mercy! (*She kneels over him.*)

MR GIBSON: Thank heaven, he's not dead. I can repay him yet.

HAWKSHAW: Men don't die so easily. He's worth a dozen dead men.

MAY: Look – he opens his eyes. Robert, speak to me – it's May – your own wife.

BRIERLY: (*faintly*) Darling, I'm glad you're here. It's only a clip on the head. I'm none the worse. It was all my game to snare those villains. Who's there? Mr Gibson? You wouldn't trust me, sir, but I was not ungrateful. You see, there may be some good left in a Ticket-of-Leave Man after all. (*Tableau.*)

CURTAIN.

The Maniac's Tear

Music by Matthew Scott
Words by Tony Harrison

A poor honest girl to a drunkard was wed,
and because of his boozing her babes went unfed,
which drove that poor woman clean off of her head.

She did a dire deed that she still can't believe,
and her groans make the Bedlamites grieve
as with each shriek and cry
they hear her deny
she chopped up her children that chill Christmas eve –

I needed the meat! (they hear her repeat)
so my babies could eat!

And the Maniac's tear it fell with a plop
on the cold Bedlam floor as she cried,
How cruel to tell me that here I must stop
and pretend that my babies have died!

And the weight of the dinner she scarcely could bear
and she served it with love to each chair,
and oh little she knew
that the steaming hot stew
was the family that should have sat there.

I needed the meat! etc.

My flock will be fed, said the smile on her face
as she served the rich stew to each place;
but there was no need
and no mouths to feed
and no children there to say grace.

I needed the meat! etc.

Now ev'ryone dreads her and fears her so much
her gaolers daren't go near or touch her,
and all night they hear
the cries they all fear
of Bessie the Bedlamite Butcher.

I needed the meat! etc.

So I crave of you kindly good sirs
to blend your tenderest tears with hers:
show your grief for her ghost,
and purchase her story
so gruesome and gory,
for two shillings a sheet from mine host!

© Matthew Scott and Tony Harrison 1981

Freely - a music hall recit.

A poor hon-est girl to a drunk-ard was wed, and be – cause of his booz-ing her

sempre c.v.

babes went un - fed, which drove that poor wo - man clean off of her head.

VERSE half spoken as in early music hall

She did a dire deed that she still can't be - lieve, and her

sempre colla voce

groans make the Bed- lam - ites grieve———— as with each shriek and cry they

hear her de-ny she chopped up her chil-dren that chill Christ-mas eve ___

___ I need-ed the meat! (they hear her re-peat) so my ba-bies could

REFRAIN

eat! And the Ma-ni-ac's tear it fell with a plop on the

cold Bed-lam floor as she cried, How cru-el to tell me that

here I must stop and pre - tend that my ba - bies have died! And the

Repeat for each verse; on last time, to CODA

CODA

died!_____ So I crave of you kind-ly good sirs to blend your ten-der-est tears_ with

hers: show your grief for her ghost, and pur - chase her sto - ry so

grue-some and go - ry, for a shil - ling a sheet from mine host!

THE PRINCIPAL PLAYS OF TOM TAYLOR

In assembling this list I have relied greatly on the work of Winton Tolles, *Tom Taylor and the Victorian Drama* (New York, 1940) and upon Allardyce Nicoll's invaluable Hand-List of Plays. I have accepted Tolles' performance dates where any uncertainty arises, and have noted the variants between the lists of Tolles and Nicoll. First London performances are recorded, plus significant first productions when they occurred outside London. Published texts are indicated in Lacy's and French's Standard editions only, abbreviated as L(vol) or F(number).

A Trip to Kissengen, Lyceum, 14 November 1844 (farce: with A. A. Knox)
Valentine and Orson, Lyceum, 23 December 1844 (burlesque: with Albert Smith and Charles Kenney)
Whittington and his Cat, Lyceum, 24 March 1845 (burlesque: with Albert Smith and Charles Kenney)
Cinderella, Lyceum, 12 May 1845 (burlesque: with Albert Smith and Charles Kenney)
Friends at Court, Lyceum, 9 June 1845 (comedietta)
The Enchanted Horse, Lyceum, 26 December 1845 (burlesque: with Albert Smith and Charles Kenney)
To Parents and Guardians, Lyceum, 14 September 1846 (comic drama) L XIII F 127
Wanted a Hermit, Lyceum, 18 May 1847 (farce)
Diogenes and His Lantern, Strand, 28 December 1849 (burlesque)
The Vicar of Wakefield, Olympic, 4 March 1850 (drama: adapted from Oliver Goldsmith's novel) L II; F 82
Novelty Fair, Lyceum, 20 May 1850 (revue: with Albert Smith) L I
The Philosopher's Stone, Strand, 20 May 1850 (extravaganza) L I
Prince Dorus, Olympic, 26 December 1850 (extravaganza) L III
Sir Roger de Coverley, Olympic, 21 April 1851 (drama: based on essays by Addison and Steele) L IV
Little Red Riding Hood, Adelphi, 26 December 1851 (burlesque)
Our Clerks, Princess, 6 March 1852 (farce) L VI
Wittikind, Princess, 12 April 1852 (extravaganza: from Grimm's story of the Seven Swans) L VI
Masks and Faces, Haymarket, 20 November 1852 (comedy: with Charles Reade) F 240
Slave Life, Adelphi, 29 November 1852 (drama: adapted from 'Uncle Tom's Cabin' by Harriet Beecher Stowe)
Plot and Passion, Olympic, 17 October 1853 (drama: 'suggested' by John Lang) L XIII
A Nice Firm, Lyceum, 16 November 1853 (farce) L XIII
Harlequin Columbus, Olympic, 26 December 1853 (pantomime)

To Oblige Benson, Olympic, 6 March 1854 (comedietta: adapted from 'Un Service à Blanchard' by Eugene Moreau and Henry Delacour)

Two Loves and a Life, Adelphi, 20 March 1854 (drama: with Charles Reade) F 165

The Barefaced Imposters, Canterbury Theatre, 15 August 1854 (farce: adapted from 'L'Ours et le Pasha' by Eugene Scribe, with George C. Bentinck and Frederick Ponsonby) L LXX

A Blighted Being, Olympic, 17 October 1854 (farce: from French vaudeville 'Une Existence decolorée') L XVI

The King's Rival, St James, 2 October 1854 (drama: with Charles Reade) F 124

Still Waters Run Deep, Olympic, 14 May 1855 (drama: from 'Le Gendre' by Charles Bernard) L XXII

Helping Hands, Adelphi, 20 June 1855 (drama) L XXII F 278

The First Printer, Princess, 3 March 1856 (drama: with Charles Reade)

Retribution, Olympic, 12 May 1856 (drama: from 'La Peine du Talion' by Charles Bernard) L XXVII F 151

A Sheep in Wolf's Clothing, Olympic, 19 February 1857 (drama: adapted from 'Une Femme qui déteste son mari' by Madame Delphine de Girardin) L XXXVII

Victims, Haymarket, 8 July 1857 (comedy) L XXXII F 186

An Unequal Match, Haymarket, 7 November 1857 (comedy) L CXVIII F 374

Going to the Bad, Olympic, 5 June 1858 (farce) L XXXVII

Nine Points of the Law, Olympic, 11 April 1859 (comedietta: based on 'Clover Cottage' by Marmion W. Savage) L XL

The House or the Home?, Adelphi, 16 May 1859 (drama: from 'Péril dans la demeure' by Octave Feuillet) L XLII

The Contested Election, Haymarket, 29 June 1859 (comedy)

Payable on Demand, Olympic, 11 July 1859 (drama) L XLI

The Fool's Revenge, Sadler's Wells, 18 October 1859 (poetic drama: adapted from 'Le Roi s'amuse' by Victor Hugo) L XLIII F 330

Garibaldi, Astley's, 24 October 1859 (hippodrame)

The Late Lamented, Haymarket, 21 November 1859 (comedy)

A Tale of Two Cities, Lyceum, 30 January 1860 (drama: from the novel by Charles Dickens) L XLV

The Overland Route, Haymarket, 23 February 1860 (comedy) L No. 1853

A Christmas Dinner, Olympic, 23 April 1860 (comic drama: from French vaudeville 'Je dine chez ma mère')

The Brigand and his Banker, Lyceum, 1 October 1860 (drama: based on 'Le Roi des montagnes' by Edmond About)

Up at the Hills, St James, 29 October 1860 (drama) L L

Babes in the Wood, Haymarket, 10 November 1860 (comedy). Also known as *Babes and Beetles*. L L

A Duke in Difficulties, Haymarket, 6 March 1861 (comedy: from 'A Duke's Dilemma' in *Blackwood's Magazine*, vol. LXXIV, September 1853)

Our American Cousin, Haymarket, 16 November 1861 (comedy). First produced at Laura Keene's Theatre, New York, 15 October 1858

The Ticket-of-Leave Man, Olympic, 27 May 1863 (drama: from 'Léonard' by Édouard Brisebarre and Eugène Nus) L LIX F 329

An Awful Rise in Spirits, Olympic, 7 September 1863 (burlesque)

Sense and Sensation, Olympic, 16 May 1864 (burlesque-morality) L LXIII

The Hidden Hand, Olympic, 2 November 1864 (drama: with Horace Wigan from 'L'Aïeule' by Adolphe Dennery and Charles Edmond) L LXV

Settling Day, Olympic, 4 March 1865 (drama) L LXXXII

The Serf, Olympic, 30 June 1865 (drama) L LXVIII

Henry Dunbar, Olympic, 9 December 1865 (drama: based on novel by Mary Elizabeth Braddon) L LXXVI

The Whiteboy, Olympic, 27 September 1866 (drama: based on novel by Mrs S. C. Hall)

A Sister's Penance, Adelphi, 26 November 1866 (drama: with Augustus W. Dubourg) L LXXV

Lesson for Life, Haymarket, 26 December 1866 (comedy)

The Antipodes, Holborn, 8 June 1867 (drama)

Narcisse, Lyceum, 17 February 1868 (Tolles describes this as 'from Brachvogel's play'. Nicoll, *History of Late Nineteenth Century Drama 1850–1900*, vol. 2, lists it under plays by Unknown Authors.

Won by a Head, Queen's, 29 March 1869 (drama)

Mary Warner, Haymarket, 21 June 1869 (drama: based on 'Margaret Meadows' by Dr William Gilbert)

New Men and Old Acres, Haymarket, 25 October 1869 (comedy: with Augustus W. Dubourg) First produced at the Theatre Royal, Manchester, 20 August 1869. L XC

'Twixt Axe and Crown, Queen's, 22 January 1870 (poetic drama: from 'Elizabeth Prinzessin von England' by Madame Charlotte Birch-Pfieffer)

Handsome is That Handsome Does, Olympic, 3 September 1870 (comedy)

Jeanne D'Arc, Queen's, 10 April 1871 (poetic drama)

Faust, Haymarket, Melbourne, Australia, 1871 (drama: from Goethe) Not listed by Nicoll.

Dead or Alive, Queen's, 22 July 1872 (drama: based on 'Le Colonel Chabert' by Honoré de Balzac)

Hamlet, Crystal Palace, 3 May 1873 (version of Shakespeare's play) Not listed by Nicoll.

Arkwright's Wife, Globe, 6 October 1873 (drama: suggested by John Saunders) First produced in Leeds, 7 July 1873.

Lady Clancarty, Olympic, 9 March 1874 (drama) F 368

The White Cockade, Croydon, 26 September 1874 (drama) Listed by Nicoll, but not by Tolles.

Anne Boleyn, Haymarket, 7 February 1876 (poetic drama)

Abel Drake, Princess, 20 May 1876 (drama: with John Saunders)

Such is the Law, St James, 20 April 1878 (drama: with Paul Merritt)

Love or Life, Olympic, 10 June 1878 (drama: with Paul Merritt, based on 'Smugglers and Poachers', *Tales of the Hall*, Book XXI, by George Crabbe)

In addition to the discrepancies between Tolles and Nicoll noted above, Nicoll attributes the following plays to Taylor, which are not recorded by Tolles:

Guy Fawkes, Olympic, 31 March 1855 (extravaganza: with Albert R. Smith, W. P. Hale, E. Draper and Arthur Smith)

William Tell, Lyceum, 14 July 1856 (pantomime: with A. R. Smith, F. Talfourd and W. P. Hale)
The Seasons, Strand, 17 March 1860 (drama)
Hearts and Hands, Manchester, 2 May 1865 (drama)

Editions

Three Dramas, 1854 (Masks and Faces, The King's Rival, Two Loves and a Life) by Tom Taylor and Charles Reade (Bentley, London, 1854)
Historical dramas (The Fool's Revenge, Jeanne D'Arc, 'Twixt Axe and Crown, Lady Clancarty, Anne Boleyn, Plot and Passion, Arkwright's Wife) by Tom Taylor (Chatto and Windus, London, 1877)

SELECT BIBLIOGRAPHY

Editions

New Men and Old Acres, in *English Plays of the Nineteenth Century, III: Comedies*, ed. Michael R. Booth (Oxford, 1973)

The Ticket-of-Leave Man, in *Nineteenth Century Plays*, ed. George Rowell, 2nd edn (Oxford, 1972) and *English Plays of the Nineteenth Century, II: Drama 1850–1900*, ed. Michael R. Booth (Oxford, 1973)

Critical Studies

Tolles, Winton, *Tom Taylor and the Victorian Drama* (New York, 1940)

There is no other full-length study of Taylor's work. Recent assessments may be found in:

Booth, Michael R. (ed.), *English Plays of the Nineteenth Century, II: Drama 1850-1900*, and *III: Comedies* (Oxford, 1973)

Nicoll, Allardyce, *A History of the Late Nineteenth Century Drama, 1850-1900*, vol. 1 (Cambridge, 1946) (see also vol. 5 of *A History of English Drama: 1660-1900* (Cambridge, 1959))

Rowell, George, *The Victorian Theatre, 1792-1914*, 2nd edn (Cambridge, 1978)

Booth, Michael R., Southern, Richard, Marker, Frederick and Lise-Lone and Davies, Robertson (eds.), *The Revels History of Drama in English, vol. VI, 1750–1880* (London, 1975)

Additional materials are to be found in various memoirs and critical studies from the nineteenth century amongst which the following are most helpful:

Bancroft, Sir Squire and Marie, *Mr and Mrs Bancroft on and off the Stage* (2 vols., London, 1888)

Burnand, Sir Francis C., *Records and Reminiscences, Personal and General* (2 vols., London, 1903)

Scott, Clement, *The Drama of Yesterday and Today* (2 vols., London, 1899)

Coleman, John, *Players and Playwrights I have Known* (2 vols., London, 1888)

Terry, Ellen, *The Story of my Life* (London, 1908)